Oxford Anthology
of Western Music

Oxford Anthology
of Western Music

Second Edition

Volume One

**The Earliest Notations to the Early
Eighteenth Century**

EDITED BY

David J. Rothenberg & Robert R. Holzer

New York   Oxford
OXFORD UNIVERSITY PRESS

Oxford University Press is a department of the University of Oxford.
It furthers the University's objective of excellence in research, scholarship,
and education by publishing worldwide. Oxford is a registered trade mark
of Oxford University Press in the UK and certain other countries.

Published in the United States of America by Oxford University Press
198 Madison Avenue, New York, NY 10016, United States of America.

ISBN: 978-0-19-060031-0

Printer number: 9 8 7 6 5 4 3 2 1
Printed by Sheridan Books, Inc., United States of America

Contents

Preface

This volume serves as a companion anthology to Chapters 1–11 of *The Oxford History of Western Music*, College Edition, by Richard Taruskin and Christopher H. Gibbs. With the essays that introduce each of the scores, we have also aimed to make it possible for the anthology to stand on its own as a text for courses, both historical and analytical, on what is commonly referred to as music of the Medieval, Renaissance, and Baroque periods. Our selection begins with ancient Greek music and Christian plainchant and ends with George Frideric Handel. In addition to a number of landmark works likely to be found in many historical surveys, we have included important pieces that are rarely anthologized, such as Jacopo da Bologna's *Osellecto selvaggio*, Févin's *Missa super Ave Maria*, Willaert's *Benedicta es*, Lully's *Atys*, Buxtehude's *Durch Adams Fall*, and Rameau's *Castor et Pollux*.

Some essays are edited excerpts from Richard Taruskin's six-volume *The Oxford History of Western Music*, and some are newly written for this anthology. Although mainly analytical in content, the essays also provide historical context for the works discussed. Because many of the works in this volume will be a student's first encounter with important formal concepts such as the "formes fixes" and "ritornello form," some essays are extensive in analytical detail. For works including sung texts in languages other than English, we provide the original text and a facing literal translation after the introductory essay. Since it has become easy to look up the meaning of terms in this age of Internet dictionaries, we have not included a glossary of terms. However, we do provide an index of names and terms, which enables students to look up the terms in the context of the essays in the anthology.

We are happy to acknowledge the many individuals who have helped this volume come to life. First, we are indebted to Richard Taruskin, whose six-volume *The Oxford History of Western Music* has served as a basis and inspiration for the present anthology, and to Christopher Gibbs, co-author of the textbook version of Taruskin's work, who has been an ideal collaborator. We are also indebted to Daniel Boomhower, who assisted in requesting permission to reproduce the scores in the Medieval and Renaissance portions of this anthology, and to the staff of the Irving S. Gilmore Music Library, Yale University, in particular, Emily Ferrigno, public services assistant, for her help in scanning noncirculating scores (and signing out still others!) in the Baroque portion.

Jan Beatty and Richard Carlin, executive editors at Oxford University Press, have been skilled coordinators and mentors of the entire project. Cory Schneider and Lauren Mine, associate editors, Jacqueline Levine, assistant editor, and Nichole LeFebvre, editorial assistant, all in Higher Education at Oxford, and Jay Crowley of Jay's Publishers Services have been models of efficiency and good cheer in helping us sort out the numerous logistical details of production.

Thank you to the following reviewers:

Stephen Allen, Rider University
Pedro Aponte, James Madison University
Candace Bailey, North Carolina Central University
Paul T. Barte, Ohio State University
Laura Basini, Sacramento State University
Glen Bauer, Webster University
Matthew Baumer, Indiana University of Pennsylvania
Jonathan Bellman, University of Northern Colorado
Lynn Wood Bertrand, Emory University
John Brobeck, University of Arizona
Lance Brunner, University of Kentucky
Gordon Callon, Acadia University
Charles Carson, University of Delaware
Mel Comberiati, Manhattanville College
Jane Dahlenburg, University of Central Arkansas
Terry Dean, Indiana State University
Silvio dos Santos, University of Florida
Ralph Dudgeon, State University of New York, Cortland
Robert Eisenstein, Mt. Holyoke, University of Massachusetts
Cathy Ann Elias, DePaul University
Sarah Eyerly, Butler University
William Gibbons, Texas Christian University
Jonathan Gibson, James Madison University
Howard Goldstein, Auburn University
David Grayson, University of Minnesota, Twin Cities
Richard Greene, Georgia College & State University
Olga Haldey, University of Maryland
L. Curtis Hammond, Morehead State University
Gregory Harwood, Georgia Southern University
Joseph Herl, Concordia University, Nebraska
Karl Hinterbichler, University of New Mexico
Julie Hubbert, University of South Carolina

Kevin Karnes, Emory University
Derek Katz, University of California, Santa Barbara
Kenneth Keaton, Florida Atlantic University
David Kidger, Oakland University
Erinn Knyt, University of Massachusetts, Amherst
Ben Korstvedt, Clark University
Jonathan Kregor, University of Cincinnati
Jonathan Kulp, University of Louisiana, Lafayette
Zoë Lang, University of South Florida
James Leve, Northern Arizona University
David Levy, Wake Forest University
Nora Lewis, Kansas State University
Melanie Lowe, Vanderbilt University
Gayle Sherwood Magee, University of Illinois, Urbana-Champaign
James Maiello, University of Manitoba
Peter Marsh, California State University, East Bay
Kerry McCarthy, Duke University
Susan McClary, Case Western Reserve University
Alyson McLamore, California Polytechnic State University, San Luis Obispo
Stephen Meyer, University of Cincinnati
Vera Micznik, University of British Columbia
Michael Miranda, Loyola Marymount University
Sharon Mirchandani, Rider University
Alexandra Monchick, California State University, Northridge
Simon Morrison, Princeton University
Caroline Polk O'Meara, University of Texas at Austin
Mathew Peattie, University of Cincinnati College Conservatory of Music
Thomas Peattie, University of Mississippi
Sanna Pederson, University of Oklahoma
Elaine Peterson, Mississippi State University
Mark A. Radice, Ithaca College School of Music
Christina Reitz, Western Carolina University
Eric Rice, University of Connecticut
Jerry Rife, Rider University
Kailan Rubinoff, University of North Carolina, Greensboro
Jennifer Saltzstein, University of Oklahoma
Anthony Scelba, Kean University
Peter Schimpf, Metropolitan State College
Douglass Seaton, Florida State University
Jacquelyn Sholes, Boston University
Timothy Snyder, Jacksonville University
Jennifer Thomas, University of Florida
Noel Verzosa, Hood College

Jacqueline Waeber, Duke University
Robin Wallace, Baylor University
Sarah F. Williams, University of South Carolina
Stephen A. Willier, Temple University
Yali You, Hamline University

1

Epitaph of Seikilos
(first century CE)

The chief contributions of the ancient Greeks to the Western musical tradition lie in their philosophical and theoretical writings. Greek philosophers, including Socrates and Plato (through whose writings Socrates's teachings are known), believed that music could have a profound influence on the innermost human emotions and that it was therefore both uniquely powerful and uniquely dangerous. The debates that they started about the moral and ethical effects of music have shaped musical thought ever since. Ancient Greek music theorists, meanwhile, described the acoustical proportions underlying musical intervals and laid out in great detail a scale that, though quite different from our own, employs the same diatonic pitch set out of which the major and minor scales—and all the other modes still in use today (Dorian, Phrygian, etc.)—can be constructed. Greek philosophy and music theory therefore show that as far back as the very beginning of recorded musical history, people have been cognizant of the emotional power of music and have internalized the diatonic pitch set as a means of organizing, receiving, and reproducing meaningful sound patterns.

But what did the music of ancient Greece actually sound like? We can offer only a partial answer. This anthology does not present a history of all music made in the past but of literate music, of music written down in the past. Only a handful of ancient Greek melodies have come down to us in writing, and most, like the one given here, date from relatively late in the history of ancient Greece. The Epitaph of Seikilos is a short composition written on a tombstone dating from the first century CE that now resides in the National Museum in Copenhagen, Denmark. Historians disagree about whether Seikilos, the man named on the tombstone whose identity remains obscure, was the composer of the piece. Still, it is one of the best-preserved pieces of ancient Greek music, and it can give us at least some idea of the ancient Greek sound world. The text is an epigram, a type of short and simple poem that was often placed on tombstones. The melody, transcribed here onto a modern musical staff, is notated on the original stone tablet using alphabetic symbols (shown here above the staff) that indicate both pitch and rhythm. Ancient Greek visual art shows a variety of commonly used instruments, including the aulos (a reeded wind instrument) and the cithara (a large lyre with a wooden soundboard), which would very likely have accompanied the singer in a composition such as this. The language is

foreign, and the instruments are no longer in use, but given that this is one of the earliest pieces of Western music to survive, its diatonic melody is surprisingly familiar to our ears two millennia later.

> As long as you live, be lighthearted.
> Let nothing trouble you.
> Life is only too short,
> and time takes its toll.
> *trans. Thomas J. Mathiesen*

Instructions for Reading Quadratic Notation

Many of the Gregorian chant examples given on the following pages are written in quadratic notation, a Medieval notational system in which the note shapes are called neumes. It is called quadratic because the basic note shape is a square (Latin quadratus). The music is usually written on a four-line staff, with two types of clef: ⬙ indicates middle C, and ⬙ indicates F a fifth below it. Some neumes consist of a single note, but many are ligatures, which include multiple notes. When quadratic notation is transcribed into modern notation, notes are generally written as unstemmed note heads, and ligatures are indicated by slurs. Quadratic notation does not indicate rhythm. All notes have roughly the same duration, and any durational variation is at the discretion of the performers.

Single notes may be given as a square note with or without a stem (⬙ and ⬙), both of which have the same rhythmic value. Notes proceed from left to right (⬙), except when two notes of exactly the same size are stacked immediately one on top of the other (⬙), in which case the lower note is sung first. Diamond-shaped notes (⬙) are used only in descending passages but have the same duration as square notes. Oblique neumes, which include diagonal pen strokes (⬙), indicate not a glissando but two notes, one on the pitch where the stroke begins, the other where it ends (⬙).

Small square notes, in what are called liquescent neumes, indicate that the mouth or tongue should close onto a voiced consonant (usually "m" or "n") on the ascending or descending note at the end of a syllable (⬙, ⬙). The squiggly note used in certain ascending neumes is called a quilisma (⬙); historically it may have indicated some sort of ornament, but its meaning remains obscure. The symbol at the end of each line (⬙), called a custos (guard), indicates what the first note of the next line will be. Asterisks (*) generally indicate where the soloist is joined by the rest of the choir, but they also sometimes indicate when two halves of the choir alternate with one another or other changes in performance. Flat signs (⬙) generally hold until the end of the word, a dividing line (bar line) of any sort, or a natural sign.

2

Psalm Verse

Justus ut palma (Ps. 92, 12) in
Four Liturgical Settings

Many central points about the history of Gregorian chant and also about its many genres and styles can be illustrated by examining several settings of a single psalm verse in various liturgical contexts. Verse 12 of Psalm 92 (according to the numbering in the standard Latin Bible, known as the Vulgate, translated by St. Jerome in the late fourth century) appears especially frequently in the liturgy. Perhaps because of its two vivid similes—comparing the righteous to a palm tree and to a cedar in Lebanon—it crops up time and again in many guises, running the full stylistic gamut of Gregorian chant, from the barest "liturgical recitative" to the most elaborate jubilation. The following four examples illustrate that stylistic range.

a. Antiphon to Full Psalm Recitation (Commemoration of a Martyr Saint)

The term for the singing of psalms is *psalmody*. In its simplest form, the *Justus ut palma* verse is part of the formulaic chanting of the psalm from which it comes, within the weekly cycle of the Divine Office. In such contexts psalms are sung to elementary reciting formulas or *psalm tones* (eight psalm tones are used in the Latin liturgy, one for each mode, plus one called the *tonus peregrinus* ["migrating tone"] because the featured reciting pitch of its first half is different from that of its second). Early in the history of Medieval psalmody, a short composition called an *antiphon* was sung before and after each verse of the psalm. Later the practice was streamlined, as shown here, so that the antiphon appears only before and after the entire psalm rather than alternating with every verse. In the present example, the full Psalm 92 is paired with an antiphon that takes as a text *Justus ut palma*, its own twelfth verse. Every single psalm that was recited in the Divine Office was sung as part of an antiphon–psalm complex like the one shown here, which is from a service commemorating a martyr saint, a class of saints to whom the similes in *Justus ut palma* apply especially well.

The performance begins with the antiphon. A soloist sings the first two words to set the pitch, and the full choir joins in for the remainder. Then the psalm is sung to the psalm tone,

which begins in the score on the second system of music. Its constituent parts function very much like punctuation marks. First there is the intonation, or *initium* ("beginning"), sung by a soloist to reestablish the pitch. The *initium* always ascends to a repeated pitch, called the *reciting tone* or *tenor* (from the Latin *tenere*, "to hold"), which is sung as many times as necessary to accommodate the syllables of the text. Since psalms are prose texts, the number of syllables varies considerably from verse to verse; in a long verse there will be many repetitions of the tenor. The longest verses (here, verses 2, 4, and 5) have a "bend" (*flexus*) as additional punctuation. The end of the first half-verse is sung to a melodic turn called the *mediant* (Latin *mediatio*), which divides the two halves of the verse. The second half-verse begins on the tenor and ends with a final turn called the *termination* (Latin *terminatio*). All the verses of the psalm are recited to the same psalm tone, but they are sung by halves of the choir in alternation with one another, in what is called *antiphonal practice*. The intonation is sung only by a soloist and only in the first verse (a half-choir joins the soloist in the first verse after the mediant); a full half-choir begins each subsequent verse directly on the tenor. Note that at the end of the psalm, a text called the Lesser Doxology has been appended and treated as an extra pair of psalm verses (verses 12 and 13). The Doxology was appended in this manner to every Office psalm as a Christianizing tag invoking the Holy Trinity (a notion assuredly unfamiliar to the Old Testament authors of the *psalter*). After the Doxology, the entire antiphon is sung again by the full choir.

In the psalm tone, the musical setting of the text is entirely syllabic, in that every note carries exactly one syllable of text. In the antiphon the text setting is sometimes syllabic, but mostly it is neumatic, in that syllables are generally set to simple two- or three-note neumes. In most Medieval chant books, the antiphon is the only portion of the antiphon–psalm complex that is written out. Monks would have had the words of the entire psalter memorized, and for the melody they needed only apply the words of a psalm to the appropriate psalm tone, generally indicated at the close of the antiphon by a few notes of music set over the letters E u o u a e (sometimes informally combined into a mnemonic, pronounced "e-VO-vay"). These notes show the ending of the psalm tone by indicating the notes for the final syllables of the concluding Doxology—the letters are the vowels in ". . . seculorum. Amen." The brief formula over E u o u a e is called the *differentia*, because it tells you which of the different available endings of the psalm tone to employ in order to achieve a smooth transition into the repetition of the antiphon. The differentia is not shown in the modern transcription but is shown at the bottom in the original quadratic notation.

Psalm 92

1. *Bonum est confiteri Domino: et psallere nomine tuo, Altissime.*

2. *Ad annuntiandum mane misericordiam tuam: et veritatem tuam per noctem.*

1. It is a good thing to give thanks unto the Lord, and to sing praises unto thy name, O most High:

2. To shew forth thy loving kindness in the morning, and thy faithfulness every night,

3. *In decachordo psalterio: cum cantico et cithara.*

3. Upon an instrument of ten strings, and upon the psaltery; upon the harp with a solemn sound.

4. *Quia delectasti me, Domine, in factura tua: et in operibus manuum tuarum exsultabo.*

4. For thou, Lord, hast made me glad through thy work: I will triumph in the works of thy hands.

5. *Quam magnificata sunt opera tua, Domine! Nimis profundae factae sunt cogitationes tuae.*

5. O Lord, how great are thy works! And thy thoughts are very deep.

. . .

12. *Justus ut palma florebit: sicut cedrus Libani multiplicabitur.*

12. The righteous shall flourish like the palm tree: he shall grow like a cedar in Lebanon.

13. *Plantati in domo Domini, in atrius domus Dei nostri florebunt.*

13. Those that be planted in the house of the Lord shall flourish in the courts of our God.

Lesser Doxology

14. *Gloria Patri et Filio, et Spiritui Sancto.*

14. Glory be to the Father, the Son, and the Holy Spirit.

15. *Sicut erat in principio, et nunc, et semper, et in secula seculorum. Amen.*

15. As it was in the beginning, is now, and ever shall be, world without end. Amen.

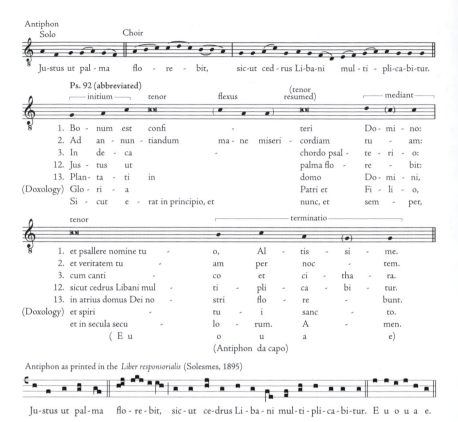

b. Introit (Commemoration of a Saint Who Was a Confessor but Not a Bishop)

The Introit is the opening chant of the Mass Proper (the part of the Mass with texts that change from service to service), during which the congregation enters. Its style is based on the psalmodic practice of the Office antiphons, but it is more elaborate than its Office counterpart because of its grander role as the first musical item of the Mass. Though they originally included recitation of entire psalms, Introits were later shortened to an antiphon (or, more specifically, the "Introit antiphon") sung before and after a single psalm verse plus the Doxology as follows: antiphon–verse–Doxology–antiphon. The example shown here is sung at Masses commemorating saints who were confessors but not bishops. The Introit antiphon sets the text of verses 12 and 13 of Psalm 92. The first time it is sung a soloist sings up to the asterisk to set the pitch before the choir joins in. Then comes the verse "Bonum est," verse 1 of Psalm 92, plus the obligatory Doxology, written in abbreviated form to save space. Both are sung to a tone that is more elaborate than the Office psalm tones but nevertheless features considerable recitation on the tenor. After the Doxology the antiphon is repeated, all of it sung by the full choir.

The antiphon is mostly neumatic, but it has several compound neumes that verge on the melismatic style. The first syllable, for instance, is set to a seven-note melisma that ends with a pulsating triple note. Over "palma" there is a three-note ascent, immediately followed by a three-note descent from the high note, which is sung twice for additional emphasis. The highest note of the antiphon—an octave above its lowest note—is reached in the syllable "-ca-" of "multiplicabitur," which is also the most melismatic word of the antiphon. The final phrase of the antiphon, "Dei nostri," returns three times to the lowest note before cadencing on D. The pair of "alleluia" exclamations that comes between the antiphon and the verse is sung when the saint's commemoration happens to fall during the fifty-day period after Easter known as Paschal Time, the gladdest season of the church year.

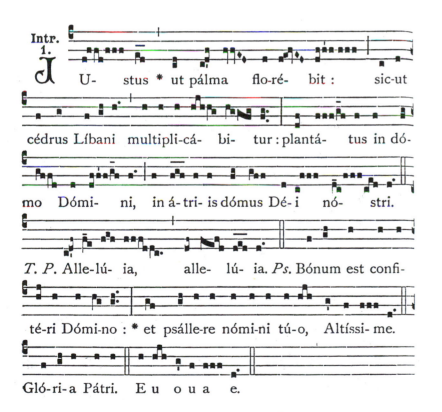

c. Offertory (Commemoration of a Church Doctor)

The Offertory and Communion are two further movements of the Mass Proper. Although they originated as psalmodic chants of the Eucharist portion of the Mass (the portion that recreated the Last Supper), they were eventually entirely shorn of their psalm verses, which in the case of the Offertory were once very elaborate indeed. They are sung as freestanding antiphons amounting to autonomous "arias" for the choir. The *Justus ut palma* Offertory comes from the mass commemorating a saint who was a "Doctor of the Church," a title reserved for only the most learned and wise of scholar saints. The style of the Offertory is fully melismatic. All of the words that were given neumatic settings in the Introit ("justus," "palma," "multiplicabitur") are now set to much longer and more effusive melodies.

d. Alleluia (Commemoration of an Abbot)

Finally, the *Justus ut palma* verse was also used in the "lesson chants" of the Mass Proper, sung between the scriptural readings (the Epistle and the Gospel) that frame the Synaxis (pre-Eucharist) portion of the Mass. These chants are sung while there is little or no liturgical action, and they are intended much more than the other chants to comment on the scriptural readings and to foster contemplation of their divine themes. These are the most melismatic of all chants in the Mass because they are the sole focus of the worshipping community while they are being sung. *Justus ut palma* appears both as a Gradual, immediately after the Epistle reading (see Vol 1-3a), and as an Alleluia verse (shown here), which precedes the Gospel. The Alleluia given here comes from a Mass commemorating a saint who was an abbot, or head of a monastery.

The Gradual and the Alleluia are *responsorial* chants, in which a skilled soloist alternates with the full choir (as opposed to antiphonal chants, in which two halves of the choir alternate with one another). In the Alleluia, the soloist sings the word "Alleluia" up to the asterisk, after which the choir begins the word again and continues through the *jubilus*, the fifty-one-note melisma that follows on the final syllable, "-a." The soloist sings most of the verse alone but is joined by the choir at the asterisk for the final word ("multiplicabitur"). The entire Alleluia (with jubilus) is then repeated by the full choir, giving the whole a "rounded" or ternary (ABA) form. Note also that the melody of the Alleluia and jubilus—essentially a textless exclamation of joy—is repeated exactly at the end of the verse on "multiplicabitur." This large-scale repetition is mirrored on a small scale by internal melodic repetitions on the words "sicut cedrus," representable as aabb. Such internal repetitions characterize many Alleluia chants.

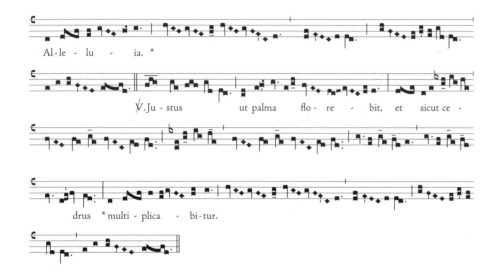

3

Two Graduals

The Gradual was, along with the Alleluia, one of the responsorial chants sung after (and in response to) the Epistle reading during the Synaxis portion of the Mass. Given here are two Graduals, each of which consists of a melismatic respond for the whole choir and an even more melismatic verse (a single psalm verse) for a highly skilled soloist. The first of these Graduals was assigned in Carolingian times to the feast of St. John the Baptist (24 June), and its respond is yet another setting of the *Justus ut palma* verse. The second Gradual is from the Mass for Easter Sunday, a very famous chant that sets a text consisting of two verses from Psalm 118, one serving as the respond, the other as the soloist's verse. As in the Alleluia, a soloist alternates with the choir. At the beginning of each chant, the soloist sings to the asterisk ("Justus" and "Haec dies") and is then joined by the full choir for the remainder of the respond. The same soloist/ choir alternation is indicated in the verse, except that the verse is given primarily to the soloist, who sings alone until the asterisks (on "per noctem" and "ejus"), after which the choir joins in for the remainder of the verse. The respond is not repeated.

The brackets placed in the music show that these two chants make heavy use of a shared group of melodic figures, which in fact appear in a whole family of Graduals that numbers more than twenty in all. What is most striking about these shared melodic phrases is that they occur most frequently at the beginnings of sections and (especially) at cadential points. How many of them are used in a given chant and how many times they are repeated are determined by the length of the text. In other words, these extremely elaborate chants still behave, despite their flowing melismatic style, very much like the psalm tones they may once have been. Scholars used to think that these shared melodic figures were indicative of an additive process of composition called *centonization* (after the Latin *cento*, "quilt"), in which composers picked and chose from a small group of melodic formulas in creating "patchwork" compositions. Today, however, most music historians prefer a different analogy or model: Instead of a fund of individual memorized formulas from which chants were assembled on the basis of artistic ingenuity and taste, one imagines a slow process in which an original repertory of simple chants within a given liturgical genre became more and more ornate over time, all of the chants in the genre being elaborated in a similar manner. The formulas shown here, for example, are found only in Graduals, but there are other, similar figures that are characteristic of other genres.

Our current concept of mode, based on a scale and defined mainly in terms of its range and final note, does not fit very well the Gregorian repertory that we have examined thus far. This concept of mode was originally the product of Frankish and Italian music theory of the tenth and eleventh centuries, long after the Graduals *Justus ut palma* and *Haec dies* were composed. Although both chants were later classified as mode 2, or "Hypodorian," melodies (transposed up a fifth so that the final is on A, not D), neither is a perfect fit within that mode—the B♭ that is the third note of *Haec dies*, for instance, implies a Phrygian, rather than a Dorian, construction. As we shall see in several subsequent examples in this anthology, the chants composed by later Frankish musicians, who had been trained according to this theory, conform much more closely to our accustomed idea of what a mode is.

a. *Justus ut palma* (Feast of St. John the Baptist)

R: *Justus ut palma florebit: sicut cedrus Libani multiplicabitur in domo Domini.*

The righteous shall flourish like the palm tree: he shall grow in the house of the Lord like a cedar in Lebanon (Ps. 92, 12).

V: *Ad annuntiandum mane misericordiam tuam, et veritatem tuam per noctem.*

To shew forth thy lovingkindness in the morning, and thy faithfulness every night (Ps. 92, 2).

b. *Haec dies* (Easter Sunday)

R: *Haec dies, quam fecit Dominus:*
exsultemus, et laetemur in ea.

This is the day which the Lord hath
made: we will rejoice and be glad in it
(Ps. 118, 24).

V: *Confitemini Domino, quoniam bonus:*
quoniam in saeculum misericordia ejus

O give thanks unto the Lord, for He is
good: because his mercy endureth
forever (Ps. 118, 1)

4

Frankish Chants for the Mass Ordinary

There were a few invariant texts of the Mass liturgy that were recited at every Mass regardless of the occasion. In the pre-Carolingian era, during which the psalmodic chants examined thus far were composed, these texts had not yet been assigned stable liturgical positions. In the ninth and tenth centuries the Franks assigned them stable positions and composed numerous melodies for them. The adoption of these texts—all of them acclamations—into the Mass reflects a Frankish love of pomp, most likely transferred from civic ceremonies, such as the *laudes regiae*, the "royal acclamations" with which Charlemagne was greeted after his Roman coronation. Once these invariant Mass texts became fixed, they could be prescribed as part of the Mass *ordo* (Latin for "order of events"), which listed things to do at a given service. Hence to musicians the term Mass Ordinary (from *ordinarium missae*) has come to mean, precisely, the five invariant texts of the Mass: Kyrie, Gloria, Credo, Sanctus, and Agnus Dei, all of which were sung, after a brief solo intonation, by the full choir. In the ninth and tenth centuries they were part of a Frankish standardization and expansion of the liturgy that also included composition of sequences, hymns, and tropes, which we will see later in this anthology (Vol 1-5–8). Starting in the fourteenth century the Mass Ordinary movements were given unified polyphonic settings, establishing the tradition of Mass composition that has lasted until the present time, to which composers of the standard concert repertoire such as Bach, Mozart, and Beethoven (to name only a few) made contributions.

a. Kyrie IV

The Kyrie has a complicated and puzzling history. That it is a special chant is evident from the language of its text: It is one of the few bits of Greek that found their way into the Latin Mass. "Kyrie eleison" means the same thing as the Latin "Domine, miserere nobis," namely, "Lord, have mercy on us" (compare the middle part of the Gloria and the Agnus Dei refrain). In early Christian times it was a common liturgical response, especially appropriate for use in the long series of petitions known as *litanies*, which often accompanied processions. Pope Gregory the Great (reigned 590–604), in one of the few musically or liturgically significant acts that may be

firmly associated with his name, wrote a letter decreeing that the refrain "Kyrie eleison" should not simply be repeated but should alternate with "Christe eleison" ("Christ [that is, Savior], have mercy on us"). By the time Frankish musicians began composing melodies for the Kyrie in the ninth century, a ninefold structure had been established: thrice "Kyrie eleison," thrice "Christe eleison," thrice "Kyrie eleison."

As in all the Mass Ordinary genres, there are simple Kyries that probably reflect early congregational singing and more decorative melodies, like the one given here, that were probably produced at the Frankish monasteries for their more highly trained choirs, beginning in the tenth century. The more elaborate Kyrie tunes often match the ninefold elaboration of the three-part Kyrie text with patterns of repetition like AAA BBB AAA' or AAA BBB CCC', as in the Kyrie *Cunctipotens genitor* shown here. The last invocation (C') repeats its opening melisma, making it more emphatic than the previous C sections. Notice that the words "Kyrie," "Christe," and "Kyrie" are set to an ABC pattern that lacks repetition, whereas the word "eleison" repeats to an AA'B pattern. The repetition of the same formula for "eleison" following the different "Kyrie" and "Christe" melodies seems to be a vestige of the refrains that were sung in earlier congregational litanies.

Kyrie eleison.	Lord, have mercy on us.
Christe eleison.	Christ, have mercy on us.
Kyrie eleison.	Lord, have mercy on us.

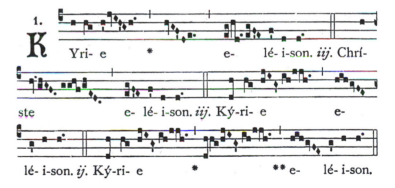

b. *Cunctipotens Genitor Deus*

In the earliest sources of Kyries, dating from the eleventh century, the chants appear twice, first in the melismatic form as shown in part a, and then syllabically texted as shown here, with words that amplify and expand on the very short Kyrie text, much as tropes—which we will see later in this anthology (Vol 1-8)—comment on the chants to which they are appended. The texted version of the Kyrie looks at first glance like a *prosula* (text added to a melisma) on the melismatic version, but it is actually unclear which came first. Sixteenth-century chant reformers assumed that the melismatic versions were the earlier and "original" ones, and so they purged all syllabic

Kyrie texts from the liturgy (along with all tropes and most sequences). Yet despite this fact, the syllabic incipits are still used to identify the Kyrie melodies in modern liturgical books. The melody given earlier is now called "Kyrie IV (*Cunctipotens genitor*)" because it is the fourth Kyrie given in modern chant books and was earlier associated with this syllabic text.

Cunctipotens genitor, Deus omnicreator, eleison.	Almighty Father, all-creating God, have mercy upon us.
Fons et origo boni, pie, luxque perennis, eleison.	Fount and source of good, kindly light eternal, have mercy upon us.
Salvificet pietas tua nos, bone rector, eleison.	May Thy mercy save us, O good guide, have mercy upon us.
Christe, Dei splendor, virtus patrisque Sophia, eleison.	O Christ, Lord, splendor, power and wisdom of the Father, have mercy upon us.
Plasmatis humani factor, lapsi reperatur, eleison.	O Redeemer of mankind, redresser of error, have mercy upon us.
Ne tua damnetur, Jesu, factura benigne, eleison.	Let us not disdain Thy deeds, O gentle Jesus; have mercy upon us.
Amborum sacrum spiramen, nexus amorque, eleison.	Sacred spirit of both, and united love, have mercy upon us.
Procetens fomes, vitae fons, pucificans vis, eleison.	Perpetual activator of life, purifying fount, have mercy upon us.
Purgator culpae, veniae largitor opimae, offenses dele, sancto nos munere, reple, spiritus alme, eleison.	Highest cleanser of sin, bestower of mercy, take away our offenses, fill us with Thy holy bounty. O nourishing spirit, have mercy upon us.

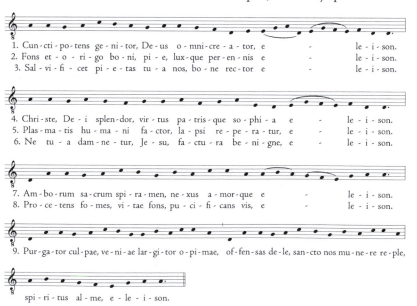

c. Gloria IV

The Gloria, also known as the *Gloria in excelsis*, or Greater Doxology (to distinguish it from the *Gloria patri*, or Lesser Doxology, inserted at the end of psalm recitation), was the first movement of the Mass Ordinary to be cultivated. Its text opens with two verses from the Gospel of Luke, which quote the angels' "Annunciation to the shepherds" on the night of Christ's Nativity. For this reason, before it was assigned to its fixed position in the Mass, the *Gloria in excelsis* was often used as a Christmas processional hymn, forming the culmination of the celebrants' entrance. (It was also used this way at Easter; after it joined the Mass, it was not sung during the penitential weeks preceding those two feasts so that its reappearance would express seasonal gladness.) After the angelic announcement come several *laudes* (praises) that may actually have originated in the worship of earthly rulers. Next comes a series of petitions ("Domine Deus . . .") and then a concluding song of praise ("Quoniam to solus sanctus . . ."). The earliest liturgical use of the Gloria seems to have been fully congregational, characterized by simple, formulaic, and mostly syllabic melodies. But the Glorias preserved in Frankish manuscripts are mostly neumatic, with occasional melismatic flourishes, and are clearly intended for a trained clerical or monastic choir. The Gloria given here is a ninth-century melody, one of the earliest of the forty or so surviving Frankish settings. Its number, IV, is the one assigned to it in modern chant books.

Gloria in excelsis Deo. Et in terra pax hominibus bonae voluntatis. Laudamus te. Benedicimus te. Adoramus te. Glorificamus te. Gratias agimus tibi propter magnam gloriam tuam. Domine Deus, Rex caelestis, Deus Pater omnipotens. Domine Fili unigenite Jesu Christe. Domine Deus, Agnus Dei, Filius Patris. Qui tollis peccata mundi, Miserere nobis. Qui tollis peccata mundi, suscipe deprecationem nostram. Qui sedes ad desteram Patris, Miserere nobis. Quoniam tu solus sanctus. Tu solus Dominus. Tu solus Altissimus, Jesu Christe. Cum Sancto Spiritu, in Gloria Dei Patris. Amen	Glory to God on high. And on earth peace to men of good will. We praise thee, we bless the, we adore thee, we glorify thee. We give thee thanks for thy great glory. O Lord God, King of heaven, God the Father almighty. O Lord, the only begotten Son, Jesus Christ. O Lord God, Lamb of God, Son of the Father. Thou who takest away the sins of the world, have mercy on us. Thou who takest away the sins of the world, receive our prayer. Thou who sittest at the right hand of the Father, have mercy on us. For thou only art holy, thou only art Lord. Thou only art most high, O Jesus Christ. With the Holy Ghost, in the glory of God the Father. Amen.

Glo - ri - a in excelsis De - o. Et in terra pax ho - mi - ni - bus bonae vo - lunta - tis. Laudamus te.

Bene - di - cimus te. Ado - ra - mus te. Glo - ri - fica - mus te.   Gra - ti - as agimus

ti - bi propter magnam glo - ri - am tu - am. Domi - ne De - us, Rex caelestis, De - us Pa - ter

omni - pot - ens. Domine Fi - li uni - geni - te Je - su Chri - ste. Domine De - us,

Agnus De - i, Fi - li - us Pa - tris.   Qui tollis pecca - ta mundi, mi - se - re - re no - bis.

Qui tollis pecca - ta mundi, suscipe depreca - ti - onem nostram. Qui se - des ad dexteram Patris,

mi - se - re - re no - bis. Quo - ni - am tu so - lus sanctus. Tu so - lus Dominus. Tu solus Altissimus,

Je - su Chri - ste. Cum Sancto Spi - ri - tu, in glo - ri - a De - i Pa - tris.

A - men.

d. Credo I

The Credo is a setting of the Nicene Creed, a statement of the basic tenets of Christianity that was adopted at the fourth-century Council of Nicaea. There are far fewer melodies for it than for the other Mass Ordinary movements. Though originally sung as part of the baptism ceremony, it was adopted by the Franks in 798 as part of the Mass, and Pope Benedict VIII (reigned 1012–24) made it part of the Mass of the entire Catholic Church in 1014, positioning it between the Gospel reading and the Offertory. It thus served as a divider between the Synaxis and Eucharist portions of the Mass. The melody given here (Credo I in modern chant books) is by far the most

common Credo melody and is one of the oldest melodies still being used in the liturgy. Unlike the other Mass Ordinary compositions given here, which have ninth- or tenth-century Frankish origins, this one has archaic Greek origins. With its regular use of B♭ and E to surround the reciting tone on G and its final cadence on E, it is a rather exotic specimen within the Gregorian chant repertoire. Yet although it seems to emphasize the odd interval of a diminished fifth, the melody nevertheless fully conforms to the intervallic structure of the diatonic pitch set. Transposed up a fifth or down a fourth it could be accommodated on the staff without accidentals.

Credo in unum Deum, Patrem omnipotentem, factorem caeli et terrae, visibilium omnium et invisibilium. Et in unum Dominum Jesum Christum, Filium Dei unigenitum. Et ex Patre natum ante omnia saecula. Deum de Deo, lumen de lumine, Deum verum de Deo vero. Genitum, non factum, consubstantialem Patri: per quem omnia facta sunt. Qui propter nos homines, et propter nostram salutem descendit de caelis. Et incarnatus est de Spiritu Sancto ex Maria virgine: et homo factus est. Crucifixus etiam pro nobis sub Pontio Pilato: passus, et sepultus est. Et resurrexit tertia die, secundum scripturas. Et ascendit in caelum, sedet ad dexteram Patris. Et iterum venturus est cum gloria judicare vivos et mortuos: cuius regni non erit finis.

I believe in one God, the Father almighty, maker of heaven and earth, and of all things visible and invisible. And in one Lord Jesus Christ, the only-begotten Son of God, begotten of his Father before all ages, God of God, Light of Light, true God of true God, begotten, not made, being of one substance with the Father, by whom all things were made; who for us and for our salvation descended from heaven, And was incarnated by the Holy Spirit through the Virgin Mary, and was made man, and was crucified for us under Pontius Pilate. He suffered and was buried, and on the third day rose again according to the scriptures, and ascended into heaven, and sits at the right hand of the Father. And he shall come again with glory to judge both the living and the dead, he whose kingdom shall have no end.

Et in Spiritum Sanctum Dominum, et vivificantem: qui ex patre, filioque procedit. Qui cum Patre, et Filio simul adoratur, et conglorificatur: qui locutus est per prophetas.

And I believe in the Holy Spirit, the Lord and giver of life, who proceeds from the Father and the Son, who with the Father and the Son together is worshipped and glorified, who spoke through the prophets.

Et unam, sanctam, catholicam et apostolicam Ecclesiam. Confiteor unum baptisma in remissionem peccatorum. Et exspecto resurrectionem mortuorum. Et vitam venturi saeculi. Amen.

And I believe in one catholic and apostolic church. I acknowledge one baptism for the remission of sins. And I look for the resurrection of the dead, and the life of the world to come. Amen.

4.

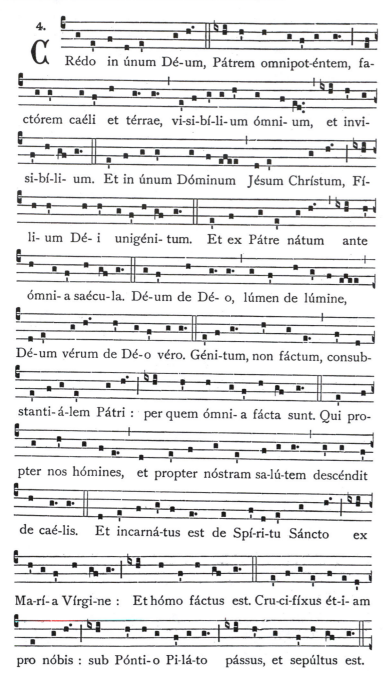

CRédo in únum Déum, Pátrem omnipot-éntem, factórem caéli et térrae, vi-si-bí-li-um ómni-um, et invisi-bí-li-um. Et in únum Dóminum Jésum Chrístum, Fí-li-um Dé-i unigéni-tum. Et ex Pátre nátum ante ómni-a saécu-la. Dé-um de Dé-o, lúmen de lúmine, Dé-um vérum de Dé-o véro. Géni-tum, non fáctum, consub-stanti-á-lem Pátri : per quem ómni-a fácta sunt. Qui pro-pter nos hómines, et propter nóstram sa-lú-tem descéndit de caé-lis. Et incarná-tus est de Spí-ri-tu Sáncto ex Ma-rí-a Vírgi-ne : Et hómo fáctus est. Cru-ci-fíxus ét-i-am pro nóbis : sub Pónti-o Pi-lá-to pássus, et sepúltus est.

Et resurréxit térti-a dí-e, secúndum Scriptúras. Et ascéndit in caélum : sédet ad déxte-ram Pátris. Et í-te-rum ventúrus est cum gló-ri-a, judi-cá-re vívos et mórtu-os : cú-jus régni non é-rit fí-nis. Et in Spí-ri-tum Sánctum Dóminum, et vi-vi-fi-cántem : qui ex Pátre Fi-li-óque procé-dit. Qui cum Pátre et Fí-li-o simul ado-rá-tur, et con-glo-ri-fi-cá-tur : qui locútus est per Prophé-tas. Et únam sánctam cathó-li-cam et apostó-li-cam Ecclé-si-am. Confí-te-or únum baptísma in remissi-ónem pecca-tó-rum. Et exspécto resurrecti-ónem mortu-ó-rum. Et ví-tam ventú-ri saé-cu-li. A-men.

e. Sanctus I

The Sanctus is an acclamation from the book of Isaiah in the Old Testament. It was adopted early on in Christian worship as the congregational part of the Eucharistic prayer of thanksgiving. The Hebrew version of it, the *Kedusha*, has been a part of Jewish worship since ancient times, and its Latin text retains two Hebrew words: "Sabaoth" ("hosts") and "Hosanna" ("save us"), which is stated twice, once after the "Pleni sunt caeli" section and once after the "Benedictus" section. The melody given here, Sanctus I in modern chant books, dates from the tenth century and is one of the earliest Frankish settings. Like the Gloria, which had also originated as a full congregational song, the Sanctus, by the time the Franks began composing melodies for it, was intended for a trained choir.

Sanctus, Sanctus, Sanctus	Holy, holy, holy, Lord
Dominus Deus Sabaoth.	God of Hosts.
Pleni sunt caeli et terra Gloria tua.	The heavens and earth are full of thy glory.
Hosanna in excelsis.	Hosanna in the highest.
Benedictus qui venit in nomine Domini.	Blessed is he who comes in the name of the Lord.
Hosanna in excelsis.	Hosanna in the highest.

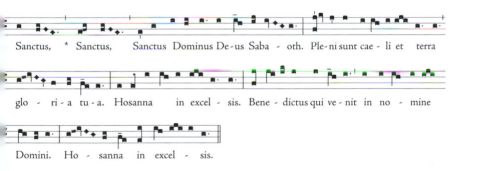

three acclamations, with the response to the third one changed to "Grant us peace" (*Dona nobis pacem*). The text and melodies of the Frankish Agnus Dei settings are thus roughly contemporaneous. The example given here, a Frankish arrangement and abridgment of the earliest (Greek) surviving melody for the Agnus Dei, is in a "rounded" or ternary (ABA) form, with each section matching one of the three sections of the text. Its style is neumatic, in the manner of an antiphon for the Divine Office.

Agnus Dei, qui tollis peccata mundi:	Lamb of God, who takest away the sins
Miserere nobis.	of the world, have mercy on us.
Agnus Dei, qui tollis peccata mundi:	Lamb of God, who takest away the sins
Miserere nobis.	of the world, have mercy on us.
Agnus Dei, qui tollis peccata mundi:	Lamb of God, who takest away the sins
Dona nobis pacem.	of the world, grant us peace.

f. Agnus Dei II

The Agnus Dei has a much shorter history in the liturgy than does the Sanctus. It was introduced into the Mass in the seventh century to accompany the breaking of the bread before Communion. At first it was a type of litany with an indefinite number of soloistic petitions to the Lamb of God (*Agnus Dei*), to which the congregation always responded "Have mercy on us" (*Miserere nobis*). Around the time the Franks began composing their melodies for the Mass Ordinary, the Agnus Dei was standardized and abbreviated so that, like the Kyrie, it consisted of

5

Two Sequences in Modern Use

The *sequence*, a new genre of musical and poetic composition cultivated by Frankish composers starting in the ninth century, became an additional movement of the Mass Proper on high feast days, where it was placed immediately after the Alleluia. Sequences are almost entirely syllabic. They demonstrate the tendency of their composers to regularize tonally and formally, to add the additional regularizing element of metrical verse, and to use these stabilizing dimensions to reinforce one another. Like tropes—which we will see a little bit later in this anthology (Vol 1-8)—most of them were purged from the liturgy by the Council of Trent in the mid-sixteenth century. Two that survived into the modern liturgy are given here.

a. *Victimae paschali laudes* (Easter)

The Easter sequence *Victimae paschali laudes* has been attributed to the German monk Wipo, who was chaplain to the Holy Roman Emperor Conrad II (reigned 1024–39). It has the paired versicle structure that was typical of the Frankish sequence from the earliest examples by Notker Balbulus of St. Gallen (ca. 840–912): a, bb, cc, dd, and so forth. The piece as given here lacks a repetition of the d phrase ("Scimus Christum . . .") because it was officially expurgated by the Catholic Church. The first of the d verse pair had read: "Credendum est magis soli Mariae veraci quam Judaeorum turbae fallaci" ("More trust is to be put in honest Mary [Magdalene] alone than in the lying crowd of Jews"). Sensible to its nastiness and aware of its bearing on a history of persecutions, the Council of Trent, the same mid-sixteenth-century congress of church reform that evicted almost all the other sequences from the liturgy, pruned the offending verse as a gesture of reconciliation with the Jews.

The constituent phrases of *Victimae paschali laudes* describe the principal parts of the Dorian (modes 1 and 2) modal scale with great regularity. The two phrases of the *a* section describe the modal pentachord above the D final, with the first phrase darkened by the Dorian lower neighbor (C), and the second compensating by adding the previously withheld top note (A). The *b* section makes a steady descent from the authentic tetrachord (A–D above the pentachord) through the "darkened" pentachord (that is, the pentachord with lower-neighbor C)

and then back to the final D. Verse *c* extends downward, to describe the plagal tetrachord (A–D below the final), proceeding through the "darkened" pentachord to the regular pentachord. The *d* section, which resembles the *b* section, begins like it, with the authentic tetrachord at the top of the modal ambitus, and again gradually descends to the final, with the final phrase (and also the paschal alleluia) colored dark by the use of the lower neighbor.

Victimae paschali laudes immolent Christiani.	Let Christians offer praises to the paschal victim.
Agnus redemit oves: Christus innocens Patri reconciliavit peccatores.	The lamb has redeemed the sheep; innocent Christ has reconciled sinners to the Father.
Mors et vita duello conflixere mirando: dux vitae mortuus, regnat vivus.	Death and life have engaged in a miraculous duel; the slain leader of life reigns living.
Dic nobis Maria, quid vidisti in via? Sepulcrum Christi viventis, et gloriam vidi resurgentis:	Tell us, Mary, what did you see in the way? I saw the tomb of Christ and the glory of the resurgent one,
Angelicos testes, sudarium, et vestes. Surrexit Christus spes mea: praecedet suos in Galilaeam.	The angelic witnesses, the shroud and the vestments. Christ, my hope, is risen; he goes before his people in Galilee.
Scimus Christum surrexisse a mortuis vere: tu nobis victor Rex, miserere.	We know that Christ truly is risen from the dead. You, our victorious King, have mercy on us.
Amen. Alleluia.	Amen. Alleluia.

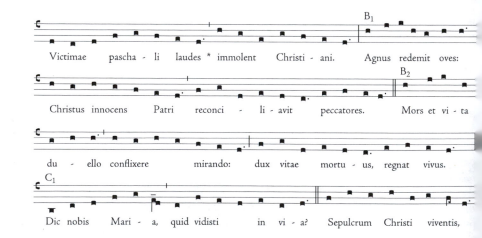

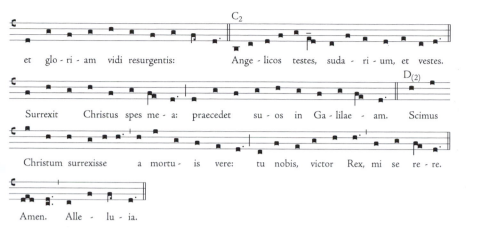

et glo-ri-am vidi resurgentis: Ange-licos testes, suda-ri-um, et vestes.

Surrexit Christus spes me-a: praecedet su-os in Ga-lilae-am. Scimus

Christum surrexisse a mortu-is vere: tu nobis, victor Rex, mi se-re-re.

Amen. Alle-lu-ia.

b. *Dies irae* (Mass for the Dead)

Dies irae, the sequence from the Mass for the Dead (called the Requiem Mass because it opens with the Introit *Requiem aeternam*), may well be the most famous of all Medieval chants. It was quoted by numerous later composers, including Hector Berlioz (1803–69) in his *Symphonie Fantastique*, as a musical signifier of death and the final judgment. The *Dies irae* text is attributed to Thomas of Celano (d. ca. 1255), a disciple and biographer of St. Francis of Assisi (1181/2–1226), and the music too probably dates from the thirteenth century. It is thus a very late chant composition. The rhymed tercets, composed of eight-syllable lines with regular patterns of accentuation, were the norm in sequence composition by the mid-twelfth century, as was their musical setting in a double versicle structure, in which all phrases, including the first, are repeated (aa, bb, cc, etc.). Within this very rigid poetic and formal scheme, Thomas's poem elaborates on the second verse— "Dies illa, die irae"—of the responsory *Libera me, Domine, de morte aeterna* ("Deliver me, O Lord, from eternal death"), sung during the graveside service that follows the Requiem Mass. The beginning of the melody even alludes to that of the responsory verse.

The full *Dies irae* chant has a melodic repetition scheme that is more rigid than the normal double versicle structure. It goes through a nearly complete triple *cursus* (threefold repetition): aabbcc/aabbcc/aabbc, after which follows a final couplet (dd) and a brief "Amen," which were added by an anonymous reviser in place of the final c section. (The score given here shows only the first cursus.) The constituent musical sections are characterized by numerous internal repetitions. The second phrase of the b section ("per sepulcra regionum"), for example, is an embellished variant of the responsory-derived opening phrase of a ("Dies irae, dies illa") and thus comes to function almost as a refrain. And once again, the melody delineates the principal parts of the Dorian mode with great clarity. The a section occupies the Hypodorian ambitus (A to A), minus the highest note; the b section stakes out the upper tetrachord (A to D), but again minus the highest note); and the c section sinks back into Hypodorian space (this is, after all, a funereal chant).

Dies irae, dies illa,
Solvet saeclum in favilla:
Teste David cum Sibylla.

Dreaded day, that day of ire,
When the world shall melt in fire,
Told by Sybil and David's lyre.

Quantus tremor est futurus,
Quando judex est venturus,
Cuncta stricte discussurus!

Fright men's hearts shall rudely shift,
As the judge through gleaming rift
Comes each soul to closely sift.

Tuba mirum spargens sonum
Per sepulcra regionum,
Coget omnes ante thronum.

Then, the trumpet's shrill refrain,
Piercing tombs by hill and plain,
Souls to judgment shall arraign.

Mors stupebit et natura,
Cum resurget creatura,
Judicanti responsura.

Death and nature stand aghast,
As the bodies rising fast,
Hie to hear the sentence passed.

Liber scriptus proferetur,
In quo totum continetur,
Unde mundus judicetur.

Then, before him shall be placed,
That whereon the verdict's based,
Book wherein each deed is traced.

Judex ergo cum sedebit,
Quidquid latet apparebit:
Nil inultum remanebit.

When the Judge his seat shall gain,
All that's hidden shall be plain,
Nothing shall unjudged remain.

Di-es irae, di-es illa, Solvet saeclum in favilla: Teste David cum Sibylla.

Quantus tremor est futurus, Quando ju-dex est venturus, Cuncta stricte discussurus!

Tuba mi-rum spar-gens sonum Per sepulcra regi-onum, Coget omnes ante thronum.

Mors stupe-bit et natu-ra, Cum resurget cre-a-tura, Judi-can-ti responsura.

Liber scriptus pro-fe-re-tur, In quo to-tum contine-tur, Unde mundus judi-ce-tur.

Judex ergo cum sedebit, Quidquid la-tet apparebit: Nil inultum remanebit.

6

Hildegard of Bingen (1098–1179)

Columba aspexit (Sequence for St. Maximinus)

Hildegard of Bingen, Abbess of the Benedictine convent of Rupertsberg in the Rhine Valley near the German city of Trier, was a famous visionary and writer and a prolific composer of chant. Her compositions are mostly antiphons, hymns, and sequences devoted to various saints—the sequence *Columba aspexit*, given here, was composed for the feast of St. Maximinus, a local saint of Trier. Hildegard's chants display a highly individual and original style that is very different from what we have seen elsewhere. Whereas late sequences like *Dies irae* reflect a formal, modal, and metrical clarity that accorded with the highly rigorous scholastic theology of Augustine, Boethius, and Aquinas, Hildegard used highly vivid poetry and music to express the "symphony of the harmony of heavenly revelation" (*Symphonia armonie celestium revelationum*), the title that she gave to her collected works, which she compiled in the late 1150s. Her melodies often have an extremely wide ambitus (sometimes spanning as much as two and a half octaves!), feature much more extended scalar melody than we have seen in other chants, and are not easily parsed into the abstract modal functions of the Frankish chant theorists. Her fantastic diction, melodic style, and imagery are all her own.

Columba aspexit is a wonderful example of Hildegard's effusive and idiosyncratic style. It features the traditional paired versicles of sequence composition, but whereas most sequence versicles form strict pairs, Hildegard's form only loose pairs with similar but not identical melodies (verse 5 has no pair at all). The process resembles melodic variation rather than rote repetition. The mode, too, with its C final, is fluid, seeming to oscillate between transposed Lydian and transposed Mixolydian (C was not recognized as a modal final in its own right until the sixteenth century). Perhaps most striking, the imagery is very vivid and appeals directly to the senses, especially the sense of smell. Derived largely from the Song of Songs (an especially sensuous book of the Old Testament), it creates a rich sensuous experience for the listener that one associates with revelation rather than analytical thought. Her musical compositions, just like her writings, reflect the divine visions for which she was famous.

Columba aspexit	The dove peered in
per cancellos fenestre	through the lattices of the window

ubi ante faciem eius	where, before its face,
sudando sudavit balsamum	a balm exuded
de lucido Maximino.	from incandescent Maximinus.

Calor solis exarsit	The heat of the sun burned
et in tenebras resplenduit	dazzling into the gloom:
unde gemma surrexit	whence a jewel sprang forth
in edificatione templi	in the building of the temple
purissimi cordis benivoli.	of the purest loving heart.

Iste, turris excelsa,	He, the high tower,
de ligno Libani	constructed of cedar of Lebanon
et cipresso facta,	and cypress,
iacincto et sardio ornata est,	has been adorned with jacinth and onyx,
urbs precellens artes	a city excelling the crafts
aliorum artificum.	of other builders.

Ipse, velox cervus,	He, the swift hart,
cucurrit ad fontem purissime aque	ran to the fountain of clearest water
fluentis de fortissimo lapide	flowing from the most powerful stone
qui dulcia aromata irrigavit.	which courses with delightful spices.

O pigmentarii	O Perfume-Makers,
qui estis in suavissima viriditate	you who are in the sweetest greenness
hortorum regis,	of the gardens of the King,
ascendentes in altum	ascending on high
quando sanctum sacrificium	when you have completed the holy
in arietibus perfecistis,	sacrifice with the rams,

Inter vos fulget hic artifex,	This builder shines among you,
paries templi,	the wall of the temple,
qui desideravit alas aquiloe,	who longed for the wings of an eagle,
osculando nutricem Sapientiam	kissing his nurse Wisdom
in gloriosa fecunditate Ecclesie.	in the glorious fecundity of the Church.

O Maximine,	O Maximinus,
mons et vallis es,	you are the mount and the valley
et in utroque alta edificatio appares,	and in both you seem a high building,
ubi capricornus cum elephante exivit,	where the goat went with the elephant
et Sapientia in deliciis fuit.	and Wisdom was in rapture.

Tu es fortis	You are strong
et suavis	and beautiful
in cerimoniis	in rites

et in choruscatione altaris,
ascendens ut fumus aromatum
ad columpnam laudis,

Ubi intercedis pro populo
Qui tendit ad speculum lucis,
Cui laus est in altis.

(Trans. Christopher Page)

and in the shining of the altar,
mounting like the smoke of perfumes
to the column of praise,

Where you intercede for the people who
stretch towards the mirror of light
to whom there is praise on high.

R ff.474^{r/v} (Sequentia de sancto Maximino)

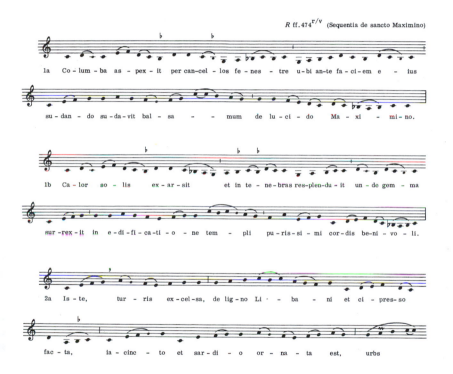

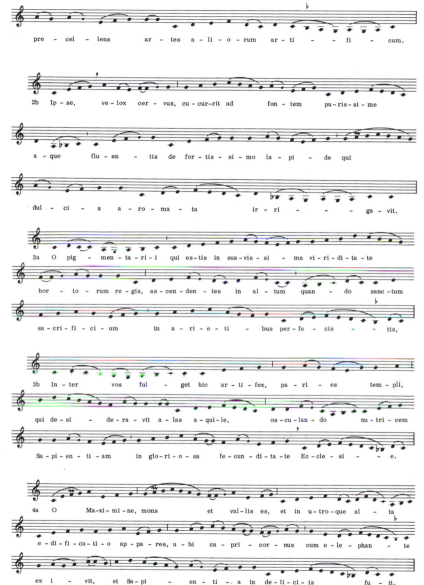

4b Tu es for - tis et sua - vis in ce - ri - mo - ni - is et

in cho - rus - ca - ti - o - ne al - ta - ris, as - cen - dens ut fu - mus

a - ro - ma - tum ad co - lump - nam lau - dis,

5 U - bi in - ter - ce - dis pro po - pu - lo qui ten - dit

ad spe - cu - lum lu - cis, cu - i laus est in al - tis.

7

Three Frankish Hymns

The *hymn* is a chant in strophic form sung most often in the various liturgical services of the Divine Office. It was yet another new type of musical composition with which the Franks adorned and amplified the Gregorian liturgy, making it their own, in the ninth and tenth centuries. The Latin liturgy had known hymnody since at least the fourth century, but for doctrinal reasons it was rejected in Rome (and so it was not part of the repertory brought north under the Carolingians in the ninth century). St. Augustine recounts that his teacher, St. Ambrose, the fourth-century bishop of Milan, had adapted hymns from Greek practice for full congregational singing during vigils (or matins), the office sung in the middle of the night. The greatest Latin hymnographer after Ambrose was a contemporary of Pope Gregory the Great named Venantius Fortunatus (d. ca. 600), an Italian who served as bishop of Poitiers in west-central France. Both Ambrose's fourth-century Milanese texts and Venantius's sixth-century "Gallican" ones remained current into the twentieth century, but no melodies can be documented before the year 1000. Once they begin appearing in monastic manuscripts, however, they appear in such profusion that most of the oldest texts are provided with as many as a dozen or more tunes. There is no telling which or how many of them date from before the ninth century, but the overwhelming majority conform so well with the modal criteria established by the ninth-century Frankish music theorists that their Frankish origin seems virtually certain.

The musical approach of hymnody is quite different from that of psalmody. Whereas psalms and their appendages (antiphons and responsories) have an elevated style that avoids textual regularity or overt musical repetition and encourages spiritual contemplation, hymns more resemble popular songs. Their texts are metrical, and they repeat a relatively short and memorable syllabic or lightly neumatic melody through numerous stanzas of text. All of this is conducive to exuberance on the part of the singers. Three of the most famous Frankish hymns are given here. In each case music is given for only the first stanza—subsequent stanzas are to be sung to the same melody. All three of these hymns were quoted frequently in later music, as, for example, in Guillaume Du Fay's *Ave maris stella* (Vol 1-37).

a. *Ave maris stella* (Veneration of the Virgin Mary)

Ave maris stella is a hymn to the Blessed Virgin Mary that was sung in many of the offices devoted to her that burgeoned in the Frankish liturgy around the time of the earliest notated manuscripts. The text is securely dated to the ninth century, but the strongly contoured neumatic melody—the most famous of several associated with the poem—makes its appearance in the extant manuscripts somewhat later. In a still primarily oral age, however, the date of a melody's earliest written source bears no reliable witness to the date of its creation. Its melody fits squarely in the first mode as first defined by Frankish theorists in the ninth century.

1. *Ave maris stella,* *Dei mater alma,* *Atque semper virgo,* *Felix caeli porta.*	1. Hail, star of the sea, Gracious Mother of the Lord, And eternal Virgin, happy gate of heaven.
2. *Sumens illud Ave* *Gabrielis ore,* *Funda nos in pace,* *Mutans Hevae nomen.*	2. Receiving that "Ave" from Gabriel's mouth, establish us in peace, changing the name of Eve.
. . .	. . .
7. *Sit laus Deo Patri,* *Summo Christo decus,* *Spiritui Sancto,* *Tribus honor unus.*	7. Praise be to God the Father, Glory to Christ, And to the Holy Spirit, One honor to three.
Amen.	Amen.

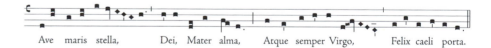

Ave maris stella, Dei, Mater alma, Atque semper Virgo, Felix caeli porta.

b. *Pange lingua gloriosi* (Feast of Corpus Christi)

The version of *Pange lingua* given here, composed by St. Thomas Aquinas (d. 1274), is not an entirely original composition. It is a contrafactum (retexting of old music) of the hymn *Pange lingua* by Venantius Fortunatus, which Aquinas adapted for the office of Corpus Christi (veneration of the Body of Christ), a feast that was brand new in the thirteenth century. Unlike *Ave maris stella*, then, the third-mode melody of *Pange lingua* is probably considerably older than its text. These two hymns demonstrate in opposite ways the fluidity of text–music relationships in the Gregorian chant repertoire.

1. *Pange lingua gloriosi*
   Corporis mysterium,
   Sanguinisque pretiosi,
   Quem in mundi pretium
   Fructus ventris generosi
   Rex effudit gentium.

1. Sing, O my tongue,
   Of the glorious mystery of the body,
   and of the precious blood,
   shed for the good of the world,
   by the fruit of a noble womb,
   the King of all peoples.

2. *Nobis natus, nobis datus*
   Ex intacta Virgine,
   Et in mundo conversatus,
   Sparso verbi semine,
   Sui moras incolatus
   Miro clausit ordine.

2. Born to us, given to us,
   From a spotless Virgin,
   And having dwelled in the world,
   Sowing the seed of the word,
   Concluded in a miraculous way
   His time of habitation.

. . .

. . .

6. *Genitori, Genitoque*
   Laus et jubilatio,
   Salus, honor, virtus quoque
   Sit et benedictio:
   Procedenti ab utroque
   Compar sit laudatio.

6. To the Begetter and the Begotten,
   Praise and jubilation,
   Health, honor, and virtue,
   And blessing as well.
   And let equal praise be to him,
   Who proceeds from Both.

Amen.

Amen.

many famous Franks, including Hrabanus Maurus (d. 856), the archbishop of Mainz, and even Charlemagne himself. (It has also been attributed to St. Gregory the Great and to St. Ambrose.) The poem makes use of the so-called "Ambrosian stanza"—used by the first great hymnodist— which consists of four lines of eight syllables each. The melody is of exemplary Frankish design, set in the eighth mode, with all phrases beginning either on the final G or the tenor/reciting tone C.

1. *Veni Creator Spiritus,*
   Mentes tuorum visita:
   Imple superna gratia
   Quae tu creasti pectora.

1. Come, Creator Spirit,
   Visit your people's souls;
   Fill with heavenly grace
   The hearts that you have created.

2. *Qui diceris Paraclitus,*
   Altissimi donum Dei,
   Fons vivus, ignis, caritas
   Et spiritalis unctio.

2. You who are called Paraclete
   Gift of the highest God,
   Living fountain, flame, charity,
   And spiritual anointing.

. . .

. . .

7. *Deo Patri sit Gloria,*
   Et Filio, qui a mortuis
   Surrexit, ac Paraclito,
   In saeculorum saecula.

7. Glory be to God the Father,
   And to the Son, who from the dead,
   Was risen, and to the Paraclete,
   In eternity.

Amen.

Amen.

c. *Veni creator spiritus* (Pentecost)

The hymn *Veni creator spiritus* is sung on Pentecost, the feast held on the seventh Sunday after Easter that celebrates the descent of the Holy Spirit upon the apostles after Christ's ascension to heaven. It first appears in tenth-century manuscripts but has been attributed honorifically to

8

Two Tropes to the Easter Introit, *Resurrexi et adhuc tecum sum*

Tropes are a large category of Frankish chants that were not self-standing but were attached to other chants—usually older, canonical chants—in various ways. Although the practice of troping, like most Frankish musical innovations, seems to have appeared first in the ninth century, it was cultivated most intensely beginning in the tenth. Often tropes were attached as prefaces to the older chants—especially the antiphonal chants of the Mass Proper—in order to explain and clarify their meaning for the community of worshippers. While troping became a very widespread practice, individual tropes were a more local and discretionary genre than the canonical chants. A given antiphon can be found with many different prefaces in various sources, reflecting local liturgical customs. Tropes are included in manuscripts or manuscript sections called *tropers*, a very large number of which come from just two monasteries: the East Frankish monastery of St. Gallen in modern-day Switzerland (which also figures prominently in the history of the early sequence) and the West Frankish monastery of St. Martial at Limoges in southwestern France (which, as we shall see, also figures prominently in the history of twelfth-century polyphony).

What follows are two tropes to the Easter Introit *Resurrexi et adhuc tecum sum* (Example 8-1), one from St. Martial and the other from St. Gallen. The Introit is shown here; its antiphon portion has the following text, drawn from verses 18, 5, and 6 of Psalm 138 in the Old Testament:

Resurrexi et adhuc tecum sum, alleluia!   I arose and am still with thee, alleluia!
Posuisti super me manum tuam, alleluia!   Thou hast laid thy hand upon me, alleluia!
Mirabilis facta est scientia tua, alleluia!   Thy knowledge is become wonderful, alleluia!

In the psalm the opening words ("I arose and am still with thee") refer to waking from sleep, but by the ninth century there was a long tradition of Christian exegesis that interpreted them as a prophecy of Christ's own words on his resurrection on the third day after his crucifixion. The beginning of the Introit can therefore be understood allegorically as Christ speaking in the first person, and one of the tasks of the trope was to reinforce this allegorical interpretation of the Old Testament words.

Example 8-1 *Resurrexi et adhuc tecum sum*, Introit for the Easter Sunday Mass

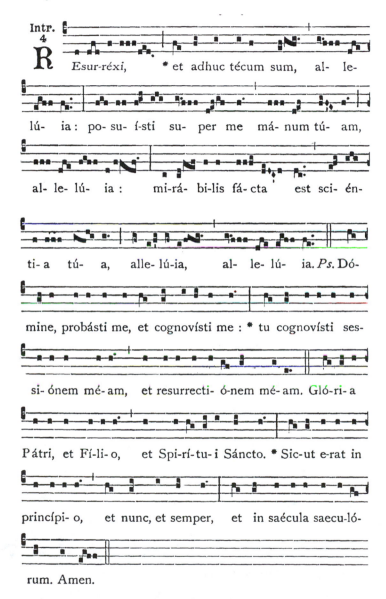

a. *Ecce pater*

At their most elaborate, tropes could function not only as a preface to a complete Introit but also as prefaces to each psalm verse in the antiphon or to the cursive verse or verses that followed or even to the Lesser Doxology formula. Thus, in practice, tropes could take the form of interpolations as well as introductions. They imitated the neumatic or even melismatic style of the chants to which they were appended, to all intents and purposes becoming part of them. The example given here, taken from a St. Martial troper, presents introductory and interpolated tropes to the Introit antiphon that make explicit the connection between the psalm verses quoted by the Introit and Christ's resurrection. Because the first words of chants are always sung by the soloist to set the pitch, it is thought that the tropes may have been assigned to soloists in order to differentiate them from the choral antiphons. When a soloist sings an introductory trope, the pitch is already set, and there is no need for a soloist to sing the intonation of the antiphon proper. After the introductory trope given here ("Ecce pater . . ."), the whole choir would enter on "Resurrexi."

Trope: *Ecce pater, cunctis, ut jusserat ordo peractis*

[**Introit Antiphon:**] *Resurrexi et adhuc tecum sum, alleluia!*

Trope: *Victor ut ad celos calcata morte redirem.*

[**Antiphon resumed:**] *Posuisti super me manum tuam, alleluia!*

Trope: *Quo genus humanum pulsis erroribus altum scanderet ad celum.*

[**Antiphon resumed:**] *Mirabilis facta est scientia tua, alleluia!*

Trope: *Behold, Father, all things having been accomplished according to your plan,*

[**Introit Antiphon:**] *I arose and am still with thee, alleluia!*

Trope: *A victor, so that I might return to heaven after trampling death.*

[**Antiphon resumed:**] *Thou hast laid thy hand upon me, alleluia!*

Trope: *By which mankind, its errors banished, might ascend to high heaven.*

[**Antiphon resumed:**] *Thy knowledge is become wonderful, alleluia!*

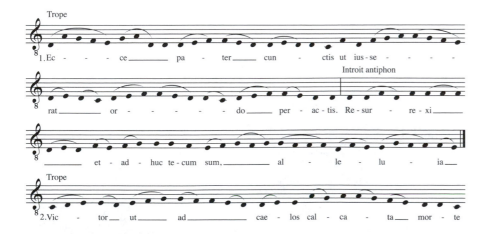

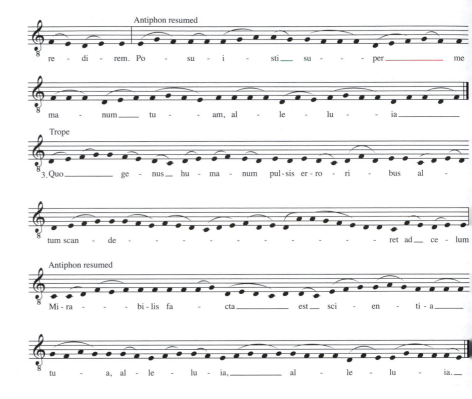

b. *Quem quaeritis in sepulchro?*

Some of the most famous of all tropes and certainly the most famous *Resurrexi* tropes are the ones that append to the beginning of the Easter Sunday Introit the *visitatio sepulchri*—the visit of the three Marys to the empty tomb of Christ on the morning after his burial. There are many different tropes in this group, but all cast the visitation scene as a dialogue between the women visiting the tomb and angelic messengers who announce that Christ has risen. These dialogues provide an apt introduction to Christ's own announcement, in the opening words of the Introit that he has risen. The trope given here is an early version from a St. Gallen manuscript dating from around 950. The text carries special directions—known in liturgical books as *rubrics*, since they were often entered in red ink made from *rubrica*, Latin for "red earth"—that specify what is a "question" (*interrogatio*) and what is an "answer" (*responsorium*). These rubrics in effect turn the trope into a theatrical script, indicating that two (or several) singers were to act out the dialogue in parts. This and similar dialogue tropes are an early and simple form of what became a significant repertory of much longer (and self-standing) Latin church plays with music, known as "liturgical dramas." The best-known liturgical dramas are the anonymous twelfth-century

Play of Daniel and the *Ordo virtutum* (Play of the Virtues) by Hildegard of Bingen, one of whose compositions we have already seen in Vol 1-6.

Interrogatio: *Quem quaeritis in sepulchro, o Christicolae?*

Responsorium: *Jesum Nazarenum crucifixum, o caelicolae.*

[**Angeli**]: *Non est hic, surrexit sicut praedixerat; ite, nuntiate quia surrexit de sepuchro.*

Introit: *Resurrexi . . .*

Question [**Angels**]: Whom do you seek in the tomb, O Christians?

Answer [**Marys**]: Jesus of Nazareth, who was crucified, O Heavenly ones.

[**Angels:**] He is not here, but has risen, as it was foretold; go and spread the word that he has risen from the tomb.

Introit: I arose . . .

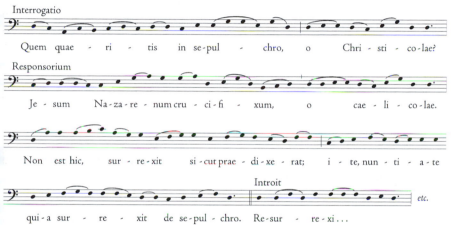

9

Two Marian Antiphons (eleventh or twelfth c.)

Votive antiphons were psalmless antiphons—in other words, independent devotional Latin songs—sung in honor of saints so that those saints might recommend to Christ the people singing them. They were composed in great numbers beginning in the eleventh century, sometimes in honor of local saints or patron saints of specific causes, but most often in honor of the Virgin Mary, the all-purpose saint for the Medieval populace. Votive antiphons to the Virgin were known as *Marian antiphons*, or "anthems to the Blessed Virgin Mary," and were the very latest genre of Medieval chant to be incorporated into the canonical liturgy. The four most famous Marian antiphons were *Alma redemptoris mater* ("Gracious mother of the redeemer"), *Ave regina caelorum* ("Hail, queen of heaven"), and the two given here: *Regina caeli laetare* and *Salve regina*. These chants appear in numerous musical manuscripts dating from as early as the late eleventh century, and by the thirteenth century they had been adopted in certain monasteries for ordinary use in a seasonal cursus as the concluding item of Compline, the last of the hours of the Divine Office, sung before bedtime. Eventually this monastic cursus was adopted by the entire Catholic Church so that each liturgical day ended with an ample song of praise to the Virgin Mary: From Advent until the Feast of the Purification (February 2) it was *Alma redemptoris mater*; from Purification until Easter it was *Ave regina caelorum*; during Paschal Time (from Easter Sunday until Pentecost, the seventh Sunday after Easter) it was *Regina caeli laetare*; and from the end of Paschal Time until the beginning of Advent (that is, from summer through fall), it was *Salve regina*.

Regina caeli laetare and *Salve regina*, which follow one another in the seasonal cursus, contrast extremely with one another in both affect and mode, showing that the doctrine of modal *ethos*, still alive today in our conventional assignment of contrasting moods to the major mode and the minor mode, existed in at least a rudimentary form in the Middle Ages. In fact, the exultant *Regina caeli laetare*, which praises the Virgin Mary as the mother of the resurrected Christ, though classified as a sixth-mode melody, is in the major mode to all intents and purposes. Its final, F, became ever more prevalent in the later Frankish genres, and when it appeared it was usually given a "signature" of one flat to "soften" progressions from B to F, which are especially frequent in *Regina caeli laetare*. The resulting "Lydian" octave species is identical to what we would call the major scale. The mode here works in tandem with other traditional earmarks of

rejoicing, notably the long melismas on "portare" and the final "alleluia," which are replete with internal repeats clearly modeled on those of the Alleluia from the Mass Proper.

Salve regina, on the other hand, is dark in both affect and mode. Like so many D-mode (Dorian) chants composed in the eleventh century or later, it spans both the authentic ambitus (from the D final to the D an octave above it) and the plagal ambitus (from the A below the D final to the A above it), though it favors the plagal end. Its official assignment to mode 1 was due, most likely, to the repeated cadences of the concluding acclamations—"O clemens: O pia: O dulcis"—on A. Although there are no real melismas, there is a great deal of melodic parallelism; indeed, the first two main phrases ("Salve Regina . . ." and "Vita dulcedo . . .") are nearly identical, producing an aab form (with the *b* section starting at "Ad te clamamus . . ."). This form, as we shall see, was a common feature of many secular love songs of the troubadours and trouvères, although it is not found in many chants. The *Salve regina* can therefore be looked upon as a love song to the Blessed Virgin Mary in the style of the troubadour canso, the first major genre of secular music to be written down, which emerged around the same time that the *Salve regina* was composed. For examples of the canso, see Bernart de Ventadorn's *Can vei la lauzeta mover* (Vol 1-10) and La Comtessa de Dia's *A chantar* (Vol 1-11).

a. *Regina caeli laetare*

Regina caeli laetare, alleluia:	Queen of heaven, rejoice, alleluia.
Quia quem meruisti portare, alleluia:	For He whom thou didst merit to bear, alleluia,
Resurrexit sicut dixit, alleluia:	has risen, as He said, alleluia.
Ora pro nobis Deum, alleluia.	Pray for us to God, alleluia.

b. *Salve regina*

Salve regina, mater misericordia:	Hail, holy Queen, mother of mercy;
Vita, dulcedo, et spes nostra, salve.	hail, our life, our sweetness, our hope!
Ad te clamamus, exsules, filii Hevae.	To thee do we cry, poor banished children of Eve;
Ad te suspiramus, gementes et flentes in hac lacrimarum valle.	to thee do we send up our sighs, mourning and weeping in this vale of tears.
Eia ergo, Advocata nostra, illos tuos misericordes oculos ad nos converte,	Turn then, most gracious advocate, thine eyes of mercy towards us; and after this our exile,
Et Jesum, benedictum fructum ventris tui, nobis post hoc exsilium ostende.	show unto us the blessed fruit of thy womb, Jesus.
O clemens:	O gentle,
O pia:	O loving,
O dulcis virgo Maria.	O sweet Virgin Mary.

10

Bernart de Ventadorn
(ca. 1130/40 to ca. 1190/1200)

Can vei la lauzeta mover ("When I see the lark flutter his wings")
(twelfth c.)

The earliest secular repertories to be written down were songs of love and feudal service composed by the troubadours, knightly poets in the southern French duchy of Aquitaine around the turn of the twelfth century. The language they used is Provençal, also known as Occitan or *langue d'oc*, from the local word for "yes" ("oc"). (Old French, spoken to the north, was called *langue d'oïl* for the same reason, "oïl" being the predecessor of the modern French "oui.") The Provençal word for poetry is *trobar*, meaning "found words," and a poet was therefore known as a *trobador*, a "finder" of words. In English we call such a poet a troubadour, which is simply a Frenchified form of this word. Troubadours worked at the courts of noblemen and -women and were sometimes nobles themselves. Their songs reflected the highly formalized social conventions of the medieval court, and as a result they are themselves highly formalized in genre and style, to the point of virtuosic complexity of design and occasional, sometimes deliberate, obscurity of meaning. The poems of the troubadours were always meant for public performance—hence the music!—not for private reading; theirs was still an eminently oral tradition.

The principal genre of troubadour song is the *canso*, which literally means simply "song" but which refers more specifically to an elaborate type of poem or song about a very specific kind of love. The troubadours called this love *fin' amors*, "refined love," which one modern authority has defined as "a great imaginative and spiritual superstructure built on the foundation of sexual attraction." Modern scholars often use the term "courtly love" (*amour courtois*). In *fin' amors* the troubadour writes in praise of a *domna* (lady) who is of higher social rank than he is and whose nobility, beauty, and worth he praises to the point of sacralization. There is a foundation of sexual attraction, yes, and the poets go to great lengths to describe the visceral effects that their love has on them. But there is no intent of actual consummation of their attraction, and the lady is most often praised from afar, offering no response or even acknowledgment to the poet. *Fin' amors* is a devotional love of lofty intention, to be expressed in self-consciously lofty lyrics.

Bernart de Ventadorn was the most famous troubadour, and the lofty style of the canso is illustrated by his *Can vei la lauzeta mover*. Cansos are composed in strophic form, meaning that several stanzas feature the same rhyme scheme and are sung to the same music (as in the Frankish hymn). In *Can vei la lauzeta moverz*, each stanza consists of eight octosyllabic lines that follow a well-defined rhyme scheme, with a unique phrase of music for nearly each line of verse (the exception being that the fourth and seventh lines of poetry are set to the same music). The rhyme scheme and musical form of each stanza line up as follows:

Rhyme Scheme	Musical Form
a	A
b	B
a	C
b	D
c	E
d	F
c	D
d	G

After the final full stanza of a canso comes the *tornada*, an abbreviated stanza that provides a dedication to a patron or a farewell. Here it follows the cdcd rhyme of the second half of a stanza and is sung to the last four lines of music. Comparison of Bernart's melody with those of late Frankish chant discloses a great similarity of style. Like the *Salve Regina* (Vol 1-9b) or Agnus Dei II (Vol 1-4f), it is an exemplary Dorian melody according to the rationalized concept of mode developed by Frankish theorists. (The composers probably picked up the style by ear on the basis of the chants they heard sung.)

But sophisticated formal construction and musical similarity to Gregorian chant are only part of the "high"-ness of the troubadour canso. Equally important is the lofty imagery that defines *fin' amors* in a way that no analytical definition can, as we see in *Can vei la lauzeta mover*. The song begins with a striking metaphor that compares the fluttering of a lark's wings and its soaring and swooping in flight to the joyful effects that love has on the poet. This joy, however, is contrasted with the poet's unhappiness at the lady's unresponsiveness, which he is condemned to suffer alone and from afar. Bernart's metaphor thus illustrates a central paradox that is built into *fin' amors*: The lover cannot have what he most desires, and the love that brings him joy must therefore also bring him sorrow.

1. *Can vei la lauzeta mover* When I see the lark flutter his wings
 De joi sas alas contra.l rai out of joy against the sun's ray,
 Que s'oblid'e.s laissa chazer and that he lingers and then swoops down
 Per la doussor c'al cor li vai, because of the sweetness that fills his heart,

 Ai, tan grans enveya m'en ve ah, such great envy fills me
 De cui qu'eu veya jauzion, towards those whom I see rejoice;
 Meravilhas ai, car desse I marvel that my heart
 Lo cor de dezirer no.m fon. does not melt with desire.

2. *Ai las! tan cuidava saber*
   D'amor, e tan petit en sai!
   Car eu d'amar no.m posc tener
   Celeis don ja pro non aurai.

   Tout m'a mo cor e tout m'a me
   E se mezeis e tot lo mon;
   E can se.m tolc, no.m laisset re

   Mas dezirer e cor volon.

3. *Pus ab midons no.m pot valer*
   Precs ni merces ni.l dreihz qu'eu ai,
   Ni a leis no ven a plazer
   Qu'eu l'am, ja mais no.lh o dirai.
   Aissi.m part de leis e.m recre;
   Mort m'a, e per mort li respon,

   E vau m'en, pus ilh no.m rete,

   Chaitius, en issilh, no sai on.

4. *Tristans, ges no.n auretz de me,*
   Qu'eu m'en vau, chaitius, no sai on.

   De chantar me gic e.m recre,
   E de joi e d'amor me'scon.

Alas! How much I thought I knew
of love, and how little I know.
For I cannot keep myself from loving
the lady from whom I will never receive
   any favor.
She has my entire heart, my whole self,
her own self and the whole world,
and when she robs me, she leaves me
   nothing
but desire and a longing heart.

Because I can win my lady
neither with mercy nor with my rights,
and since it does not please her
that I love her, I will speak of it no more.
I depart from her and her service;
she has killed me, and with death I
   respond.
And since she will not have me in her
   service,
miserable, I go into exile, I know not where.

Tristan, you will hear no more of me,
for I go, miserable, into exile, I know not
   where.
I forsake singing and turn away from it,
and I flee from love and from joy.

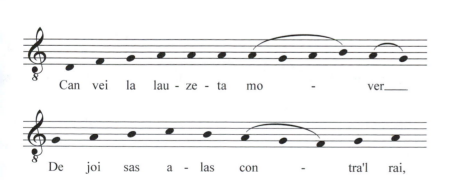

11

La Comtessa de Dia
(*fl* late twelfth/early thirteenth c.)

A chantar m'er de so qu'ieu non volria ("I must sing of that which I would rather not") (late twelfth c.)

Manuscripts of troubadour songs contain *vidas*, short biographies of the poet-composers whose works are contained therein, and these *vidas* tell us of at least twenty lady troubadours, for which the Provençal word was *trobairitz*. The trobairitz composed courtly songs in the same genres as their male counterparts—with similar emphasis on the canso—but they took a modified approach to *fin' amors* that resulted from the fact that the woman, venerated as a *domna* in poetry composed by males, was now the one singing of love. It was not gender-appropriate in Provençal courtly culture for a woman to place herself low in relation to an elevated male beloved, and so the trobairitz often focused their poetry on what they shared with the troubadours, namely, the strong visceral effect that their love had on them and the confusion and unhappiness that accompanied it. This is what we see in the canso *A chantar*.

Although the texts of numerous trobairitz songs have survived, only this single poem has come down to us with a melody. Its composer, La Comtessa de Dia (the Countess of Dia), is a woman whose identity remains a mystery. Her *vida*, which does not give her first name, says that she was married to Guilhem de Poitiers, but there is no historical record of a Guilhem de Poitiers who was married to a Countess of Dia. It is possible that she was the daughter of Count Isouard II of Dia, who is called "Beatrix comitissa" in various documents and may have been married to Guilhem de Poitiers, Count of Viennois. As a result, musicologists sometimes refer to the trobairitz as "Beatriz de Dia," a name that appears nowhere in the Medieval sources of her songs.

What does appear in the sources is a canso that sits between the lofty, chant-based style of Bernart de Ventadorn's *Can vei la lauzeta mover* (Vol 1-10) and the low, mock-popular style that we will see in Moniot D'arras's pastoral song *Ce fut en mail* (Vol 1-13). The strict strophic form and closing tornada are typical of the elevated canso, and the melody, like Bernart's, fits the profile of a first-mode chant. And yet the rhyme scheme of each stanza is much simpler, and the music has a "rounded" form in which there is a repeated opening couplet (AB), the latter phrase of which returns at the end of the stanza. The rhyme scheme and musical form line up as follows:

Rhyme Scheme	Musical Form
a	A
a	B
a	A
a	B
b	C
a	D
b	B

The first four musical phrases alternate cadences on the pitches E (not the final) and D (the final) in a fashion never encountered in first-mode chants but common in the dances and dance songs of a slightly later period. Such endings would be designated open and closed cadences in thirteenth-century dance manuscripts; they correspond to, and prefigure, what we would now call half and full cadences.

1. *A chantar m'er de so qu'ieu non volria*

   I must sing of that of which I would rather not,

   Tant me rancur de lui cui sui amia,
   So bitter am I toward him whose love I am,

   Car ieu l'am mais que nuilla ren que sia;
   For I love him more than anything else.

   Vas lui no.m val merces ni cortesia
   With him mercy and courtliness are of no use,

   Ni ma beltatz ni mos pretz ni mos sens,
   Nor my beauty, nor my merit, nor my sense,

   C'atressi.m sui enganad'e trahia
   And so I am deceived and betrayed,

   Com degr'esser, s'ieu fos desavinens.
   As I should be if I were ungracious.

2. *D'aisso.m conort car anc non fi faillenssa,*
   I take comfort in the fact that I was never false,

   Amics, vas vos per nuilla captenenssa,
   My love, in my behavior towards you.

   Anz vos am mais non fetz Seguis Valenssa,
   Instead I love you more than Seguin loved Valensa,

   E platz me mout quez eu d'amar vos venssa,
   And it pleases me that my love is greater than yours,

   Lo mieus amics, car etz lo plus valens;
   My love, because you are the most valiant.

   Mi faitz orguoill en ditz et en parvenssa,
   You are contemptuous towards me word and deed,

   E si etz francs vas totas autras gens.
   And yet you are kindly towards others.

3. *Meravill me com vostre cors s'orguoilla*
   Amics, vas me, per qu'ai razon qu'ieu.m
   *   duoilla*
   Non es ges dreitz c'autr'amors vos mi tuoilla

   Per nuilla ren qe.us diga ni acuoilla;
   E membre vos cals fo.l comenssamens
   De nostr'amor ja Dompnedieus non vuoilla
   Qu'en ma copa sia.l departimens.

4. *Proesa grans qu'el vostre cors s'aizina*
   E lo rics pretz qu'avetz m'en ataina,
   C'una non sai, loindana ni vezina,
   Si vol amar, vas vos non si'aclina;

   Mas vos, amics, etz ben tant conoissens
   Que ben devetz conoisser la plus fina,
   e membre vos de nostres covinens.

5. *Valer mi deu mos pretz e mos paratges*
   E ma beltatz e plus mos fis coratges,
   Per qu'ieu vos man lai on es vostr'estatges

   Esta chansson que me sia messatges.
   Ieu vuoill saber, lo mieus bels amics gens,
   Per que vos m'etz tant fers ni tant salvatges,
   Non sai, si s'es orguoills o maltalens.

6. *Mas aitan plus voill qe.us diga.l messatges*

   Qu'en trop d'orguoill ant gran dan main-
   *   tas gens.*

I marvel at how arrogant you are,
My love, towards me, for which I have
   reason to grieve.
It is not right that another love should take
   you from me,
No matter what she may say to you.
And remember how it was at the beginning
Of our love. God forbid
That I should be the cause of our parting.

The great prowess that you possess
And your merit retain me.
For I know no woman, far or near,
Who would not, if she wants to love, be
   drawn to you.
But you, my love, are so discerning
That you must discern the finest,
And remind yourself of our agreement.

My merit and my lineage should help me,
And my beauty, and above all my faithfulness,
Which is why I send to you where you
   dwell
This song, so that it might be my messenger.
I want to know, my most noble love,
Why you are so harsh and cruel towards me.
I don't know whether it is arrogance or
   malice.

But above all I want you to tell him,
   messenger,
That too much pride has harmed many.

A chan - tar m'er__ de so q'ieu no__ vol - ri - a,

Tant me ran - cur__ de__ lui__ cui sui a - mi - a,

Car eu__ l'am mais__ que nuil - la ren__ que si - a,

Vas lui no'm val__ mer - ces__ ni cor - te - si - a,

Ni ma bel - tatz, ni mos pretz, ni__ mos sens,

C'a - tres - si'm sui en - ga - nad' e__ tra - hi - a,

Cum degr'es - ser,__ s'ieu__ fos__ de - sa - vi - nens.

12

Richard the Lionheart (1157–99)

Ja nun hons pris ("No captive can tell his story") (1192–94)

By the late twelfth century, troubadour song had spawned a hardy successor in northern France, despite hostilities between the northern courts and those of the south. The northern French poets who adapted the tradition of the troubadours to their own northern language, known as Old French, or *langue d'oïl* (from their word for "yes," "oïl," precursor of the modern French "oui"), were called trouvères (in direct translation from the Occitan *trobador*). Their tradition grew stronger over the course of the thirteenth century, just as the troubadour tradition was declining. Eleanor of Aquitaine (1122–1204) was an important figure in this northward migration of the tradition. Her grandfather was William IX of Aquitaine (1071–1126), the first troubadour, and she was the patron of Bernart de Ventadorn, the most famous troubadour, whom she brought with her to northern France. She was, at various times in her life, both Queen of France and Queen of England, and her son, Richard the Lionheart, most famous for becoming King Richard I of England (r. 1189–99), was also one of the first trouvères. Though he was born in England and became King of England, he spent most of his life in Aquitaine and never learned to speak English. His poems are found in both Provençal and French manuscripts, but the only one to survive with a melody, *Ja nun hons pris*, is in French.

The song is cast in the form of a *chanson courtoise*, the descendent of the troubadour canso, but it is not about courtly love. Instead, it is about honor. While Richard was returning home from the Third Crusade, Leopold V of Austria took him hostage and held him for the proverbial "king's ransom," which Richard's English subjects were eventually able to raise and pay. But Richard spent 1192–94 in captivity waiting for them to raise the funds. It was during his time as a prisoner that he composed *Ja non hons pris*, which is classified in its thirteenth-century sources as a *retrouenge*. Modern scholars have not yet succeeded in defining this term, which may mean no more than a song in the vernacular rather than in Latin, but it probably has to do with the use of a concluding tag line or refrain (every stanza ends with the word *pris*, "prisoner"). The melody, to which each stanza is sung, consists of two main sections, the first of which is repeated. This produces the familiar aab form, which we first encountered in the *Salve regina* chant of Vol 1-9b (it can be traced further back yet, all the way to the classical Greek ode) and which we will reencounter again and again in later repertories. Richard's chanson courtoise is closely modeled on the Provençal canso, and, indeed, as long as trouvère song remained an art

of the castle and the court, its chief (and sometimes only) difference from troubadour song was its language.

1. *Ja nun hons pris ne dira sa raison*
   Adroitement, se dolantement non;
   Mais par esfort puet il faire chançon.

   Mout ai amis, mais povre sunt li don.
   Honte I avront, se por ma reançon
   Sui ça deus yvers pris.

2. *Ce sevent bien mi home et me baron,*
   Ynglois, Normanz, Poitevin et Gascon

   Que je n'ai nul si povre compaignon
   Que je lessaisse, por avoir, en prison.

   Je nou di mie por nule retraçon,
   Car encor sui pris.

3. *Or sai je bien de voir, certeinnement*
   Que je ne pris ne ami ne parent,
   Quant on me faut por or ne por argent.
   Mout m'est de moi, mès plus m'est de ma gent;
   Qu'après ma mort avront reprochement,
   Se longuement sui pris.

4. *N'est pas mervoille se j'ai le cuer dolant,*
   Quant mes sires mest ma terre en torment.
   S'il li membrast de nostre soirement
   Que nos feïsmes andui communement,
   Je sai de voir que ja trop longuement
   Ne seroie ça pris.

5. *Ce sevent bien Angevin et Torain,*
   Cil bacheler qui or sont riche et sain,
   Qu'encombrez sui loing d'aus, en autre main,

   Forment m'aidessent, mais il n'en oient grain.

   De beles armes sont ore buit et plain,

   Por ce que je suis pris.

No captive can tell his story
skillfully if he does not tell it sadly;
but then he can compose a more powerful song.
I have many friends, but their gifts are small.
They will be shamed if, for lack of ransom,
I am a *prisoner* here for two winters.

This my men and my barons know well,
Englishmen, Normans, Poitevins, and Gascons:
that I have no companion so poor
that I would let him languish in prison on account of money.
I do not say this as a reproach,
but I am still a *prisoner*.

This I know with certainty:
that I should prize neither friend nor family
when they abandon me for gold or for silver.
I am concerned for myself, but even more for my people
who will be blamed after my death
if I am a *prisoner* for long.

It is no wonder that I have a grieving heart
when my lord torments my land.
If he remembered our vow
that we swore together,
I know truly that I would not
be a *prisoner* here for so long.

This Anjou and Touraine know well,
those young men who are rich and safe:
that I am held captive far away, in the hands of others.
They could help me, but they do not care at all.
The battlefields are stripped bare of gallant arms,
since I am a *prisoner*.

6. *Mes compaignons que j'amoie et que j'ain,*

   Cés de Chaën en cés de Percherain:
   Di lor, chançon, qu'il ne sunt pas certain.
   C'onques vers aus ne oi faus cuer ne vain.
   S'il me guerroient, il feront que vilain,
   Tant con je serai pris.

My companions whom I loved and whom
   I love,
these men of Chaën and Percherain:
tell them, song, that they are not reliable.
I have never been false or vain towards them.
If they fight against me, they are traitors,
while I remain a *prisoner*.

7. *Contesse suer, vostre pris soverain*
   Vos saut et gart cil a cui je m'en clain;

   Et por ce suis je pris!
   Je ne di mie a celle de Chartrain,
   La mere Loëys.

Countess, Sister, may your sovereignty
be defended and preserved by him to
   whom I address my appeal;
I am a prisoner for his sake.
I say not a word to that Chartrain lady,
the mother of Louis.

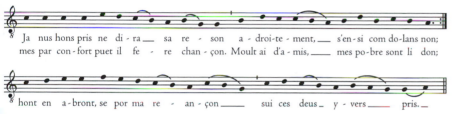

Ja nus hons pris ne di - ra__ sa re - son a - droi-te - ment,__ s'en-si com do-lans non;
mes par con-fort puet il fe - re chan - çon. Moult ai d'a - mis,____ mes po-bre sont li don;

hont en a-bront, se por ma re - an - çon____ sui ces deus_ y - vers____ pris.__

13

Moniot d'Arras
(fl 1213–39)

Ce fut en mai ("It was in May") (early thirteenth c.)

Rhyme Scheme	Musical Form
a	A (m. 1)
a	
b	
a	A' (m. 9)
a	
b	
c	B (m. 17)
c	
d	
c	B' (m. 25)
c	
d	

Although trouvère song grew directly out of troubadour song, there were from the very beginning some subtle but significant differences between the two, both on the level of form and style and on that of social attitude and practice, differences that became more pronounced with the passage of time. In the thirteenth century, the main centers of musico-literary activity in France shifted from castle and court to city and town, reflecting a general shift in society as well. Urbanization, on the rise since the eleventh century, had begun to gallop. Over the century ending around 1250, the city of Paris doubled in size. The episcopal town of Arras to the north, meanwhile, was granted a commercial charter in 1180 and soon became a major center of banking and commerce. Musical and literary culture flourished among Arras's (and Paris's) emerging class of city-dwelling freemen, the *bourgeoisie*—in the term's original meaning. The old type of courtly love song, the chanson courtoise, continued to be popular among the new urban poet-musicians, but it was rivaled by a genre of narrative song based on the pastorela, a folk-like idiom of the troubadours. In French it was known as the *pastourelle*.

Moniot d'Arras, whose pseudonym means "The Little Monk of Arras," composed *Ce fut en mai*, the most famous pastourelle in the repertory. Typical for a pastourelle, it is set in springtime, and its characters, which include knightly nobles wandering in the meadow and a peasant maiden who lives there, take part in a merry dance. The edition given here assumes that Moniot's composition is itself a dance song, and it transcribes the melody, written in the original manuscript in rhythmless neumes, in a regular alternation of long and short syllables, yielding a sort of iambic meter that fits the text perfectly. From the text we can also glean some useful information about how pastourelles were performed: It describes the knight and the damsel dancing to the accompaniment of a fiddle (*vielle*), indicating that Moniot's song, too, might be accompanied by a fiddle that either doubles the vocal melody or improvises some sort of accompaniment.

The musical structure is more regularized than anything we have seen thus far. There are two musical sections of equal length, each of which is repeated with contrasting open and closed cadences. The musical form, which resembles the "binary" form of later musical dances, lines up with the rhyme scheme as follows:

The open cadences are on the pitches A (m. 8) and G (m. 24), while the closed cadences are both on the F final (mm. 16 and 32). The dance-like form of the piece plus the use of the major mode (Lydian with B♭) makes this a consummate imitation folk song. There is little left here of the high Latinate style seen in Bernart de Ventadorn's *Can vei la lauzeta mover* (Vol 1-10).

Ce fut en mai	It was in May,
au douz tens gai,	in the sweet and merry time,
Que la seson est bele;	when the season is beautiful.
Main me levai,	I rose up one morning
Jöer m'alai	and went out to play
Lez une fontenele,	by a stream
En un vergier	in an orchard
Clos d'esglentier	enclosed by a hedge.
Oï une vielle;	I heard a fiddle
La vi dancier	and saw a knight
Un chevalier	and a damsel
Et une damoisele.	dancing there.
Cor erent gent	Their bodies were graceful
Et avenant,	and comely,
Et Deus! Tant biau dançoient!	and my God, how beautifully they danced!
En acolant	Embracing
Et en besant,	and kissing,
Mult biau se deduisoient.	they were enjoying themselves.

En un destour,	After the dance,
Au chief du tor,	they went off together
Dui et dui s'en aloient;	to an isolated spot,
Desor la flor,	where, on top of a flower,
Le gieu d'amor	they played the game of love
A lor plesir fesoient.	to their hearts' pleasure.
J'alai avant,	I approached,
Trop redoutant	completely fearful
Que nus d'aus ne me voie	that one of them might see me,
Maz et pensant	sad and pensive
Et desirant	and wishing
D'avoir autretel joie.	to have such joy.
Lors vi lever	Then I saw one of them
Un de lor per,	stand up
De si loign con g'estoie,	and call out to me
A apeler,	from far away
A demander	to ask
Qui sui et qui queroie.	who I was and what I wanted.
J'alai vers aus,	I went up to them
Dis lor mes maus:	and told them of my woes:
Que une dame amoie	that I loved a lady
A qui loiaus,	to whom I would be loyal
Sanz estre faus,	and true
Tout mon vivant seroie,	all my life.
Por qui plus trai	For her I endure
Paine et esmai	More pain and suffering
Qui dire ne porroie.	than I could ever say.
Las, or morrai,	Alas, I will soon die—
Car bien le sai,	I know it well—
S'ele ne mi ravoie.	if she does not console me.
Cortoisement	Courteously
Et gentement,	and politely,
Chascun d'aus me ravoie	each one of them consoled me
Et dïent tant	and said
Que Deus briément	that God would soon
M'envoit de cele joie	send me some of that joy,
Por qui je sent	without which I feel
Grant marrement;	such great sadness.
Et je lor en rendoie	I offered them
Merciz mult grant	great thanks
Et, en plorant,	and, weeping,
A Deu les conmandoie.	commended them to God.

14

Adam de la Halle
(1245/50 to ca. 1307)

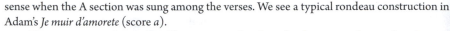

Three Dance Songs with Refrains (ca. 1300)

Adam de la Halle, the last of the great trouvères of Arras, was known as "Adam le Bossu"—Adam the Hunchback—by his contemporaries ("although I am not one," he wrote in one of his poems). Adam studied at the University of Paris as a young man and was trained in the various types of "university music" (conductus and motet) that we will see later in this anthology (Vol 1-19–22). What he learned in Paris equipped him to compose polyphonic music, and he became the only trouvère to do so. He was famous for his unique set of poetic and musical skills, which allowed him to follow an international career path that brought him to Italy and England. There is a large chansonnier from the late thirteenth century that consists almost entirely of a retrospective collection of Adam's works, organized by genre. First come the traditional chansons courtoises (the bread and butter of the trouvère tradition), then the debate songs, and finally the polyphonic chansons.

These last consist of French songs notated in score and harmonized the way Latin conductus was often harmonized in the thirteenth century: in a relatively strict chordal and homorhythmic (note-against-note) style. Polyphonic composition was extremely unusual for a trouvère, and the university genres from which Adam borrowed were very "learned." It is somewhat surprising, then, that Adam's polyphonic chansons are not chansons courtoises but, rather, dance songs, or *caroles*. Such dance songs are cast in a folksy and mock-naive character, especially the type known as the *rondeau* (or *rondel*), which, despite its quasi-pastoral character, is actually quite a sophisticated poetic form. The name rondeau, which means "round" or "circular," may originally have referred to the circle dances it accompanied, but the form of the poem is also "rounded." Within it, a "contained refrain" frames the verses but also appears in truncated form within the verses. The form can be represented with letters as follows: AB a A ab AB, where a capital letters stands for refrain text, and a lowercase letters stands for new text sung to the same music. The "A" music (mm. 1–3 in score *a*) and the "B" music (mm. 4–6) are each written out only once, to be repeated with appropriate text according to the form just outlined. The poet's task in composing a rondeau was to create a poem in which the refrains (AB) framed the verses when placed at the beginning and the end of the song but also made linear

sense when the A section was sung among the verses. We see a typical rondeau construction in Adam's *Je muir d'amorete* (score *a*).

There were two other types of dance song with refrain that became widespread in chanson composition in the late thirteenth century, beginning with Adam's works, and they continued to dominate chanson composition into the fifteenth century. They differed from the rondeau primarily in how they used refrains, but what they had in common with the rondeau was just as significant. If one takes away the refrains (the sections indicated by capital letters) from a rondeau, one is left with the aab form familiar to us from older trouvère chansons courtoises, including Richard the Lionheart's *Ja nun hons pris* (Vol 1-12). Thus:

$$[AB] \ a \ [A] \ ab \ [AB] \rightarrow aab$$

By adding a refrain—not a "contained" refrain but one with unrelated music—before and after the basic aab stanza, we get the form of Adam's *Dieus soit en cheste maison* (score *b*), which was called a *ballade*:

$$R \ aab \ R \ [aab \ R \ aab \ R \ aab \ R, \ etc.]$$

Rather quickly, however, the ballade shed its refrain when set as a fancy polyphonic composition; in doing so, of course, it merely reverted to the basic aab shape, which would come to define the fourteenth- and fifteenth-century ballade.

The third form, called the *virelai* (from the Old French verb *virer*, "to turn around"), was created by giving the refrain sung before and after the basic stanza the same music as the non-repeating *b* section of the stanza, thus making it another type of "contained" refrain:

$$B \ aab \ B \ [aab \ B \ aab \ B \ aab \ B, \ etc.]$$

This is the form of Adam's *Fines amouretes* (score *c*). Since it is conventional to begin an alphabetical formal scheme with the letter *A*, the virelai form is usually given as A bba A bba A, and so forth, which disguises the basic aab stanza within it. (Adam actually varies his musical sections slightly; the sections A, b, b, and a begin on mm.1, 5, 7, and 9, respectively.)

The three forms—ballade, virelai, rondeau—that we see in Adam's polyphonic chansons came to be known as the *formes fixes*, French for "fixed forms." They dominated chanson composition over the next 200 years, with the lyrics of the individual lettered sections and the music to which they were set becoming ever more elaborate. We will see the formes fixes next in the mid-fourteenth-century compositions of Guillaume de Machaut (Vol 1-25–26).

a. *Je muir, je muir d'amorete* ("I die, I die of love"), Rondeau

A	*Je muir, je muir d'amorete, Las! aimi!*	I die, I die of love, ah weary, ah me!
B	*Par defaute d'amiete de merchi.*	it is my beloved's want of all mercy!
a	*A premiers le vi douchete, Las! aimi!*	At first she was demure and attractively docile;
A	*Je muir, je muir d'amorete, Las! aimi!*	I die, I die of love, ah weary, ah me!

a	*D'une atraiant manierete, adont le vi,*	With that catching little way she has, I saw her then;
b	*Et puis le truis si fierete, quant li pri,*	but since I've found her so proud when I beg for loving,
A	*Je muir, je muir d'amorete, Las! aimi!*	I die, I die of love, ah weary, ah me,
B	*Par defaute d'amiete de merchi.*	it is my beloved's want of all mercy!

b. *Dieus soit en cheste maison* ("God, be in this house"), Ballade

R	*Dieus soit en cheste maison,*	God, be in this house,
	Et biens et goie a fuison!	And send it wealth and joy.
a	*Nos sires Noueus*	Lord Christmas
	Nous envoie a ses amis,	sends us to his friends.
a	*Ch'est as amoureus*	to lovers,
	Et as courtois bien apris	and to the courtly and well-born,
b	*Pour avoir des pairesis*	to collect
	A nohelison.	a Christmas penny

R	*Dieus soit . . .*	God, be in this house . . .
a	*Nos sires est teus*	Our lord is such
a	*Qu'il prieroit a envis,*	that he would beg only against his will,
	Mais a frans honteus	but to the unworthy,
b	*Nous a en son lieu tramis*	he sent us to his place,
	Qui sommes de ses nouris	who are his family
	Et si enfançon.	and children.
R	*Dieus soit . . .*	God, be in this house . . .

Pour a - voir des____ pai - re - sis   A no - he - li - son.
Qui som - mes de____ ses nou - ris   Et si   en - fan - çon.

Back to refrain

Verse

1. Or man-de - rai   m'a - mi - e - te,   Qui est____ coin - te et   jo - li - e - te
2. Et   s'ele est de   moi   en - chain - te,   Tost de - ven - ra   paile et____ tain - te;
3. Mieus vaut que je   m'en   as - tien - gne   Et   pour__ li   jo - li   me - tien - gne

Et____ s'est   si   sa - ve - rou - se - te,   clas - te - nir   ne m'en por - rai.
S'il en____ est   es - clan - de - le et____ plain - te,   Des - hon - ne - ré - e   l'ar - rai.
Et____ que   de   li   me__ sou - vien - gne   Car____ s'on-nour   li   gar - de - rai.

Back to refrain

c. *Fines amouretes* ("I have many fine lovers"), Virelai

A	*Fines amouretes ai, Dieu!*	I have many fine lovers, God knows!
	Si ne sai, quant les verrai.	Such that I don't know when I will see the like again.
b	*Or manderai m'amiete,*	Now I will send for my little friend,
b	*Qui est cointe et joliete*	who is pretty and refined
a	*Et s'est si saverousete,*	and so tasty a dish
	Clastenir ne m'en porrai.	that I won't be able to hold myself in!
A	*Fines amouretes ai ...*	I have many fine lovers ...
b	*Et s'ele est de moi enchainte,*	But if she should become pregnant by me,
b	*Tost devenra paile et tainte;*	and gets pale and sickly,
a	*S'il en est esclandele et plainte,*	and should a scandal and an outcry ensue,
	Des honnerée l'arrai.	then I shall have dishonored her.
A	*Fines amouretes ai ...*	I have many fine lovers ...
b	*Mieus vaut que je m'en astiengne*	It would be better if I abstained,
b	*Et pour li joli me tiengne*	and, for the pretty one's sake,
a	*Et que de li me souviengne*	contented myself with merely remembering her.
	Car s'onnour li garderai.	Thus does her honor protect her.
A	*Fines amouretes ai ...*	I have many fine lovers ...

Refrain

Fi - nes   a - mou - re - tes__ ai,   Dieu!   si____ ne sai,   quant les   ver - rai.

Fine

15

Anonymous

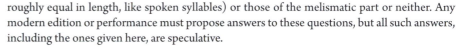

Jubilemus exultemus (ca. 1100)

Jubilemus exultemus is an example of *melismatic organum*, which, along with discant (Vol 1-16), was one of two styles of twelfth-century Aquitanian polyphony. It comes from a manuscript that was long kept in the library of the Abbey of St. Martial at Limoges, the biggest monastery in Aquitaine (the same region where troubadour song emerged at about the same time). St. Martial was already a center of trope and *versus* composition in the tenth century, and the lower voice of *Jubilemus exultemus* is in fact a metrical versus composed as an embellishment of the end of matins on Christmas Day. The melismatic upper voice, then, is an embellishment of an embellishment of the liturgy, or, in other words, a polyphonic trope. It is a new type of trope, though, sung not before another chant, after it, or in between its verses, but simultaneously with it, providing a literal amplification (that is, a sonic enhancement) of the liturgy.

In the earliest polyphony the chant-bearing voice had been called the *vox principalis* (principal voice), but from now on we will call it the *tenor*, from the Latin infinitive *tenere* ("to hold"). The additional voice, which was called the *vox organalis* (organal voice) in earlier polyphony, we will now call the *duplum* (literally "second voice"). The notation of "St. Martial"–style polyphony (the quotes here are a reminder that the music was written into manuscripts held at the Abbey of St. Martial but not necessarily composed there) is like that of Gregorian chant, in that it specifies pitch but not rhythm. We are reminded by this lack of notational specificity that this music was "composed," learned, and performed by oral methods. Modern musicians, who must read this notation in order to sing the music that the twelfth-century singers committed to memory, face much greater challenges here than with chant because they now need to know not just how to sing each part but also how the two parts line up. In particular, the singer of the tenor part has to know when to change to the next note—or else the singer of the duplum part has to know when to cue his colleague on the tenor. The only clue that the manuscript sources give us is the rough—*very* rough—vertical alignment of the two voices in the manuscript "score." To that we can add the twelfth-century contrapuntal rule that the sustained part should move only when it can create a perfect consonance against the more rapidly moving part. Even with these clues we cannot arrive at a definitive text, assuming there was such a thing (which is a great deal to assume). Nor do we know if it is the tenor's notes that are meant to be "equipollent" (that is,

roughly equal in length, like spoken syllables) or those of the melismatic part or neither. Any modern edition or performance must propose answers to these questions, but all such answers, including the ones given here, are speculative.

What is clear is the twelfth-century preference for perfect intervals—unisons, octaves, fifths, and fourths. These had been the favored intervals since the earliest written-down polyphony from the ninth century, and they would continue to be the fundamental harmonic building blocks of polyphonic music until the early fifteenth century.

Jubilemus exultemus, intonemus canticum,	Let us rejoice, let us exult, let us sing a song
Redemptori plasmatori, salvatori omnium.	to the redeemer, the maker, the savior of all.
Hoc nathali salutari omnis nostra turmula	For this saving birth, let our whole congregation
Deum laudet sibi plaudat per eternal secula. *Qui hodie de Marie utero progrediens*	praise God and applaud him in eternity. The one coming forth today from Mary's womb,
Homo verus rex atque herus in terris apparuit.	a true man, a king and Lord appeared on earth.
Tam beatum ergo natum cum ingenti gaudio	Therefore, for such a blessed birth, with great delight,
Conlaudantes, exultantes benedicamus Domino.	praising and exulting together, let us bless the Lord.

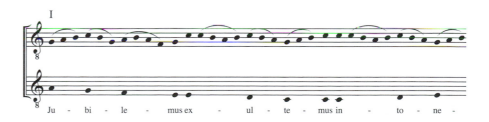

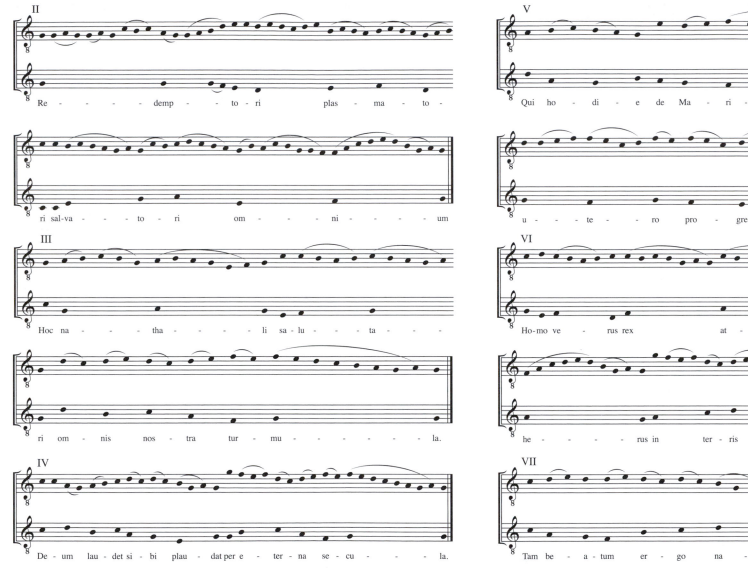
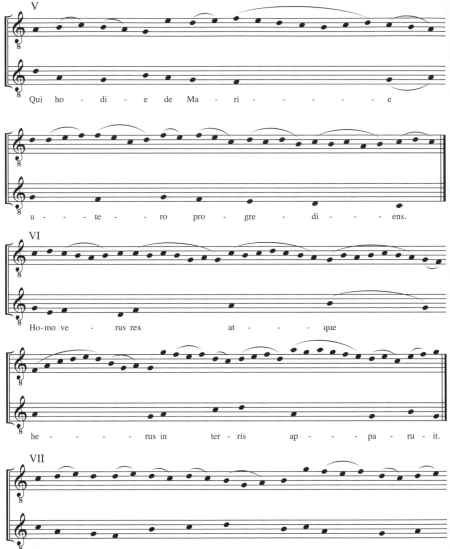

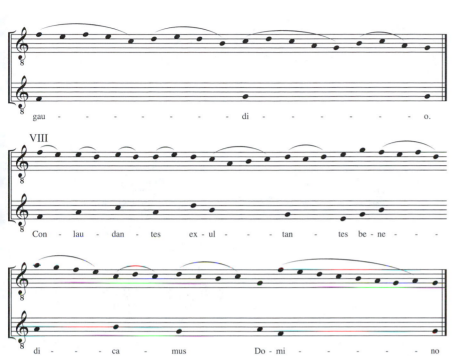

16

Anonymous

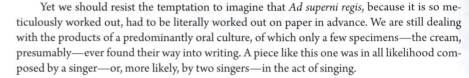

Ad superni regis (early twelfth c.)

Not all the polyphonic pieces in the St. Martial style present modern performers with as many difficulties as *Jubilemus exultemus*. This is because, along with melismatic organum settings, the St. Martial sources contain numerous versus and hymn settings in *discant* style, in which the two frequently crossing voices move at roughly the same speed. Even when not precisely note-against-note, they are at least rhythmically similar. In *Ad superni regis* and other such settings it is not often possible to identify a preexisting tune in either part; thus there is nothing in them to distinguish a tenor from an organal voice. In such cases the two parts were in all likelihood conceived as a pair.

The texture is "neume-against-neume" rather than note-against-note. The slurs in the modern edition given here indicate ligatures in the original notation, and we can see that the original notation consisted of ligatures of two, three, four, and sometimes more notes. The transcription given here follows the "isosyllabic" principle, which assumes that every neume lasts the same amount of time, corresponding to a quarter note in the transcription. It is unlikely that performances of the piece held strictly to this principle, but they could very well have held loosely to it. At the beginning of the piece this neume/quarter-note duration corresponds to the duration of syllables of text, but at the ends of verses there are decorative melismas in which final syllables are set to multiple neumes—and therefore last longer. Notice the way the melismas "accelerate" through the piece from two-note to four-note to five-note patterns. This seems to argue in favor of the isosyllabic scheme, in which ligatures actually gather speed as they grow in size. Notice, too, the repetitive or sequential patterns into which the melismas are organized and the way the voices complement one another's contour by the use of contrary motion. For a third thing, notice the way in which the two voices exchange roles in the first two measures, but also notice the slight differences between them that ensure variation within repetition, small irregularities within a larger regularity (the ligature G–F in the first measure, upper part, is answered in the second measure by a single G in the lower; the two-note ligature F–E in the first measure, lower part, is answered in the second measure by a three-noter, E–F–E, in the upper). Fascination with abstract patterning here produces a fascinating result.

Yet we should resist the temptation to imagine that *Ad superni regis*, because it is so meticulously worked out, had to be literally worked out on paper in advance. We are still dealing with the products of a predominantly oral culture, of which only a few specimens—the cream, presumably—ever found their way into writing. A piece like this one was in all likelihood composed by a singer—or, more likely, by two singers—in the act of singing.

Ad superni regis decus *qui continet omnia*	To the jewel of the king who possesses all things,
celebramus leti tua, *Iacobe, sollempnia.*	we happily celebrate, James, your feast.
Secus litus galilee *contempsisti propria.*	From the shore of Galilee you scorned worldly possessions.
Sequens Christum predicasti *ipsius imperia.*	Following Christ, you foretold his kingdom.
Tu petisti iuxta Christum *tunc sedere nescius,*	You sought to be near Christ, without knowing,
Sed nunc sedes in cohorte *duodena alcius.*	but now you sit with the twelve on high.
Prothomartir duodenus *fuisti in patria.*	You were the first martyr of the twelve in your land.
Primam sedem duodenam *possides in gloria.*	You hold the first seat of the twelve in glory.
Fac nos ergo interesse *polo absque termino.*	Let us therefore be present in the infinite heavens,
Ut mens nostra regi regum *benedicat Domino.*	that our mind may bless the king of kings, the Lord.

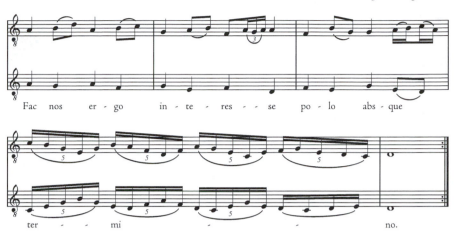

qui con - ti - net om - ni - - - a.

Fac nos er - go in - te - res - se po - lo abs - que

Se - cus li - tus Ga - li - le - e con - temp - sis - ti

ter - mi - no.

pro - pri - a. Tu pe - tis - ti iux - ta Chris - tum

tunc se - de - re nes - ci us.

Pro - tho mar - tir du - o - de - mus fu - is - ti in

pa - tri - a.

17

Leonin
(*fl* 1150s to ca. 1201)

Viderunt omnes (late twelfth c.)

Leonin's organum duplum (two-voice organum) *Viderunt omnes* is the opening piece of the *Magnus liber organi* ("Great Book of Organum") of the cathedral of Notre Dame in Paris. It is based on the chant *Viderunt omnes* (Example 17–1), the Gradual from the Mass for Christmas day, and it is the first item in the book because the *Magnus liber* is organized according to the church calendar, which begins with Advent, the lead-up to the Christmas season. The tenor (lower voice) corresponds to the chant, and the duplum (upper voice) sings a newly composed melody against it. The first two words are set polyphonically, but then the polyphony stops until the beginning of the chant verse ("Notum fecit . . ."). The verse is set almost completely to polyphony, but the final two words ("justitiam suam") are once again sung as chant. The reason for this alternation between polyphony and monophony is that Leonin divided up the Gradual exactly as the choir and soloist would have in the original responsorial chant. After the soloist's intonation on the words "Viderunt omnes," the opening respond belongs to the choir. The verse, excepting the final two words, belongs to the soloist. The composer set as polyphony only the soloist's portions of the chant, so that the two-voice polyphony represents multiple soloists, so to speak, while the chant portions represent a monophonic choir.

Looking at the piece in more detail, we see that the duplum begins with a series of extremely long melismas above relatively few notes in the tenor. The first syllable of text ("Vi-"), for example, lasts more than forty notes in the duplum while the tenor holds a single note. When the tenor is held long, the texture is called *organum purum* (a new term for what we have previously called *melismatic organum*). But when the soloist's portion of the chant has its own melismas (for example at "om-" of "omnes" in mm. 34–57 of the respond and especially at "Dominus" in mm. 38–93 of the verse), the tenor notes move along at roughly the same speed as those of the duplum, and both voices are given definite rhythm. These are the first examples of notated rhythm in the history of Western music. The main reason for shortening and rhythmicizing the tenor notes at these points is primarily practical: The music would be interminable if every tenor note were held as long as the first few. But it is in these sped-up, rhythmicized sections that we see the greatest creativity from Notre Dame composers. *Discant* is the word to describe the texture in which the tenor voice is melismatic and both voices use definite rhythm,

and portions of organa in which discant is used are called *clausulae* (singular *clausula*). Notre Dame clausulae display the clear organization of ligatures into the patterns of the rhythmic modes, of which there were six in theory, though in practice fewer than that were used (in this modern edition, ligatures are indicated by brackets above the notes). All of the clausulae (to the two just mentioned, add "-tum gentium revelavit" in mm. 154–207 of the verse and "-runt om-" in mm. 12–23 of the repetition of the respond) feature primarily the first rhythmic mode (repeating long-short patterns of notes) in the duplum, and all but the first feature the fifth mode (a series of long notes) in the tenor.

In organum purum, rhythm is not organized as it is in discant. Instead, the notes are sung "freely," as in chant, but not entirely freely. Guides to organum emphasize that notes forming consonances with the tenor were or could be sung longer than those forming dissonances. This habit, or rule, was probably what prompted the adoption of the trochaic (long-short) pattern of the first rhythmic mode as the rhythmic norm: The note that in the added voice intervenes between two harmonic consonances is often dissonant (a "passing" or "neighbor" tone, as we now call such things), hence sung short. In this and other works of Notre Dame polyphony, we see not only the first examples of rhythmic notation but also the first examples of rhythm acting as a guiding parameter of harmony and counterpoint.

R: *Viderunt omnes fines terrae salutare Dei nostri. Jubilate Deo omnis terra.*

V: *Notum fecit Dominus salutare suum; ante conspectum gentium revelavit justitiam suam.*

All the ends of the earth have seen the salvation of our Lord; sing joyfully to God, all the earth (Ps. 98, 3–4).

The Lord hath made known his salvation; he hath revealed his justice in the sight of the Gentiles (Ps. 98, 2).

Example 17-1 *Viderunt omnes*, **Gradual from the Mass for Christmas Day**

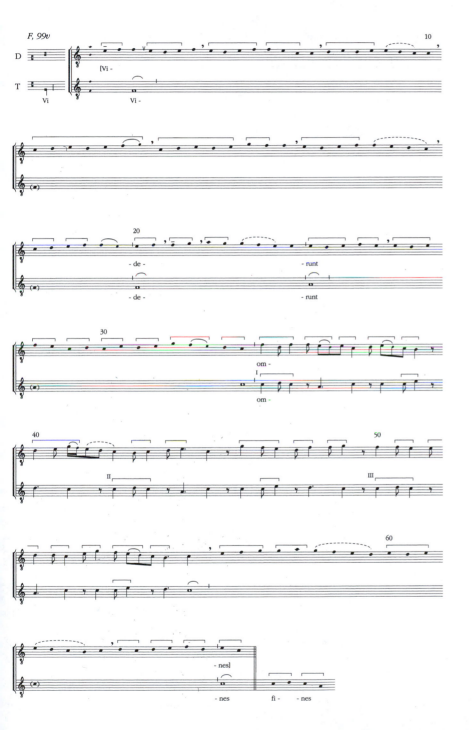

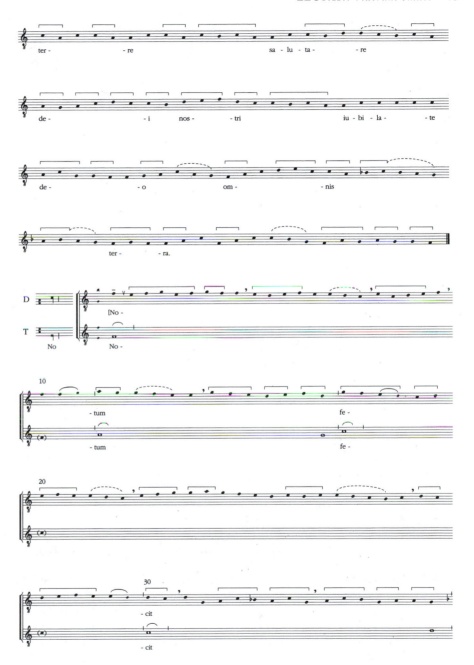

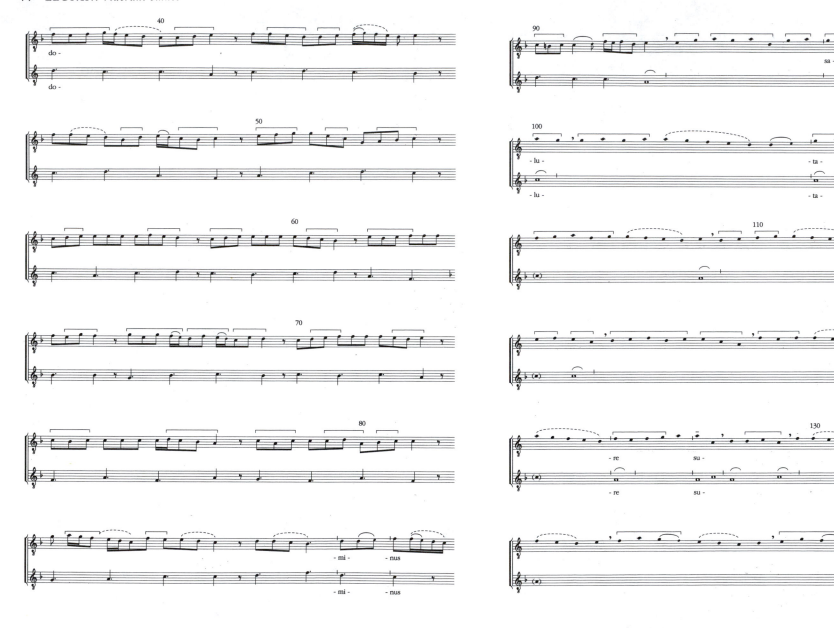

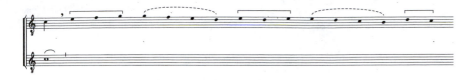

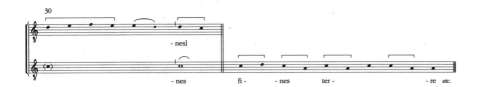

- nes]

- nes   fi -   - nes   ter -   - re *etc.*

18

Perotin
(*fl* ca. 1200)

Viderunt omnes (1198)

Thirteenth-century theorists distinguished between *organum per se* ("organum by itself") and *organum cum alio* ("organum with another [voice]"). In Leonin's *Viderunt omnes* we saw a splendid example of *organum per se*. In Perotin's *organum quadruplum* (four-voice organum) on the same Christmas Gradual, we see an example of *organum cum alio* at its most elaborate. Like Leonin, Perotin sets the solo portions of the chant as polyphony and leaves the choral portions to be sung as chant. But the presence of the third and fourth voices (called the *triplum* and the *quadruplum*) changes everything, because they move at the rate of the duplum, not that of the tenor. Two or three parts moving at a similar rate are in effect in discant with one another, regardless of whether there is a long-held tenor note, and so they had to be notated throughout in strict modal rhythm.

Perotin's composition moves throughout in an especially stately version of the trochaic (first-mode) meter we first observed in Leonin's setting. What makes it "stately" is the liberal admixture of perfect and duplex longs (dotted quarter notes and dotted half notes in the modern edition) into the rhythms of the upper parts. The first note in the duplum, triplum, and quadruplum is a duplex long, and the long-held chord they create is a composite of all the *symphoniae* (consonant intervals). There is a unison between the duplum and the quadruplum, an octave between the tenor and the triplum, a fifth between the tenor and both the duplum and the quadruplum, and a fourth between the triplum and both the duplum and the quadruplum. This harmony—essentially a three-voice sonority consisting of an octave and a fifth over the lowest-sounding note—is a sort of Pythagorean summary, and it became the normative consonance for polyphony in three or more voices until the sixteenth century.

Notice how at the outset every successive phrase ends on that normative perfect consonance (e.g., mm. 7, 11, 15, and 19). And notice, too, how in every phrase the perfect long (dotted quarter note) preceding it is constructed so as to make the greatest degree of dissonance, both with respect to the tenor and among the upper voices themselves. In the first phrase (ending in mm. 6–7), the next-to-last note in the quadruplum is D, a major sixth from the tenor (the least consonant of the imperfect consonances as then classified). The penult in the triplum is E, a major seventh from the tenor and a major second from the quadruplum; its dissonance

speaks for itself. The duplum's penult is B♭, a tritone from the triplum's E. If isolated from its context and banged out at the keyboard, the chord would startle even a twenty-first-century ear. In context, of course, the chord is heard as implying its resolution to the normative consonance. Note that in making the resolution, every voice proceeds by step. The dissonant major second between the triplum's E and the quadruplum's D, for example, arises not out of some "nonharmonic" Medieval way of hearing, but out of the implied rule of voice-leading that dissonant notes should proceed by step to consonant notes. We see in this voice leading the beginnings of a cadential practice, in which the melodic motion of individual voices is subordinated to an overall harmonic function. It is the beginning—the very beginning, in a very rudimentary form—of tonal harmony.

To see textural integration, control, and planning from another perspective, compare the identical or nearly identical melodic figures in the triplum in mm. 4–7, the triplum in mm. 12–15, the duplum in mm. 16–19, the triplum in mm. 24–27, and finally the quadruplum in mm. 28–31. Now compare the triplum in mm. 8–11 with the duplum in mm. 12–15, the triplum in mm. 16–19, and the quadruplum in mm. 20–23 and 24–27. This kind of elaborate voice exchange—the passing of melodic motives back and forth between various voices—is the most conspicuous of integrative devices and can be traced throughout the piece.

For yet another perspective, look at the music starting in m. 95, halfway through the syllable "-de-" (of "Viderunt") in the tenor. Here the motion has slowed down to an alternation between perfect longs (the fifth rhythmic mode) and the normative trochees (the first rhythmic mode). The figure C–D–C in longs and its trochaic variant C–D–E–D–C are tossed back and forth between the duplum and the triplum. Their exchanges are now dovetailed so that the first note in one voice coincides with the last note in the other. In between, a note in one voice coincides with a rest in the other. This kind of exchange between notes and rests (done slowly here, but sometimes done with lightning speed) was a specialty of *organum cum alio* and its derivative genres. The controlled textural fragmentation was great fun for the singers, as we can tell by the name they gave it: *hoquetus*—hocket in English—from the Latin for "hiccup," no doubt because of the way the rests interrupt the melodic lines like spasms. An even more radically fragmented hocket texture comes over the first tenor note of the syllable "-runt" starting in m. 125.

To see *organum cum alio* at its most rhythmically intense, look at the points in this composition where melismas in the tenor are set to modal rhythm rather than being held long. The three most splendid of these appear on the syllables "om-" of "omnes" (mm. 225–241), "Do-" of "Dominus" (mm. 274–330 of the verse), and the word "revelavit" (mm. 553–589 of the verse), the same bits of text on which discant clausulae appear in Leonin's setting. The propulsive energy in these passages far surpasses anything in *organum per se* and is arguably not seen again until the Baroque period.

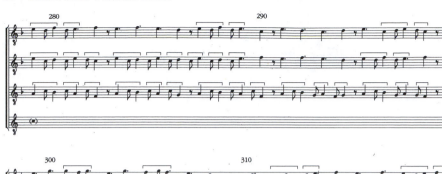

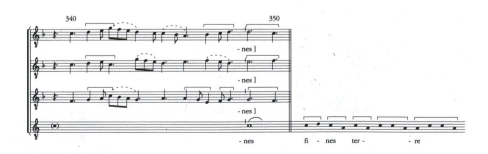

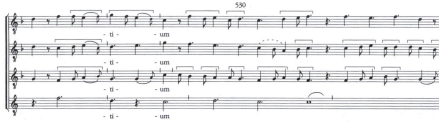

19

Anonymous

Vetus abit littera (early thirteenth c.)

The conductus was the only one of the Notre Dame genres that was not based on a preexisting chant. Instead, it was a setting of a Latin poem composed from scratch. It was also the only Notre Dame genre that was syllabically texted. In contemporary parlance it was *musica cum littera* ("music with words"), and that meant it had to be notated in "simple notes" (*notae simplices*) rather than in ligatures, because ligatures functioned in Notre Dame notation just as they did in plainchant with respect to the text. They were used only to carry melismas, that is, music without text (*musica sine littera*), and there was no standard method for applying text to notation in ligatures. In the conductus we therefore encounter the central shortcoming of the system of modal rhythm pioneered in Notre Dame polyphony, which used groupings of ligatures to indicate rhythm. The four-voice Christmas conductus *Vetus abit littera* shows how the conductus exposed this shortcoming and also a possible attempt to remedy the situation.

The notation, until the last syllable of text, consists almost entirely of single notes. If read strictly according to the rules of modal rhythm, they are all perfect longs, casting the setting in a very heavy spondaic (fifth-mode) meter throughout. But that final syllable has a sizable melisma in all voices, called a *cauda* ("tail"). Being a melisma, the *cauda* is written in ligatures. As a second glance at them will show, the ligatures in question could hardly form a clearer trochaic (first-mode) pattern. No question, then, that the *cauda* is supposed to go tum-ta-tum-ta-tum-ta-tum in good modal fashion. And so the question arises: Is the first-mode *cauda* supposed to contrast with the fifth mode of the rest of the piece? Or, perhaps, is the *cauda* there not simply to embellish the otherwise-syllabic composition but also to convey the otherwise-unconveyable information that the whole piece is to be sung in first mode? The edition given here transcribes the whole piece into first mode, which turns the accentual pattern of the entire poem quite convincingly into a quantitative musical meter. But there is no authority to back up that decision; it is simply a preference.

Vetus abit littera,
Ritus abit veterum,
Dat virgo puerpera

The old word has passed away,
The ancient rite is gone,
The child-bearing virgin gives

Novum nobis puerum,
Numis salutiferum,
Regem et presbyterum,
Qui complanans aspera,
Firma pacis foedera,
Purgator et scelerum,

(Trans. Alexander Blachly)

To us a new son,
A life-giving gift,
A king and priest,
Who smoothes the rough places
And strengthens the pacts of peace:
He is the cleanser of sin.

Qui com-pla-nans a-spe-ra   Fir-mat pa-cis foe-de-ra   Pur - ga-tor _ et sce-le-rum.

(cauda)

20

Anonymous

Ex semine rosa/Ex semine Habrahe/EX SEMINE
(early to mid-thirteenth c.)

The earliest *motets*, as we may surmise from the genre's earliest sources, were simply prosulated bits of discant—that is, discant to which a syllabic text has been grafted onto the added duplum and/or triplum voice in the manner of a prosula. The motet *Ex semine rosa/Ex semine Habrahe/ EX SEMINE* is based entirely on the music of a clausula (the beginning of which is shown in Example 20-1) on the words "Ex semine" from an organum triplum by Perotin on the *Alleluia Nativitas* chant from the Mass for the Nativity of the Virgin Mary (8 September). Strip away the text of the triplum and the *motetus* (the second voice, which in organum had been called the duplum), and the motet is identical to the clausula.

The syllabic text in the motetus is a Latin poem about the Virgin Mary's own birth and about the birth of her son. It opens with a quotation from the text of the *Alleluia Nativitas* at the very point where the clausula begins ("Ex semine Abrahe," "from the seed of Abraham") and closes with a repetition of the word "semine." These, along with yet an additional allusion to the Alleluia text (on "de tribu Iuda"), are italicized in the transcription of the prosula-poem given here. The poem glosses—that is, expands and clarifies—the text of the Alleluia in the manner of

a trope, and it may have been intended for performance within the organum in the place of the textless clausula. The triplum too is outfitted with its own text, which also glosses the *Alleluia Nativitas* text in a similar manner. It begins and ends with the same textual allusions to the chant and was clearly composed as a partner voice to the motetus. What we have, then, is a three-voice clausula in which each of the non-chant-bearing voices has its own prosula. This type of motet, with two different texts in addition to the tenor, is called a *double motet*.

Eventually motets were weaned from their incubator within organum compositions and began to be performed as freestanding pieces of texted music rather than as mere textual grafts onto existing discants. It is as these freestanding miniatures—which could have Latin or French texts above the tenor—that they come down to us in manuscript sources. What is endlessly fascinating and at the same time puzzling about the motet is that it was "polytextual," with as many different texts as it had voices over the Gregorian tenor. The words were clearly important to the composers—as the highly planned text of *Ex semine rosa/Ex semine Habrahe/EX SEMINE* shows—but they are difficult to hear when all sung together. We must therefore ask ourselves whether motets were meant only to be heard or perhaps were also to be read.

Triplum

Ex semine	From the seed
Rosa prodit spine;	of a thorn, a rose comes forth.
Fructus olee	The olive fruit
Oleastro legitur;	is plucked from the olive tree.
Virgo propagine	A Virgin comes forth
Nascitur Judee.	from Judah's line.
Stelle matutine	The morning star's
Radius exoritur	radiance shines forth
Nubis caligine;	from the cloudy gloom;
Radio sol stelle;	The sun, from the star's ray;
Petra fluit melle	A stone flows with honey;
Parit flos puelle	A flower of maidenhood gives birth
Verbum sine semine.	to the Word, without *seed*.

Motetus

Ex semine	From the seed
Abrahe, divino	of Abraham, by divine
Moderamine,	control,
Igne pio numine	in the holy fire of your presence,
producis domine,	Lord, you bring forth
Hominis salutem,	the salvation of mankind
Paupertate nuda,	from stark poverty,

Example 20-1 Excerpt from Perotin's three-voice *Alleluia Nativitas* on the words "Ex semine"

Virginis nativitate   by the birth of a Virgin
de tribu Iuda.   from the tribe of Judah.
Iam propinas ovum   And now you proffer an egg
Per natale novum,   for an additional birth,
Piscem, panem dabis,   by which you will give fish and bread
Partu sine semine.   all delivered without *seed*.

Tenor

Ex semine   From the seed

21
Anonymous

L'autre jour/Au tens pascour/IN SECULUM
(late thirteenth c.)

In the late thirteenth century, the motet became the genre that reveled more than any other in its polyphonicness. *L'autre jour/Au tens pascour/IN SECULUM* is an example of the fully evolved late-thirteenth-century motet, the development of which was facilitated by the emergence of "Franconian" notation, the first system of mensural rhythmic notation. First described about 1280 by Franco of Cologne, a German scholar resident in Paris for whom it is named, this notational system indicated rhythmic durations with specific note shapes rather than with patterned groupings of ligatures as modal notation had done. Mensural notation allowed composers to notate the familiar modal rhythms while also texting them fully (a new syllable could not begin in the middle of a ligature, and so modally notated melodies were untextable). The basic note shapes were the *long*, which could either be "perfect" (transcribed as a dotted quarter note) or "imperfect" (transcribed as a quarter note); the *breve*, which could be "normal" (transcribed as an eighth note) or "altered" (transcribed as a quarter note); and the *semibreve* (transcribed as a sixteenth note).

L'autre jour/Au tens pascour/IN SECULUM is clearly discant- or clausula-derived, although the actual clausula counterpart to it has not survived. The triplum and motetus voices are both in trochaic meter (the first rhythmic mode), notated as alternating longs and breves. They are accompanied by a spondaic (fifth-mode) tenor borrowed from a Gregorian chant melisma that comes from the Easter Gradual, *Haec dies,* already encountered in Vol 1-3b. The *IN SECULUM* tenor is taken from the final phrase of the chant—"quoniam *in seculum* misericordia ejus" ("for His mercy endureth *forever*")—and the complete chant melisma is stated twice (starting in mm. 1 and 23), its notes cut up into alternating groups of two and three longs (dotted quarter notes) or maximas (double longs, transcribed as dotted half notes).

That much is *à la* clausula, but the French motetus and triplum texts are not. Both are pastourelles of the sort that we have encountered in trouvère song (see Moniot d'Arras's *Ce fut en mai*, Vol 1-13), which were not only secular but also in a low style. Such pastourelle texts were common in French motets of the thirteenth century, which often invoked, as this one does, the shepherd character Robin and the cliché beginning ("the other day . . .") that goes all the way back to pastoral troubadour poetry. The texted voices may seem naive and folksy, but they are

placed within a very literate composition that belies their rustic nature. That incongruity was meant to amuse and—along with the polytextuality—intensify the essential heterogeneity of the motet genre. We see in this composition a delightful example of the *ars combinatoria* (the art of combining things) and *discordia concors* (the harmonization of contrarieties). The harmonization of diverse elements to which motet composers aspired extends to the words as well as to the music, including the liturgical Latin tenor. The duplum text, which begins by setting the scene in the "tens pascour"—translatable as "springtime" or "Eastertime"—makes an oblique reference to the Easter chant *Haec dies*, from which the tenor's melisma is drawn. This amusing little piece is thus a tightly wrought web of referentiality in which liturgy, organum, and secular song all comment on one another in very sophisticated ways.

Triplum

L'autre jour par un matin	The other day at morn
dejouste une valée	down by a valley
A une ajournée	at the break of day
Pastourelle ai trovée,	I spied a shepherdess
Je l'ai regardée;	and watched her a while.
Seule estoit,	She was all alone,
D'amours chantoit;	singing of love,
Et je dis:	and I said:
"Simple et coie,	"Guileless and bashful girl,
Volentiers seroie,	gladly would I be,
Se il vous agrée,	if it would pleasure you,
Vos amis."	your lover."
Ele respont cum senée:	She replied, thoughtfully:
"Sire, laissiés moi ester,	"Sir, let me be,
Ralés en vo contrée,	go back where you came from.
J'aim Robin sans fausseté,	I love Robin without deceit;
m'amor li ai donnée,	I've pledged him my love.
Plus l'aim que riens née;	I love him more than any born thing.
Il s'en est alés juer	He's gone off to play
au bois, sous la ramée;	in the woods 'neath the trees;
Villenie feroie,	I'd do an awful thing
Se je ne l'amoie,	if I didn't love him back,
Car il m'aimme sans trechier,	For he has loved me faithfully,
Ja pour vous ne le quier laissier."	And I'd never leave him for the likes of you."

Motetus

Au tens pascour	At Eastertime
Tuit li pastour	All the shepherd folk
D'une contrée	from one locale
Ont fait assemblée	gathered together

Desous une valée.	at the bottom of a valley.
Hebers en la prée	Herbert, in the meadow,
A de la pipe et dou tabour	with pipe and tabor
la danse demenée;	led the dance.
Robin pas n'agrée,	Robin did not like it
Quant il l'a esgardée;	when he saw it,
Mais par aatie	but out of conceit
Fera mieudre estampie.	thought he'd do a better estampie.
Lors a saisi son fourrel,	So he grabbed his bagpipe,
Prist son chapel,	put on his hat,
S'a sa cote escourcie,	tucked in his coat,
S'a fait l'estanpie	and did an estampie,
Jolie	a jolly one,
Pour l'amour de s'amie.	to impress his girl.
Rogers, Guios et Gautiers	Roger, Guy and Gautier
en ont mont grant envie,	are right full of jealousy,
N'i a nul qui rie,	They none of them laugh,
Ains font aatie,	but say defiantly
K'ains ke soit l'avesprée,	that come nightfall
Iert sa pipe effondrée.	his pipe is going to be in pieces.

Tenor

In seculum   Forever

"Si - re, lais - siés moi es - ter, ra - lés en vo con - tre - e, j'aim Ro - bin sans

Lors a sai - si son four - rel, prist son cha - pel, s'a sa cote es - cour - ci - e,

faus - se - té, m'a - mor li ai don - ne - e, plus l'aim que - riens ne - e; il s'en est a -

s'a fait l'es - tan - pi - e jo - li - e pour l'a - mour de s'a - mi - e. Ro - giers, Gui - os

lés ju - er au bois sous la ra - me - e; vi - le - ni - e fe - roi - e, se je ne l'a -

e Gau - tiers en ont mout grant en - vi - e, n'i a nul qui ri - e, ains font a - a -

moi - e, car il m'aim - me sans tre - chier, ja pour vous ne le quier lais - sier."

ti - e, k'ains ke soit l'a - ves - pre - e, iert sa pipe ef - fon - dre - e.

22
Anonymous

On parole/A Paris/FRESE NOUVELE
(ca. 1300)

Johannes de Grocheio, a theorist writing at the very end of the thirteenth century, had this to say about the motet:

> This kind of song ought not to be propagated among the vulgar, since they do not understand its subtlety nor do they delight in hearing it, but it should be performed for the learned and those who seek after the subtleties of the arts. And it is normally performed at their feasts for their edification, just as the song they call rondeau is performed at the feasts of the vulgar.

Grocheio's exclusionary prescription for the motet illustrates the way in which the newly emerging urban and literate elite aspired to the status of the older, established aristocracy. The "learned" class that Grocheio represents gave the motet genre an initiated audience that encouraged composers to create witty and ingenious combinations of materials within the genre's polyphonic and polytextual structure (as we have seen in Vol 1-20). Even the tenor, which had always given the motet its sacred link to the organum tradition and by extension to chant, was not immune from the combinatorial games.

The motet *On parole/A Paris/FRESE NOUVELE* is precisely the sort of composition that Grocheio did not want propagated among the vulgar, who were not initiated to the subtleties of learned composition. Semibreves (transcribed here as eighth notes) can be found in all parts. The triplum and motetus texts describe just the sort of "feasts of the learned" that Grocheio says are the proper setting for motet performance, at which literate clerics gather to feast on capons, guzzle wine, cavort with girls, and despise manual labor but also to discuss intellectual topics and share learned compositions. The texts also praise Paris, the center of this intellectual good life. The tenor states a fourfold repetition of a tune that is not of a piece of chant but of the cry of a street vendor selling fruit—"Fresh strawberries, nice blackberries!" Appropriation of preexisting material is the norm for the genre, but the untraditional source of that material, which Grocheio's learned elite would have understood as witty, is precisely the sort of thing that Grocheio feared the uninitiated might have viewed as sacrilegious.

Both the musical material and the subject matter in this motet are entirely urban and entirely secular. The piece no longer has any direct relationship to the traditions of liturgical polyphony and courtly song out of which motet composition originally grew; its connection to the clausula or the trouvère chanson can be better demonstrated historically than stylistically. The motet had become independent of its traditions and ready to nurture the growth of new ones.

Triplum

On parole de batre et de vanner	The talk is of threshing and winnowing,
Et de foïr et de hanner,	of digging and ploughing.
Mais ces diduis trop me desplaisent,	Such pastimes are not at all to my liking.
Car il n'est si bone vie que d'estre a aise	For there is nothing like having one's fill
De bon cler vin et de chapons,	of good clear wine and capons,
Et d'estre aveuc bons compaignons.	and being with good friends,
Liés et joians,	hale and hearty,
Chantans,	singing,
Truffans,	joking,
Et amorous,	and in love,
Et d'avoir, quant c'on a mestier,	and having all one needs
Pour solacier	to give pleasure
Beles dames a devis:	to beautiful women to one's heart's content.
Et tout se truev' on a Paris.	And all of this is to be had in Paris.

Motetus

A Paris soir et matin	Morning and night in Paris
Truev' on bon pain et bon cler vin,	there is good bread to be found and good, clear wine,
Bone char et bon poisson,	good meat and fish,
De toutes guises compaignons,	all manner of friends
Sens soutie, brant baudour,	of lively mind and high spirits,
Biaus joiaus, dames d'ounour;	fine jewels and noble ladies
Et si truev' on bien en tredeus	and, in the meantime,
De menre feur pour homes desiteus.	prices to suit a poor man's purse.

Tenor

Frese nouvele! Muere france! Muere!	Fresh strawberries! Nice blackberries!
Muere france!	Blackberries! Nice blackberries!

23

Attributed to Philippe de Vitry (1291–1361)

Tribum/Quoniam/MERITO (early fourteenth c.)

The motet *Tribum/Quoniam/MERITO* is one of the earliest surviving pieces in *Ars Nova* rhythmic notation. It is one of 126 musical compositions, including 24 motets, that are interpolated into a manuscript source of a famous allegorical poem, the *Roman de Fauvel*. The musical items in this manuscript, compiled about 1316, illustrate the theme of the poem, which is ferocious civil and political satire. The texts of the triplum and motetus, like the *Roman de Fauvel* itself, are full of allegorical references to the fate of Enguerrand de Marigny, the corrupt finance minister to King Philippe IV (Philip the Fair) of France, who was hanged on 30 April 1315 following the death of the king. Marigny's death is held up as an *admonitio*, a warning about the fickleness of Fortune and the dangers of usurping political power. The "fox" of the motetus voice is Marigny, the "cock" is the nation of France (*Gallus* is the Latin word for both rooster and France), and the blind Lion is the ineffectual king who allowed Marigny to operate as he did.

This motet is thought to be an early work of Philippe de Vitry, who was a contemporary of the authors of the *Roman de Fauvel* and who, with this piece and others that he composed around the same time, established the norms of the so-called *isorhythmic motet*, the standard type of fourteenth-century motet that would serve as the basis for more than a century of stylistic development. The differences between Philippe's motet and the late-thirteenth-century motets we have already seen will virtually define the prototype. Its texts are in Latin, not French (the language of most late-thirteenth-century motet texts), and its subject matter is political, not courtly or religious. Whereas thirteenth-century motets began with all the voices together, *Tribum/Quoniam/MERITO* begins with the triplum, which is joined by the motetus (m. 4) before the all-important tenor finally enters (m. 7). This sort of introductory section before the entrance of the tenor became so standardized that it was given a name: the *introitus*. By now the tenor has become the most important structural voice of a motet, and it is therefore chosen with care to reflect its liturgical dignity on the texted parts. The tenor *MERITO* is drawn from a matins responsory sung during the pre-Easter penitential season of Lent, and it invokes the words of the chant from which it is drawn: "Merito hec patimur" ("We suffer this deservedly"). These words are clearly an additional gloss on Enguerrand de Marigny's just desserts.

In Vitry's composition the tenor melody is stated twice (beginning in mm. 7 and 43). It is cast, moreover, in easily recognizable (even if slowed down) "second mode," or iambic (short-long), groupings. Most fourteenth-century motet tenors feature this sort of repeating rhythmic pattern, known as a *talea*, although in later motets the patterns became much more complex. Modern scholars use the term *isorhythm* ("same rhythm") to denote the application of a recurrent talea, often quite long and cunningly constructed, to a repeating melodic pattern, or *color*. An isorhythmic tenor, like the tenor seen here, is thus built on two periodic cycles, the one governing pitch (color), the other, duration (talea).

Composers of isorhythmic motets took special delight in constructing tenors with subtle patterning that organized and unified the still polytextual and heterogeneous surface of their works. One can bring this aspect of *Tribum/Quoniam/MERITO* to light by comparing mm. 10–13 with mm. 34–37 and mm. 58–62, which are all nearly identical. This repetition initiates an interlocking series of periodicities in the upper voices that crosscut the more obvious periodicity of the tenor. The triplum–duplum combination in mm. 22–25 will recur in mm. 46–49 and again in mm. 70–73. Every one of these spots, all of which correspond to a progression in the tenor from E to D, crosscuts the tenor's more obviously repeating rhythmic talea, because in every case the E is the end of a talea and the D is the beginning of another. And the thrice-recurring pair of alternating repetitions in the upper voices—mm. 10–13/22–25, 34–37/46–49, and 58–62/70–73 (ABABAB)—crosscuts the double cursus of the tenor's color, the second statement of which begins right between the members of the middle pair in m. 43. This is an especially significant hidden periodicity, for it imposes on the structure of the motet at its most encompassing level a "perfect/imperfect" duality (three repeated pairs vs. two tenor statements) that reflects the duality of note–value relationships at the heart of the Ars Nova system.

Triplum

Tribum que non abhoruit	Furious Fortune did not fear
indecenter ascendere	to turn quickly against the tribe
furibunda non metuit	that did not recoil from a shameless rise [to power]
Fortuna cito vertere,	when she did not spare
dum duci prefate tribus	the governing leader of the tribe
in sempiternum speculum	from the pillory,
parare palam omnibus	to be established as
non pepercit patibulum.	an eternal public example.
Populus ergo venturus	Therefore if future generations
si trans metam ascenderit,	should ascend across the limit,
quidam forsitan casurus,	let them fall.
cum tanta tribus ruerit,	When such a tribe has been ruined,
sciat eciam quis fructus	may it know what a result it would be,
delabi sit in profundum.	to fall into the depth.
Post zephyros plus ledit hyems, post	Winter harms more after the western
gaudia luctus;	wind, grief more after joy.

unde nichil melius quam nil habuisse
secundum.

Motetus

Quoniam secta latronum
spelunca vispilionum
vulpes que Gallos roderat
tempore quo regnaverat

leo cecatus subito
suo ruere merito
in mortem privatam bonis:
concinat Gallus Nasonis
dicta que dolum acuunt:
omnia sunt hominum tenui pendencia filo

et subito casu que valuere ruunt.

Tenor

Merito hec patimur

It is therefore better never to have had
anything than to have had something
favorable and been left with nothing.

Since with the plots
of thieves and
the den of shady dealers
the fox, which gnawed at the cocks (the
French)
in the time when the blind lion reigned,
has suddenly been hurled down
to his reward in death.
Let the cock (France) sing Ovid's words,
which sharpen the deceit:
"All human affairs hang by a slender
thread,
and those who were strong fall with sudden misfortune."

We suffer this deservedly

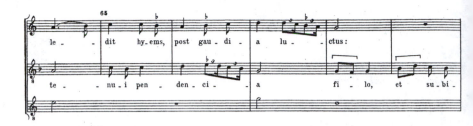

24

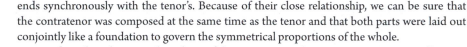

Guillaume de Machaut
(ca. 1300–77)

Felix virgo/Inviolata /AD TE SUSPIRAMUS (ca. 1360)

Machaut was the greatest poet and musician of mid-fourteenth-century France. He was the chief heir to the trouvère tradition of courtly song, but he also composed numerous isorhythmic motets that built on the tradition founded by Philippe de Vitry. *Felix virgo/Inviolata genitrix/AD TE SUSPIRAMUS* is a grandly conceived work with a polyphonic texture that is expanded to four voices. In addition to the by-now-familiar complement of Gregorian tenor plus newly composed motetus and triplum, it has a *contratenor* that moves "against the tenor" and in the same melodic range. Machaut's motet has a more formal introitus than Vitry's *Tribum/Quoniam/MERITO*: It comes to a full cadence (in m. 40), supported by the contratenor and the tenor, the latter playing "free" notes (that is, not drawn from the *cantus firmus* or color) for no other purpose than sonorous enhancement. The color, which begins in m. 42, is drawn from the *Salve regina* chant, which we have already encountered earlier (Vol 1-9b). Machaut excerpted a forty-eight-note passage of the version of the chant that he knew by heart, setting the words "to you we sigh, mourning and weeping in this vale of tears. O, therefore, [be] our advocate." Both upper voices sing Marian prayers that echo the devotional sentiments of the tenor.

To his color Machaut applied a talea consisting of sixteen notes and four rests, which must be stated three times to get through each of the two statements of the color (3 × 16 notes = 48 notes). The isorhythmic structure of the tenor is as follows:

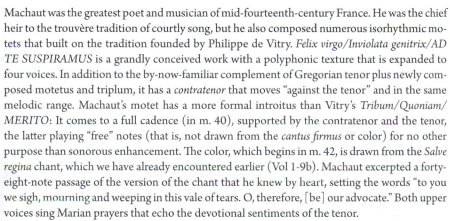

Measure:	41	77	113	149	167	185
Talea:	I	II	III	IV	V	VI
Color:	A————————————			B————————————		

The second statement of the color/talea complex (starting in m. 149) is in rhythmic diminution, moving twice as fast as the first statement. This isorhythmic layout in the tenor is mirrored by the contratenor. Although it is a newly invented part rather than a cantus firmus, the contratenor consists of a color that moves in double cursus against the tenor's color, also in diminution during the second cursus and also subdivided by a threefold talea that begins and

ends synchronously with the tenor's. Because of their close relationship, we can be sure that the contratenor was composed at the same time as the tenor and that both parts were laid out conjointly like a foundation to govern the symmetrical proportions of the whole.

And yet the other special attribute of the motet was its heterogeneity, its power of harmonizing contradictions. What made the genre so seductive in Machaut's hands was an extraordinary harmonic idiom that, while emulated somewhat by the next generation or two of French composers, nevertheless remained Machaut's unique and inimitable signature. Look now at the introitus to Machaut's motet (mm. 1–40). In m. 11, when the motetus first enters, the triplum sings a C♯. This note follows a D, and one would expect it to return to D. But instead it skips to a G♯, a surprising note not called for by any rule of counterpoint. Its only purpose is to create a "purple patch" in the harmony, especially in view of the weird interval it creates against the F natural in the motetus. But it is also there for "tonal" reasons. All of the signed accidentals in the introitus are C♯s or G♯s, tones which at once depart from and emphasize the basic Dorian pitch set of the motet because they are "tendency tones," pitches altered chromatically in such a way as to imply—hence demand—cadential resolution to the crucial mode-defining tones D and A. When the resolution is evaded or delayed—as it is in the case of the triplum's first C♯ (and even the G♯, whose resolution to A is interfered with by a rest where one is least expected)—a harmonic tension is created that will not be fully discharged until the introitus reaches its final cadence in m. 40. That cadence incorporates both the C♯ and the G♯, resolving in parallel to D and A, the defining notes of the Dorian pentachord. The two "structural" notes are therefore each provided with a leading tone, and for this reason such a cadence (with the tenor proceeding downward by step to the final) is called a *double leading-tone cadence*. Although it may sound odd to ears more accustomed to later tonal music, its great stabilizing power made it the standard cadence—and one of the most characteristic sounds—of fourteenth- and early-fifteenth-century music. It can be seen once again at the very end of this motet.

Triplum

Felix virgo, mater Christi,	Happy Virgin, Mother of Christ,
Que gaudium mundo tristi	Who brought joy to a sad world
Ortu tui contulisti,	By your birth,
Dulcissima,	O sweetest one,
Sic hereses peremisti	You thus destroyed heresies
Dum angelo credidisti	When you believed the angel
Filiumque genuisti,	And bore a Son,
Castissima.	O most chaste one.
Roga natum, piissima,	Beseech your Son, most pious one,
Ut pellat mala plurima,	That He drive away the many evils
Tormentaque fravissima,	and harshest torments
Que patimur;	That we suffer;
Nam a gente ditissima,	For by the wealthiest tribe,
Lux lucis splendidissima,	O most splendid light of light,

De sublimi ad infima	From the heights to the depths,
Deducimur;	We are brought down.
Cunctis bonis exuimur,	We are deprived of all good things,
Ab impiis persequimur,	We are persecuted by the impious,
Per quos jugo subicimur	Through whom we are brought
Servitutis,	Into servitude,
Nam sicut ceci gradimur	For we proceed as if blind
Nec directorem sequimur,	And do not follow a leader,
Sed a viis retrahimur	But are drawn back
Nobis tutis.	From our safe paths.
Gracie fons et virtutis,	Font of grace and virtue,
Sola nostre spes salutis,	Sole hope of our salvation,
Miserere destitutis	Have mercy on those deprived
Auxilio,	Of help,
Ut a culpis absolutis	So that, freed from sin,
Et ad rectum iter ductis	And led to a righteous path,
Inimicisque destructis	And our enemies destroyed,
Pax sit nobis cum gaudio.	Peace with joy may be ours.

Motetus

Inviolata genitrix	Inviolate Mother,
Superbie grata victrix,	Gracious conqueress of pride,
Expers paris,	Lacking any peer,
Celestis aule janitrix,	Gatekeeper of the celestial temple,
Miserorum exauditrix,	You who hear the prayers of the wretched,
Stella maris,	Star of the sea,
Que ut mater consolaris,	You who console like a mother,
Et pro lapsis deprecaris	And pray humbly
Humiliter,	For the fallen
Gracie fons singularis	Singular font of grace,
Que angelis dominaris,	You who rule the angels,
Celeriter	Prepare a safe path for us
Para nobis tutum iter,	Swiftly,
Juvaque nos viriliter	And aid us vigorously,
Nam perimus,	For we perish,
Invadimur hostiliter,	We are invaded with hostility,
Sed tuimur debiliter,	But guarded weakly,
Neque scimus	Nor do we know
Quo tendere nos possimus,	Which way we are able to go,
Nec per quem salvi erimus	Nor by whom we will be saved
Nisi per te;	If not by you;
Eya! Ergo poscimus	Eya! Therefore we pray

Ut sub alis tuis simus	That we might be under your wings
Et versus nos te converte.	And that you might turn yourself towards us.

Tenor

Ad te suspiramus gementes et flentes	To you we sigh, mourning and weeping.

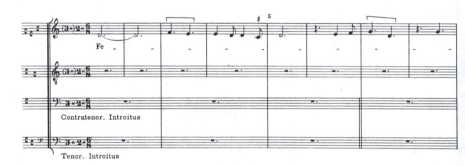

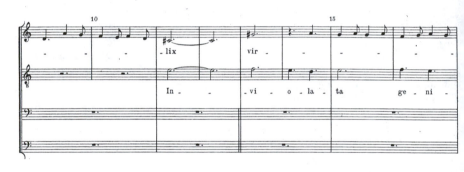

Tenor. Ad te suspiramus gementes et flentes etc.
A I

25

Guillaume de Machaut (ca. 1300–77)

Three Virelais (mid-fourteenth c.)

Guillaume de Machaut gave the dying art of the knightly poet-lover a new birth in the mid-fourteenth century, distinguished in part by his codification of the *formes fixes* (rondeau, ballade, virelai) and in part by the use of polyphonic music in the latest style—the isorhythmic motet having been the principal vehicle for this latest style in the first part of the fourteenth century. Whereas Adam de la Halle's polyphonic chansons were cast in as simple and straightforward a polyphonic texture as could be—that of the syllabic conductus setting—Machaut's were subtle, ornate, and full of a very refined lyricism that made decorative use of chromaticism. He incorporated many elements of motet composition into his chansons but turned the method of motet composition on its head. The motet, which had evolved from earlier organum, was composed "from the bottom up"—that is, starting with a preexisting Gregorian tenor and adding upper voices to it. In the chanson, Machaut composed "from the top down," starting with a *cantus* ("song") voice that bears the main text and melody and adding textless voices below it when he so desired. The three virelais given here—for one, two, and three voices—illustrate this new way of composing. All consist of two musical sections (an *A* and a *B* section, each written out only once) following the standard AbbaA repetition scheme.

Let us begin with the monophonic example, *Douce dame jolie* (score *a*), which is a very early instance of an Ars Nova-style composition in duple time on all levels of *mensuration*. Like many of Machaut's pieces in imperfect (i.e., duple) mensuration, it emphasizes syncopes (upbeats) that give it an especially lively rhythmic character. With its monophonic texture and clearly demarcated phrases, its AbbaA form is exceptionally easy to follow. The *b* section, beginning in m. 17, has open and closed cadences, the open one ending on D a fifth above the final, and the closed one ending on the final G. The *A* section sets four lines of poetry, the first three of which are given four-measure musical phrases that are almost, but not completely, identical, their subtle variations making clear that this is a piece of literate music. Although there is only a single cantus voice, notice that the cadences at the ends of both musical sections approach the G final from below, whereas all the monophonic music we have seen previously tended to approach the final from above. This will be characteristic of all Machaut cantus voices.

Only eight of Machaut's thirty-nine virelais are polyphonic. Of these, six have only two voices, a texted cantus and an untexted tenor, which unlike the tenor of a motet was not based on preexisting material. The names of the voices indicate that the tenor has been added to a monophonic "song" or at the very least that the cantus can be performed without the tenor as a self-sufficient monophonic piece. *En mon cuer* (score *b*) is found as a two-voice composition in all of its manuscript sources except the earliest one, where its cantus is entered, like *Douce dame jolie*, as a monophonic dance song. That is how it probably was originally composed. Its cantus is a self-sufficient voice, in that it has a stable and satisfying cadence structure, and, unlike its eventual accompanying tenor, it has enough notes to accommodate all the syllables of the text. Like *Douce dame jolie*, it approaches the final cadences of the *a* and *b* sections by step from below (mm. 22 and 32). When the tenor voice is added, it harmonizes the cadential notes at the octave below and approaches this lower octave by step from above. This sort of cadence, in which a sixth opens to an octave by stepwise contrary motion, became the standard mark of musical closure in Machaut's two-voice music.

Tres bonne et belle (score *c*) is the only one of Machaut's virelais to appear in all of its sources as a three-voice composition, and it can serve as an example of the three-voice *cantilena* texture that became standard for polyphonic secular song from the mid-fourteenth century to the mid-fifteenth. To the texted cantus and untexted tenor of the two-voice chanson texture is added a textless contratenor in the same range as the tenor. Although it occupies the same pitch space, the contratenor is not functionally equivalent to the tenor. The tenor, and only the tenor, always makes the true cadence against the cantus, moving out from sixth to octave, whether on the C final (mm. 3–4, 23–24, and 34–35, the closed cadence of the *b* section) or on some subsidiary degree (D in mm. 8–9 and 13–14 and E in m. 32–33, the open cadence of the *b* section). At such moments the behavior of the contratenor is also mandated: It invariably fills in the octave sonority of the tenor and cantus with a fifth, and it approaches that fifth from below by half step to create a double leading-tone cadence. That subsidiary role is what defines it as a contratenor; a contratenor (or a tenor or a cantus) is as a contratenor (or a tenor or a cantus) does. Thus, even if Machaut composed all three voices of *Tres bonne et belle* at once, and there is no reason to suppose that he did not, he nevertheless composed the three voices according to a structural hierarchy so that there are three—and only three—grammatically correct performance possibilities: The cantus voice can be sung alone, in a duet with the tenor, or in a trio with the tenor and the contratenor.

a. *Douce dame jolie* ("Fair, sweet lady")

A *Douce dame jolie,*
Pour Dieu ne pensés mie
Que nulle ait signourie
Suer moy, fors vous seulement.

Fair, sweet lady,
for God's sake do not think
that any woman has mastery
over me other than you alone.

b *Qu'adès sans tricherie chierie*
Vous ay, et humblement

For without deceit, I have always
held you dear and humbly

b *Tous les jours de ma vie servie*
Sans vilein pensement.

served you all the days of my life,
without any bad thought.

a *Helas! Et je mendie*
D'esperance et d'aïe;
Dont ma joie est fenie,
Se pité ne vous en prent.

Alas! I beg
for hope and aid,
and so my joy is ended
if you do not take pity on me.

A *Douce dame jolie . . .*

Fair, sweet lady . . .

b *Mais vo douce maistrie maistrie*
Mon cuer si durement

But your sweet mastery masters
my heart so harshly

b *Qu'elle le contralie et lie*
En amours, tellement

that it torments and blinds it
with such love

a *Qu'il n'a de riens envie*
Fors d'estre en vo baillie;
Et se ne li ottrie
Vos cuers nul aligement.

that it desires nothing
other than to be in your power;
and yet your heart
grants it no relief.

A *Douce dame jolie . . .*

Fair, sweet lady . . .

b *Et quant ma maladie garie*
Ne sera nullement

And since my malady
will not be cured at all

b *Sans vous, douce anemie, qui lie*
Estes de mon tourment,

without you, sweet enemy,
who are happy about my torment,

a *A jointes mains deprie*
Vo cuer, puis qu'il m'oublie,
Que temprement m'ocie,
Car trop langui longuement.

with clasped hands I pray
that your heart, because it forgets me,
might soon kill me,
for I have languished for too long.

A *Douce dame jolie . . .*

Fair, sweet lady . . .

b. *En mon cuer* ("In my heart")

A *En mon cuer a un descort*
Qui si fort le point et mort
Que, sans mentir.
S'Amours par son doulz plaisir
N'i met accort
Aveuc ma dame, pour mort
Me doy tenir.

There is discord in my heart,
which so strongly pierces and wounds it
that if Love,
without lying, by his sweet pleasure
does not make accord
with my lady, I must consider myself
dead.

b *C'est de mon loyal Desir*
Qui me wet faire gehir
Le mal que port

It is from my faithful Desire,
which wants to make me confess
the wrongs I commit,

b *Et comment j'aim et desir*
Ma dame sans repentir
Et sans confort.

and how much I love and desire
my lady without regret
and without comfort.

a *Mais Paour s'oppose fort*
Et dit que Desirs a tort
De ce querir.
Qu'elle crient Refus oir
Qui pas ne dort,
Et Dangiers qui fait a mort
L'amant venir.

But Fear resists strongly
and says that Desire is wrong
to seek this.
For she fears hearing Refusal,
she who never sleeps.
and Rejection, which makes a lover
come to his death.

A *En mon cuer a un descort . . .*

There is discord in my heart . . .

b *Si ne say que devenir*
Quant de ma dame remir
Le gentil port.

If I do not know what will become of me
when I admire my lady's
kind bearing.

b *Car Paour me fait fremir*
Et trambler et tressaillir
Par son enort.

For Fear makes me quiver
and tremble and shake
by his suggestion.

a *Et Desirs, san nul deport.*
Fait mon cuer par son effort
Taindre et palir;
Biaute me vient assaillir.
Douceur m'endort.
Mais Amours me fait au fort
Taire et souffrir.

And Desire, without any respite,
makes my heart, by his effort,
fade and turn pale;
Beauty comes to assail me.
sweetness puts me to sleep.
But Love firmly
silences me and makes me suffer.

A *En mon cuer a un descort . . .*

There is discord in my heart . . .

b *Las! einsi m'estuet languir.*
Pleindre, plourer et gemir
En desconfort.

Alas! I must thus languish,
Lament, weep, and groan
In discomfort.

b *Ne bien n'ay fors souvenir.*
Dous penser et li servir.
La me confort.
a *La seulement me deport.*
La sont gete tuit mi sort
Et la me tir;
La weil je vivre et morir
Et la m'acort;
La seront tuit mi ressort
Jusqu'au morir.

A *En mon cuer a un descort . . .*

I have nothing good but memory,
sweet thoughts, and my service to her.
There I find comfort.
Only there do I rejoice.
There I cast all my fate
And towards there I lead myself.
There I wish to live and die,
And there I agree to this.
All my support will be there
until I die.

There is discord in my heart . . .

c.   *Tres bonne et belle* ("Very good and beautiful lady")

A *Tres bonne et belle, mi oueil*
Joyeuse pasture
Prennent en vostre figure,
Simple et sans orgueil.
Et mes cuers en vostre acueil
Vie et douce norreture.

b *Quant vo maniere meure,*
Rassise et seure
Voy, d'onneur sui en l'escueil;

b *Et quant vo regardeure,*
Riant par mesure,
Vient sur moy, tout bien recueil,

a *Car je sui si a mon weil*
Qu'en moy joie dure
Qui de plus grant m'asseure.
Adont le fruit cueil
D'espoir, se vrais estre weil
Vers vous, dame nette et pure.

A *Tres bonne et belle . . .*

Very good and beautiful lady, my eyes
find joyful sustenance
in your face,
which is simple and without pride,
and my heart takes from your greeting
life and sweet nourishment.

When I see your refined,
calm, and secure bearing,
I feel my own honor increase.

And when your gaze,
smiling modestly,
comes upon me, it is a wonderful reward,

for I have what I want;
joy endures within me
and I am greatly reassured.
Thus I enjoy the fruits
of hope, and I will be true
to you, distinguished and pure lady.

Very good and beautiful lady . . .

1.,5. Tres bonne et bel - le, mi oueil   Joy - eu - se pa -
4. Car je sui si a mon weil   Qu'en moy joi - e

Contratenor

Tenor

manie - re me - ure,   Ras - sise et se - u - re   Voy, d'on -
vo re - garde - u - re   Ri - ant par me - su - re   Vient seur

stu - re   Pren - nent en vos - tre fi - gu - re,   Simple et
du - re   Qui de plus grant m'as - se - u - re.   A - dont

1.
neur   sui en l'es - cueil;
moy,   tout

2.
bien re - cueil;

sans or - gueil,   Et mes   cuers en vostre ac -
le fruit   cueil   D'es - poir,   se vrais es - tre

cueil   Vie et dou - ce nor - re - tu - re.   2. Quant vo
weil   Vers vous, da - me nette et pu - re.   3. Et quant

26

Guillaume de Machaut
(ca. 1300–77)

Rose, liz ("Rose, lily") (ca. 1360)

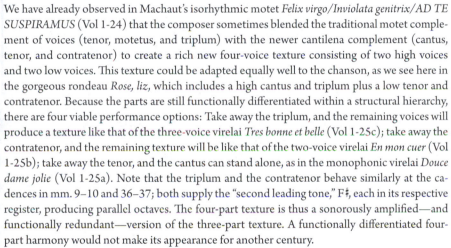

We have already observed in Machaut's isorhythmic motet *Felix virgo/Inviolata genitrix/AD TE SUSPIRAMUS* (Vol 1-24) that the composer sometimes blended the traditional motet complement of voices (tenor, motetus, and triplum) with the newer cantilena complement (cantus, tenor, and contratenor) to create a rich new four-voice texture consisting of two high voices and two low voices. This texture could be adapted equally well to the chanson, as we see here in the gorgeous rondeau *Rose, liz*, which includes a high cantus and triplum plus a low tenor and contratenor. Because the parts are still functionally differentiated within a structural hierarchy, there are four viable performance options: Take away the triplum, and the remaining voices will produce a texture like that of the three-voice virelai *Tres bonne et belle* (Vol 1-25c); take away the contratenor, and the remaining texture will be like that of the two-voice virelai *En mon cuer* (Vol 1-25b); take away the tenor, and the cantus can stand alone, as in the monophonic virelai *Douce dame jolie* (Vol 1-25a). Note that the triplum and the contratenor behave similarly at the cadences in mm. 9–10 and 36–37; both supply the "second leading tone," F♯, each in its respective register, producing parallel octaves. The four-part texture is thus a sonorously amplified—and functionally redundant—version of the three-part texture. A functionally differentiated four-part harmony would not make its appearance for another century.

Note also the open cadence at the end of the *A* section (m. 25) and the closed one at the end of the *B* section (m. 37). Since the *A* music (which starts in m. 1) always leads into something else—either another statement of the *A* music or the *B* music (which starts in m. 26)—its *Phrygian cadence* on D creates a tonal tension that is not resolved until the double leading-tone cadence on the C final at the end of the *B* music. This resolution is especially satisfying at the end of the *b* section of the ABaAabAB form, before which the *A* music, with its open cadence, has been stated three times in a row.

A	*Rose, liz, printemps, verdure,*	Rose, lily, springtime, greenery,
	Fleur, baume et tres douce odour,	Flower, balm, and sweetest fragrance,
B	*Belle, passes en doucour.*	Lovely Lady, you surpass them all in sweetness.
a	*Et touz les biens de Nature,*	And you possess all the goodness
	Avez dont je vous aour.	of Nature, for which I adore you.
A	*Rose, liz, printemps, verdure,*	Rose, lily, springtime, greenery,
	Fleur, baume et tres douce odour.	flower, balm, and sweetest fragrance.
a	*Et quant toute creature*	And, since your virtue surpasses
	Seurmonte vostre valour,	all other creatures,
b	*Bien puis dire et par honnour:*	I can honestly say:
A	*Rose, liz, printemps, verdure,*	Rose, lily, springtime, greenery,
	Fleur, baume et tres douce odour,	flower, balm, and sweetest fragrance,
B	*Belle, passes en doucour.*	Lovely lady, you surpass them in sweetness.

27

Guillaume de Machaut
(ca. 1300–77)

Messe de Nostre Dame (Mass of Our Lady), Kyrie (ca. 1360)

The *Messe de Nostre Dame* (Mass of Our Lady) by Machaut is the earliest single-authored setting of the entire Mass Ordinary. It is a votive mass, one that the composer himself endowed with a bequest, to serve as a memorial to "Guillaume and Jean de Machaux [*sic*], both brothers and canons of the church of Our Lady (*l'eglise de Notre Dame*) of Reims." That is what the preface to an eighteenth-century copy of the composer's cathedral epitaph tells us, and it goes on to quote a provision of his will stating that he had left 300 florins to ensure "that the prayer for the dead, on every Saturday, for their souls and for those of their friends, may be said by a priest about to celebrate faithfully, at the side altar, a Mass *which is to be sung*" (italics added). In fact, the will was honored (though not always with the music originally provided) until the middle of the eighteenth century.

Although it is the work of a single composer, Machaut's mass is not a *cyclic mass* but, rather, a composite. Its six movements—it includes a setting of the *Ite missa est*, an item of the Mass Ordinary generally omitted from polyphonic settings—are modally disparate (the first three having a D final, the last three an F final) and are based on different styles of contemporary learned polyphony. The Kyrie, Sanctus, Agnus Dei, and Ite missa est are based on the motet, the Gloria is like a cantilena or chanson, and the Credo is like a conductus.

The Kyrie, given here, adapts the style of an isorhythmic motet to its liturgical context. It is built around the famous Kyrie *Cunctipotens genitor* melody (Vol 1-4a), which has an AAA BBB CCC′ form and which we have encountered by now in multiple guises. In the first section of Machaut's setting, the *A* section of the chant melody, carried of course by the tenor, serves as a color that is cut up into bite-sized taleae of archaic cast: They actually correspond to the third rhythmic mode (long-short-short-long) that was common a century earlier. The contratenor, too, is composed of short recurring rhythmic "cells," although they are not strictly enough organized to be considered isorhythmic. Isorhythmic or no, there is a great deal of rhythmic repetition: The active rhythms of the triplum at mm. 7–12, for example—which include two measures of syncopation and one of hocket with the motetus—are mimicked exactly in mm. 20–24; moreover, two measures in the same repeated passage—compare mm. 10–11 and mm. 22–23—are pan-isorhythmic (rhythmically identical in all parts). The *Christe* section (m. 28)

introduces a new level of rhythmic energy—syncopated, hockety figures—into the two uppermost parts. In the triplum it is the extremes of rhythmic activity—full-measure longs and rapid hockets—that recur most strictly.

The taleae in each subsequent section get progressively longer and more complex. The "third-mode" talea in the *Kyrie I* is four measures long in transcription; the *Christe* section, which starts in m. 28 and takes the *B* phrase of the chant as its color, has a talea that is seven measures long; the *Kyrie II*, which starts in m. 50 and is based on the *C* phrase of the chant, has a talea that is eight measures long; and the *Kyrie III*, which starts in m. 67 and is based on the *C′* phrase of the chant, has one that is fourteen measures long. In performance, Machaut's musical sections can be repeated in order to achieve the ninefold structure of the complete Kyrie, or they can alternate with sections of plainchant in what is known as *alternatim practice*. The two performance options are as follows.

Chant Form	Performance Option 1	Performance Option 2
Kyrie (A)	**Machaut *Kyrie I* (A)**	**Machaut *Kyrie I* (A)**
Kyrie (A)	**Machaut *Kyrie I* (A)**	Kyrie Chant (A)
Kyrie (A)	**Machaut *Kyrie I* (A)**	**Machaut *Kyrie I* (A)**
Christe (B)	**Machaut *Christe* (B)**	Christe Chant (B)
Christe (B)	**Machaut *Christe* (B)**	**Machaut *Christe* (B)**
Christe (B)	**Machaut *Christe* (B)**	Christe Chant (B)
Kyrie (C)	**Machaut *Kyrie II* (C)**	**Machaut *Kyrie II* (C)**
Kyrie (C)	**Machaut *Kyrie II* (C)**	Kyrie Chant (C)
Kyrie (C′)	**Machaut *Kyrie III* (C′)**	**Machaut *Kyrie III* (C′)**

For text, see Vol 1-4a.

79

28

Philippus de Caserta
(*fl* ca. 1370–90)

En remirant ("While admiring") (late fourteenth c.)

Of all the formes fixes, the ballade in three stanzas was for Machaut and his followers the noblest and most exalted—and musically, therefore, the most elaborate. The example given here is by Philippus de Caserta, a composer who was born in Italy and was active from around 1370 to 1390 at the papal court of Avignon, where technical virtuosity became the primary focus of musical composition. Philippus, also a theorist, wrote a treatise on advanced notation (*Tractatus de diversis figuris*, "Treatise on diverse note shapes"), which went beyond the limits of Ars Nova practices. In earlier Ars Nova theory, both *tempus* (Latin for "time," division of the breve into semibreves) and *prolation* (division of the semibreve into minims) could be either triple or duple, creating four basic mensural combinations, only one of which could be used at any one time. Philippus wanted to be able to use different mensurations simultaneously, combining them vertically and creating proportional relationships between them. In order to make these relationships as explicit as possible, he borrowed or invented many note shapes, some of them utterly bizarre, to be used in addition to the standard note shapes and time signatures. The style seen in *En remirant* and similar pieces—with their greater refinement, greater decorativeness, greater sophistication, and especially with ever-more-flamboyant technique than had ever been seen before—has been known since the 1960s as the *Ars Subtilior* (Subtler art).

For Ars Subtilior composers, the ballade had replaced the isorhythmic motet as the preferred genre of elevated composition. In *En remirant*, Philippus casts himself demonstratively as Machaut's heir by quoting the text incipit from one of Machaut's ballades (*De triste cuer*) and the refrain of another (*Plouréz, dames*), but he extends Ars Nova techniques far beyond anything we encounter in Machaut's music. (Philippus's own incipit—both words and music—was later quoted in Johannes Ciconia's *Sus un fontayne*.) *En remirant* is actually a relatively subdued example of Ars Subtilior composition that shows the kinds of notational and rhythmic techniques that composers like Philippus enjoyed contriving—there are other works that push these techniques to much more outlandish extremes. Philippus's ballade is cast in the usual *a* and *b* musical sections (beginning in mm. 1 and 24, respectively), the *a* section ending with open and closed cadences (first and second endings). Notice that mm. 16–23 of the second statement of the *a* section and mm. 47–51 of the *b* section are musically identical (though

barred differently in the modern edition), creating what is known as a *musical rhyme* between the two sections. Note also that all three stanzas end with the same two lines of text (that is, with a refrain), another common feature of the fourteenth-century grand ballade.

The tenor is the most rhythmically and notationally straightforward voice, and the other voices use it as an anchor for their rhythmic and notational "subtleties," which are of four main types. (1) There are extended syncopated passages in which unusually placed "dots of division" and rests working in conjunction with one another at the beginning and ends of these passages shift the rhythms off from the prevailing beat; for example, the cantus in mm. 2–5 sings typical $\frac{9}{8}$ rhythms but seemingly a quarter note too late. (2) Perfect (triple) and imperfect (duple) note values are set against each other through the use of red ink (indicated in the modern edition by open brackets), which stands for the opposite of whatever the prevailing mensuration is. This red ink is used, among other places, in mm. 38–40 in the cantus and contratenor to denote a duple passage against the prevailing triple meter. (3) Proportional time signatures are used throughout, which create juxtapositions of diverse meters, including a lovely little passage in mm. 12–15, in which the three voices all go into diminished imperfect ($\frac{3}{4}$-like) time, but not together—the cantus goes first, on the words "en laquele" (m. 12), then the contratenor (later in m. 12), and, finally, as if nudged by the other parts, the tenor (m. 14) in its only mensural change of the entire piece. (4) Finally, there are the newly invented note shapes that more than any other feature define Ars Subtilior composition. Philippus uses two novel note shapes in *En remirant*, both borrowed, as it happens, from contemporary Italian notation. The first one is a curious red note with both ascending and descending stems (called a *dragma*) that creates a 4:3 relationship at the level of the minim (m. 15 in the cantus). The other creates the same 4:3 relationship at the level of the breve (as in mm. 17 and 47 in the cantus).

a	*En remirant vo douce pourtraiture*	While admiring your sweet portrait
	En laquele est tout doulz ymaginer	In which all good can be seen,
a	*M'a point au cuer d'une tele pointure*	I have been pierced in my heart with such a wound
	D'ardant desire si que mon cuer durer.	Of burning desire that my heart cannot survive.
b	*Las, si ne puet doulce dame sans per*	Alas, sweet lady without peer,
	Se vo douçour ne me va secourant	If your sweetness does not come to save me.
	Pour vostre amor dame	*For your love, lady,*
	vois languissent.	*I shall languish.*
a	*He bel acueil ou je prens noureture*	Oh fair welcome where I take nourishment,
	Vo cuer vueilliez de m'amor alumer	May your heart be illuminated with my love,
a	*Car se mon cuer de vois en grant ardure*	For if my heart must, with great passion,
	Ardre bruir a tous jorns sans finer	Burn ardently forever without end,
b	*Si ne lairay que ne vous doie amer*	Still I would not abandon your love,
	Mes vo mercy me va trop detriant	But your mercy would destroy me completely.
	Pour vostre amor dame	*For your love lady,*
	vois languissant.	*I shall languish.*

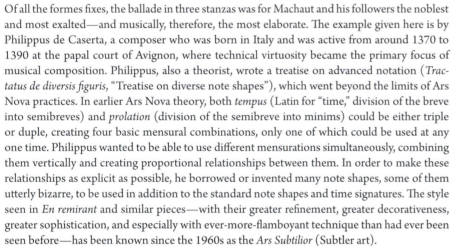

a *A vous me plains car sui en aventure*   I protest to you because I am likely
   De tous mourir pour loyalement amer   To die for loving faithfully.
a *Se Dieus e vous ne me prenez en cure*   If God and you do not cure me,
   En face amour le dur en doulz muer.   May love turn the harsh into the sweet.
b *Tels mauls ne puis longuement endurer*   I cannot endure such suffering any longer.
   De triste cuer dire puis en plourant   With a sad heart, I therefore say, crying:
   Pour vostre amor dame   *For your love lady,*
   vois languissent.   *I shall languish.*

29

Solage
(*fl* late fourteenth c.)

Fumeux fume ("A smoker smokes") (late fourteenth c.)

In addition to the papal court at Avignon, Ars Subtilior composition flourished in several other centers, including the court of Jean, the Duke of Berry (1340–1416), which was located in the city of Bourges. We do not know exactly when Solage lived or even what his first name was, but he was the most productive poet-composer associated with Jean's court. Seven of his ten extant works are ballades (three of them make reference to Jean), but his best-known work is the strange rondeau *Fumeux fume*. Whereas most Ars Subtilior compositions explore complicated mensural constructions, *Fumeux fume* is mensurally tame while pushing fourteenth-century harmony to its chromatic limits. As we have seen, Machaut employed a certain amount of chromaticism in creating his distinctive voluptuous sound, and Solage appears deliberately to have emulated Machaut's style in several works. The "smoke" featured in the *Fumeux fume* poem provides an indirect historical connection to the earlier master. The *Fumeux* (Smokers) were an obscure and exclusive literary society presided over by the poet Eustache Deschamps (1346–1406), who declared himself Machaut's poetic heir. The *Fumeux* met at least from 1366 to 1381 and tried to outdo one another in complicated and arcane—that is, "smoky"—poetic conceits.

Solage's text and musical construction straightforwardly follow the conventions of the rondeau, but the unusually low vocal ranges and extremely chromatic harmonies are as "smoky" as the poem. Note that the accidentals drift flatward ("*fa*-ward") in the *A* section (mm. 1ff) and sharpward ("*mi*-ward") in the *B* section (mm. 29ff). To place the composition within one of the modes would be impossible. It starts on a G sonority and ends on an F sonority, and the fermata at the end of the *A* section—which is stated five times in the rondeau form—is on an E♭ sonority (m. 22) that can only be created through *musica ficta*. This is musical "smoky speculation" indeed!

A	*Fumeux fume par fumee*	A smoker smokes through smoke.
B	*Fumeuse speculacion.*	A smoky speculation
a	*Qu'antre fum met sa pensee;*	Is, between puffs, his thought:
A	*Fumeux fume par fumee*	A smoker smokes through smoke.
a	*Quar fumer molt li agree:*	For smoking suits him very well

b	*Tant qu'ill ait son entencion,*	As long as he keeps his intention.
A	*Fumeux fume par fumee*	A smoker smokes through smoke
B	*Fumeuse speculacion.*	A smoky speculation.

me - e -
se - e:
gre - e:
2.8. fu - meu - se
6. tant qu'il ait

spe - cu - la - ci - on.
son en - ten - ci - on.

30

Jacopo da Bologna

(*fl* 1340–?1386)

Two Settings of *Osellecto selvaggio* ("A wild bird") (mid-fourteenth c.)

a. Madrigal

The most common type of vernacular song of the Italian fourteenth century—called the *trecento*—was the *madrigal*. Formally, the madrigal consisted of two or more three-line stanzas called *terzetti* (tercets) and a single concluding one- or two-line *ritornello* in a contrasting rhyme scheme. The music, composed in two sections, reflected this contrast. The first section of music was repeated for all the terzetti, and the second section, which generally contrasted with the first in meter, set the ritornello. There are commonly two voices, a cantus and a tenor, which, unlike the tenor of contemporary French chansons, is usually texted. Madrigal texts typically describe the bucolic scene—the "pleasant place" (in Latin, *locus amoenus*)—inherited from the classical authors of "idylls" and "eclogues," such as Virgil and Theocritus: a stream, a shade tree, flowers in bloom.

The madrigal *Osellecto selvaggio*, by Jacopo da Bologna, the leading composer of the mid-trecento, is in many ways typical. It has two texted voice parts, and its text has three terzetti and a ritornello, set to two contrasting musical sections (mm. 1–58 and 59 to the end). What is unusual is that the subject matter of its text is music itself, and what it says about music can tell us much about trecento composition. The first line of the poem seems to be establishing the expected pastoral setting by describing the wild songbird, a standard image in pastoral poetry. But the bird immediately becomes a metaphor for song, and the text as a whole becomes a sermon on the art of singing and composing. This is an entirely unconventional use of a conventional genre, but one that is tied intelligibly to the convention that is being "bent" or "sent up." Jacopo's music, since it is the medium for the sermon, must demonstrate the sweetness and moderation it proclaims, avoiding the melodic virtuosity that is often seen in madrigals and that its text decries. It is cast in a meter—*senaria perfecta*, as Italian theorists would have called it—in which the fixed breve is divided into six semibreves grouped in pairs, which are transcribed as eighth notes within a $\frac{3}{4}$ meter. One particular melodic feature that is especially characteristic of trecento music arises directly out of this meter. Note how frequently the paired notes take the

form of descending seconds in the cantus part, cast in sequences, with the first note in each pair repeating the second note of its predecessor in a sort of stutter. The first instance of this is the delightfully syncopated initial "clump" of words in mm. 9–10, but more typical—and more rhythmically straightforward—is the clump in mm. 44–45. This type of melodic motion is called a "sigh-figure" in later music; it symbolizes emotion by mimicking the behavior of a person responding to emotion.

Osellecto selvaggio per stagione	A wild bird during the season
Dolci versetti canta con bel modo	sings sweet lines in a fine style.
Tale che grida forte chi non lodo.	I do not praise a singer who shouts loudly.
Per gridar forte non si canta bene	Loud shouting does not make good singing,
Ma con soav'e dolce melodia	but with smooth and sweet melody
Si fa bel canto e ci vuol maestria.	lovely singing is produced, and this requires skill.
Pochi l'hanno e tutti si fan maestri	Few people possess it, but all set up as masters
Fan ballate, madriali'e motteti	and compose ballate, madrigals, and motets:
Tutti enfioran Filipi e Marchetti.	all try to outdo Philippe [de Vitry] and Marchetto [of Padua].
Ritornello:	
Sì si è piena la terra di magistroli	Thus the country is so full of petty masters
Che loco più non trovano discepoli.	that there is no room left for pupils.

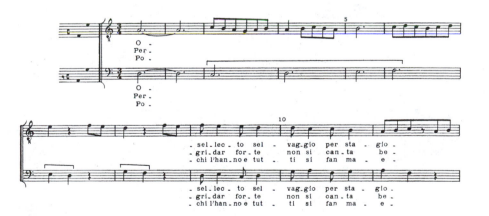

b. Caccia

Although typical in its form and two-voice texture, Jacopo's madrigal is much more restrained stylistically than most madrigals. But now a new irony, a new twist: Jacopo ostensibly eschewed virtuosity in his "wild bird" madrigal only to indulge it to the hilt in another setting of the same poem, in which it is cast as a *caccia*. The caccia was a type of madrigal (that's why Jacopo could recycle a madrigal poem in writing one), which meant that it had a musical form in two sections (the terzetti, all in one section, and the ritornello in another) and a texture consisting of a cantus, generally running against itself in canon, plus a tenor. The caccia was thus a three-voice genre. Unlike the tenors of madrigals, those of caccias never carry the text, which may indicate that they were performed by instruments. Indeed, the word "caccia" ("chase" or "hunt") had extramusical associations with hunting and the horns that accompanied it, and the subject matter of these compositions often involved the hunt. So again, the standard definition of the genre enabled a sophisticated composer like Jacopo to play ironically on the genre's implications. In the context of the madrigal, the "wild bird" represents those who sing, while in the caccia it is also the animal being hunted. Here, too, the topic was appropriate and relevant to the genre, and so its instant transformation into a metaphor in the text is again suitably ironic. Also ironic, of course, is the insistence on sweet, soft, and elegant singing, since the usual caccia text contained exactly the sorts of invitations to "loud shouting" that the text decries. To sing the virtuosic music in Jacopo's caccia smoothly and in "lovely" fashion requires (as the poem warns) the ultimate in vocal control. Notice, too, that in the caccia setting of *Osellecto selvaggio*, sixteenth notes in transcription—rhythms that were possible in Italian notation but not in the contemporary French Ars Nova notation—often carry individual syllables of text that must be spit out extremely quickly. In its caccia guise, Jacopo's song could well have been a test for singers—or a contest piece.

31

Francesco Landini
(ca. 1325–1397)

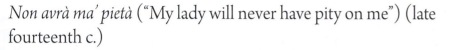

Non avrà ma' pietà ("My lady will never have pity on me") (late fourteenth c.)

In the *Osellecto selvaggio* text Jacopo da Bologna mentions a third musico-poetic genre besides the motet and madrigal: the *ballata* (pl. *ballate*). *Ballata* is the past participle of *ballare*, "to dance," and indeed the ballata is a dance song with a refrain, much like the French *chanson balladée* or virelai, with which it shares the AbbaA form. Over the second half of the trecento it gradually displaced the madrigal as the leading genre of Italian vernacular music. As it did so, it showed increasing influence of the French virelai, until we find in the last generation of trecento composers a truly Gallicized style—that is, with their form adapted to the French manner by means of a "contained" refrain, with open and closed cadences for the inner verses and a three-voice texture that (unlike the madrigal) included a contratenor. The great master of such ballate—regarded by all his contemporaries as the greatest musician of the trecento—was the blind Florentine organist Francesco Landini. Unlike earlier madrigals, Landini's ballate do not so much evoke bountiful pastoral surroundings or extol voluptuary pleasures or narrate venereal conquests as communicate personal feeling—often the conventionalized love-longing that had first emerged in the songs of the troubadours.

One of Landini's most popular ballate, and one of the most thoroughly Gallicized as well, was *Non avrà ma' pietà*. There is a texted cantus voice accompanied by an untexted tenor and contratenor, exactly as one might find in a three-voice virelai. The open and closed (Italian *verto* and *chiuso*) cadences of the musical *b* sections (first on the "supertonic" A, then on the final G) recall Machaut's cadential practice. The text, of course, is in Italian, and Landini follows the distinctly Italian practice of setting lines of poetry with melismas at the beginnings and ends of lines, with mostly syllabic clusters in the middle. Landini's highly personal musical style, moreover, is unmistakable, largely due to the frequent use of a cadential ornament that has come to bear his name. Every one of the three standard double leading-tone cadences in the refrain or *A* section (mm. 3–4, 16–17, 28–29) and the final cadences (both open and closed) in the *b* section show the same melodic progression to the final, in which the *subtonium* (the note below the final), instead of resolving up to the final, proceeds down an additional scale step—from the seventh degree above the final to the sixth—before leaping up to the cadential note. Such motion resembles what we would now call an "escape tone." A cadence featuring this 7–6–1

motion in the upper voice is commonly called a *Landini cadence*. While Landini was the first to use it extensively, it became a stylistic commonplace in the international continental style of the early fifteenth century that we will see later. As the counterpoint in *Non avrà ma' pietà* shows, it is often allied with a hemiola pattern ($\frac{6}{8}$ in the cantus against $\frac{3}{4}$ in the tenor and contratenor) that produces a characteristic precadential syncopation (e.g., mm. 10–11, 16–17, 28–29, etc.). The syncopation, too, would become a standard feature of fifteenth-century counterpoint, eventually emphasized by a characteristic dissonance that we now call a suspension.

A *Non avrà ma' pietà questa mie donna,*   My lady will never have pity on me,
   Se tu non fai, amore,   If you, Cupid, do not
   Ch'ella sia certa del mio grande ardore.   Make her sure of my great passion.

b *S'ella sapesse quanta pena i' porto*   If she but knew how much pain I bear
   Per onestà celata nella mente   hidden, out of propriety, in my mind

b *Sol per la sua bellecça, chè conforto*   On account of her beauty (for comfort
   D'altro non prede l'anima dolente,   my sad soul can take only in this),

a *Forse da lei sarebbono in me spente*   Perhaps she herself would put out
   Le fiamme che la pare   The flames she kindles
   Di giorno in giorno acrescono'l dolore.   And which increase my torment from day to day.

A *Non avrà ma' pietà . . .*   My lady will never have pity . . .

32

Johannes Ciconia
(ca. 1370–1412)

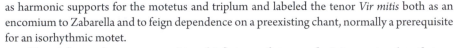

Doctorum Principem/Melodia Suavissima/VIR MITIS (ca. 1410)

By the turn of the fifteenth century the isorhythmic motet had become preeminently a grand ceremonial genre and a vehicle for propaganda. The tradition reached its culmination in the early decades of the century in works by composers who were from the north (France and the Low Countries) and received their training there but moved south to seek lucrative employment in Italian cities and courts. The first in this long and distinguished line of "Franco-Flemish" composers was Johannes Ciconia, who was born and educated in the Belgian city of Liège but by 1401 was employed at the Cathedral of the city of Padua in northern Italy, where he died in 1412.

Ciconia's most important patron in Padua was the chief canon of the cathedral, Francesco Zabarella (1360–1417), who was also a university professor of canon law and an accomplished diplomat. Zabarella became bishop of Florence in 1410 and later a cardinal, and it has been suggested that Ciconia wrote his grand isorhythmic motet *Doctorum Principem/Melodia Suavissima/VIR MITIS* in honor of Zabarella when he left Padua to assume the bishopric. The triplum and motetus texts are of equal length and sung at the same speed, often playing off one another in hocket-like manner. They are each laid out in three strophes that define the three clearly demarcated sections of the composition (beginning at mm. 1, 45, and 89). Each section begins with a textless introitus in the style of a fanfare, suggesting outdoor performance by wind instruments, perhaps in the Paduan cathedral square.

The tenor and contratenor follow a mensural scheme that is a virtual summation of Ars Nova practices. In each of the three sections of the piece they present the same color and talea in notationally identical form. In fact, both voices are written out only once, with a "canon" ("rule" or "special direction") that instructs the performers to read their parts each time under a different mensuration sign—C, O, and C, respectively. Thus despite their notational congruence, the actual rhythms of each presentation not only differ but undergo a progressive compression from perfect (triple) time to imperfect (duple) time. The tenor is labeled *Vir mitis* ("gentle man"), but its unusual contour, with numerous alternating leaps up and down a fifth (mm. 1–5) and a scalar descent through an entire octave (mm. 36–41), is entirely uncharacteristic of any known chant. Instead, it seems that Ciconia has newly composed the tenor and contratenor

as harmonic supports for the motetus and triplum and labeled the tenor *Vir mitis* both as an encomium to Zabarella and to feign dependence on a preexisting chant, normally a prerequisite for an isorhythmic motet.

The triplum and motetus are written chiefly in semibreves and minims, note values that are not affected drastically by the mensural diminution of the tenor and contratenor. Each stanza, though setting new words, is similar to the others in its melodic contour and overall form, creating what resembles a set of strophic variations. At the beginning of each section, after the introitus but before the tenor and contratenor reenter, short snippets of text are brought to the fore by the textural reduction. In the first stanza the triplum sings, unaccompanied, "Doctorum principem super ethera" ("The foremost teacher above the skies," mm. 8–9), to which the motetus responds, "Melodia suavissima cantemus" ("With the sweetest melody let us sing," mm. 10–13). At the corresponding point in the second section, the voices engage in a similar hocket, except that they both declaim the same words, "O Francisce Zabarelle" (mm. 52–55), a call to the dedicatee whom they had addressed only indirectly at the opening of the piece. At the same point in the final stanza they avoid hocket and sing together, but they both sing the same word, making them just as audible as if each sang alone. The conspicuously audible words are once again the name of the honoree, "Francisce Zabarelle" (mm. 96–99).

The beginning of each section of the piece is marked by a sustained sonority on the syllable "O," which provides repose before and after the passages of restless rhythmic drive that dominate the remainder of each section. At the end of the third section—that is, at the very end of the composition—the tenor and contratenor are extended by two notes (G and F in the tenor, B [natural] and C in the contra), over which the motetus and triplum create a densely voiced and slow-moving double leading-tone cadence. This stately cadence balances out the "O" sonorities at the beginning of the section and brings the ceremonial motet to a grand close.

Triplum

Doctorum principem super ethera,	The worthy merits of his virtues
Revocant virtutum digna merita,	call the foremost teacher above the skies.
Ergo vive voci detur opera,	Therefore let praise be given to the living voice;
Promat mentis fervor intus concita.	Let the fervor of our inner minds express excitement.
O Francisce Zabarelle, Gloria,	O Francesco Zabarella, the Glory,
Doctor, honor et lumen Patavorum,	Teacher, honor, and light of the Paduans,
Vive felix de tanta victoria,	Live happy from such victory;
Per te virescit fama Patavorum.	Through you the fame of the Paduans flourishes.
O Francisce Zabarelle, pabula,	O Francesco Zabarella, you have prepared
Parasti pastoribus armentorum,	nourishment for the shepherds of flocks,

93

Quibus pascant oves; grata secula

from which the sheep may graze; grateful generations

Te pro munere revocant laborum.

recall you for the rewards of your labors.

Motetus

Melodia suavissima cantemus,
Tangant voces melliflue sidere
Concorditer carmen lira sonemus,

With the sweetest melody, let us sing,
Let our mellifluous voices touch the stars,
Let our song sound concordantly on the lyre,

Resonet per choros pulsa cithara.

Let the plucked cithara resound through the chorus.

O Francisce Zabarelle, protector
Imo versus pater rei publice,
Illos ad se vocat rerum conditor,
Qui fortune miserentur lubrice.

O Francesco Zabarella, protector,
indeed, father of the republic,
The creator calls those to him
who have mercy on fickle fortune.

O Francisce Zabarelle, causas
Specularis omnium creatorum;
Tuas posteri resonabunt musas
Per omnia secula seculorum.

O Francesco Zabarella, you
examine the causes of all creators.
Posterity will echo your learning
through all eternity.

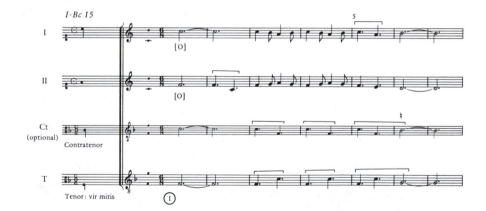

33

Guillaume Du Fay
(1397–1474)

Nuper rosarum flores/TERRIBILIS EST LOCUS ISTE (1436)

Although Guillaume Du Fay is generally considered to be a composer of "The Renaissance," his career very closely resembled that of Philippe de Vitry a century earlier. He was a churchman who eventually became a canon of the Cathedral of Cambrai, and his musical horizons were shaped by the decidedly Medieval ideas transmitted in the writings of Boethius and Guido of Arezzo as well as Vitry and the other theorists of the Ars Nova. Some of his early compositions, then, while perhaps having a "Renaissance" sound, are clearly "Medieval" in conception. Such is the case with *Nuper rosarum flores.*

Du Fay was born in French-speaking Cambrai and followed in Ciconia's footsteps, pursuing early employment in Italy. In 1428 he joined the papal choir and became a favored musician of Gabriele Cardinal Condulmer, who in 1431 became Pope Eugenius IV and in 1434 was exiled—along with his entire retinue—to Florence after a rebellion in Rome. While the pope and Du Fay were in Florence, the massive cathedral of the city, which had been under construction since 1294, was finally ready for dedication. Its crowning architectural feature is the massive neoclassical dome designed in 1420 by the great architect and artist Filippo Brunelleschi (1377–1446), which soars above the already-grand gothic structure. When Brunelleschi's dome was completed, the cathedral was ready to be dedicated to the Virgin Mary under the denomination Santa Maria del Fiore (St. Mary of the Flower), and the pope, who was already resident by force of circumstance in Florence, performed the dedication ceremony himself on the feast of the Annunciation (25 March) in 1436. It was for this ceremony that Du Fay composed *Nuper rosarum flores,* an isorhythmic motet in the tradition of Ciconia's *Doctorum Principem/ Melodia Suavissima/VIR MITIS* (Vol 1-32) but even grander.

The motet has four large musical sections (beginning in mm. 1, 57, 113, and 141) plus a melismatic "Amen." Each section begins with an introitus for the two upper voices that lasts twenty-eight *tempora* (units of time equivalent to a breve and represented at first by one bar in the transcription). After the introitus in each section, a pair of tenors enters. It is a pair of tenors, not a tenor plus a contratenor, because both voices are based (though at different pitch levels) on the same piece of chant: the first fourteen notes of *Terribilis est locus iste,* the Introit from the mass for the dedication of a church (shown in Example 33-1). The tenors and the upper voices

then sing together in each of the four sections for twenty-eight more *tempora,* mirroring the 28 (14 + 14) total notes sung by the two tenors and also the 28 *tempora* of the introitus.

As in Ciconia's motet, the tenors are written out only once, with the instruction to sing them four times in four different mensurations (O, C, ₵, and ϕ), which create a significant proportional relationship among the sections of the piece. A breve of O contains six minims; a breve of C has four. The line through the signature halves the value of the breve, so a breve under ϕ contains three minims as sung by the texted parts running above, and a breve under ₵ contains two. Comparing these signatures in the order in which Du Fay presents them gives the durational proportions 6:4:2:3 to the four sections of the piece. These same numerical proportions, when considered within the realm of pitch rather than of duration, describe the harmonic ratios of the most common and most consonant intervals. Given a fundamental pitch X, Du Fay's numbers represent the octave (2X), the compound fifth, or twelfth (3X), the double octave (4X), and the twice-compound fifth (6X). Moreover, the complex of durational ratios also contains a symbolic perfect fifth (3:2) and a perfect fourth (4:3). Through its durational proportions, then, Du Fay's motet embodies the harmony of the universe that Medieval theorists—claiming Pythagoras as the founder of their tradition—believed was represented by the acoustical proportions of consonant intervals.

But there is also symbolism in these numbers that is much more specific to the occasion for which *Nuper rosarum flores* was composed. The first book of Kings in the Bible describes the building of the temple of Jerusalem as follows: "The house which King Solomon built to the Lord, was three-score cubits in length, and twenty cubits in width, and thirty cubits in height" (1 Kings 6:2). It goes on to say that the inner sanctuary was forty cubits long (1 Kings 6:17) and that the dedicatory feast lasted "seven days and seven days, that is, fourteen days" (1 Kings 8:65). These numbers are precisely the numbers, in a slightly different order, that give Du Fay's motet its structure. The durational proportions of the tenor taleae are the same as those governing the dimensions of Solomon's temple (6:4:2:3 minims to a breve; 60:40:20:30 cubits to the parts of the temple), and the fourteen notes of the tenor melody (the isorhythmic color) correspond to the fourteen days of the dedication feast. At the dedication of the cathedral of Florence this symbolism carried special import because of a theological tradition that cast Rome as the new Jerusalem and the Church—the Catholic Church generally and its cathedrals specifically—as the new temple of God. Indeed, the proportions of Solomon's temple (and of Du Fay's taleae) are built into the dimensions of the Florence cathedral itself and of the campanile (bell tower) and baptistry that stand beside it. The facets of the cathedral tribunes, each side of the octagonal baptistry, and the width of the campanile all measure 24 ($= 6 \times 4$) *braccia* (the plural of *braccio*, meaning "arm," the standard unit of length in Florence at the time). The width and height of the cathedral nave and the diameter of Brunelleschi's dome all measure 72 ($= 6 \times 4 \times 3$) *braccia*. Finally, the length of the nave and the height of Brunelleschi's dome both measure 144 ($= 6 \times 4 \times 2 \times 3$) *braccia*.

The motet text, too, is fraught with numerical symbolism. It is cast in a rare poetic meter with seven syllables per line and seven lines per stanza. The four stanzas yield twenty-eight total lines, just as the introitus before the tenor entrance in each musical section lasts 28 (4×7) *tempora*, as does the section after the tenors enter. Seven is the number most often mystically associated with the Virgin Mary in Christian symbolism, and it is to the Virgin Mary, as the text affirms, that the cathedral was dedicated. Mary had numerous sevenfold attributes, including seven sorrows, seven joys, seven acts of mercy, seven virginal companions, and seven years of exile in Egypt. The number four, by contrast, represented the temple, which, as described in the Old Testament, had four cornerstones and four walls, which in turn correspond in the New Testament to the four points on the cross, on which all cathedral floor plans were modeled. The number 28 (4×7) thus mystically unites the cathedral of Florence, built in the image of Solomon's temple, with the Virgin Mary, to whom it was dedicated and whose womb that bore the son of God was also thought of in medieval theology as a symbolic temple.

Du Fay reinforces this intricate symbolic scheme with harmonic symmetries, like the striking "D major" sonorities he creates by writing in F♯s in mm. 31–32 and mm. 87–88, the places in the first and second sections where the tenors enter. These F♯s, moreover, are made even more striking by the B♭s and "G-minor" sonorities that precede them, and they both lend harmonic emphasis to important words—"grandis templum" ("grand temple") and "Florentiae" ("Florence"). Amid all the praise of Florence's grand temple, Du Fay is also sure to pay tribute to his patron, Pope Eugenius, who presided over the dedication ceremony and whose name bubbles to the aural surface when the upper voices sing it in declamatory homorhythm in mm. 46–47.

Triplum/Motetus

Nuper rosarum flores   Recently rose blossoms,
Ex dono pontificis   a gift from the pope—
Hieme licet horrida   the terrible winter having gone—
Tibi, virgo celica,   were given to adorn unceasingly
Pie et sancte deditum   the temple of grand structure
Grandis templum machinae   dedicated piously and with holiness
Condecorarunt perpetim.   to you, heavenly Virgin.

Hodie vicarious   Today the vicar
Jesu Christi et Petri   of Jesus Christ and
Successor Eugenius,   successor of Peter, Eugenius,
Hoc idem amplissimum   has deigned to consecrate
Sacris templum manibus   this same most splendid temple
Sanctisque liquoribus   with sacred hands
Consecrare dignatus est.   and holy oils.

Igitur, alma parens   Therefore, kind parent
Nati tui et filia   and daughter of your son,
Virgo decus virginum,   decorous virgin of virgins,
Tuus te Florentiae   your devoted populace
Devotus orat populus   of Florence prays to you
Ut qui mente et corpore   that whoever pleads for anything
Mundo quicquam exorarit,   with pure mind and body,

Oratione tua   through your prayer
Cruciatus et meritis   and through the merits
Tui secundum carnem   of your son the Lord
Nati domini sui   and his bodily torments,
Grata beneficia   might be worthy to receive
Veniamque reatum   gracious benefits
Accipere mereatur.   and forgiveness for transgressions.

Amen.   Amen.

Tenors

Terribilis est locus iste   Awesome is this place

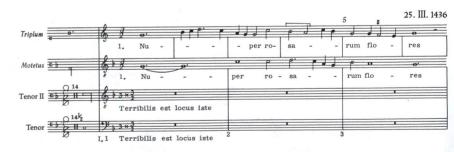

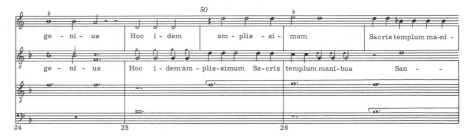

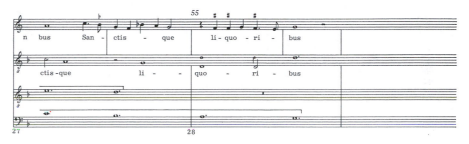

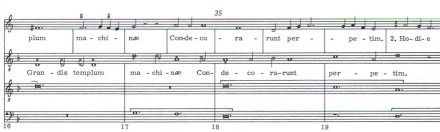

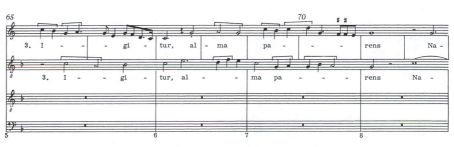

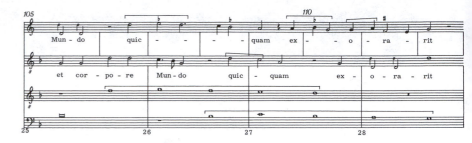

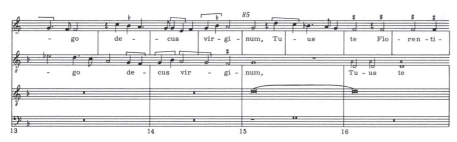

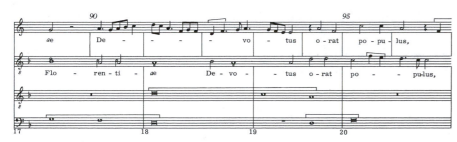

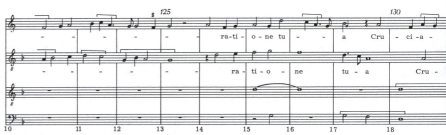

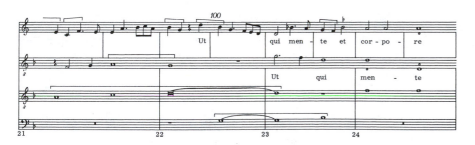

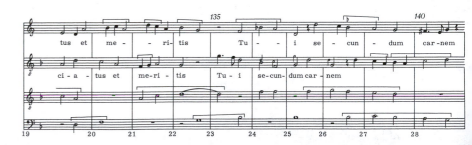

34

Anonymous

Sumer is icumen in ("Summer has come")
(ca. 1250)

Sumer is icumen in is one of the most famous pieces of Medieval music and has been ever since modern histories of music began to be written in the late eighteenth century. Its catchy melody, cheery text, and mellifluous multivoiced texture have made it popular with many who have otherwise never run into any early music at all. The piece is found in a single manuscript that was probably compiled in the mid-thirteenth century at the Benedictine abbey of Reading, a town in south central England about fifty miles west of London. It has two texts in two different languages, the first a song in English (the local Wessex dialect) that celebrates the arrival of summer, the second a Latin *versus* written below it that celebrates the Resurrection. Both texts fit the music equally well, and either can be sung. A rubric explains how the piece is to be performed:

> This round can be sung by four companions, but not by less than three (or at least two), in addition to the ones on the part marked *pes* ["foot" or "pacer" or, better yet, "ground"]. Sing it thus: While the rest remain silent, one begins together with the singers of the *pes*, and when he comes to the first note after the cross, another begins, and so on. Pause at the rests, but nowhere else, for the length of one long note.

A round is a canon that has a beginning but no specified end—that is, it can be repeated indefinitely. This round is to be sung by up to four voices, and it is to be sung over what the rubric calls a *pes*, a repeating phrase or ostinato, which in this case is itself split like a round between two voices. When all the voices get singing, what results is an accompanied round in as many as six separate voices! There is no other piece from the period with this many voice parts, and the next six-voice pieces to be preserved in writing date from the late fifteenth century, more than 200 years later.

Yet despite the fact that a lot of voices sing at once, they are organized according to a very simple harmonic pattern. The repetitive two-voice pes implies a harmonic oscillation between a perfect fifth built on the final F and a minor third built on its "supertonic" G. This is not so different from the harmony we have seen in other Medieval polyphony. But once the second upper voice enters, the harmony thickens so that full F major or G minor triads sound on just about every strong beat. That basic harmonic to and fro so pervades the texture of the Sumer Canon that anyone with half an "ear" (that is, the least bit acculturated into the idiom) could easily get into the swing of things and extend the piece by ear with additional simple counterpoints beyond the written ones, the way kids at the piano do with "Chopsticks" or "Heart and Soul."

So, is the Sumer Canon a uniquely complex and forward-looking musical composition that an anonymous English composer genius created without precedent, or is it simply a rare written record of a common oral tradition that has otherwise been lost to the historical record? If we assume the latter—and the catchiness of its simple "chord progression" might incline us to do so—then a great deal of what is otherwise strangely unique about early English music seems to fit into a historical pattern. We cannot be certain that this oral tradition existed, but, whatever the case, the thirds, sixths, and triads that pervade *Sumer is icumen in* characterized much English polyphony of the thirteenth and fourteenth centuries and would have an enormous impact when they were finally imported to the Continent in the early fifteenth century.

Sumer is icumen in—	Summer has come in—
lhude sing, cuccu!	loudly sing, cuckoo!
Groweth sed and bloweth med	The seed grows and the meadow blossoms
and springth the wude nu.	and the wood now puts forth shoots.
Sing cuccu!	Sing, cuckoo!
Awe bleteth after lomb,	The ewe bleats for the lamb,
lhouth after calve cu;	the cow lows for the calf;
bulluc sterteth, bucke verteth—	the bullock leaps, the buck farts—
murie sing, cuccu!	merrily sing, cuckoo!
Cuccu, cuccu—	Cuckoo, cuckoo!—
wel singes thu, cuccu!	Well do you sing, cuckoo!
Ne swik thu naver nu.	Do not ever cease now.
Perspice, christicola—	Pay heed, Christian—
que dignacio!	what an honor!
Celicus Agricola,	The heavenly husbandman,
pro vitis vicio,	because of a blemish in the vine branch
filio	did not spare
non parcens exposuit	his son but exposed him
mortis exicio;	to the destruction of death!
qui captivos semivivos	and he (the Son) restores from torment
a supplicio	to life
vite donat	the half-living captives (of hell)
et secum coronat	and crowns them together
in celi solio.	with himself on the throne of heaven.

35

Anonymous

Thomas gemma Cantuariae/Thomas cesus in Doveria (fourteenth c.)

As a marvelous summation of everything from the Middle Ages that is identifiable as English, consider the motet *Thomas gemma Cantuariae/Thomas caesus in Doveria*. Discovered by fortunate accident in the flyleaves of an English (nonmusical) manuscript from the fourteenth century that was acquired by the Princeton University Library around 1950, it is a dual martyrs' commemoration. The motetus text honors Thomas de la Hale, a monk from the Benedictine priory at Dover, the chalk-cliffed port on the English channel. He was killed in August 1295 in a French raid that prefigured the drawn-out conflict between France and England that came to be known as the Hundred Years War (it lasted from 1337 to 1453). The triplum honors a different Thomas, Thomas à Becket (1118–70), the Archbishop of Canterbury whose murder in Canterbury Cathedral was ordered by King Henry II. He came to be known as St. Thomas of Canterbury after his canonization in 1173. The two motet texts draw parallels between the lives of the two martyrs named Thomas, often sharing or paraphrasing each other's lines. The triplum and motetus are paired; they share the same range, cross each other frequently, and engage in frequent hockets. They are accompanied by a tenor and contratenor (the latter actually labeled "secundus tenor") that are paired in the same way, producing a double twin-song texture. That is already an English trademark, the first of many.

Like the Sumer Canon, the piece unfolds as a set of variations over a pes. But that pes, even more explicitly than the one in the Sumer Canon, is essentially a harmonic rather than a melodic idea. It is never repeated literally even once, but its harmonic framework is restated more than twenty times in a remarkably consistent manner. That framework consists of a slightly more complex version of the same alternation or oscillation we have observed in the Sumer Canon, between the final F (the "closed-cadence" note) and its upper neighbor G (the "open-cadence" note). They alternate in a regular four-measure pattern as follows: I | I–ii | ii | ii–I ("I" meaning F and "ii" meaning G).

The reason for using the anachronistic roman numerals I and ii (reminiscent of much later harmonic analysis), rather than their letter names F and G, to label the notes is that G is not always the lowest note in the "ii" sonority. When G is the lowest note, the cadences are of the double leading-tone type that was standard in the fourteenth century. But sometimes the other voice in the tenor pair sings the C a fifth below the G, producing against the upper-voice leading

tone not a $^6_3$ harmony but a characteristically English $^{10}_5$ sonority with the G in the middle (e.g., m. 6). At such cadences the actual "bass progression" is not ii–I but V–I. These are the first occurrences in this anthology of a "V–I" cadence, the most familiar harmonic progression to our modern ears. Just what the *historical* significance of that (to us) striking and significant progression may have been on its debut is a matter of considerable debate among historians—a debate that cuts very deep into the question of what the word "historical" really means. For the moment, it will be enough merely to take note of the freedom with which the $^{10}_5$ open-spaced triad is deployed in this motet, along with all the other full-triad sonorities (mostly of the $^6_3$ variety) that pervade this piece and indeed all of fourteenth-century English music.

Triplum

Thomas gemma Cantuariae primula	Thomas, the foremost jewel of Canterbury,
fide pro tuenda cesus in ecclesia,	slain in the church for holding fast to the faith,
a divina repentina mira caritate fulgens,	shining suddenly with divine, miraculous love
matutina vespertina lucis increate gratia	morning and evening in the grace of uncreated light.
late tibi nova reparate	Great things were newly restored to you.
sublimaris curia regis	You are elevated to the court of the King
pro fidelitate tua;	because of your fidelity.
a ruina leti bina	Those rejoicing were liberated twice
per te liberate	by you from the destruction of death,
sunt a fece et ab amaro	from filth and from bitterness,
malo, frivolo	evil, and frivolity,
a sentina serpentina gentes expiate et a viciis	cleansed of the filthy serpent and of sins.
singularis nuncupatis	You alone are said to be
gratia dictatus super	distinguished in grace.
hinc perfectos et electos	You are raised up to this place
tu es sublimatus,	above the perfect and the elect,
rivulo madido pie sanans egros,	curing the sick compassionately with a river of tears,
preciosis generosis gemmis tumulatus aureis	and buried in your tomb where precious gems and abundant gold
modulo, tumulo,	are measured out.
cum decore vel honore	With elegance and honor,
pie laureatus in celis	rightfully crowned with the laurel in heaven,
inter cives celicos digne	most highly venerated among heavenly citizens,
veneratus Thomas	you, Thomas,
nunc pro populo, stimulo	now pray with fervid charity on behalf of the

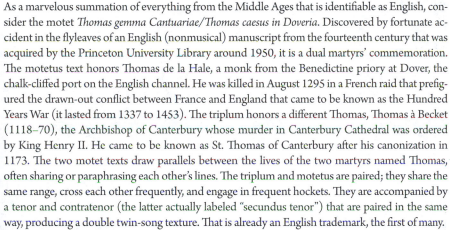

tempestatis caritate fervida rogatus.

people, inspired by these tempestuous times.

Motetus

Thomas cesus in Doveria emulo
lesus a divina repentina
mira caritate fulgens

Thomas, wounded by the enemy and slain in Dover, shining suddenly with divine, miraculous love morning and evening

matutina vespertina lucis increate gratia,
rivulo, patulo
sublimaris curia manens
in eternitate patris;
a ruina repentina
per te liberate sunt sane
tu doctrina medicina serva sanitate

in the grace of uncreated light, like a vast river you are raised to the court of the father, remaining there for eternity. Through you the healthy are freed from sudden destruction. You preserve fragile health with your knowledge of

tremulo, sub dolo,
purga a sentina serpentina gentes

medicine, without fraud. Purge the forgiven people of the filthy serpent,

expiate dirige;
singularis nuncuparis
gratia dictatus super
Remo atque Romulo tremulo
tu per sanctos
et electos pie sublimatus
merito peris in ecclesia decora tumulatus
stimulo,
primulo de sancto,
in honore et decore
pie laureatus
gaudiis inter cives celicos summe
veneratus querulo
celo sine fine manens tam beatus.

and guide them. You alone are said to be distinguished in grace, above Remus and Romulus. You were justly raised up among the holy and the elect. You deserved to be entombed in the beautiful church when you died. Because of your preeminent sanctity, with honor and grace, you were joyfully crowned with the laurel, most highly venerated among heavenly citizens, remaining blessed in the stormy sky without end.

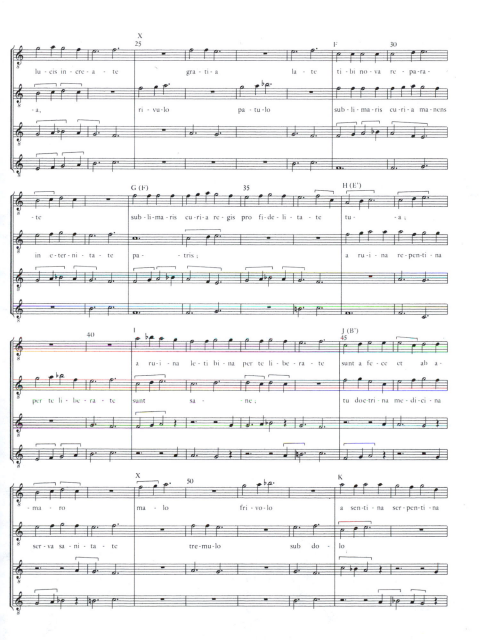

36

John Dunstable
(ca. 1390–1453)

Quam pulchra es (ca. 1420)

John Dunstable, an English musician, mathematician, and astronomer, spent considerable time in France in the early fifteenth century because his English patrons traveled there, along with their court personnel, for the latter stages of the Hundred Years War (1337–1453), a protracted conflict between England and France that was fought on and off for over a century, mostly on French soil. It was Dunstable, more than any other, who was responsible for bringing the characteristic sounds of England—especially the English preference for thirds, sixths, and triads—to the continent, altering the course of fifteenth-century music and profoundly influencing the next generation of continental composers, including Guillaume Du Fay (1397–1474) and Gilles Binchois (ca. 1400–60).

No work illustrates the *contenance angloise*, the "English guise" that swept through the continent in Dunstable's wake, better than the motet *Quam pulchra es*, his most famous composition then as now. It sets several verses from the Song of Songs, a book of the Bible containing love lyrics attributed to King Solomon. The Song of Songs had become very popular in the late Middle Ages, especially in England, where its texts were used as votive antiphons in an ever-growing number of paraliturgical services in honor of the Virgin Mary. Mary was considered the "neck" that connected (and mediated between) the Godhead and the body of the faithful, and the music sung in her praise often appealed to her with an intensity that reflected the sensuous, even erotic verses of the Song of Songs. Dunstable's *Quam pulchra es* is representative of a new type of discant setting that emerged out of these Song of Songs antiphons; it is often called a "declamation motet" in the scholarly literature because all of its voices declaim the text simultaneously, but it is best known simply as a "cantilena motet" because of its similarity to the texture of the continental courtly chanson, which in Latin was called the *cantilena*. As in the fourteenth-century chansons we have already seen, Dunstable's cantus (top) and tenor (bottom) voices create a structural pair that always forms octaves at cadences (e.g., on C in m. 9 and on F in m. 15). The contratenor (middle voice), meanwhile, leaps around, frequently crossing the tenor and filling out the harmony.

Quam pulchra es has an exceedingly sweet sound because its dissonance is very carefully controlled. There are only nine dissonant notes in the entire composition, and they all follow the highly regulated rules of dissonance treatment still taught in counterpoint classes. There is, for example, an "incomplete neighbor," or "escape tone," on "pulchra" (m. 2); there are unaccented passing tones on "ut" (m. 20) and "eburnea" (m. 28); there is an accented passing tone on "videamus" (m. 40); and there are four 7–6 suspensions at various cadences. It took considerable effort to limit dissonance to this degree, and the extreme consonance of the piece reminds us that we normally take for granted a much higher level of dissonance than Dunstable gives us here. The full triads are most conspicuous of all when they come in chains of parallel $^6_3$ sonorities—for example, on the phrases "assimilata est palme" (mm. 12–14) and "ubera mea" (mm. 52–54). Those chains were a standard feature of English discant in the thirteenth and fourteenth centuries; in Dunstable's work they are absorbed into a more varied and subtly controlled compositional technique.

Dunstable's careful text declamation is also highly expressive. The words that are set to strict speech-like homorhythm include "carissima" ("dearest," mm. 5–6), "collum tuum" ("your neck," m. 23, perhaps symbolic as well as erotic), and "ubera" ("breasts"), this last singled out twice, once toward the beginning (mm. 16–17) and another time at the end (mm. 52–54). The most dramatic moment of the entire piece is the lover's command "Veni dilecte mi" ("Come, my beloved," mm. 31–34), which is set off by long note values, homorhythm, and fermatas that cause the musical time momentarily to stand still.

Quam pulchra es et quam decora,	How beautiful thou art, and how graceful,
carissima in deliciis.	my dearest in delights.
Statura tua assimilata est palme,	Your stature I would compare to the palm tree,
et ubera tua botris.	and your breasts to clusters of grapes.
Caput tuum ut Carmellus,	Your head is like Mount Carmel,
collum tuum sicut turris eburnean.	your neck just like a tower of ivory.
Veni, dilecte mi, egrediamur in agrum,	Come my love, let us go out into the field,
Et videamus si flores fructus parturierunt,	and see whether the flowers have yielded fruit,
Si floruerunt mala punica.	and whether the pomegranates are in bloom.
Iba dabo tibi ubera mea.	There will I give my breasts to you.
Alleluia!	Alleluia!

37

Guillaume Du Fay
(1397–1474)

Ave maris stella (ca. 1430)

Du Fay's setting of the Marian hymn *Ave maris stella*, which we have already seen as a chant (Vol 1-7a), employs *fauxbourdon*, a technique of deriving three parts from two to achieve an instant-English effect. In fauxbourdon, only the outer two voices (cantus and tenor) are written, and a third voice is created by doubling the higher voice a perfect fourth below (that is why the middle voice is written in smaller notes in this edition). The technique, with its numerous parallel $\frac{6}{3}$ sonorities and occasional $\frac{8}{5}$ sonorities, seems to be derived from *faburden*, an older English practice of harmonizing a chant at sight in three voices. In the English practice, the chant is carried in the middle voice, doubled at the perfect fourth above, and harmonized below with a voice that moves mostly in parallel thirds with it but sometimes in contrary motion to create a fifth below the chant-bearing voice. In addition to the fact that fauxbourdon is written out (at least in two voices) whereas faburden is not, another important distinguishing feature is that in fauxbourdon the top voice, not the middle voice, carries the original chant (transposed up an octave).

Dufay embellishes the chant melody (or *paraphrases* it, as we now usually say) so that the chant-bearing cantus conforms to the contrapuntal conventions of the contemporary "top-down" genre, the chanson. It seems no accident, then, that Du Fay, one of the most prolific masters of fauxbourdon, was also one of the leading chanson composers of his generation. He fills in the chant's opening leap of a fifth with an original, chanson-like, melody. The cadential structure of Dufay's setting too turns this chant-based composition into something more closely resembling a chanson. The first cadence, for example, joins the finishing note of "maris" to the first note of "stella" (mm. 2–3), creating a stopping point on C, a note to which no cadence is made in the original chant, on the way to a cadence on the chant's final, D, on "alma" (mm. 6–7). This alternation of cadences on C and D is then repeated in the second half of the piece (C on "virgo" in mm. 9–10, D on "porta" in mm. 11–12). The bipartite structural symmetry that results is not at all typical of chant melodies, but it is very typical of fifteenth-century chansons, whose *formes fixes* always consist of two main sections.

For text see Vol 1-7a.

38

Gilles Binchois
(ca. 1400–60)

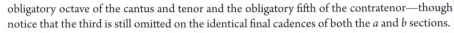

Deuil angoisseux ("Anguished grief") (1430s)

Binchois was his generation's great specialist in the courtly chanson. He composed more than sixty chansons, which constitute more than half his surviving output, and he was famous as a melodist in his own day as he is in ours. He composed mainly rondeaux, but his greatest achievements were ballades. By the early fifteenth century, the ballade, the oldest and most distinguished of the formes fixes, had become a genre of special grandeur, reserved for special occasions, chiefly commemorative and public. An especially grand ballade poem was *Deuil angoisseux* by Christine de Pizan (1364 to ca. 1430), one of the leading poets of the late fourteenth and early fifteenth centuries and perhaps the first great French woman poet. Christine composed her ballade on the death of her husband, Etienne Castel, a notary at the French royal court, in 1390. By the time Binchois set it to music for performance at the court of Burgundy, where he was employed, it was old and very well known.

In Binchois's setting we find an almost-overwhelming influence of the contenance angloise. The harmony changes slowly, it is triadic throughout, and the dissonance treatment is extremely careful. The first three measures of the song consist entirely of arpeggiations of the "F-major" triad in both cantus and tenor (the top two voices in the edition), supported by a pair of droning contratenors (the lower two voices) on the F final and the C a fifth above. When the tenor sings a high A at the end of the word "angoisseux" (m. 3), the resulting harmony is the most resonant possible spacing of an F-major triad: 10/8/5 over the final. This ravishing four-voice texture, a richer sound than we have seen in earlier chansons, is achieved by replacing the contratenor from a three-part version of the song—which itself adds harmonious sonority to a thin-sounding but self-sufficient structural pair—with a pair of complementary contratenors. The lowest voice in the transcription could still function correctly as a contratenor by itself. It regularly sounds the fifth between the cantus-tenor octave at cadences, approaching these notes by octave leap from below: see mm. 11–12, 21–22, 34–35, and 53–54 (= 21–22), the final of these recapitulating an earlier cadence as a result of musical rhyme, in which the ending of the *b* section (mm. 46–54) quotes the ending of the *a* section (mm. 13–23). The presence of the fourth voice makes it possible to complete the triad at each cadence by adding a third to the

obligatory octave of the cantus and tenor and the obligatory fifth of the contratenor—though notice that the third is still omitted on the identical final cadences of both the *a* and *b* sections.

Binchois's *Deuil angoisseux* tells us that the aesthetics of fifteenth-century courtly song are quite different from the aesthetics of later music with which we are more familiar. The song is a marvelously intense expression of grief, but it includes none of the qualities we have come to expect of a lament: slow tempo, a low range, dark (i.e., "minor") or dissonant harmonies. Instead, its bright F-majorish tonality, extreme consonance, and high tessitura (especially in the tenor) convey a public proclamation of grief rather than internal anguish. The register is one of elevation, or "high-ness" (*hauteur* in French)—a highness of tone, diction, and delivery that reflects the elevated social setting in which it would have been performed.

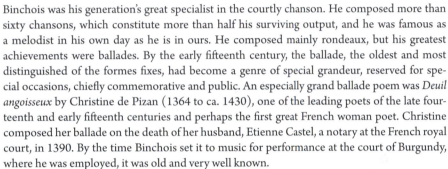

a *Deuil angoisseux, rage desmesurée,*
   Grief desespoir, plein de forsennement,
a *Langour sanz fin et vie maleurée*
   Pleine de plour, d'angoisse et de tourment,
b *Cuer douleureux qui vit obscurement,*
   Tenebreux corps sur le point de partir
   Ay, sanz cesser, continuellement;
   Et si ne puis ne garir ne morir.

a *Fierté, durté de joye separée,*
   Triste penser, parfont gemissement,
a *Angoissse grant en las cuer enserrée*
   Courroux amer porté couvertement,
b *Morne maintien sanz resjoïssement,*
   Espoir dolent qui tous biens fait tarir,
   Si sont en moy, sanz partir nullement;
   Et si ne puis ne garir ne morir.

a *Soussi, annuy qui tous jours a durée*
   Aspre veillier, tressaillir en dorment,
a *Labour en vain, à chiere alangourée*
   En grief travail infortuneéement,
b *Et tout le mal, qu'on puet entierement*
   Dire et penser sanz espoir de garir,
   Me tourmentent desmesuréement;
   Et si ne puis ne garir ne morir.

Text by Christine de Pizan

Anguished grief, unmeasured fury,
despairing grief, full of madness,
languor without end and life of misfortune,
full of tears, of anguish, and of torment,
dolorous heart, which lives in darkness,
shadowy body at the point of death,
I have these continuously;
and thus I can neither be cured nor die.

Disdain, separated from joy,
sad thoughts, profound sighs,
great anguish locked in a weary heart,
bitter pain endured covertly,
mournful demeanor without joy,
foreboding which takes away all goodness,
these are in me without ever leaving;
and thus I can neither be cured nor die.

Perpetual worry and emptiness,
bitter waking, turmoil in sleep,
labor in vain, with great languidness,
tormented work in grief,
and all the bad that one could ever
say or think, without hope of being cured,
torment me without measure;
and thus I can neither be cured nor die.

ment;   Et   si   ne   puis   ne

ga - rir   ne   mo - rir.

39
Anonymous

Missa Caput, Kyrie (ca. 1440)

Around 1440 an anonymous English composer wrote a four-voice *cantus firmus mass* that was much grander in scale than any that had come before it. Its cantus firmus is the long melisma on "caput" ("head"), the final word of the antiphon *Venit ad Petrum* (He came to Peter), which was sung for the ceremony of "washing the feet" on Maundy Thursday during Holy Week before Easter at the Cathedral of Salisbury. The antiphon draws its text from a passage in the Gospel of John in which Jesus says to Peter, "Do not wash only my feet, but also my hands and my *head*."

The *Missa Caput* is a true *cyclic mass*, in that its movements are musically unified. For starters, the *caput* melisma (shown in Example 39-1) appears in the tenor voice of each movement. In addition, all movements have the same overall bipartite structure articulated through the same contrast of perfect (triple) and imperfect (duple) mensurations, each of which governs a full statement of the enormous cantus firmus so that each movement embodies a double cursus of what is already a very lengthy melody. The two sections of the Kyrie—*Kyrie* (mm. 1ff) in perfect time and *Christe* (mm. 105ff) in imperfect time, both prosulated, as was still the practice in fifteenth-century England—are composed to satisfy the requirements of the structural plan. But they do not satisfy the requirements of the liturgy, for in the actual liturgical performance of any mass the words "Kyrie eleison" must be repeated following the words "Christe eleison"; and so we may assume that in the liturgical performance of this mass, either the missing words were shoehorned into the *Christe*, or the first section was performed *da capo* in order to complete the liturgical text.

Just as important as the length of the mass is its texture. Four voices, in precisely the configuration found here, became the norm for a century or more of intense Mass Ordinary composition, and we can therefore witness in the *Caput* mass the birth of "four-part harmony." The *Caput* melisma is an unusually high-lying melody, and the tenor's high tessitura puts it in a range far closer to, and more apt to cross with, the contratenor above it than the "second tenor" below. Indeed, at its peaks it even crosses the cantus at times—sometimes quite dramatically, as when it makes its ascent above the cantus E to the high G in m. 31, while the second tenor descends to its lowest note, putting a maximum distance of a twelfth between these two parts that in earlier music used to cross so freely. Although the sources that include the mass retain

the nomenclature of voice parts with which we are familiar, scribes in the mid-fifteenth century responded to the newly stratified four-part texture by adopting a new nomenclature. The now-obligatory voice that stays consistently below the tenor came to be thought of as a second contratenor rather than a second tenor. To distinguish the two contratenors, one was called "high" (*altus*) and the other "low" (*bassus*). The term *contratenor altus* metamorphosed into the Italian *contralto*, and *contratenor bassus* into *contrabasso*—terms that have long since been anglicized as "alto" and "bass." The highest voice, which till now has been called the *cantus* or *triplum*, became known as the *superius* ("top voice"), from which the Italian word *soprano* is derived. We now have our four familiar voice parts—soprano, alto, tenor, and bass (SATB).

The bassus voice, which now occupies its own pitch space below the tenor's, features the same disjunct motion that previous contratenor voices had. But because it lies below the tenor, it defines the harmony much more strongly than they did, and it behaves in a newly standardized way at cadences. A cadence, we may recall, is defined theoretically as stepwise movement by the "structural pair" (cantus and tenor) in contrary motion from an imperfect to a perfect consonance, generally a sixth to an octave. That criterion is met at the end of both the *Kyrie* and *Christe* sections (mm. 103–104 and 178–179), in which the superius moves from F♯ to G and the tenor from A to G. The only way two additional voices can be added to the "imperfect" part of this cadence that will be both consonant with the structural pair and independent of it is to have them both sing D. At the resolution of the cadence, the D above the tenor remains stationary, and the D below goes the only place it can—to G. The progression in the bass, from the fifth scale degree to the final, is congruent with what we nowadays call a V–I or dominant–tonic progression. Such an approach and such a harmony became a perceptual part of virtually every final cadence from the mid-fifteenth century on.

Example 39-1 The melisma on *caput* from the antiphon *Venit ad petrum*

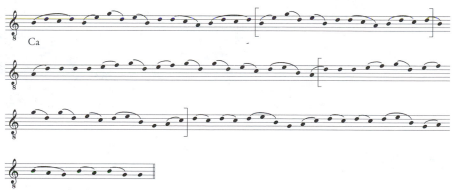

Bracketed repetitions omitted in Ockeghem's Mass.

115

*Kyrie, Deus creator omnium, tu Theos ymon
nostri pie eleison.*

*Kyrie, tibi laudes conjubilantes regum rex
magne oramus te eleison.*

*Kyrie, laus, virtus, pax et imperium cui est
semper sine fine eleison.*

*Christe, rex unice, patris almi nate
coeterne eleison.*

*Christe, qui perditum hominem salvasti, de
morte reddens vite, eleison.*

*Christe, ne pereant pascue oves tue Jesu,
pastor bone, eleison.*

Lord, God, creator of all things, you our
merciful God, have mercy on us.

Lord, singing great praises to you, great
king of kings, we pray to you, have
mercy on us.

Lord, to whom praise, virtue, peace, and
dominion are due, always and without
end, have mercy on us.

Christ, only king, son coeternal with the
gracious father, have mercy on us.

Christ, who saved fallen man, restoring
him from death with life, have mercy
on us.

Christ, so that your pastured sheep
should not perish, Jesus, good
shepherd, have mercy on us.

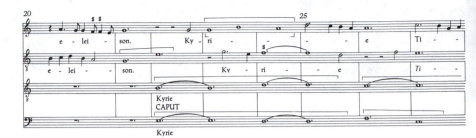

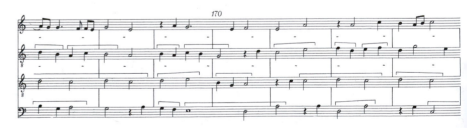

40

Johannes Ockeghem
(ca. 1410–97)

Missa Caput, Kyrie (1450s?)

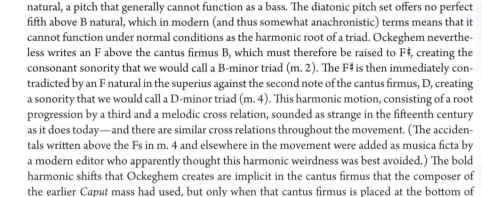

Johannes Ockeghem spent most of his long career at the French royal court and was a leading composer in every major genre of the later fifteenth century. His *Caput* mass, which probably dates from relatively early in his career, is composed in emulation of the anonymous English *Caput* mass we have just seen, which it both pays homage to and in very clear ways seeks to surpass. Ockeghem's Kyrie, given here, is more compressed than the Kyrie of the anonymous mass because the latter had a full set of prosulas, as English (but not continental) Kyries still tended to do in the fifteenth century. To accommodate these prosulas, the English mass had provided a very spacious musical treatment. Ockeghem, because he had only the eighteen words of the canonical Kyrie text to set (3 × Kyrie eleison; 3 × Christe eleison; 3 × Kyrie eleison), streamlined his setting by pruning away several lengthy internal repetitions in the cantus firmus melody (the *Caput* melisma is shown earlier in Example 39-1). He then laid out his abridged cantus firmus in a single cursus that runs through the whole Kyrie, divided into three parts in accordance with the liturgical form (*Kyrie–Christe–Kyrie*). These three musical sections retain the mensural contrast of the original *Caput* mass; the first is in perfect time (triple meter), the second (mm. 23ff) in imperfect time (duple meter), and the third (mm. 53ff) once again in perfect time, making explicit the "da capo" resumption of the initial mensuration that was implied but not actually stated in the older mass.

Ockeghem's chief way of departing from—and surpassing—the cantus firmus treatment of his model was to transpose the tenor down an octave, making it the lowest-sounding voice—in effect, the bass. It was likely originally sung by the composer himself, who is known to have had an especially deep voice. In the original manuscript, the lowest-sounding voice is labeled *bassus tenorizans* (Latin for "bass playing tenor"), and it is provided with a rubric: *Alterum caput descendendo tenorem per diapason et sic per totam missam* ("Another head [appears] by lowering the tenor an octave, and thus for the entire mass"). It will not be missed that the "head" (*Caput*) has now become the "foot" of the texture. That sort of playful cleverness was part of the emulation game; and yet that playfulness gave rise to music of high seriousness and eloquence.

Any fifteenth-century musician would have been impressed with Ockeghem's sheer audacity in transposing this particular cantus firmus melody down an octave because it begins with B

natural, a pitch that generally cannot function as a bass. The diatonic pitch set offers no perfect fifth above B natural, which in modern (and thus somewhat anachronistic) terms means that it cannot function under normal conditions as the harmonic root of a triad. Ockeghem nevertheless writes an F above the cantus firmus B, which must therefore be raised to F♯, creating the consonant sonority that we would call a B-minor triad (m. 2). The F♯ is then immediately contradicted by an F natural in the superius against the second note of the cantus firmus, D, creating a sonority that we would call a D-minor triad (m. 4). This harmonic motion, consisting of a root progression by a third and a melodic cross relation, sounded as strange in the fifteenth century as it does today—and there are similar cross relations throughout the movement. (The accidentals written above the Fs in m. 4 and elsewhere in the movement were added as musica ficta by a modern editor who apparently thought this harmonic weirdness was best avoided.) The bold harmonic shifts that Ockeghem creates are implicit in the cantus firmus that the composer of the earlier *Caput* mass had used, but only when that cantus firmus is placed at the bottom of the texture. By discovering this implicit effect and exploiting it, Ockeghem proclaims himself a worthy heir to his distinguished predecessor in the *Caput* tradition.

For text, see Vol 1-4a.

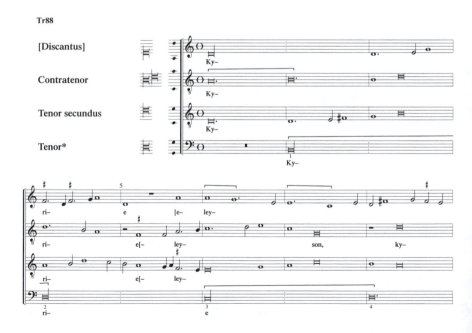

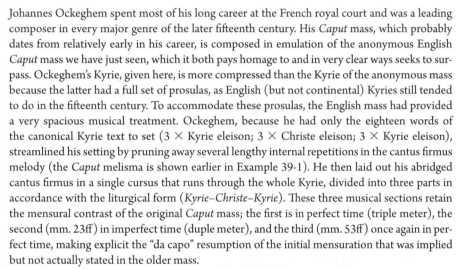

41

Antoine Busnoys
(ca. 1430–92)

Missa L'Homme armé (ca. 1460), Sanctus, Agnus Dei

The *Missa L'Homme armé* of Antoine Busnoys, a French composer who spent the latter part of his career at the court of Burgundy, is an example of the fifteenth-century cantus firmus mass at its most characteristic, most regular, and most fully developed. It may be taken as a type-work for the "high" style of the third quarter of the century. What contributes most to its high-ness are the multiple techniques by which the movements of the mass are musically unified. The most obvious of these is the consistent use throughout of the cantus firmus, here not a sacred chant but the French tune *L'Homme armé* ("The man at arms"), which served as the model for over forty polyphonic masses, of which Busnoys's is one of the earliest (shown in Example 41-1). Each of the five movements sends the *L'Homme armé* tune through the tenor part, in augmented note values, in a cursus that joins the various subsections in an overarching continuity. The Sanctus may fairly represent all its fellows, the more so because all five movements begin identically, with a head motive consisting of a duo for the superius and altus, three measures in length, in which the lower part anticipates the cantus firmus tune, adding yet another level of unity. The first three measures of the Sanctus are (but for the words) identical to the first three measures of the Kyrie, the Gloria, the Credo, and the Agnus Dei.

Busnoys, surprisingly, does not divide the cantus firmus within the mass movements according to its own very clearly articulated three-part (ABA) form, even though two sections of the Mass Ordinary (the Kyrie and the Agnus Dei) are themselves tripartite in textual structure. His precise treatment of the cantus firmus varies from movement to movement according to the length and nature of the various Ordinary texts, but in all movements it is deployed in conjunction with the other voices to create a sense of climax. In the Agnus Dei (as in the Kyrie not given here), the single cursus of the cantus firmus is split right down the middle and alternates with a subsection, the Agnus II, in which "the tenor is silent" (*tenor tacet*). That alternation creates an A-B-A feel that underscores the tripartite form of the Agnus Dei text. The sense of climax is achieved in this and every other movement apart from the Kyrie by accompanying the cantus firmus, on its resumption, with voices notated in diminution (see the *Hosanna* section of the Sanctus and the Agnus III). Speeding along against an unchanged tactus in the tenor, they reach a really dizzy pitch of virtuosity in bringing movements to a close.

In the Sanctus the form is somewhat expanded. The cantus firmus is divided between the *Sanctus* and *Hosanna* sections, the tenor is silent in the *Pleni sunt caeli* and the *Benedictus*, and the *Hosanna* section is repeated after the *Benedictus*, creating sort of an A-B-A-C-A effect in which the last two A sections both sound climactic. In the final Agnus Dei, Busnoys, following a custom that was already well established, provides a cap to the entire Ordinary setting by manipulating the cantus firmus with a special "canon," or transformation rule ("gimmick" might actually be the best translation, flippant though it may seem). The tenor appears to carry the tune in its usual form, but a jesting puzzle-rubric—*Ubi thesis assint ceptra, ibi arsis et e contra* ("Where [the armed man's] scepter is raised, there go lower and vice versa")—tells the singers to exchange roles with the basses, who are to sing the cantus firmus down an octave and with all of its intervals inverted. This means that for the final section of the mass, the cantus firmus is displaced from its usual position in the tenor voice and sung upside down! From Busnoys's time through the end of the sixteenth century it remained common to use some sort of special technique to set the final Agnus Dei apart from the rest of the mass.

For text, see Vol 1-4e and Vol 1-4f.

Example 41-1 The *L'Homme armé* tune

Sanctus

12) **Chigi**: signa congruentiae in superius and altus.

13) **Chigi**: ; corrected after **SMM**.

14) **Chigi**:

17) **Chigi**: Benedictus untexted; underlay roughly follows **SMM**.

18) **Chigi**: signum congruentiae to signal entrance of bassus.

Agnus Dei

Canon: Ubi thesis assint ceptra,
ibi arsis et e contra.

19) **Chigi**: signa congruentiae in superius and altus to signal entrance of cantus firmus.

42

Philippe Basiron
(ca. 1449–91)

Salve regina (1470s)

In the second half of the fifteenth century, the motet became increasingly a votive genre, most often praising the Virgin Mary, the most favored saint of clergy and laity alike. A four-voice texture became standard, and although motets continued to be built on plainchant, the manner in which they used their plainchant models changed. Paraphrase technique, which had been used to great effect in early fifteenth-century fauxbourdon settings to turn an old chant melody into a song-like cantus voice, came to dominate the motet just as cantus firmus technique was being appropriated by the mass. Textual and expressive concerns became more important in both the large-scale structure and surface-level style of the late-fifteenth-century motet. The result was a "middle style," to use the term of theorist Johannes Tinctoris (ca. 1435–1511), that redirected the motet from the altogether transcendent plane of the isorhythmic motet and cyclic mass traditions to a lower, more human level.

Philippe Basiron's setting of the *Salve regina* chant (see Vol 1-9b) provides an excellent introduction to the late-fifteenth-century Marian motet. The aab form of the chant, as we have seen earlier, resembles that of some troubadour cansos and also of one of the descendants of the canso with which Basiron would have been familiar, the polyphonic ballade. The repeated phrase is in fact paraphrased nearly identically on both of its appearances in Basiron's superius voice (mm. 1–9 and 10–18), pointing up the composer's awareness of the melody's resemblance to a secular love song. There are other generic resonances in the *prima pars* (the "first part" of the piece) as well. When the superius paraphrases the opening line of the chant, it is accompanied only by the altus, in a duet that looks like the sort of introitus that one sees in cyclic Mass Ordinary settings or older isorhythmic motets before the entrance of the tenor cantus firmus. And indeed, when the superius repeats the opening phrase of the chant (mm. 10ff), the tenor enters as if it is a cantus firmus—its note values are slow compared to those of the opening duo, and it is accompanied by an equally slow-moving bassus voice. But the source of the tenor melody has never been identified and probably never will be. Basiron creates an aural expectation of a cantus firmus in the tenor, when all the while it is the superius that bears the chant. He has composed a paraphrase motet disguised as a cantus firmus motet! The disguise

is playful, of course, meant to amuse rather than to deceive. The motet creates its "middle style" precisely by juxtaposing a paraphrased superius in "pseudo-vernacular" (i.e., "low") style with a tenor in pseudo-cantus firmus (i.e., "high") style. Basiron displays an awareness of the stylistic registers available to him and an ability to exploit them that are beyond anything we have seen to this point.

In the *secunda pars* ("second part"), Basiron shows a budding concern for choral "scoring." The cantus firmus migrates into the altus and even the tenor (mm. 12–21 and 64–70, respectively), and there is a great deal of interplay among various duos and trios drawn from the four-part texture, with full four-part "tuttis" assuming in such a context a rhetorical, emphatic role. Particularly calculated for oratorical effect is the concluding triple acclamation to the Virgin—"O clemens, O pia, O dulcis" ("O gentle, O loving, O sweet")—in a progression from two to four voices (mm. 59–85), with the three-voice passage in the middle cast as a slightly modified fauxbourdon (mm. 64–69).

For text, see Vol 1-9b.

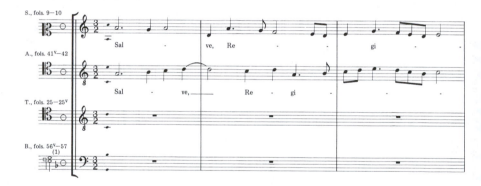

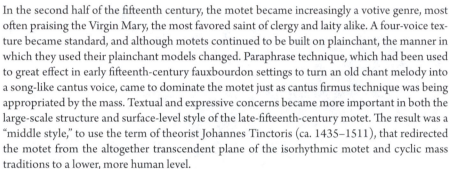

[Secunda pars]

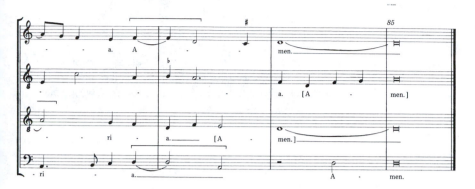

43

Loyset Compère
(ca. 1445–1518)

Ave Maria (1480s?)

In the 1470s a custom was instituted in Milan of substituting votive motets addressed to Mary, more rarely to Christ or to local saints, for all of the items of the Mass Ordinary (and, in larger cycles, parts of the Mass Proper as well). These cycles of *motetti missales*, or substitute motets for the Mass, contributed to a further "lowering" of motet style. Their composers were mostly northern musicians who worked at the court of the Sforzas, a family of mercenary soldiers who in the middle of the fifteenth century had risen from the lower class and become by violent insurgency and advantageous marriage-making the ruling family of Milan. Duke Galeazzo Maria Sforza, who ruled the city from 1466 until he was assassinated in 1476, was an especially enthusiastic patron of the arts. The *motetti missales* composed for his court display a style so distinctly at odds with the lofty architectural masses and motets of the Franco-Flemish tradition that scholars have often postulated an influence of oral, unwritten Italian popular styles and genres. There is no real evidence to warrant the assumption that the music of the *motetti missales* is truly "popular" in style, but there is plenty of evidence that its style is "low." There is also evidence that the liturgical practice of substituting votive motets for mass sections—and indirectly, then, the musical style of the result—was dictated by Galeazzo Maria himself, the grandson of an illiterate farmer, and may have reflected his plebeian personal tastes.

Loyset Compère was a French composer who worked at Galeazzo's court in the 1470s and composed numerous substitute motets. His motet *Ave Maria*, though not itself one of the *motetti missales*, is a Marian pastiche that shows the influence of their stylistic low-ness. In the *prima pars*, a cantus firmus appears in the altus voice, an unexpected place for it because the altus is the least "essential" voice of the counterpoint. It is, moreover, paraphrased in such a way that it is virtually inaudible, moving at the same speed as the other voices and disappearing into the dense polyphony (mm. 1–9). The quoted melody, however, was a familiar one and no doubt was meant to be noticed (at second hearing, perhaps, with a furtive smile of recognition). It comes from *Ave Maria . . . virgo serena*, a sequence for the feast of the Annunciation that was often appropriated for votive purposes, as it is here. The opening of the chant, which begins with the familiar words of the daily *Ave Maria* ("Hail Mary!") prayer, is given in Example 46-1 (which accompanies Vol 1-46, Josquin des Prez's motet *Ave Maria . . . virgo serena*, in which it is

also quoted). Meanwhile, the tenor, the voice most likely to carry significant preexisting material, is confined to a monotone recitation of the prayer that the sequence quotes, as if mimicking the mumbling of a distracted communicant saying the rosary. After the tenor text arrives at the name of Jesus in m. 15, the prayer shifts over to a patchwork of all-purpose litanies: "Kyrie eleison" ("Lord have mercy"), "Sancta Maria, ora pro nobis" ("Holy Mary, pray for us"), and so on (mm. 17ff). At this point the polyphony that has been spinning out in a leisurely manner shifts to a series of duets, alternating between high and low voices (mm. 20–35) and ending in bold homorhythm on the pleading words "O Christe audi nos" ("O Christ hear us," mm. 35–37).

The *secunda pars* continues the litany. After invoking the warrior angel St. Michael with full-textured homorhythm (m. 38), it calls to a varied assortment of saints with a pervasively imitative texture in which the order and interval of entries is likewise varied and unpredictable—unpredictable, that is, until all voices begin to call to the entire community of saints ("omnes sancti Dei") in declamatory homorhythm (mm. 57–61). After the music from mm. 35–36 is reprised in m. 61 on the words "O Christe audi nos," the piece then abruptly breaks into a long and virtuosic closing section in triple meter that calls out emphatically to the Virgin and Christ (mm. 62–71). The sound is almost humorous, but the humor is pious. It is piety that hearers could understand—as opposed to the piety of earlier Franco-Flemish polyphony that was pitched way over its listeners' heads.

Ave Maria, gratia plena,	Hail Mary, full of grace,
Dominus tecum, Virgo serena.	the Lord is with you, serene Virgin.
Benedicta tu in mulieribus, et benedictus	You are blessed among women, and
fructus ventris tui Jesus.	blessed is the fruit of your womb, Jesus.
Kyrie eleison, Christe eleison.	Lord have mercy, Christ have mercy.
O Christe audi nos.	O Christ hear us.
Sancta Maria, ora pro nobis ad Dominum.	Holy Mary, pray to the Lord for us.
O Christe audi nos.	O Christ hear us.
Sancta Dei genitrix, ora pro nobis ad	Holy mother of God, pray to the Lord for
Dominum.	us.
O Christe audi nos.	O Christ hear us.
Sancte Michael, ora pro nobis ad Dominum.	Saint Michael, pray to the Lord for us.
O Christe audi nos.	O Christ hear us.
Sancte Gabriel, Sancte Raphael, Omnes sancti	Saint Gabriel, Saint Raphael, all Angels
Angeli et Archangeli Dei, orate pro nobis ad	and Archangels of God, pray to the
Dominum.	Lord for us.
O Christe audi nos.	O Christ hear us.
Sancte Ludovice, Sancte Francisce, Sancte	Saint Louis, Saint Francis, Saint Nicholas,
Nicolae, Sancte Quintine, Sancte Martine,	Saint Quentin, Saint Martin, Saint
Sancte Augustine, Sancte Benedicte, Sancte	Augustine, Saint Benedict, Saint Anthony,
Anthoni, (Sancti Nicolae), omnes sancti	all holy Martyrs, all holy Confessors,
Martyres, omnes sancti Confessores, omnes	all male and female Saints of God, pray

Sancti et Sanctae Dei, orate pro nobis ad Dominum.
O Christe audi nos.
Beata es Maria, Virgo dulcis et pia, candore vincis lilia, et rosa sine spina, Sanctorum melodia.

O Christe audi nos.
Amen.

to the Lord for us.

O Christ hear us.
You are blessed Mary, sweet and pious Virgin, you are purer than the lily, and a rose without thorns, melody of the Saints.

O Christ hear us.
Amen.

44

Johannes Ockeghem
(ca. 1410–97)

Ma bouche rit ("My mouth laughs") (1460s)

The emergence of whimsy, even humor, in some religious music of the later fifteenth century suggests the upward-trickling influence of the secular, vernacular genres of literate music—most notably, the chanson. The chanson, too, was changing significantly at this time, becoming both higher and lower in stylistic register than it ever had been before. Part of this development was the emergence of a new type of chanson, called the *bergerette*, which literally means "shepherdess," although it originated in French court circles rather than in peasant gatherings. It was a synthesis of two of the formes fixes that we have already encountered, the virelai and the rondeau. Its stanzaic structure (AbbaA) was identical to the virelai, but like the rondeau the bergerette consisted of a single puffed-up stanza, in which the *A* section alone consisted of an ample five lines of poetry, whereas in the virelai there were multiple shorter stanzas that could go on forever.

Ockeghem, the eminent composer to the French king, was the bergerette's first great practitioner. His *Ma bouche rit* is an early example that was well known in its day. It was disseminated widely and emulated by numerous composers, including one (Johannes Martini) who used it as the tenor of a cantus firmus mass. Its most novel stylistic feature is its use of almost-systematic imitation between the cantus and tenor, the voices that had made up the structural pair in chanson composition since the time of Machaut. We can call this *structural* imitation, as opposed to *pervasive* imitation, in which all voices of the polyphonic texture take part (we will see pervasive imitation often later in the anthology, starting with Vol 1-44). The incipits of both musical sections are imitations at the interval of an octave at a time interval of two measures (mm. 1ff and 47ff). In the three-voice texture they could hardly be more conspicuous. From the "tonal" point of view, too, *Ma bouche rit* is novel and exceptionally lofty for a chanson. It is one of the earliest polyphonic compositions to incorporate a final Phrygian cadence (m. 46), by way of a sighing tenor half step down to E, as an emblem of special melancholy or seriousness. The surviving sources, on which alone we can base our knowledge of the past, indicate that Phrygian polyphony was a special predilection of Ockeghem, who bequeathed it as a standard resource to succeeding generations. The earliest Phrygian masses and motets, as well as the earliest Phrygian chansons (all bergerettes), were by Ockeghem.

A *Ma bouche rit et ma pensée pleure,*
Mon oeil s'esjoye et mon cueur mauldit l'eure
Qu'il eut le bien qui sa santé deschasse

Et le plaisir que la mort me pourchasse
Sans resconfort qui m'aide ne sequeure.

b *Ha, cuer pervers, faulsaire et mensonger,*
Dictes comment avez osé songer
Que de faulser ce que m'avez promis.

b *Puis qu'en ce point vous vous voulez venger,*
Pensez bien tost de ma vie abreger;
Vivre ne puis au point ou m'aves mis.

a *Vostre rigueur veult doncques que je meure,*
Mais Pitié veult que vivant je demeure;
Ainsi meurs vif et en vivant trespasse,
Mais pour celer le mal qui ne se passe
Et pour couvrir le dueil ou je labeure,

A *Ma bouche rit ...*

My mouth laughs and my thoughts weep,
my glance is gay, but my heart curses the hour
when it received the prize that now banishes its well-being
and the pleasure that buys me death
without hope of aid or consolation.

Ah, devious, lying, fickle heart,
How, pray, did you dare dream
of making such false promises to me?

Since you seek vengeance in this way,
Think first of all of shortening my life;
I cannot live in the predicament you have put me in.

Your cruelty, then, wills me to die,
but Pity wishes that I go on living;
thus alive I die and dead I live,
only to hide the incessant pain
and mask the sorrow I endure.

My mouth laughs ...

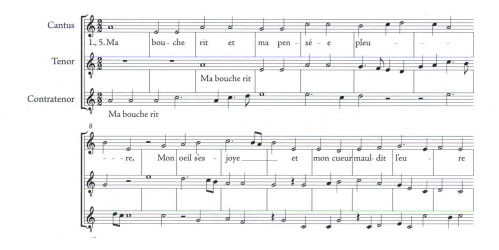

45

Johannes Ghiselin
(*fl* 1491–1507)

La Alfonsina (1490s)

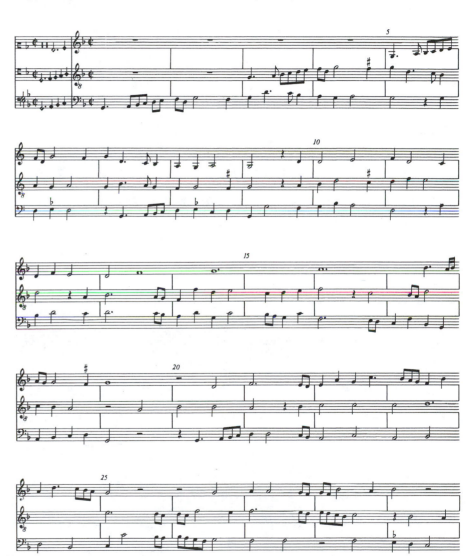

Instrumental music, which for centuries had been primarily an improvisational and unwritten genre, finally became literate in the second half of the fifteenth century. The earliest written instrumental compositions were built on the tenors (or, less frequently, the cantus voices) of well-known chansons, and they likely resembled the sorts of improvisations that skilled performers frequently rendered over these well-known melodies. As these instrumental chanson reworkings came to be written down, composers began to display literate virtuosity in their treatment of their chanson models, in addition to the sort of instrumental virtuosity that performer-improvisers had long since mastered. The next type of instrumental composition, which emerged in the 1480s and '90s, was the "tenor tacet" *Benedictus* portion of the Sanctus from a cantus firmus mass. In these *Benedictus* sections, the cantus firmus–bearing tenor was silent, and the superius, altus, and bassus voices tended to engage in pervasive imitation. Many of these *Benedictus* sections were transmitted independent of the masses in which they appear and were presumably performed as instrumental compositions. The final type of fifteenth-century instrumental composition to emerge resembled chanson reworkings and tenorless *Benedictus* movements stylistically but was not based on a preexisting song or originally composed as part of a mass. These were freestanding compositions, or songs without words, intended for an audience of connoisseurs—those who knew the stylistic idiom well either by playing it or listening to it. Such pieces make up the earliest repertoire of instrumental "chamber music."

For these songs without words we can use the term *carmen* (pl. *carmina*), which came to be applied with more regularity to them in the first decades of the sixteenth century. *La Alfonsina*, published in Ottaviano Petrucci's *Odhecaton* (Venice, 1501), the earliest printed collection of polyphony, was the work of Johannes Ghiselin (alias Verbonnet), a Picard or northern French composer, who, like Josquin des Prez (whose work we will see next) and Jacob Obrecht (1457/8–1505), traveled to Italy and worked alongside them at the court of Ferrara. The piece is named after Ghiselin's patron, Alfonso I d'Este, the Duke of Ferrara (and husband of the notorious Lucrezia Borgia). Its title means simply "Alfonso's little piece," and it does not specify which instruments should perform it—such decisions were still made by performers, not composers. The opening point of imitation ascends through the entire rising octave for virtuoso

verve not imaginable in vocal music and is passed upwards from voice to voice, starting with the bassus. In mm. 30–41 the two lower parts are cast in imitative sequences against the superius, which plays descending dotted longs that crosscut the prevailing meter. Ghiselin adroitly tightens things up into a pair of *strettos* (points of imitation at a reduced time lag and with overlapping entries) in mm. 52ff and mm. 57ff to conclude the piece.

46

Josquin des Prez
(ca. 1450/55–1521)

Ave Maria . . . virgo serena (ca. 1485)

Josquin des Prez was born in northern France, where he received his musical training. He found employment early in his career with various French nobles, later traveled to Italy to work in Milan, Rome, and Ferrara, and finally retired to Condé-sur-l'Escaut, near where he was born, as the most famous musician in Europe. The motet *Ave Maria . . . virgo serena* has been his most famous work since the early sixteenth century, when he first acquired the reputation as the supreme composer of his age. This work exemplifies new approaches to counterpoint and text setting that emerged in the late fifteenth century and formed the basis of the *ars perfecta* ("perfected art") of sixteenth-century sacred music that we will trace through the next several pieces in this anthology. Josquin's composition was widely disseminated, studied by music theorists, and, as we shall see, emulated by later composers.

The core of the text is a five-stanza votive antiphon to the Blessed Virgin Mary, cast as a metrical hymn that commemorates the five major events in Mary's life that were celebrated on the five most important liturgical feast days in her honor: the Immaculate Conception (8 December), the Nativity (8 September), the Annunciation (25 March), the Purification (2 February), and the Assumption (15 August). The antiphon is introduced by an opening quatrain drawn from a sequence for the Feast of the Annunciation, the occasion on which the archangel Gabriel uttered the original "Hail, Mary!" as recounted in the first chapter of the Gospel of Luke (we have already encountered this chant in Compère's *Ave Maria*, Vol 1-43), and a closing couplet that was a common devotional refrain in Josquin's time.

The setting of the opening quatrain (mm. 1–31) is based not only on the text of the sequence chant but also on its melody. Instead of being treated as a traditional cantus firmus of the sort we have seen to this point, however, its four phrases are paraphrased and each turned into a point of imitation in all voices (this is pervasive imitation, as opposed to the structural imitation we saw in Ockeghem's *Ma bouche rit*). The first phrase is quoted directly from the chant, which in subsequent phrases is paraphrased more decoratively (but to maintain the intelligibility of the text, even in these later phrases melismas tend to come at or near the end of the phrase,

and the accented syllables of text are set to longer notes). The first three points of imitation (beginning in mm. 1, 8, and 16, respectively) present their subjects first in the superius voice and proceed downward through the altus, tenor, and bassus, mirroring Gabriel's descent from heaven to earth to deliver the news to Mary that she would be impregnated by the Holy Spirit. In the fourth point of imitation, on "virgo serena" (mm. 23ff), the voices finally enter in a different order, and the time interval between the entries is shorter, with the tenor entering only one measure after the superius (mm. 25–26). The cadence in m. 30 (which the bassus takes an extra measure to reach) brings the introductory quatrain to a close.

Each stanza of the votive antiphon that follows is shaped carefully around its text and is brought to a close with a cadence similar—but never identical—to the cadence in m. 30. The first stanza ("Ave, cujus conceptio . . . ," mm. 31–54) begins with a declamatory duo in the superius and altus that is immediately echoed by an identical duo in the tenor and bassus, in what is known as paired imitation (mm. 31–39). During the second duo, however, the altus joins the tenor and bassus in a fauxbourdon-like passage (mm. 36–39), which creates a smooth transition into the stark four-voice homorhythm on "solemni plena gaudio . . ." (mm. 40ff) that follows. This homorhythmic passage begins with slow rhythms but gradually accelerates into a glorious cadence at m. 53, with the altus embellishing the cadential sonority as if to slow the momentum that has been gathered. The second stanza, on "Ave, cujus nativitas . . ." (mm. 54–77), begins with more paired imitation, although this time each member of the pair itself consists of close imitation at the fifth, rather than at the octave or the unison as we have seen to this point (mm. 54–65). More imitation at the fifth sets the phrase "Ut lucifer . . ." (mm. 64–77) with a prevailing three- or four-voice texture that arrives at a strong cadence in m. 77. The third stanza ("Ave, pia humilitas . . . ," mm. 78–93) presents more paired imitation between high and low voices, but the text is now split between the voice pairs, accelerating the pace of the stanza. The fourth stanza ("Ave, vera virginitas . . . ," mm. 94–110) is in a lilting triple meter, with a quasi-homorhythmic texture that disguises the canon at the fifth between the cantus and the tenor at a temporal interval of one whole note. The fifth stanza ("Ave, praeclara . . . ," mm. 111–141) returns to the duple meter and high–low paired imitation of the first stanza. The suitability of the melodic ascent in the superius and the tenor to the meaning of the word *assumptio* ("Assumption") in mm. 127–133 is self-evident, just as the floridity of the other voices matches the word *glorificatio* ("glorification") in mm. 134–141.

The varied texture of the fifth stanza creates a stark contrast with the total homorhythm of the concluding prayer ("O mater Dei . . . ," m. 143 to the end). This section begins and ends on "open" sonorities that lack a third and contain only perfect consonances, which make the voices sound even more like a single unit. The motivation for the rhythmic coming together of the voices in this coda-like section is textual: For the first and only time in the motet, the text is cast in the first-person singular, with *mei* ("me") replacing *nostra* ("our"). After praising the Virgin as a group, the singers conclude by praying to her as individuals.

Ave Maria,	Hail, Mary,
gratia plena,	full of grace,
Dominus tecum,	the Lord is with thee,
Virgo serena.	virgin serene.

(1) *Ave*, cujus CONCEPTIO, Hail, thou whose conception,
solemni plena gaudio,   full of solemn joy
coelestia, terrestria,   fills all things in heaven and earth
nova replet laetitia.   with renewed gladness.

(2) *Ave*, cujus NATIVITAS   Hail, thou whose birth
nostra fuit solemnitas,   became our solemn rite,
ut lucifer lux oriens   a light arising like the morning star
verum solem praeveniens. going before the true sun.

(3) *Ave*, pia humilitas,   Hail true humility,
sine viro fecunditas,   fruitfulness without man,
cujus ANNUNTIATIO   whose annunciation
nostra fuit salvatio.   has become our salvation.

(4) *Ave*, vera virginitas,   Hail, true virginity,
immaculata castitas,   immaculate chastity,
cujus PURIFICATIO   whose purification
nostra fuit purgatio.   has become our cleansing.

(5) *Ave*, praeclara omnibus   Hail, most glorious one
angelicis virtutibus,   in all angelic virtues,
cujus ASSUMPTIO   whose assumption
nostra fuit glorificatio.   has become our glorification.

  O mater Dei,   O mother of God,
  memento mei. Amen.   remember me. Amen.

Example 46-1 Opening of chant sequence *Ave Maria . . . virgo serena*

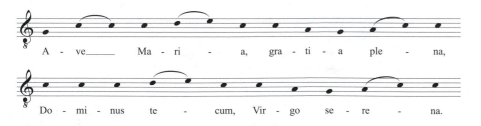

47

Antoine de Févin
(ca. 1470–1512)

Missa super Ave Maria, Kyrie (1515)

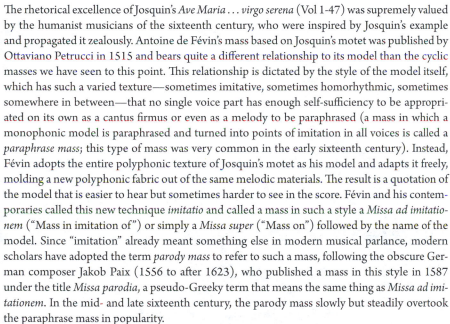

The rhetorical excellence of Josquin's *Ave Maria . . . virgo serena* (Vol 1-47) was supremely valued by the humanist musicians of the sixteenth century, who were inspired by Josquin's example and propagated it zealously. Antoine de Févin's mass based on Josquin's motet was published by Ottaviano Petrucci in 1515 and bears quite a different relationship to its model than the cyclic masses we have seen to this point. This relationship is dictated by the style of the model itself, which has such a varied texture—sometimes imitative, sometimes homorhythmic, sometimes somewhere in between—that no single voice part has enough self-sufficiency to be appropriated on its own as a cantus firmus or even as a melody to be paraphrased (a mass in which a monophonic model is paraphrased and turned into points of imitation in all voices is called a *paraphrase mass*; this type of mass was very common in the early sixteenth century). Instead, Févin adopts the entire polyphonic texture of Josquin's motet as his model and adapts it freely, molding a new polyphonic fabric out of the same melodic materials. The result is a quotation of the model that is easier to hear but sometimes harder to see in the score. Févin and his contemporaries called this new technique *imitatio* and called a mass in such a style a *Missa ad imitationem* ("Mass in imitation of") or simply a *Missa super* ("Mass on") followed by the name of the model. Since "imitation" already meant something else in modern musical parlance, modern scholars have adopted the term *parody mass* to refer to such a mass, following the obscure German composer Jakob Paix (1556 to after 1623), who published a mass in this style in 1587 under the title *Missa parodia,* a pseudo-Greeky term that means the same thing as *Missa ad imitationem.* In the mid- and late sixteenth century, the parody mass slowly but steadily overtook the paraphrase mass in popularity.

Févin's mass was one of the earliest true parody masses and gives a good idea of the new genre and its possibilities. Its Kyrie is set in three parts, following the structure of the text (*Kyrie–Christe–Kyrie*). The first section opens with a superius/altus duo on the opening motto phrase of Josquin's motet, with a melismatic extension that takes it one scale degree higher for its climax (to F). The tenor enters with what sounds like a repetition of the same point, but in fact it sings an elision of the first two phrases from the motet (mm. 5–7), imitated by the altus (mm. 6–8) and then by the superius (mm. 8–10), while the bassus enters at the lower fifth (mm.

5ff), providing a harmonization that reemphasizes the F reached by the superius in the first phrase. The closing phrase (mm. 15–18) reiterates the opening, but only in the superius. The other voices sing nonimitative counterpoints, the tenor making a brief recollection (mm. 17–19) of "gratia plena" from the motet just before the final cadence.

The *Christe* appears to begin with a new point woven out of the "gratia plena" motive, but it is actually the altus counterpoint, derived from "cujus assumptio" near the end of Josquin's motet, from which most of the fabric is woven. The final *Kyrie* is especially ingenious. The motivic material for its first point of imitation is provided by the tenor's version of the third phrase ("Dominus tecum . . .") in Josquin's motet. What had been an accompanying melisma—part of the background, as it were—in the original motet is moved here into the foreground. Févin's final point (mm. 41ff) is woven more straightforwardly out of Josquin's "Virgo serena" phrase. In its general effect, Févin's Kyrie is a reworking of the opening quatrain from the motet, but with subtle variants and digressions at the reworker's discretion.

For text, see Vol 1-4a.

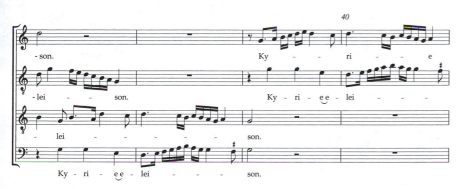

48

Josquin des Prez
(ca. 1450/55–1521)

Benedicta es (ca. 1510)

In *Ave Maria . . . virgo serena* (Vol 1-46) Josquin turned away from the cantus firmus technique that had dominated mid-fifteenth-century sacred composition and focused instead on newer techniques of pervasive imitation and rhetorical homorhythm. These would overtake cantus firmus technique almost entirely by the mid-sixteenth century, but for a few decades around the turn of the century, the old and the new coexisted happily. *Benedicta es*, a six-voice chant-based motet that Josquin composed toward the end of his life, shows not only that cantus firmus, canon, imitation, and rhetorical homorhythm can coexist but that they can reinforce one another, to stunning effect.

The chant model is a sequence for the Feast of the Annunciation of the Virgin (25 March) that features the usual paired versicle structure (shown in Example 48-1). Josquin quotes the entire melody of his model but does not follow its formal divisions. Instead, he divides the motet into three sections: The *prima pars* (first part) sets the first two versicle pairs; the *secunda pars* (second part) sets the single versicle 3a; and the *tertia pars* (third part) sets the single versicle 3b. The structure of the motet and its treatment of the chant are shown in the following table.

Section of Motet	Prima pars (mm. 1–107)	Secunda pars (mm. 108–135)	Tertia pars (mm. 136–176)
No. of Voices	6	2	6
Versicles of Chant	1a–2b	3a	3b
Treatment of Chant	Canonic cantus firmus in superius and tenor voices	Paraphrased and turned into points of imitation	Paraphrased and turned into points of imitation

The use of more than four voices was rare in the first decade of the sixteenth century, and when large performing forces were called for, some sort of scaffolding device was generally employed in order to give structure to the additional voices. In the *prima pars* a combination of cantus firmus technique and canon provides that structure. Ever since the thirteenth century it had been standard to place the borrowed melody in the tenor voice, and so it is striking when

Example 48-1 Chant sequence *Benedicta es*

Benedicta es begins with the chant stated in long note values in the superius voice (mm. 1–7). Rather than hidden in the middle of the texture, it is right there on top, clear to the ear both because it is the highest-sounding voice and because there is only one voice sounding below it at first. When the third and fourth voices enter in m. 5, the tenor sings exactly the same music that the superius just sang, making Josquin's compositional conceit clear: The superius and the tenor are engaged in a structural canon. What is more, the bassus primus (first bass) accompanies the tenor cantus firmus in mm. 5–9 with exactly the same melody the altus had used to accompany the superius in mm. 1–5, creating paired imitation between the superius/altus and the tenor/bassus primus. The structural canon between the superius and tenor continues through most of the *prima pars*, with a short break in mm. 68–86. As it proceeds, the other voices sometimes imitate the canonic voices, further saturating the polyphonic texture with motives from the chant melody (as, for instance, in the upper four voices on "tu praeclara" in mm. 37–46). When the structural canon finally breaks down, it is for rhetorical purposes: In m. 95 all the voices come together in homorhythm on the words "sic salutavit" ("thus saluted you"), which are stated twice and followed by a grand pause in m. 98. All of this stresses the importance of *how* the Virgin was saluted: with the words "Ave plena gratia" ("Hail full of grace"), set in mm. 99–106. These are the words of salutation that the Archangel Gabriel utters to the Virgin Mary in the Gospel of Luke to inform her that she will be impregnated by the Holy Spirit and will give birth to the son of God. They are vitally important on the Feast of the Annunciation, and Josquin sets them with appropriate solemnity. The rhythm slows noticeably, the voices move together in homorhythm, and all the while the superius continues to quote the chant melody in long note values. Cantus firmus technique and rhetorical text setting come together here effortlessly.

After this striking conclusion to the *prima pars*, the *secunda pars* offers a moment of repose. The texture is reduced to only the two highest voices, and the superius paraphrases each phrase of the chant versicle in succession, always imitated or fore-imitated by the altus. In the *tertia pars* the full six-voice complement of voices returns, presenting the last versicle of the chant now as paraphrased points of imitation in all voices (mm. 136–153). In mm. 154–158 there are quasi-imitative homorhythmic trios on the words "Et regnum det nobis paratum" ("and grant us the kingdom prepared for us"), followed in mm. 158–162 by similar but bigger and more rapid imitative quartets on "in caelesti patria" ("in the heavenly realm"). These passages accelerate into the concluding "Amen," which is essentially a giant authentic cadence stretched out over mm. 166–76. The voices sing imitative scalar flourishes before all arriving at a fermata on a D harmony in m. 174. The concluding G sonority that follows it, which sounds very final indeed, is the first final sonority in this anthology to include a third. By the early sixteenth century the last holdout against the incursion of imperfect consonances—the final chord—had finally let them in.

1a. Benedicta es, caelorum regina,
  et mundi totius domina,
  et aegris medicina

Blessed are you, Queen of heaven,
mistress of the entire world,
and balm for the sick.

1b. Tu praeclara maris stella vocaris,
  quae solem justitiae paris,
  a quo illuminaris.

You are called the bright star of the sea,
who brings forth the sun of justice,
by whom you are illuminated.

2a. Te Deus Pater, ut Dei mater
  fieres, et ipse frater
  cujus eras filia,

God the Father, so that you might become
the mother of God, and He your brother,
whose daughter you were born,

2b. Sanctificavit, Sanctam servavit,
  et mittens sic salutavit:
  "Ave plena gratia."

Sanctified you and kept you holy,
and by His messenger thus saluted you:
"Hail, full of grace."

3a. Per illud "Ave" prolatum
  et tuum responsum gratum
  est ex te Verbum incarnatum,
  quo salvantur omnia.

By that proclamation of "Ave" [Hail],
and by your gracious reply,
the Word was made flesh from you,
so that all might be saved.

3b. Nunc mater exora Natum
  ut nostrum tollat reatum,
  et regnum det nobis paratum
  in caelesti patria. Amen.

Now Mother pray to your Son
that he take away our sin,
and grant us the kingdom prepared for us
in the heavenly realm. Amen.

49

Adrian Willaert
(ca. 1490–1562)

Benedicta es (1545)

Josquin and his contemporaries went a long way toward perfecting and "classicizing" counterpoint, but their dissonance treatment was not yet fully rationalized and codified. It became so in the mid-sixteenth century thanks in large part to Adrian Willaert, a northerner who spent most of his career at St. Mark's Basilica in Venice, and his student Gioseffo Zarlino (1517–90), who also worked at St. Mark's and became the single most authoritative and influential theorist of the mid-sixteenth-century art of counterpoint—the *ars perfecta*. It is largely because Willaert's music is held up as the model of perfection in Zarlino's *Le istitutioni armoniche* (1558) that he looms in history as the great midcentury stylist. Willaert's counterpoint is balanced, refined, and much less idiosyncratic than anything that had come before. He took the basic elements of Josquin's style and modified them slightly to make a leaner, cleaner, more consistent idiom that Zarlino could easily codify and that could then become a true lingua franca. Thus it was Willaert, above all, who made Josquin a truly representative sixteenth-century composer.

Willaert's motet *Benedicta es* draws its text and melodic material from the same plainchant sequence that Josquin had already set (see Vol 1-48). The *prima pars* of Josquin's six-voice setting observes a radical functional distinction between the cantus firmus voices and the "free" ones, each group treated separately, if equally, in imitation. In Willaert's setting, on the other hand, each phrase of the chant is similarly paraphrased and turned into a point of imitation in all four functionally equivalent voices (this is the type of paraphrase one sees in the paraphrase mass). But this observation, even as it puts distance between the two settings of *Benedicta es*, points to a similarity between Willaert's motet and the opening of Josquin's oft-emulated *Ave Maria . . . virgo serena* (Vol 1-46). Both use pairs of voices and manipulate the texture so that tuttis, on the rare occasions when they do occur, achieve a high level of sonic prominence. Texting is more often on the semibreve (half note in transcription) than on the minim (quarter note), and it is more nearly syllabic (hence more intelligibly declaimed) than in the work of Willaert's immediate predecessors. There are even suggestions, at times, of Josquin's rhetorical use of homorhythm for emphasis (e.g., on "cujus eras filia" at mm. 65–70 or "Ave plena gratia" at mm. 81–89).

Willaert's harmony, however, shows him clearly to be of a younger generation than Josquin. The final chord of the piece is a full triad—as Josquin's were only late in his life and even then only occasionally—and is approached through a *plagal cadence*, which remains to this day the most common type of cadence for the word "Amen." There is also more disciplined and regular handling of dissonance. The most important way in which Willaert's style differs from Josquin's is in the regularity of rhythmic flow. The four voices, once they get going, maintain a near-constant stream of quarter-note motion that comes to rest only at the end of a section. In order to maintain this gently forward-driving motion, Willaert mitigates, elides, or even evades cadences, sometimes through what later came to be called the "deceptive cadence," as in mm. 7–8. The altus drops out instead of sounding its octave G against the one in the superius, and at the same time the bassus sounds an unexpected E a third below the final. That E, however, while unexpected harmonically, is very much expected melodically: The deceptive cadence arises right out of the bassus/tenor statement of the opening imitative subject. Sometimes the avoidance is more subtle, such as when the phrase "Et mundi . . ." (first heard in the altus and superius in mm. 12ff) is calculated to enter against, and draw attention away from, cadences that have been prepared in the other parts (in mm. 14 and 17). An especially ingenious cover-up is the one that hides the literal repeat of the opening superius/altus duo in mm. 28ff behind continuing, harmonically diversionary action in the lower parts.

Where earlier composers, including Josquin, had often inclined toward overtly modeling the shape of their chant-derived motets on that of the chant itself (in this case the paired versicles of the sequence), Willaert, while actually honoring the melodic repeat, tries to obscure the fact. The aim seems always to be the avoidance of anything that will sectionalize the music, except where the composer expressly wishes to sectionalize it. The abstractly conceived, "purely musical" or composerly form of the polyphonic motet, in two cadentially articulated halves expressly labeled "first part" (*prima pars*) and "second part" (*secunda pars*), takes precedence over the form of the liturgical model. The result is a music that is carefully and expertly controlled in every dimension, yet one without a hint of flashy tour de force. That is as good a description as any of a "classic" style.

For text and chant model, see Vol 1-48.

W 1545 b No. 16

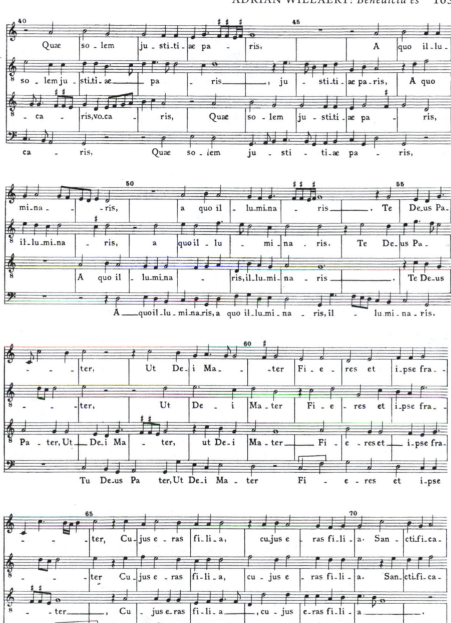

50
Giovanni Pierluigi da Palestrina (1525/6–1594)

Missa Papae Marcelli ("Mass of Pope Marcellus"), Kyrie, Gloria, and Credo (1567)

By the 1540s some church officials had taken a negative view of the sacred music of the generation after Josquin because its learned imitative counterpoint did not, in their opinion, fulfill the central duty of religious music. They believed that in its preoccupation with abstract musical constructions like pervasive imitation, it fell short in its obligation to deliver the text clearly and modestly to the listener. Pope Marcellus II, during his extremely brief (twenty-day) reign as pope in 1555, reportedly told the Sistine Chapel Choir, of which Palestrina was a member at the time, that the music for holy week should be sung in such a way that all the words would be clearly audible. It is possible that Palestrina composed his *Missa Papae Marcelli* (Mass of Pope Marcellus) in 1555 as a response to the Pope's words, but it is far more likely that he composed it closer to 1567, when it was published in Palestrina's second book of masses. By that time Pope Marcellus's demand for textual intelligibility had been echoed by the Council of Trent (1545–63), which demanded in its "Canon on Music to Be Used in the Mass" (1562) that "the whole plan of singing in musical modes should be constituted not to give empty pleasure to the ear, but in such a way that the words be clearly understood by all, and thus the hearts of the listeners be drawn to desire of heavenly harmonies, in the contemplation of the joys of the blessed."

Palestrina was born near Rome and spent his entire career working for major musical establishments in Rome, including the choirs of the Sistine Chapel and St. Peter's Basilica. His musical voice was, more than anyone else's, the voice of the Catholic Church authorities in the second half of the sixteenth century. Most of his masses incorporate preexisting material using either paraphrase or parody technique, but the six-voice *Missa Papae Marcelli* is "freely composed." In the absence of an external scaffold, it was up to Palestrina to provide a musical shape that holds the mass together. The Kyrie, Sanctus, and Agnus Dei movements—that is, the ones with the short texts that would be difficult to obscure—are composed in a free, often-imitative texture that adorns the Mass Ordinary text with perfected counterpoint, the artifice of which was not a hindrance to their textual intelligibility. The Kyrie, given here, opens with an imitative subject that returns in the *Agnus Dei I* and in the concluding seven-voice *Agnus Dei II*, where it is part of a three-voice canon. This opening subject begins with long, repeated notes that emphasize the upward leap of a fourth that follows, which is itself followed by a gentle stepwise

descent back to the starting point. This subject defines the opening *Kyrie*. The *Christe* begins (m. 25) with looser imitative writing that builds rhythmic momentum into a point of imitation on a stepwise descending subject that starts in the tenor I in m. 32 and is picked up in *stretto*-like fashion by the other voices throughout the remainder of the section. The final *Kyrie* starts again with a lucid point of imitation (m. 52) on a subject that begins with long notes and creates gradual acceleration into a cadence (m. 65). This cadence is elided by a final energetic point of imitation that leads to an emphatic authentic cadence in m. 75, which is reinforced by a plagal cadence to conclude the movement.

In the "talky" movements of the Mass (the Gloria and the Credo), special post-Tridentine (that is, post–Council of Trent) qualities emerge that make their much longer texts easier to hear. Polyphonic Glorias and Credos generally leave the first few words to a soloist to intone, and so the polyphony generally begins, as in the movements given here, on "et in terra . . ." and "patrem omnipotentem . . . ," respectively. In both of the movements here, the full six-voice choir is divided into varying ensembles of three to five voices that declaim the text in homorhythm that is decorated only over long-held syllables, allowing the words to remain clear at all times. These varying ensembles often form pairs that alternate phrases of text with one another (as in the two different four-voice ensembles that declaim "Et in terra pax hominibus" and "bonae voluntatis" in mm. 1–8 of the Gloria). The structure of these long-texted movements can be described as a series of musical units that correspond to phrases of text declaimed by a portion of the six-voice choir and are marked off by clear cadences. The full complement of six voices is generally reserved for important bits of text, such as the words "Jesu Christe" in mm. 101–107 of the Gloria or "Et incarnatus est" in mm. 59–62 of the Credo.

In the middle section of the Credo ("Crucifixus . . . ," mm. 74ff), Palestrina apes the tenor-tacet sections of old by scaling down the performing forces to a four-voice "semichoir," but the nature of the writing does not differ; it still consists of a kaleidoscopic interplay of homorhythmically declaimed, cadenced phrases. The third and last part ("Et in spiritum . . . ," mm. 116ff) returns to the full six-part texture, which is deployed more frequently than before at full strength, reaching a climax at the concluding "Amen" (mm. 186–197). This final word having been reached, Palestrina departs from the declamatory homorhythm that he had used up to this point and returns to the imitative texture and melismatic writing of the outer movements. To set this last word he indulges in a glorious point of imitation based on a descending pentachord. The subject is passed through all six voices—starting with bassus I—and outlines a final authentic cadence on C in mm. 193–194 and a reinforcing plagal cadence in mm. 195–197. Palestrina's *Missa Papae Marcelli*, even in the Gloria and the Credo, is thus not a chastened, ascetic, quasi-penitent affair, but a masterpiece of expressiveness.

For texts, see scores Vol 1-4a, Vol 1-4c, and Vol 1-4d.

Gloria

Credo

51

Giovanni Pierluigi da Palestrina (1525/6–1594)

Tui sunt caeli (1593)

The practice of *ars perfecta* polyphony reached a stage of ultimate refinement in a book of Offertory settings that Palestrina published in the last year of his life. The motets in this collection display the smoothest and most consistent voice leading imaginable, harmony that is completely saturated with triads, and extremely economical motivic construction. It is a "classical" style at its most classical. Illustrative of the collection as a whole is *Tui sunt caeli*, the offertory for Christmas, in which the imitative subjects all begin with slow motives that have a strong rhythmic profile, feature wide melodic leaps, and are carefully modeled on the pronunciation of the text that they set. Many of these openings ("et tua est terra . . ." in mm. 13ff, "orbem terrarum . . ." in mm. 20ff, etc.) are in fact nearly syllabic. Rhythmic activity increases in the freely formed melismas that follow and drive each point of imitation toward a cadence, but the melodic motion always increases gradually and spins effortlessly out of the head motive, with stepwise motion becoming ever more common as a phrase proceeds. The text is concentrated in the head motives, so it stands out to the ear even though each voice declaims it at a different time. Every entrance of an imitative subject, therefore, stands out in note lengths, melodic profile, and texting style, even as it remains part of a seamless contrapuntal texture.

In Palestrina's late compositions it is the norm, rather than the exception, to have imitation that is tonal instead of literal. The setting of the text incipit ("Tui sunt caeli"), for example, contains entries on the final (D) and on the reciting tone (A). In every case, the downward contour is adjusted so that the two notes in question will define its limits: Either A proceeds downward to D by way of G (producing the intervallic succession step + fourth) or D proceeds downward to A by way of C (producing the intervallic succession step + third). In a way that is almost shocking for Palestrina, the next interval (on the words "sunt caeli"), while reversing direction as expected, does so by means of a spectacular leap of a minor sixth that emphatically requires a full "recovery." The ensuing stepwise melismatic "tail" supplies precisely that. And it does not come to rest until full recovery—return to the starting note—is achieved, which is how Palestrina is able to maintain melodic tension over a considerable melismatic span and why the tunes in his late compositions, however decorative, always have a pressing sense of direction. The altus, for example, entering first, has to recover the whole sixth from B♭ to D in its

descending melisma (mm. 3–8); it proceeds immediately as far as E, but it then reverses direction; next it overshoots its top and skips down from C so as to require another recovery before it can go farther; that recovery having been made, it teasingly moves down again to the E; finally it gives the ear the D it craves, through a circle of fifths. The D having at last been regained, the voice now—and only now—can rest. The line is complex and tortuous, but as it keeps making and (eventually) keeping promises, it sounds at all times purposeful, never meandering.

The high tonal definition and tonal stability established at the outset is maintained throughout the motet, and the projecting and achieving of tonal goals are among the factors contributing fundamentally to the impression of the music's overall "shape," the coherence of its unfolding. We are, in other words, just about at the point where it makes sense to start replacing the old modal terms like *final* and *reciting tone* with modern terms like *tonic* and *dominant*, which refer to harmonic functions. Although a fully functional tonality does not come into existence until almost a century later, it can be argued that the age of functional tonality begins in pieces like this one, late-sixteenth-century imitative compositions that construct their counterpoint within a highly focused tonal space.

> *Tui sunt caeli et tua est terra: orbem terrarum et plenitudinem ejus tu fundasti: justitia et judicium praeparatio sedis tuae.*
>
> *(Psalm 89, verses 11 and 14)*

Thine are the heavens, and thine is the earth: the world and the fullness thereof thou hast founded: justice and judgment are the preparation of thy throne.

52

William Byrd
(1543–1623)

Two Settings of the Agnus Dei

Byrd was younger than Palestrina, lived far longer, and was a much more versatile composer. He composed in every sacred and secular genre of his day and made especially important contributions to the development of instrumental chamber music and keyboard music, realms about as far from Palestrina's sphere as can be imagined. But he was also one of the last great masters of vocal polyphonic music in the Catholic tradition. Whereas Palestrina worked in Rome, where the Catholic Church consolidated its power, Byrd worked in England, where the Catholics were on the losing side of a religious war. Byrd was one of the so-called *recusants,* or *refusers,* loyal Catholics in a country where the Pope's authority was not recognized and his followers persecuted. Byrd's latest—and quite possibly his best—music, including his three masses (for four, three, and five voices), was written for an underground church where services were celebrated privately and secretively.

Byrd effectively retired from the English Royal Chapel at the age of fifty and moved to a country home, where he joined a recusant community headed by a noble family named Petre. His three masses were evidently composed for this community and others like it. The tradition of mass composition in England—which included the highly influential *Caput* mass from the mid-fifteenth century (Vol 1-39)—had continued unbroken through the early sixteenth century, but the Reformation ended it. Byrd was therefore left to start the tradition anew, and he did it based on his own experience composing motets and related genres, in which he used a very personal and idiosyncratic mix of *ars perfecta* imitation and rhetorical, declamatory homorhythm. He approached the text of the mass in an entirely new way that did not at all resemble settings by continental composers, who took the text for granted. His mass movements are basically free-form motets that respond closely to the text they set. As a recusant unable to proclaim the mass text freely, Byrd was extremely sensitive to its semantic content and reflected this content with unusual directness in his music. Thus although Byrd, like Palestrina, played imitation off against homorhythm, he did so with greater terseness and sensitivity to the meaning of the words.

a. The Mass in Four Parts (1593)

The Mass in Four Parts has a tortured sound that seems to reflect the tortured mood of its composer. The mode—transposed Dorian, but with a specified E♭ that turns it into something more nearly resembling plain G minor—contributes to the mood, of course; but more potent by far is the astonishing degree of dissonance, which grates most where it is least expected, in the Agnus Dei, a text outwardly concerned with gentleness, deliverance from sin, and peace. Unlike continental settings, which divide the Agnus Dei into three subsections for the three invocations of the lamb, Byrd's is a continuous, seamless movement in which the three invocations run one into the next. All three are strictly imitative, but they are set apart from one another by a progressively denser texture: The first is sung by two voices (mm. 1–12), the second by three (mm. 12–27), and the last, with its new words "dona nobis pacem" ("grant us peace"), by all four voices (mm. 27ff). The most striking moment of the piece comes when those final words are set, beginning in m. 40, to a stretto based on an imitative subject that creates a suspension on every beat, emphasizing the most strident dissonances (major seventh, minor second, minor ninth). The result is almost painful to the ears, underscoring a contradiction between the meaning of the word "peace" and the unsettledness of Byrd's harmonies. This seeming irony is more likely representative of what was a simple truth for recusants: They needed to beg for peace from the Lamb of God because in England of their time they had none.

For text, see Vol 1-4f.

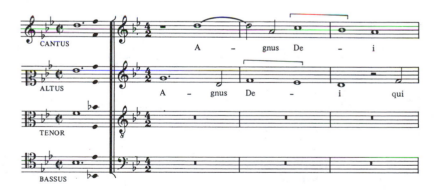

Prefatory stave: 𝄴 (B)

major third) in the second (m. 32). In the third acclamation, the whole choir joins in a pair of homorhythmic outbursts (mm. 33–42) that literally "call" to the Lamb with an emotional immediacy not seen in the work of other Catholic composers. We are again reminded of the plight of the persecuted recusants, but in this Mass the words "dona nobis pacem" sound resolved and display a confidence in the Catholic faith despite the difficult circumstances of the Catholics who sang it.

b. The Mass in Five Parts (1595)

The Mass in Five Parts interprets the text of the Agnus Dei quite differently, yet with equal sensitivity. Once again it sets it as a single unbroken movement, and once again there is a progression over the three invocations of the lamb from sparse to dense texture—beginning with three voices in the first acclamation and moving to four in the second and five in the third. The first invocation (mm. 1–18) uses a shift in harmonic color to distinguish the "Agnus Dei" ("Lamb of God," but figuratively Christ) from the prayer to him, "Miserere nobis" ("Have mercy on us"). By suppressing the B♭ on the rising figure that addresses him (e.g., m. 4) but emphasizing it in the prayer (mm. 10–18), Byrd reminds us that the flat has, ever since Guido of Arezzo, been a "softening" device. (*Mollis*, the Latin word for "flat," literally means "soft"; *durus*, the word for "sharp" or "natural," literally means "hard.") In the second invocation (mm. 18–32), like a magician, Byrd retains the conflict of B♭ and B natural, but in the opposite order, moving from the "soft" B♭ to the "hard" B natural by transposing the closing cadence from F in the first acclamation (m. 18) to G (with a

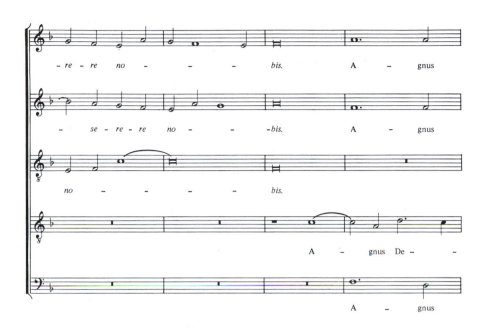

40 - 42 IV: tol^{mm}-lis^{m} pec^{m}-ca^{c}-ta^{s} mun^{m}-di^{b}

53

Johann Walther
(1496–1570)

Christ lag in Todesbanden ("Christ lay in the bonds of death")
(1524)

The Lutheran Church broke with the musical practices of the Catholic Church most definitively by advocating the use of full congregational singing where previously service music had been sung by a trained choir. Eliminating the trained choir eliminated any musical hierarchy, which accorded well with the communitarian ideals of Martin Luther's religious reforms—which also included translating the Bible from Latin into vernacular languages that members of the congregation could understand. The entire lay congregation thus became the choir, just as the entire community of the faithful—not just an ordained clergy—now constituted the Lutheran priesthood. A service in which the minister's preaching was answered by congregational singing would be more than a mere sacramental ritual; it would become "evangelical"—an occasion for actively and joyously proclaiming the Gospel anew and affirming the bonds of Christian fellowship.

The standard genre of Lutheran congregational song was the strophic German hymn known as the *chorale*. Chorales replaced the corpus of Gregorian chant as the music of the Lutheran church, and many of the earliest ones were adapted from well-known chants, particularly (but not only) hymns. Others were freer adaptations. One of the most famous Lutheran songs from the sixteenth century forward is the Easter chorale *Christ lag in Todesbanden*, derived from the Latin Easter sequence *Victimae paschali laudes* (Vol 1-5a), which had already been adapted as a German Easter song called *Christ ist erstanden* ("Christ is risen") that was sung mainly in street processions rather than in church. Only the first line of the Latin sequence is retained in *Christ lag in Todesbanden* (shown in Example 53-1), and it is immediately balanced by an answering phrase in the complementary modal pentachord. The melody thus created is immediately repeated in conformity with the traditional *Bar form* (aab) that pervaded sixteenth-century German secular music, including the *Tenorlied*, which was the German counterpart of the Italian frottola and Parisian chanson but which, in a manner unique among secular genres, carried the main melody in the tenor voice.

The first publication of Lutheran chorales arranged polyphonically was Johann Walther's *Geystliches gesangk Buchleyn* ("Little sacred songbook"), which was published in 1524 and boasted a preface by Luther himself. Essentially a collection of sacred Tenorlieder that carry the chorale melody in the tenor voice, Walther's collection was intended for use at religious schools, so that "young people," as Luther put it in the preface, "who should and must be trained in music and other proper arts, would free themselves from love songs and other carnal music and learn something wholesome instead." Walther's setting of *Christ lag in Todesbanden* treats the chorale tune as a cantus firmus in the tenor voice, but it anticipates the tenor's entrance with imitation in the bassus and discantus (mm. 1–5). When the tenor does enter in m. 6, it creates a canon with

Example 53-1 Lutheran chorale *Christ lag in Todesbanden.*

the altus (which actually enters first, in m. 5); these two voices remain pretty strictly imitative throughout the entire piece. Despite Walther's contrapuntal artifice, the composition remains true to the communal spirit of the Lutheran chorale. The texture is clearly organized around the chorale cantus firmus, and, although the other parts are texted, they could just as easily be (and often were) played on the organ or by other instruments. This tradition of mixing voices and instruments in polyphonic chorale settings led to an important instrumental genre called the "chorale prelude" (*Choralvorspiel*), an often-improvised type of cantus firmus chorale setting that composers up to and including Bach cultivated as a way of ornamenting and elaborating on the melodies of the Lutheran Church.

Christ lag in Todesbanden,	Christ lay in the bonds of death,
für unser Sünd gegeben.	handed over for our sins.
Der ist wieder erstanden,	He is risen again,
und hat uns bracht das Leben.	and has brought us life.
Des wir sollen fröhlich sein,	We should therefore be happy,
Gott loben und dankbar sein,	praise God and be thankful,
und singen Alleluia.	and sing, "Alleluia!"

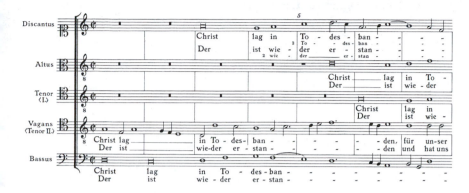

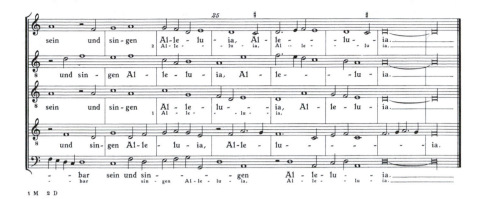

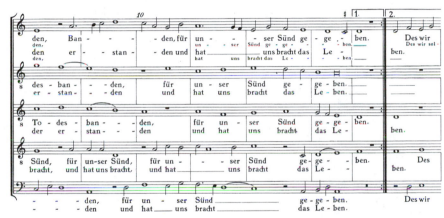

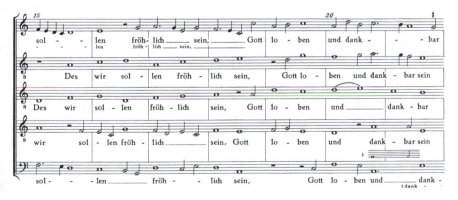

54

Giovanni Gabrieli
(ca. 1554/7–1612)

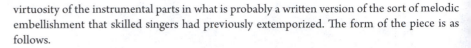

In ecclesiis (1615)

virtuosity of the instrumental parts in what is probably a written version of the sort of melodic embellishment that skilled singers had previously extemporized. The form of the piece is as follows.

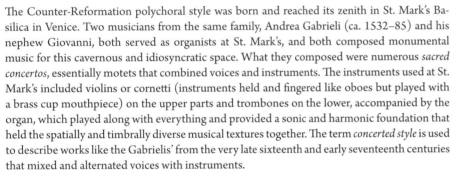

Verse	1	2	Sinfonia	3	4	5
Measures	1–12	13–31	31–39	39–68	68–101	102 to end
Performing forces (organ always plays)	Soprano soloist, choir	Bass soloist, choir	Instrumentalists	Alto and tenor soloists, choir, instrumentalists	Soprano and bass soloists, choir	Tutti

The Counter-Reformation polychoral style was born and reached its zenith in St. Mark's Basilica in Venice. Two musicians from the same family, Andrea Gabrieli (ca. 1532–85) and his nephew Giovanni, both served as organists at St. Mark's, and both composed monumental music for this cavernous and idiosyncratic space. What they composed were numerous *sacred concertos*, essentially motets that combined voices and instruments. The instruments used at St. Mark's included violins or cornetti (instruments held and fingered like oboes but played with a brass cup mouthpiece) on the upper parts and trombones on the lower, accompanied by the organ, which played along with everything and provided a sonic and harmonic foundation that held the spatially and timbrally diverse musical textures together. The term *concerted style* is used to describe works like the Gabrielis' from the very late sixteenth and early seventeenth centuries that mixed and alternated voices with instruments.

In some of his concerted works, Giovanni Gabrieli specified for the first time in the history of Western music exactly which instruments should play which parts—choices that previously had been left to the performers. Gabrieli could therefore be said to be the first composer who practiced the art of orchestration. *In ecclesiis*, composed after 1605 and published in his posthumous second book of *Sacrae Symphoniae* ("Sacred Symphonies") in 1615, displays Gabrieli's concerted polychoral practice at its absolute grandest. There are fifteen performing parts, which are divided into three choirs (no doubt meant to be placed in three different locations in St. Mark's), plus a single organ part that combines the roles of *basso continuo* and *basso seguente* in what was called the "basso generale" ("general bass"). The three choirs consist of distinct performing forces. At the top of the score is a choir of four parts (SATB), each labeled *voce* (voice), that are sung by vocal soloists. Next is a choir of four parts (SATB) labeled *cappella* (choir), sung by a vocal chorus. The third choir, at the bottom of the score, consists of instruments, which Gabrieli specifies: three cornetti on top, a *violino* in the middle (its range suggesting that it was of a size more like that of a modern viola), and two trombones on the bottom. Gabrieli creates a clear stylistic distinction between the vocal chorus and the instrumental ensemble, tasking the instrumentalists with many more rapid notes and scalar passages. The vocal soloists seem to occupy a middle ground, moving more rapidly than the choral parts and adopting some of the

Verse 1 begins more or less like a solo concerto or a piece of monody of the sort we will see later in this anthology (first in Vol 1-65). The soprano solo voice sings in speech-like rhythm supported by an accompanimental organ line in mm. 1–3. In mm. 4–5 it adopts a clearer duple-time feel, driving to a cadence on A. The chorus then responds in m. 6 with the word "Alleluia," its music creating a complete contrast, in both its homorhythmic texture and bouncy triple meter, with what the soloist has just sung. The soloist and choir alternate in rapid-fire Alleluias in mm. 6–10 before joining forces in a stately duple-meter Alleluia in mm. 10–12. The varied performing forces—soloist plus organ on the one hand, full choir on the other—thus enter separately and engage in dialogue with one another before finally and emphatically coming together. The whole process is repeated for the second verse, this time with a bass soloist played off against the choir. The bass's music in mm. 13–24 differs from what the soprano had sung at the opening, but its rapid-fire dialogue with the chorus (mm. 25–29) and their collective proclamation on "Alleluia" (mm. 29–31) are the same as they had been earlier. The Alleluias, therefore, function throughout the piece as a refrain, or, as Gabrieli would have called it, a *ritornello*.

After the soprano and bass soloists have had their turn dialoguing with the chorus, the choir of instrumentalists enters simultaneously with the cadential resolution in m. 31. What they play is marked *Sinfonia*, one of the terms used at the time for a purely instrumental composition, and in mm. 32–39 they display the articulations—dotted rhythms, sixteenth notes—that they, with their tongues and bows, can produce far more effectively than can singers. The two remaining vocal soloists—the alto and the tenor—join the instrumentalists for the third verse. Here is where the soloists' lines begin to approach the virtuosity of the instrumental parts, spinning out sixteenth notes as if in competition with the cornetti (mm. 57–61). The instrumentalists sit out the fourth verse, but the competition they had entered into with the vocalists in the third verse is now picked up by the soprano and bass soloists in mm. 68–94. The "Alleluia" ritornelli that follow the third and fourth verses (mm. 62–68 and 95–101) are by now predictable.

For the final verse, Gabrieli pulls out all the stops, so to speak. All three choirs sing together for the first time on the word "Deus" (mm. 102–103), which is further emphasized by the chromatic "madrigalian" harmony to which it is set—an F-major chord, a D-major chord, a

G-major chord, and an E-major chord in succession. The climax of the composition is reached when the vocal soloists revive their highest level of virtuosity on top of the mass of sonic texture on the word "aeternum" (mm. 115–118). The final ritornello maintains the tutti texture to the end, stating the final authentic cadence, with the cornetti soaring at the top of their range, twice for emphasis (mm. 125 and 127). A half rest by the full ensemble (m. 127) allows the cadential sonority to resound throughout the basilica before a massive plagal cadence (mm. 127 to the end) brings the entire composition to a close.

In ecclesiis benedicite Domino. Alleluia!	In the churches, bless the Lord. Alleluia!
In omni loco dominationis benedic anima mea Dominum. Alleluia!	In every place of his dominion, my soul, bless the Lord. Alleluia!
In Deo salutari meo et gloria mea, Deus, auxilium meum et spes mea in Deo est. Alleluia!	In God is my salvation and my glory, O God, and my aid and my hope is in God. Alleluia!
Deus noster, te invocamus, te laudamus, te adoramus. Libera nos, salva nos, vivifica nos. Alleluia!	Our God, we call on you, we praise you, we adore you. Free us, save us, give us life. Alleluia!
Deus adiutor noster in aeternum. Alleluia!	God is our helper in eternity. Alleluia!

55

Marco Cara
(ca. 1465–1525)

Mal un muta per effeto ("One cannot really change") (early sixteenth c.)

The *frottola* was a native Italian genre of part song from the beginning of the sixteenth century that most likely grew out of improvised practices of musical poetry recitation from the previous century. Formally speaking, it was very much like the trecento Italian ballata, which consisted of a number of strophic stanzas and a refrain, with music corresponding to part of the stanza, though the various repetition schemes encountered in the frottola are somewhat more complex and various than the AbbaA form seen in the ballata. And although the frottola also resembles the fifteenth-century chanson in its use of rigid formal schemes, its poetic and musical style was noticeably less lofty. The name was derived from the Latin word *frocta*, which meant a diverse group of trifling objects, and the term *frottola* might best be translated as "a trifling song."

The charming and simple frottola given here was included in Petrucci's seventh book of frottole (1507). The composer, Marco Cara, was one of the two leading frottolists (along with Bartolomeo Tromboncino, 1470 to after 1534) employed at the smallish but musically important court of Mantua in north-central Italy, which would later employ several prominent madrigalists, including Claudio Monteverdi (1567–1643). Everything about Cara's song suggests an origin in oral practice. Oral genres are formulaic genres, and the attractively lilting or dance-like rhythms in Cara's frottola are all stock formulas, common to dozens of frottole, that were originally devised for the musical recitation of poetry in the so-called *ottonario*, a popular eight-syllable trochaic pattern favored by Italian court poets and musicians. The text of *Mal un muta* consists of an eight-line stanza plus a two-line refrain with the rhyme scheme ababbccdDE. Cara's music consists of three basic phrases, *A* (mm. 1–3), *B* (mm. 4–6), and *C* (mm. 16–18), plus a decorative flourish *D* (mm. 31–33) for the end of the refrain, each of which ends with a cadence, made emphatic by a pitch repetition on the last trochee. These basic musical phrases are repeated to align with the rhyme scheme as follows:

Rhyme Scheme	Musical Form	Rhyme Scheme	Musical Form
a	**a** (mm. 1–3)	c	**c** (mm. 19–21)
b	**b** (mm. 4–6)	d	**a** (mm. 22–24)
a	**a** (mm. 7–9)	*Refrain*	*Refrain*
b	**b** (mm. 10–12)	D	**A** (mm. 25–27)
b	**b** (mm. 13–15)	E	**B** (mm. 28–30)
c	**c** (mm. 16–18)	(E)	**D** (mm. 31–33)

The original rhyme scheme of *ottonario* verse is ababbcca, and although Cara's poetry diverges somewhat from this, his music follows it exactly. One could easily imagine a performer extemporaneously applying Cara's formulaic phrases, set apart by their clear cadences, to different texts with similar verse patterns.

Cara's songs appear in Petrucci's publication as four-part polyphonic settings in correct, if rudimentary, counterpoint. This might seem to contradict the improvisatory hypothesis, because improvisation is generally a soloist's domain, but closer inspection of the music lessens the apparent contradiction. Only the cantus part is texted, and the other parts do not always have enough notes to accommodate the words, particularly at cadences. There is no reason to think that singers could not easily have adapted the lower parts to the words for a fully texted vocal rendition, but that does not seem to have been the primary medium for these songs. Rather, publishing them as part songs was just the most versatile or adaptable or presentable (or—perhaps more to the point—saleable) way of marketing them. They were almost certainly originally solo songs for virtuoso singers, to be accompanied by the lute or other instruments, which is why the edition of *Mal un muta* given here presents it as a solo line with chordal accompaniment.

Ogni cosa sua natura
Seguitar e di mestiero;
Non è arte nè misura
Che mai faci el falso vero;
Non è biancho quel ch'è nero,
Come chiar vede la vista;
Non si pente un alma trista
Cangie el tempo per suo aspecto.
   Mal un muta per effecto
   El suo proprio naturale.

Everything follows its own nature
And performs its own task.
Neither art nor science
Ever made what is false true.
What is white is not what is black,
As all can see clearly.
A sad soul does not repent,
Even as time marches on.
   One cannot really
   Change one's own nature.

L'armelin per non manchiarse	The ermine, to avoid being marked,
Pria al nemico vien in mano;	Comes into hand when faced with its enemy.
Mal la rana vile aparse	The cowardly frog is not
Lieta fori del paltano;	Happy outside its pond.
Chi è gentil, chi è vilano	Those who are good and those who are bad
Ala fin si manifesta;	Show themselves in the end.
Non arar la regal vesta	Do not pawn the royal robe,
Cangie el tempo per suo aspecto.	Even as time marches on.
Mal un muta per effecto	*One cannot really*
El suo proprio naturale.	*Change one's own nature.*
Orna ben di sella e freno	A bejeweled saddle and bridle
Lassi nel misero e vile,	Are miserable and vile shackles,
Chè per questo non è apieno	Which in this regard are not
Un caval acto e gentile;	Befitting a noble and kind horse.
Sta el porcho nel porcile,	A pig lives in a pigsty,
Gli convien che gli è el suo loco;	Which is its proper place.
Sempre da calore el focho	Fire always gives off heat,
Cangie el tempo per suo aspecto.	Even as time marches on.
Mal un muta per effecto	*One cannot really*
El suo proprio naturale	*Change one's own nature.*

56

Claudin de Sermisy
(ca. 1490–1562)

Tant que vivray ("As long as I live") (1528)

In the fifteenth century, the French-texted chanson had been an international genre of courtly song that always followed the *formes fixes*. Its stylized conventions were practiced by composers from anywhere in Europe, and it was performed in England, France, Germany, Italy, Spain, and beyond. The French chanson was thus nearly as ecumenical, or "travelable," a genre within its rarefied social domain as the Latin motet. The age of printing, however, brought with it a new type of chanson that was distinctly French and intended for a French audience. It was generally known as the *Parisian chanson*, and its best-known composer was Claudin de Sermisy, music director of the Royal Chapel of King François I (r. 1515–47). Claudin furnished the voracious presses of the printer Pierre Attaingnant (ca. 1494–1551/2) with dozens of chansons for publication as household music.

Attaingnant printed his first songbook in 1528, and Claudin's chansons account for the first eight selections plus another nine scattered later in the volume for a total of seventeen, more than half the total contents. *Tant que vivray*, the second item in the collection, sets a poem by Clément Marot (?1496–1544), the king's court poet, and has always been the classic example of the Parisian chanson because of its memorable tune and the beautiful manner in which it is harmonized. It was so well known and liked that it was reprinted many times as a four-voice chanson, an accompanied solo song, and a lute or keyboard intabulation. Its four-voice, homorhythmic, "popular" style is quite different from that of the fifteenth-century chanson. Perhaps this new style shows the influence of the Italian musicians who served François I after his conquest of Milan in 1515 (compare Marco Cara's frottola *Mal un muta*, Vol 1-55). Or perhaps it shows that court musicians, possibly spurred by the king's taste, began to copy the style of urban popular music. It is also possible that the print market and the chance to make a quick profit caused musicians to lower their sights (this could be called the "sell-out theory").

What is clear is that Claudin's musical setting closely follows the verse and stanza structure of the poem that it sets—part of a poetic idiom known as the *chanson rustique* ("country song"). Note that the first three lines of poetry are set to rhythmically identical and clearly demarcated phrases in mm. 1–4, 5–8, and 9–12. The long–short–short rhythm that opens the piece became an identifying tag, a sort of trademark that identified the Parisian chanson and some later

derivations from it. The second half of the piece is only slightly less formulaic in its setting of the second half of the poetic stanza, declaiming the syllables more rapidly to patter-song effect (mm. 13ff). The last five measures, which recapitulate the harmonic progression from mm. 1–2, constitute a *petite reprise* ("little refrain") that could be repeated if the performers so desired.

Tant que vivray en âge florissant	As long as I live able bodied,
Je serviray d'amours le roy puissant	I shall serve the almighty king of love
En fais en ditz en chansons et accords.	through deeds, words, songs, and harmonies.
Par plusieurs fois m'a tenu languissant	Many times he made me languish,
Mais après deuil m'a fait réjouissant	but after mourning, he let me rejoice,
Car j'ay l'amour de la belle au gent corps.	because I have the love of the beauty with the lovely body.
Son alliance, c'est ma fiance	Her alliance is my betrothal.
Son coeur et mien, le mien est sien,	Her heart is mine, mine is hers.
Fy de tristesse, vive liesse,	Away with sadness, long live joy,
Puisqu'en amour a tant de bien.	For in love there is so much goodness.
Quant je la veulx servir et honorer	When I wish to serve her and honor her,
Quand par escripts veux son nom décorer	When I wish to adorn her name with writings,
Quand je la veoy et visite souvent.	When I see her and visit her often,
Ses envieux n'en font que murmurer	Her enviers can do nothing but complain.
Mais notre amour n'en scauroit moins durer	But our love will not endure any less,
Autant ou plus en emporte le vent.	As long as the wind still blows.
Malgré envie, toute ma vie,	In spite of envy, all my life
Je l'aimeray et chanteray,	I will love her and sing:
C'est la première, c'est la dernière	This is the first, this is the last
Que j'ay servie et serviray.	That I have served and will serve.

text by Clément Marot

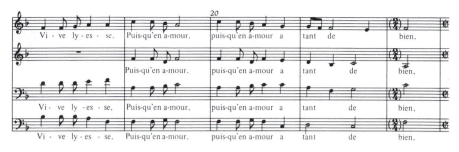

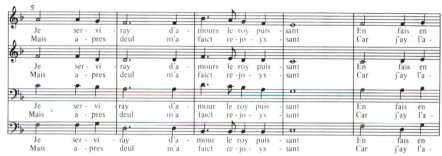

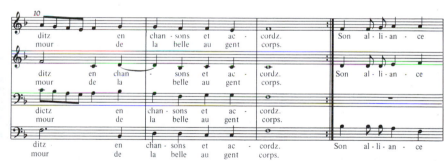

57

Orlando di Lasso (1532–94)

Four Compositions

Lasso was the last of the great peripatetic northerners. He was born in Mons, now an industrial town in the southern (French-speaking) part of Belgium, and was therefore baptized with the French name Roland de Lassus. By the time he was twelve years old, he was already a professional singer in the service of the Duke of Mantua and had adopted the Italian name—Orlando di Lasso—by which he remains best known. From 1556 until his death in 1594 he served the court of the Dukes of Bavaria in Munich, where he eventually rose to the position of Kapell-meister. By the 1570s he was the most famous musician in all of Europe. As a musician born in French-speaking lands, educated in Italy, and employed for most of his career in Germany, he was in his time the very model of the cosmopolitan musician. Lasso spent most of his career at a secular court, but his position required him to write vast quantities of religious music, and he always had a dual allegiance: to his patrons (with whom he was on terms of unprecedented familiarity and from whom he actually received a patent of nobility in his own right) and to his many publishers in numerous cities. The seventy-nine printed collections devoted entirely to his own music that were issued during his lifetime far surpass the total of any other sixteenth-century composer, and his music appeared in forty miscellaneous publications as well as numerous manuscripts produced exclusively for the Bavarian court. He composed music in every possible sacred and secular genre of his age: masses (almost all of them parody settings), motets (including many full calendrical cycles in various genres), and vernacular settings in all the languages he spoke.

From his vast and varied output, any selection at all would be unrepresentative. So without undue handwringing we will limit ourselves to what was most representative of the age rather than of the man. The following four examples forego his magnificent legacy of Catholic church music (where, after all, he had competitors and counterparts, such as Palestrina and Byrd, whose work we have already seen) and sample the full range of his secular work, which was unique. They include pieces in four different languages, all of which illustrates the chameleon-like Lasso's bent for witty mixtures and juxtapositions of styles.

a. *Je l'ayme bien* ("I love her") (1555)

Je l'ayme bien appeared in Lasso's very first publication, a miscellany published in Antwerp by Tylman Susato in 1555, when the composer was twenty-three years old. The collection contains various French and Italian vernacular compositions as well as motets. In this chanson Lasso elegantly reconciles the Parisian chanson style, by then a quarter century old, to the *ars perfecta*, by then reaching its zenith in Palestrina's early music. At the beginning and ending of Lasso's setting, a striking melody that Claudin de Sermisy might have given a rich chordal harmonization is instead given an elaborate imitative exposition (mm. 1–13 and 23 to the end). Yet notice that the imitation, though pervasive, is not nearly as systematic as Palestrina's. Whereas Palestrina's imitative subjects are replicated nearly exactly throughout a point of imitation, Lasso modifies his subjects at will in order to gain the greatest possible degree of harmonic flexibility. In the middle Lasso yields to a homorhythmic patter-song-like texture that had been a hallmark of the Parisian style and remained one in Lasso's time (mm. 13–18).

Je l'ayme bien et l'aymeray,	I love her and shall love her,
En ce propos suis et seray,	Thus I am and shall be,
Et demourray toute ma vie	And shall remain for all my life,
Et quoy que l'on me porte envie.	And no matter how much one should envy me,
Je l'ayme bien et laymeray.	I love her and shall love her.

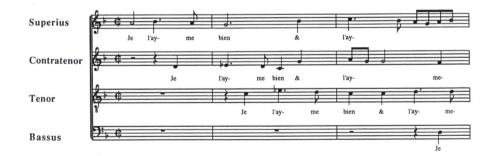

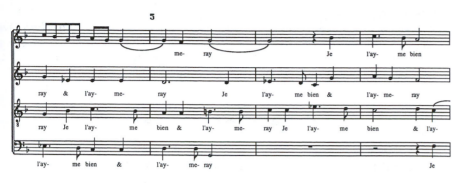

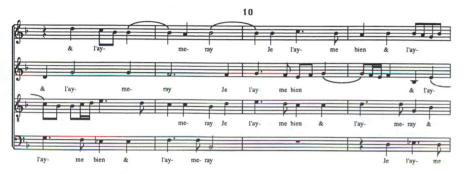

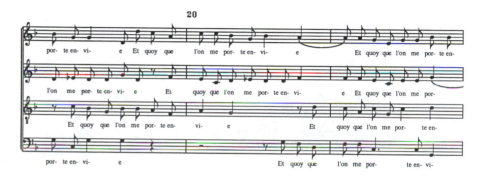

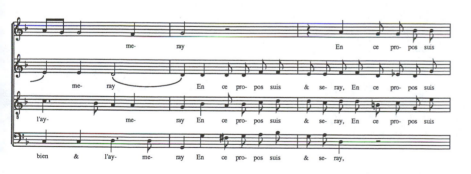

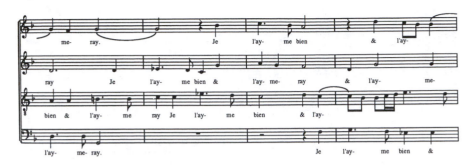

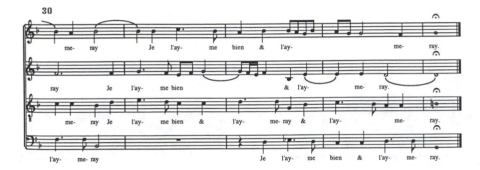

b. *Matona mia cara* ("My lady, my darling") (1581)

Matona mia cara, informally known as "the lansquenet's serenade," was printed rather late in Lasso's career, in a 1581 volume of "low style" Italian songs published in Paris. It is thought, however, to date from an earlier period, perhaps Lasso's earliest, when he accompanied his first employer, Ferrante Gonzaga of Mantua, on expeditions throughout Italy. Lansquenets were Swiss or German lance-bearing mercenaries (soldiers of fortune) who enlisted as infantrymen in foreign parts. The word itself is a jocular French corruption of *Landsknecht*, German for "trooper" or "foot soldier." There was also an Italian variant, *lanzichenecco*, and Italian armies such as Ferrante's were full of them. (The singer in Lasso's composition uses yet another variant, *Lantze*, which seems to lie somewhere between the German and Italian versions.)

No composition could better illustrate Lasso's witty cosmopolitanism than this one, a silly song written by a northerner in imitation of a German soldier's clumsy attempts to seduce a lady in Italian. It belongs to the genre of low Italian song called *villanella*, or town song, which featured strophic form and lighthearted refrains—a direct and deliberately debased descendant of the frottola, or "trifling song," of the early sixteenth century (see Marco Cara's *Mal un muta*, Vol 1-55). A villanella refrain is usually nonsensical or onomatopoetic; here "Don don don, diri-diri-don" (first statement in mm. 17–23) represents the lovesick lansquenet's feeble strummings

on his lute as he attempts to serenade his lady. The humor of the song lies in the soldier's mispronounced and ill-formed Italian. His d's become t's, and his v's become f's, as they do in English spoken by someone with a strong German accent. "Madonna, mia cara" ("My lady, my darling") thus becomes "Matona mia cara" (mm. 1–3 and 7–9), and "Io voglio cantare una canzone" ("I would like to sing a song") becomes "Mi follere canzon cantar" (mm. 4–6 and 10–13; in addition to the mispronunciation in this example, the infinitive is moved to the end of the phrase, as it would be in German). The soldier's increasingly confused language is full of double entendre and innuendo, reaching a peak in the last verse, which says that he will "stick it in all night, bang like a ram." The Italian verb "ficcar(e)" (m. 80) does indeed mean "stick it in," but it also bears a sonic resemblance to a certain German word—and its English cognate—that is too profane to print here and which is reflected in the increasingly urgent rhythms of the music.

Matona, mia cara,	My lady, my darling,
mi follere canzon	me vant to sing
Cantar sotto finestra,	song under vindow.
Lantze buon compagnon.	Soldier is good companion.
Don don don, diri-diri-don.	Dum dum dum, ditty-ditty dum.
Ti prego m'ascoltare,	Please listen to me,
Che mi cantar de bon,	zat me sing so good,
E mi ti foller bene,	and me luff you
Come greco e capon,	as much as vine and capon.
Don don don, diri-diri-don.	Dum dum dum, ditty-ditty dum.
Com' andar alle cazze,	Ven me go on hunt,
Cazzar con le falcon.	me hunt vis falcon.
Mi ti portar beccazze	Me bring you a voodcock
Grasse come rognon.	fat as a kidney.
Don don don, diri-diri-don.	Dum dum dum, ditty-ditty dum.
Si mi non saper dire	Yes, me don't know how to say
Tante belle rason,	many fine sings.
Petrarcha mi non saper,	Me don't know Petrarch
Ne fonte d'Helicon.	or ze fount of Helicon.
Don don don, diri-diri-don.	Dum dum dum, ditty-ditty dum.
Si ti mi foller bene,	Yes, you luff me,
Mi non esser poltron,	me not lazy.
Mi ficcar tutta notte,	Me stick it in all night,
Urtar come monton!	bang like a ram!
Don don don, diri-diri-don.	Dum dum dum, ditty-ditty dum.

c. *Audite nova* ("Hear the news") (1573)

Audite nova, a German *Lied*, is another humorous piece. It begins in the solemn manner of a motet but quickly shifts over to a preposterous tale about a dimwitted "farmer from Jackass-Church" and his honking goose, whose sound is faithfully reproduced by the choir ("gyri-gyri ga-ga Gans"). The song comes from a volume of miscellaneous items in various languages that Lasso published in Munich in 1573. The opening two words are in Latin and are set to a point of imitation following the standard procedure for sacred motets (mm. 1–5). But then the song abruptly breaks into a homorhythmic German patter song that more closely resembles the style of *Matona mia cara* or a Parisian chanson. The goose's "long, fat, thick, sturdy neck" is reflected in the longer note values of mm. 11–14, and the call to "rip it, pluck it, boil it, roast it, tear it, devour it" is intensified by the triplet rhythms in mm. 17–19, which also feature sharp (= *durus*, or "hard") accidentals. What at first sounds like a reverent devotional work is revealed to be a drinking song about revelry, a feast of roasted goose, and generous servings of good wine and beer.

Audite nova:	Hear the news:
Der Bawr von Eselskirchen,	The farmer from Eselskirchen
	(Jackass-Church),
der hat ein faiste ga-ga Gans,	he has a fat goo-goo goose.
das gyri-gyri ga-ga Gans,	The gaga-gaga goo-goo goose,
die hat ein langen, faisten, dicken,	it has a long, fat, thick,
weidelichen Hals.	sturdy neck.
Hab dirs, mein trauter Hans,	Take it, my trusty Hans,
rupff sie, zupf sie, seud sie, brat sie,	rip it, pluck it, boil it, roast it,
zreiss sie, friss sie!!!	tear it, devour it!!!
Das ist Sanct Martins Vögelein,	That is St. Martin's bird—
dem können wir nit feind seyn;	which we cannot disrespect.
Knecht Haintz, bring her ein guten Wein	Servant Heinz, bring us a good wine
und schenk uns dapfer ein!	and fill our glasses generously!
Lass umbher gahn in Gottes Nam,	Pass it around in God's name;
trincken wir gut Wein und Bier	let's drink good wine and beer
auff die gsotne Gans, auff die bratne Gans,	to the stewed goose, to the roasted goose,
auff die junge Gans,	to the young goose,
dass sie uns nit schaden mag.	that it do us no harm.

d. *Prophetiae Sibyllarum*: Prologue (ca. 1560)

In serious Latin settings, as in vernacular settings, there were genres in which Lasso stood virtually alone by virtue of his wit and intellectual elan. One of them was the setting of classical or classicistic texts, the latter being the work of humanist writers in imitation of the classics. His most adventurous work in this category was the *Prophetiae Sibyllarum* ("The sibylline prophecies"), published posthumously in 1600 but perhaps written as early as 1560. They were performed before King Charles IX of France, whom they astonished, in 1571.

The sibyls were women in antiquity who, in states of ecstasy, foretold future events, generally unpleasant ones. Over the formative years of the Christian religion, the tradition of the sibyls was assimilated to that of biblical prophecy, their words read increasingly as foretelling not natural disasters or the like but the coming of Christ and the Last Judgment (hence the reference to the sibyl in the sequence *Dies irae*, given in Vol 1-5b). In the fifteenth century, the number of sibyls was stabilized at twelve. They are best known today from Michelangelo's rendering of them on the ceiling of the Sistine Chapel. The twelve anonymous prophetic poems Lasso set to music appeared for the first time as a supplement to a 1481 Venetian edition of a treatise on the sibyls as prophets of Christ by Filippo Barbieri, the Inquisitor of Sicily. They were reprinted in Basel, Switzerland, in 1545, and that, presumably, is how they found their way to the composer.

These venerable quasi-pagan mystical texts as summarized by a Christian classicistic poet demand some sort of special musical treatment, and Lasso delivers it. Drawing on a strain of humanistic musical speculation that was just then emerging in Italy, Lasso adopts a style of extreme and tonally disorienting chromaticism, as he proudly proclaims in the three-line poetic prologue of his own contriving. In his setting of the prologue, Lasso couples the extreme chromaticism with stark homorhythm to create a vehemently declamatory texture that emphasizes the strange words and even stranger harmonies. The brash expository sweep by fifth and third relations from triadic harmonies on the extreme sharp side (as far as B major in m. 3) to as far flatward as E♭ major (m. 19) is hair-raising. This sort of extreme chromaticism would not be equaled until the end of the century in the Italian madrigal.

Carmina Chromatico, quae audis modulata tenore,	These songs proceed by chromatic progressions.
Haec sunt illa, quibus nostrae olim arcane salutis	They tell of how the twelve Sybils, one after the other,
Bissenae intrepido, cecinerunt ore sibyllae.	Once sang the hidden mysteries of our salvation.

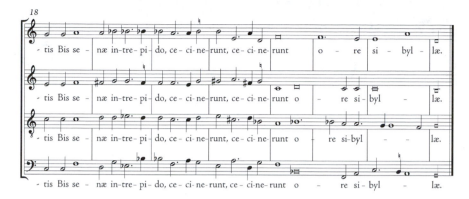

58

Jacques Arcadelt (1504/5–68)

Il bianco e dolce cigno ("The white and sweet swan") (1539)

Jacques Arcadelt, yet another in the long line of northern composers who sought employment in Italy, spent most of the 1530s and 1540s in Florence and Rome. His first book of madrigals, published for the first time in 1539, was the most frequently reprinted music book of the whole sixteenth century (it was printed some fifty-three times, the last in 1642!). *Il bianco e dolce cigno* was its first and best-known item. Many people knew the piece by heart, and countless composers emulated it. It may have been the most famous single piece of art music of the entire century. Like most madrigal poems, Arcadelt's text, composed by the Marquis of Vasto and governor-general of Milan Alfonso d'Avalos, is *inordinato,* meaning that it consists of a single stanza in lines of varying length, without any refrain or other obvious formal scheme. Nor does Arcadelt impose one in his music. This lack of an imposed formal scheme is in fact the principal difference between the madrigal and the earlier frottola. Composers of Arcadelt's generation tended to recite the poem fairly straightforwardly, mostly in approximate homorhythm, aiming at a general mood of gravity or charm—as Arcadelt does through most of this composition. But the poem of *Il bianco e dolce cigno* is built, in the manner of the revered poet Petrarch (1304–74), around a complex antithesis between the swan's sad death, at which it sings its "swan song," and the poet's happy "death" in love, at which he weeps. Arcadelt highlights this antithesis at two prominent points in the music using compositional procedures that had been available to composers of the past but that had never been used to such particularizing effect. His text setting would become the model for ever-more-adventurous experiments in madrigalistic text setting over the remainder of the sixteenth century.

The first highly affective word, "piangendo" ("weeping"), is set to the first chromatic harmony in mm. 6–7, which is repeated in mm. 11–12 as part of a wholesale (though differently voiced) repetition of the entire phrase (mm. 5–10 and 10–15). There is nothing intrinsically sad or unusual about the E♭ major chord on "piangendo," but both times that the chord is stated it stands out against the diatonic norm of the F-mode piece, and by standing out it creates a weepy effect. The end of the composition highlights the poem's antithesis in an even more ingenious way, using perhaps the most ordinary and usually unexpressive device in sixteenth-century composition: imitation. Arcadelt repeats the last line of text, "di mille morte il di . . ." ("a

thousand deaths a day . . . ," mm. 34–47), three times to a bountiful point of imitation that, like the E♭ major chord on "piangendo," stands out from the homorhythmic norm of the piece and becomes "marked." The numerous statements of the imitative subject—which persist through an authentic cadence (m. 39) and a repeated phrase (mm. 35–39 and 40–43)—underscore a charming double entendre: *lo piccolo morte* ("the little death") was in Italian of the time a euphemism for sexual climax. In harmonic terms, the "thousand deaths" resolve to a final authentic cadence in m. 43 and are brought gently to repose over an extended plagal cadence in the last four measures.

Il bianco e dolce cigno	The white and sweet swan
Cantando more. Et io	dies singing. And I,
Piangendo giung' al fin del viver mio.	weeping, come to the end of my life.
Stran'e diversa sorte,	Strange and different fates,
Ch'ei more sconsolato,	that it dies disconsolate,
Et io moro beato,	and I die happy,
Morte che nel morire,	a death that in dying
M'empie di gioia tutt'e di desire.	fills me fully with joy and with desire.
Se nel morir' altro dolor non sento,	If when I die I feel no other pain,
Di mille mort'il di sarei contento.	then a thousand deaths a day I would be content to die.

text by Alfonso d'Avalos

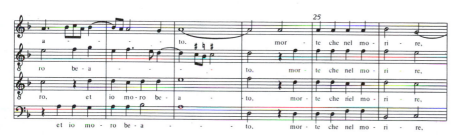

59

Cipriano de Rore
(1515/16–65)

Da le belle contrade d'oriente ("From the fair regions of the east") (1566)

We begin to see serious infractions against the contrapuntal and harmonic rules of the *ars perfecta* in works composed in the 1560s by Cipriano de Rore, who preceded Zarlino as *maestro di cappella* at St. Mark's in Venice and spent much of the later part of his career at the court of Ferrara in northern Italy. Rore, a northerner, was unusual among his contemporaries for the enthusiasm with which he followed the literary premises of the madrigal into uncharted musical terrain—especially in his use of chromaticism. *Da le belle contrade d'oriente* comes from his fifth and last book of madrigals, published posthumously in 1566. As in Arcadelt's *Il bianco e dolce cigno* (Vol 1-58), a sustained antithesis lies at the heart of the poem being set: Here it is the male lover's recollection of physical pleasures at the beginning and end set against his female beloved's outpouring of anguish in the middle, which she expresses in "direct discourse" (actual quoted speech). Rore expresses the antithesis with unprecedented, even violent, harmonic contrast. The madrigal opens with a rather conventional point of imitation (mm. 1–5), but after that the narrative portions at the beginning and end of the madrigal feature delightfully descriptive effects: rising scalar passages to represent the rising morning star ("Chiara e lieta . . . ," mm. 5–9); rocking rhythms where the lover recounts the bliss that he enjoyed in his lover's arms ("fruiva in braccio . . . ," mm. 11–13); and tightly wound imitative polyphony where the intertwining of the lovers' limbs is compared with the tangled growth of ivy vines or acanthus leaves ("Iterando gl'amplessi in tanti nodi . . . ," mm. 62–67).

The middle section (mm. 26–56) adopts a completely different approach when setting the direct speech of the disconsolate woman. Here the representation is no easy matter of analogy or metaphor—though it is sometimes that too, as when the soprano voice sings alone on the words "sola mi lasci" ("you leave me alone," mm. 33–34). The woman's sighs and sobs become especially powerful when she blurts out a harmonically adventurous and rhythmically syncopated curse upon Eros ("Ahi, crudo Amor . . . ," mm. 41–56). In keeping with the agonized mood, the soprano part (corresponding in range to the lady's voice) makes a direct "forbidden" progression through a "minor semitone" from C♯ in m. 40 (as the third of an A-major triad) to C natural in m. 41 (as root of a C-minor triad). This chromatic construction, though highly calculated, is nevertheless made to resemble a spontaneous outburst. And after cursing Eros over a

C-minor triad, the top voice continues with mostly diatonic stepwise motion that nevertheless moves downward through an A♭ in m. 47 to an F in m. 48, harmonized with a D♭ (!) triad on the words "your pleasures" ("le tue dolcezze"). This move to "soft" (*mollis*) flat harmonies could hardly create a greater harmonic contrast with her "ardent sigh" ("sospir ardente") on the "hard" (*durus*, or sharp) A-major triad that had sounded just eight measures earlier.

Rore's expression of a single subject's extreme personal feeling by the use of extreme chromatic excursions is quite novel and, judged according to the aims of the *ars perfecta*, full of exaggeration and distortion. But his harmonies sound tame in comparison to those of the last generation of madrigalists, who worked around the turn of the seventeenth century and offered the *ars perfecta* its final challenge in the "a cappella" polyphonic idiom.

Da le belle contrade d'oriente	From the fair regions of the east,
Chiara e lieta s'ergea Ciprigna, et io	Clear and joyful rose the morning star, and I
Fruiva in braccio al divin idol mio	was enjoying, in the arms of my divine idol,
Quel piacer che non cape humana mente	That pleasure that the human mind does not grasp,
Quando sentii dopo un sospir ardente:	When I heard, after an ardent sigh:
"Speranza del mio cor, dolce desio,	"Hope of my heart, sweet desire,
T'en vai, haimè, sola mi lasci, adio.	You go, alas! You leave me alone! Farewell!
Che sarà qui di me scura e dolente?	What will become of me here, gloomy and sad?
Ahi crudo Amor, ben son dubbiose e corte	Alas, cruel love, how false and brief
Le tue dolcezze, poi ch'ancor ti godi	Are your pleasures, for it even pleases you
Che l'estremo piacer finisca in pianto."	That the greatest pleasure should end in tears."
Nè potendo dir più, cinseme forte	Unable to say more, she held me tightly,
Iterando gl'amplessi in tanti nodi,	Repeating her embraces in entwinings
Che giamai ne fer più l'edra o l'acanto.	More than ivy or acanthus ever made.

RISM 1566[17], No. 2

60

Luca Marenzio
(ca. 1554–99)

Solo e pensoso ("Alone and thoughtful") (1599)

The sixteenth-century madrigal had been brought to maturity by northerners, but in its later stages the genre reached its greatest heights of chromaticism and expressive text setting at the hands of Italian-born composers. The first great madrigalist to have been born in Italy was Luca Marenzio, who spent most of his career in Rome, with short forays in other Italian centers and, at the end of his rather short life, at the royal court of Poland. The madrigal *Solo e pensoso*, from his ninth and last book, published in 1599, has for its text a famous sonnet by Petrarch, one that was frequently set by madrigalists.

Marenzio's setting of the opening couplet, the most radical part of his composition, illustrates an ingenious way of "painting" a text musically. The text describes wandering through deserted fields thoughtfully, with "slow and heavy steps," and the steady quarter-note motion in the imitative accompanying voices suggests the steps pretty clearly. But they are accompanying something much more novel: a soprano voice moving in steady whole notes through a complete chromatic scale—possibly the first in the history of European art music. In mm. 1–24 it ascends through fifteen semitonal progressions, covering more than an octave, and descends through eight. The soprano's half steps are, moreover, unpredictably treated as diatonic or chromatic, as sixteenth-century terminology would have it. In modern terms, and perhaps somewhat oversimply, the diatonic semitone (for example, B–C or C♯–D) is the one that progresses from one scale degree to another (every diatonic scale has two), and the chromatic semitone (for example, B♭–B or C–C♯) is the one that inflects a single degree and therefore cannot be found in any diatonic scale. Using chromatic semitones is obviously incompatible with modal integrity, though it would be a gross overstatement to call madrigalistic chromaticism "atonal," as some have done. Marenzio takes care to bring things into tonal focus at the end of the first couplet by extending the last note long enough to sustain a normal authentic cadence on F in m. 24. But the overt lack of tonal focus as the soprano sings up and down its unpredictable chromatic scale provides a musical analogy for the narrator's plodding and uncertain steps through deserted fields.

The remainder of the piece proceeds somewhat less radically, but it continues to create, with more conventional techniques, an extreme of textural contrast beyond anything in the works of earlier madrigalists. Such extremes, though new to music, match the abundant contrasting imagery in Petrarch's poem. To cite just one example from Marenzio's madrigal, when the poet writes that he can find no other shield that might protect him, bold homorhythmic declamation represents the shield ("altro schermo," mm. 44–47), while a sparsely textured and rambling point of imitation without a proper cadence represents his failure to find it ("non trovo . . . ," mm. 48–55).

Solo e pensoso i più deserti campi	Alone and thoughtful I pace the most deserted fields
Vo misurando a passi tardi e lenti,	with slow and heavy steps,
E gl'occhi porto per fuggir intenti	and I glance around so as to flee
Dove vestiggio human l'arena stampi.	from where human imprint leaves its trace.
Altro schermo non trovo che mi scampi	I find no other shield that might protect me
Dal manifesto accorger de le genti;	from the open attention of other people;
Perché ne gl'atti d'allegrezza spenti	for in my deeds bereft of happiness,
Di fuor si legge com'io dentr'avampi.	from outside one can tell how I burn from within.
Si ch'io mi cred'homai che monti e piagge	So that by now I think that the mountains, the shores,
E fiumi e selve sappian di che tempre	the rivers and the woods know the temper of my life,
Sia la mia vita, ch'è celata altrui.	which is hidden from others.
Ma pur sì aspre vie né sì selvagge	But now I know not how to seek paths
Cercar non so, ch'Amor non venga sempre	harsh or savage enough that Love does not
Ragionando con meco, et io con lui.	always come discoursing with me and I with him.

Text by Petrarch

(Trans. Kathryn Bosi)

223

61

Claudio Monteverdi (1567–1643)

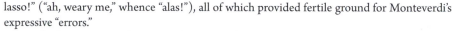

Cruda Amarilli ("Cruel Amaryllis") (1605)

Monteverdi spent most of his very long career in Mantua (1590–1613) and Venice (1613–43). He made groundbreaking contributions to the Italian madrigal as well as to new seventeenth-century genres that we will encounter later in this anthology. His madrigals, which he composed early in his career but late in the history of the genre, received an especially hostile reaction from conservative factions, who saw his rhetorical techniques and the dissonances they produced as a threat to the *ars perfecta*. *Cruda Amarilli* was published in his fifth book of madrigals in 1605, but it had been well known in learned musical circles at least as far back as 1600, when it was pointedly attacked by Giovanni Maria Artusi (1540–1613), a pupil of Zarlino and defender of his teacher's *ars perfecta*, in a treatise titled *L'Artusi, overo Delle imperfettioni della moderna musica* ("Artusi's Book Concerning the Imperfections of Modern Music").

In his critique of *Cruda Amarilli*, Artusi includes seven excerpts from the madrigal as musical examples, each of which breaks one or more of the rules of counterpoint as described by Zarlino and practiced by Willaert, Palestrina, and others. The most famous infraction, in the first excerpt, is a skip in m. 13 in the most exposed voice, the soprano, from an A that enters as a dissonance against the bass G to an F that is also a dissonance: two sins at a single stroke. But what Artusi leaves out of his musical quotations, and what he fails to consider in this and all the other passages from Monteverdi's madrigal that he criticizes, is precisely what motivated the offenses against Zarlino's rules of counterpoint: the text. The all-determining text of *Cruda Amarilli*, like those of countless other madrigals, is an excerpt from *Il Pastor Fido* ("The Faithful Shepherd"), a play by the contemporary courtly poet Giovanni Battista Guarini (1538–1612). A classic of the "pastoral" mode, in which the purity and simplicity of shepherd life is implicitly contrasted with the corruption and the artificiality of court and city, Guarini's "tragicomic" play (i.e., a play about the sufferings of "low" characters) was one of the most famous Italian poems of the sixteenth century. What Monteverdi and other madrigal composers found so conducive to vivid musical setting in Guarini's poetry was a new "affective" style that depicted the *affetti*, or sentiments, of suffering lovers. In addition to pointed words, they used sighs and nonverbal outpourings like "ohimè!" ("oh me oh my!"), "ahi!" ("ah!"), or its more elaborate cousin "ahi lasso!" ("ah, weary me," whence "alas!"), all of which provided fertile ground for Monteverdi's expressive "errors."

Indeed, every example in Artusi's treatise of Monteverdi's "improper" counterpoint is inspired precisely by Guarini's text. In m. 19, the tenor's F is dissonant against the bass, but it sets the words "ahi lasso!" An improperly prepared dissonance in m. 21 and the chain of harsh suspensions that follows set the word "amaramente" ("bitterly"). The Bs in mm. 36 and 38, dissonant against the bass's C, describe the "deaf asp" ("l'aspido sordo"). The forbidden sonority in m. 41—equivalent to a dominant-seventh chord in inversion, which in later centuries would cease to be forbidden—represents fierceness ("fera"). And, finally, the unprepared dissonances in mm. 53–54 on the text "t'offendo" ("I offend you") were designed precisely to offend the proponents of the *ars perfecta*, whose beloved counterpoint lacked the means to depict the vivid *affetti* of Guarini's poem.

Monteverdi did not take Artusi's charges idly. He addressed them in a letter included at the beginning of his fifth book of madrigals, in which he called Zarlino's *ars perfecta* the *prima pratica* ("first practice"), while his own music belonged to a *seconda pratica* ("second practice"). Monteverdi did not fully explain what he meant by *seconda pratica*, but in the preface to a collection he published in 1607, his brother Giulio Cesare Monteverdi explained that for practitioners of the *prima pratica*, harmony was the mistress and text the servant, whereas in Monteverdi's *seconda pratica* text was the mistress and harmony the servant. With music subservient to the words, the composer had license to break the established contrapuntal rules in the service of dramatic expression of the text. Artusi had disagreed with Monteverdi's premise—that's why he left out Monteverdi's text in his treatise—but the argument hardly turns on this philosophical dispute, for ultimately Monteverdi's greatest persuasiveness was offered not by his reasoning but by the rhetorical excellence of *Cruda Amarilli* and other madrigals that challenged all that Artusi held dear.

Cruda Amarilli che col nome ancora	Cruel Amaryllis, who, even with your name,
D'amar ahi lasso! amaramente insegni.	teach, alas!, to love bitterly.
Amarilli del candido ligustro,	Amaryllis, than the white privet
Più candida e più bella,	whiter and more beautiful,
Ma dell'aspido sordo	but than the deaf asp
E più sorda e più fera e più fugace.	deafer and fiercer and more fleeting.
Poi che col dir t'offendo	Since by speaking I offend you,
I mi morrò tacendo.	I shall die silently.

text by Giovanni Battista Guarini

62

Carlo Gesualdo
(ca. 1561–1613)

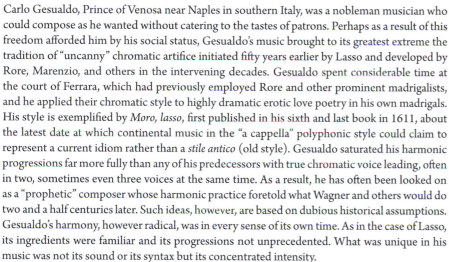

Moro, lasso ("I shall die, O miserable me") (1611)

Carlo Gesualdo, Prince of Venosa near Naples in southern Italy, was a nobleman musician who could compose as he wanted without catering to the tastes of patrons. Perhaps as a result of this freedom afforded him by his social status, Gesualdo's music brought to its greatest extreme the tradition of "uncanny" chromatic artifice initiated fifty years earlier by Lasso and developed by Rore, Marenzio, and others in the intervening decades. Gesualdo spent considerable time at the court of Ferrara, which had previously employed Rore and other prominent madrigalists, and he applied their chromatic style to highly dramatic erotic love poetry in his own madrigals. His style is exemplified by *Moro, lasso*, first published in his sixth and last book in 1611, about the latest date at which continental music in the "a cappella" polyphonic style could claim to represent a current idiom rather than a *stile antico* (old style). Gesualdo saturated his harmonic progressions far more fully than any of his predecessors with true chromatic voice leading, often in two, sometimes even three voices at the same time. As a result, he has often been looked on as a "prophetic" composer whose harmonic practice foretold what Wagner and others would do two and a half centuries later. Such ideas, however, are based on dubious historical assumptions. Gesualdo's harmony, however radical, was in every sense of its own time. As in the case of Lasso, its ingredients were familiar and its progressions not unprecedented. What was unique in his music was not its sound or its syntax but its concentrated intensity.

Within the terms of sixteenth-century style, Gesualdo's greatest audacities are not harmonic per se, but consist, rather, in the frequent pauses that disrupt the continuity of his lines, often followed by harmonically disconnected resumptions that coincide with the affective or downright suggestive exclamations of desire, such as "ahi!" (e.g., mm. 10, 25, and 35–36). The opening line of the poem, "I shall die, O miserable me, in my suffering" (mm. 1–3), is set to good old homorhythm, but in an extremely low register and with as much chromatic voice leading as possible, all to represent the misery and suffering in the text. The second line, "and she who give me life . . ." (mm. 3–10), is set to a point of imitation of the sort that we have seen countless times before, but now in a strikingly high register and with more jagged and angular rhythms (mm. 3–10) that create the maximum possible contrast between what is being represented here ("life") and what had come before ("death"). These starkly contrasting opening lines set the stage for the remainder of

the piece, in which Gesualdo's fragmented, discombobulated music completely devours the poem in the course of realizing its *affetti*, turning it into what often sounds like fairly inarticulate prose. But it does so in the name of linguistic realism, betokening emotional realism and even stark physiological realism that might make some uncomfortable when listening to this music in public. The tradition of expressive chromaticism had no farther to go.

Moro, lasso, al mio duolo	I shall die, O miserable me, in my suffering,
E chi me puo dar vita,	and the one who could give me life,
Ahi, che m'ancide	alas, kills me and is unwilling
e non vuol dar mi aita!	to give me aid.
O dolorosa sorte,	O painful fate!
Chi dar vita me puo,	The one who could give me life,
ahi, mi da morte!	alas, gives me death.

235

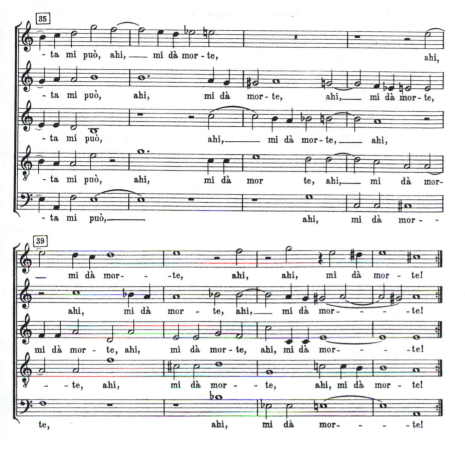

63

John Dowland
(1563–1626)

Flow My Tears (1600)

Both the music printing business and the cultivation of vernacular art music had a relatively slow start in England. Little of the English song literature that circulated in manuscript during the sixteenth century was set for vocal ensembles, as the madrigal was in Italy. Rather, it consisted of instrumentally accompanied solo "ayres," either with "consorts" of viols or with lute as backup. Whether for viols or for lute, the accompaniments were often contrapuntally intricate, the texts melancholy, and the style basically motet-like, but respectful of the structure of the poem in a way that the madrigal was not.

The most important sixteenth-century composer of English verse settings untouched by madrigalian influence was the lutenist John Dowland, who, like William Byrd, was a recusant Catholic. Upon being refused the post of lutenist to the court of Elizabeth I in 1594 (because of religious discrimination, he claimed), he went abroad and spent the early years of the seventeenth century at various German and Danish courts, returning to England in 1609 and finally securing appointment as one of the King's Lutes at the court of James I in 1612. Dowland was a supreme virtuoso of his instrument and could write for it in a strict contrapuntal style. For this reason, he found it easy to arrange his lute ayres for publication as vocal ensemble works after the madrigal had caught on in England (for an example of the English madrigal, see Vol 1-64). But his work belongs to the earlier tradition, a tradition that goes back (like most pre-madrigalian continental vernacular genres) to the strophic dance song.

Most of Dowland's ayres are cast in the form of one of the two main ballroom dances of Elizabeth's time: the stately duple-metered pavan and the lively triple-metered galliard, with which the pavan was often paired. Both pavan and galliard consisted formally of three repeated "strains" or cadenced sections, the cadence (or half cadence) of the middle strain being on a contrasting harmony. *Flow My Tears* is the most famous of all pavans. Although shown here as a lute ayre from his *Second Book of Ayres* (1600), Dowland also arranged it for solo lute and transcribed it for a five-part consort of viols without voice under the title "The Lachrymae Pavan" (*lachrimae* being Latin for "tears"). Its three strains (mm. 1–7, 8–15, and 16–21) follow the tonal template outlined above, with cadences on A minor, E major (a half cadence), and A minor, respectively. The first two strains have different text for the musical repetition,

whereas the third repeats its text along with the music. The melancholy tone of the verse is typical of the lute ayre tradition as a whole and of Dowland's output in particular. He was as well known for his ability to communicate sadness in music as for his virtuosity on his instrument.

Lute music is written in tablature, a form of notation that indicates where the performer should place his hands, rather than abstract pitches (the second and third staves in the score are a modern transcription for piano of Dowland's original lute part, shown below them). Dowland's lute had seven courses (a course is either a single string or a double string played as if it were one), pitched g–d–a–F–C–G–DD from top to bottom. The top line of the staff indicates the highest-pitched course, the second line the second highest, and so on through the seventh course, which is shown below the staff on the few occasions it is used. The letter *a* indicates that the course is to be played open, *b* that its first fret is to be depressed, *c* its second fret, and so on. Rhythms are indicated with stems and beams above the staff, showing when a note is to be struck but not when it is to be released. The performer must therefore infer release points from the harmonic context, although this is usually not critical because the lute is not capable of sustaining notes for long—thus the rapid passagework that often fills in long-sustained harmonies.

Flow, my tears, fall from your springs!
Exiled for ever let me mourn;
Where night's black bird her sad infamy sings,
There let me live forlorn.

Down, vain lights, shine you no more!
No nights are dark enough for those
That in despair their lost fortunes deplore.
Light doth but shame disclose.

Never may my woes be relieved,
Since pity is fled;
And tears and sighs and groans my weary days
Of all joys have deprived.

From the highest spire of contentment
My fortune is thrown;
And fear and grief and pain for my deserts
Are my hopes, since hope is gone.

Hark! you shadows that in darkness dwell,
Learn to contemn light.
Happy, happy they that in hell
Feel not the world's despite.

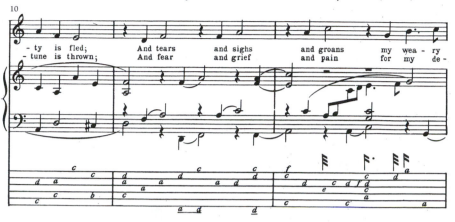

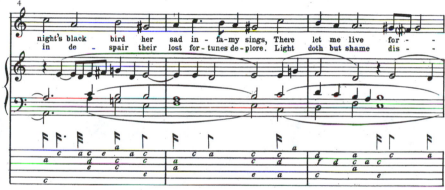

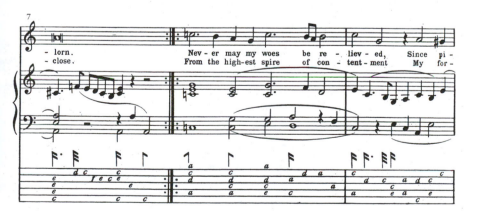

dwell, Learn to con-temn light.

Hap – py, hap – py they

that in hell Feel not the world's de – – spite.

64

Thomas Weelkes
(1576–1623)

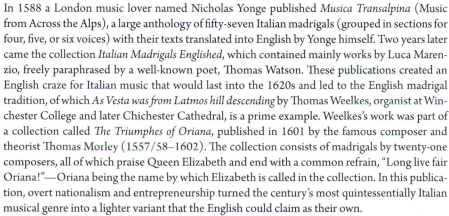

As Vesta was from Latmos hill descending (1601)

In 1588 a London music lover named Nicholas Yonge published *Musica Transalpina* (Music from Across the Alps), a large anthology of fifty-seven Italian madrigals (grouped in sections for four, five, or six voices) with their texts translated into English by Yonge himself. Two years later came the collection *Italian Madrigals Englished*, which contained mainly works by Luca Marenzio, freely paraphrased by a well-known poet, Thomas Watson. These publications created an English craze for Italian music that would last into the 1620s and led to the English madrigal tradition, of which *As Vesta was from Latmos hill descending* by Thomas Weelkes, organist at Winchester College and later Chichester Cathedral, is a prime example. Weelkes's work was part of a collection called *The Triumphes of Oriana*, published in 1601 by the famous composer and theorist Thomas Morley (1557/58–1602). The collection consists of madrigals by twenty-one composers, all of which praise Queen Elizabeth and end with a common refrain, "Long live fair Oriana!"—Oriana being the name by which Elizabeth is called in the collection. In this publication, overt nationalism and entrepreneurship turned the century's most quintessentially Italian musical genre into a lighter variant that the English could claim as their own.

The English madrigalists composed with much less emotional intensity than the Italians and referred to sex only with jocular intent. In their hands, therefore, what had fueled moments of extreme seriousness in Italian madrigals led merely to lighthearted diversions. There is also generally far less interest in chromaticism among the English than among the Italians, with the focus instead on overt and exaggerated text painting, examples of which are often called *madrigalisms*. Weelkes's text describes the goddess Vesta (goddess of hearth and home) descending from Mount Latmos and seeing a Virgin Queen (Elizabeth) ascending with the all the shepherds and their flocks to take her place. Then the Vestal Virgins ("Diana's Darlings") run to join the Queen, and all the shepherds and Virgins sing together, "Long Live Fair Oriana!" There is ample opportunity here for madrigalism, and Weelkes does not disappoint.

At the very beginning of the piece, "Latmos hill" is sung to a rising figure that reaches a high G in the soprano (m. 4). The word "descending" is then set to descending musical lines (mm. 4–9), and "ascending" to equally obvious—and amply repeated—ascending lines (mm. 12–22). Diana's darlings come running down, again to descending figures (mm. 36–46), first "two by two," sung by a duet (mm. 48–49), then "three by three," sung by a trio (mm. 50–51), and finally all "together," sung

by the full choral complement (m. 52). The goddess is left "all alone" in the unaccompanied soprano voice in mm. 56–57, and eventually the whole ensemble proclaims "Long live fair Oriana" to a point of imitation that is extended to the point of ridiculousness (mm. 79–114). Each voice states the imitative subject many times, and the bass states it twice in augmentation, first in absurdly long notes in mm. 83–99 and then up a fifth and in merely very long notes in mm. 102–108. The subtle turns of the Italian madrigal are absent, and the message could not be less nuanced: Long live the Queen!

> As Vesta was from Latmos hill descending,
> She spied a maiden Queen the same ascending,
> Attended on by all the shepherds' swain,
> To whom Diana's darlings came running down amain,
> First two by two, then three by three together,
> Leaving their Goddess all alone, hasted thither,
> And mingling with the shepherds of her train,
> With mirthful tunes her presence entertain.
> Then sang the shepherds and Nymphs of Diana:
> "Long live fair Oriana."

* 'and' in both editions.

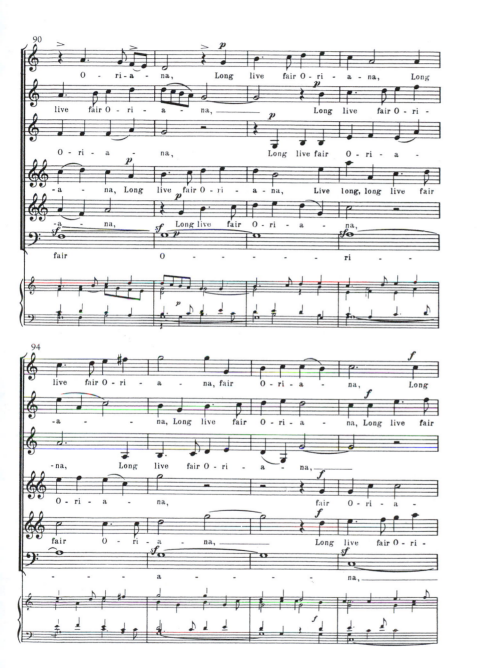

65

Giulio Caccini
(1551–1618)

Le nuove musiche: *Amarilli, mia bella* ("Amaryllis, my beautiful one") (1602)

Giulio Caccini's *Amarilli, mia bella*, likely composed in the 1580s, is a setting for solo voice and basso continuo of a madrigal by Alessandro Guarini (ca. 1565–1636), son of the celebrated poet Giambattista (1538–1612). In lines 1–3 of the text, the poetic speaker questions Amaryllis, asking her if she does not believe that she is his true love. The delivery of that question is twice delayed, by a short qualifier in line 1 ("my beautiful one") and a long one in line 2 ("my heart's sweet desire"). The remainder of the poem is more insistent, lines 4–6 each beginning with an imperative ("Believe . . . ," "take . . . ," "open . . ."), the final line literally showing what Amaryllis would find were she to follow said commands, the phrase "Amaryllis is my love" written upon the speaker's heart. The striking conclusion, in which the opening interrogative is restated as a simple declarative sentence—the only one in the poem—caps the increasing urgency of the last four lines.

In the preface to *Le nuove musiche* Caccini claimed to have forged a style that allowed one "almost to speak in music" and to have achieved "the imitation of the words' conceits." The means by which he did so were in part negative: Avoid contrapuntal complexity, and, if musical speech required it, renounce orthodox dissonance treatment. This latter Caccini characterized as "a certain noble nonchalance [*sprezzatura*] in song." Later in the preface he described this nonchalance a bit differently, as short notes to be performed "without submitting oneself to strict time," all the better to mimic speech and to capture the sense of the words. Finally, though he did not say so, Caccini avoided obvious madrigalisms: The word *strale* ("arrow"), which might have led a sixteenth-century composer to suggest its potential motion in rapid rhythms, is here set as one might declaim it, to a pair of half notes in m. 16 and again in m. 33. Those madrigalisms he did deploy are more subtle, such as the voice's descending leap of a diminished fourth (m. 2), a common symbol of pain (here, amorous languor occasioned by physical beauty), and the basso continuo's E♭ under the word *dolce* (m. 6), flatted notes a no less common symbol of sweetness.

For Caccini, though, the principal means for moving emotion was a positive one. An "exclamation" (*esclamazione*), a decrescendo followed by a crescendo, was to be applied to the long initial note—a dotted half or dotted quarter—of a melodic descent. He laced his music, including *Amarilli, mia bella*, with gestures that call for them. Measures 1–10 and 11–27 (the latter repeated in mm. 28–44), the music for the poem's two principal sections, both begin in this way, their exclamations nicely complementing the call of Amaryllis's name in line 1 (*Amarilli*) and the imperative (the command that she *Credilo*, "believe") in line 4. In the latter section Caccini further unites sound and sense by deploying exclamations for the succeeding imperatives in mm. 15/32 (*Prendi*, "take") and 17/34 (*aprimi*, "open"). For the last and most urgent of these commands he gives the voice its first high D since m. 7, and from there he launches the most wide-ranging phrase in the piece, a descent that ends an octave lower in m. 20/37. Caccini also makes liberal use of short rhythms throughout the three imperative phrases, thus allowing for the speech-like nonchalance that he also prized.

Heightened speech was not the only means by which Caccini sought to move his listeners. Melismas permeate the music for the final line of the poem (mm. 21/38 and 23/40) and after the repeat (mm. 45–47). That they appear here and nowhere else in the piece bears witness to Caccini's concern—some might say obsession—with their judicious use. Properly formed and placed, ornaments were "effects of that grace, which is most sought after in order to sing well." Indeed, Caccini published *Le nuove musiche* in part to restrain his colleagues' excesses, to establish a correct performing text, and to advise on proper embellishment. Thus, for example, the ornaments in *Amarilli, mia bella* all fall on accented syllables ("A-ma-*ril*-li," and "a-*mo*-re"), the only place Caccini deemed them permissible. They also make considerable use of dotted rhythms, which he held to be more graceful than unchanging equal values. Finally, the repeated dotted figure in the first half of m. 47 gives rise to a trill-like "restriking of the throat" (*ribattuta di gola*), an effect he found especially powerful.

The big finish that Caccini provides is of course a boon to singers, but it too is attentive to Guarini's poem. As we have seen, the text ends with a climax of its own, a simple declaration of love after six lines of amorous sophistry. Out of this well-wrought dialectic—music becoming more difficult as its verse becomes less so—tension grows. "Amarilli" is declaimed afresh in m. 20, the longest note falling on its third syllable rather the first syllable, as in m. 1, a change that underscores the word's changed case, nominative instead of vocative. Its repeated intonations, however, delay the arrival of the predicate, and with it the resolution of the poem: What will be written on the speaker's heart? "Amaryllis . . . Amaryllis . . . Amaryllis . . . is my love."

In addition to its novel text-setting practices, *Amarilli, mia bella* is notable for being among the first published works to include figured bass—numbers that indicate intervals to be sounded above the basso continuo. A note without figures generally takes a third and a fifth, a root-position triad in the language of latter-day harmonic analysis. The number 6, as in m. 1, beat 3, and m. 2, beat 4, indicates a third and a sixth above the bass, a first-inversion triad to subsequent centuries. Figured bass was also used to indicate voice leading. The "11 ♯10" in m. 3 means that half-note G followed by quarter-note F♯ are to be played over the first two Ds in the bass, a 4–3 suspension that delays the resolution of the Phrygian cadence until the third beat of m. 3 (in later practice, the figures "4 ♯3" or "4 ♯" would be used; composers of Caccini's time used the larger numbers to designate register precisely). Caccini uses 4–3 suspensions to prepare perfect authentic cadences as well, at the end of lines 2 (mm. 6–7), 3 (mm. 9–10), 6 (mm. 19–20/36–37), and 7 (mm. 26–27/43–44 and 48–49). In all but the first of these he deploys the more elaborate "11 ♯10 14," which indicates that after the resolution of the suspension, a second dissonance is sounded, either a passing tone from an octave through a seventh or a leap from the freshly resolved third up to a seventh. Thus in m. 9, a D two octaves above the bass descends to a C on the last eighth note of the measure and resolves to a B♭ on the downbeat of m. 10.

The harmonies on which these cadences arrive, finally, illustrate yet another means of text expression. Caccini saves the strongest closure, perfect authentic cadences on the "tonic" G, for the end of the poem's two sections, line 3 (m. 10) and line 7 (mm. 27/44 and 49). Closure on the latter is further strengthened by longer preparation: The whole notes in mm. 26/43 and 48 are the only ones found on the next-to-last measure of a phrase. Caccini also uses perfect authentic cadences at the end of the penultimate line of each section, in m. 7 and mm. 20/37. Both times, however, he brings the music to an "off-tonic" close, first on B♭, then on D, complementing the strong but inconclusive statements of lines 2 and 6. Less strongly closed gestures, instead, such as the aforementioned Phrygian cadence in m. 3, match open-ended utterances, in this case the call to Amaryllis in line 1.

Amarilli, mia bella,	Amaryllis, my beautiful one,
Non credi, o del mio cor dolce desio,	Do you not believe, oh my heart's sweet desire,
D'esser tu l'amor mio?	That you are my love?
Credilo pur, e se timor t'assale,	Believe it indeed, and if fear assails you,
Prendi questo mio strale,	Take this arrow of mine,
Aprimi 'l petto, e vedrai scritto il core:	Open my breast, and you will see written upon my heart:
"Amarilli è 'l mio amore."	"Amaryllis is my love."

66

Jacopo Peri
(1561–1633)

Le musiche … sopra l'Euridice, Excerpt from Scene 2 (1601)

Jacopo Peri's opera *Euridice* was first performed in Florence on 6 October 1600, as part of the festivities honoring the marriage of Maria de' Medici to the King of France, Henri IV; it was published the following year. Like his jealous rival, Caccini, Peri was a virtuoso tenor, and he sang the part of Orpheus himself. And, as did Caccini in *Le nuove musiche,* Peri wrote a preface to the printed edition. Here he argued for a similar goal, "to imitate with song one who speaks," and described a similar means of achieving it: "I made the bass move in time to those [emotions], now faster, now slower, according to the affects, I held it steady amidst dissonances and consonances until the speaker's voice passing through various notes arrived to that which intoned in ordinary speech opens the way to a new harmony." Both statements remind us, though, that Peri was setting dramatic poetry, a choice whose origins and consequences differed from those of the lyric verse set in *Le nuove musiche.* As Peri explained, his "new manner of song" (*nuova maniera di canto*) began in the 1590s, a decade or more after Caccini composed such madrigals as *Amarilli mia bella.* It was, moreover, arrived at through collaboration, experiment, and a high regard for the practical. Peri praised Emilio de' Cavalieri (ca. 1550–1602), a Roman aristocrat who oversaw music at the Medici court, for being the first who "made our music heard on stage." (Cavalieri, incidentally, described the style as "to act through singing" [*recitar cantando*]; soon after, others called it *stile recitativo,* literally "the acting style," better known to English speakers by its cognate, "recitative.") Peri composed his *Dafne* (1597–98) "to make a simple trial of that which the song of our age is capable." His insistence on adapting contemporary styles—*our* music, *our* age—bespeaks perfect awareness that the ancients were inspiration, not model. "I would not dare affirm this to be the song used in Greek and Roman plays," he wrote, even as he invoked their example in forging a new music that lay between speech and song.

Peri claimed as his principal collaborator Ottavio Rinuccini (1562–1621), a fine poet whose authorship of both *Dafne* and *Euridice* the composer noted in the preface and whose name he included on the latter's title page. He praised him further in the dedication to Maria de' Medici, declaring that "in arranging and in narrating such a noble fable, adorning it with a thousand graces and a thousand charms, with the marvelous union of those two things that go together with such difficulty, gravity and sweetness, he has shown to be the equal of the most

famous ancients, a poet in every way admirable." Again, moderns match the ancients, but on their own terms: The joining of serious and pleasing, *gravità* and *piacevolezza,* was one of the great desiderata of sixteenth-century Italian poetics. Peri likely referred as well to the most obvious feature of Rinuccini's text, in which the story is revised to end happily. Tragedy herself appears in the prologue to say that, while her usual role is to draw sighs, shed tears, and "make the faces and expressions of a crowd in an amphitheater pale with pity," just this once she is going to relent in honor of the wedding pair and their friends in attendance: "For the royal wedding I too adorn myself with a serene aspect, and set my song to happier strings, sweet delight to the noble heart." Thus Orpheus gets Eurydice back with no strings attached; there is no second death, no second loss. It remains within the boundaries of the dramatized *favola pastorale,* the pastoral play, a light genre that did not exist in classical times.

The excerpt given here comes from the scene in which Orpheus gets the news of Eurydice's death from Daphnis. The latter's long speech, some thirty-three lines (mm. 310–408), is followed by a brief interjection by the shepherd Arcetro (mm. 408–419) and a powerful lament by Orpheus (mm. 420–454). The musical imitation of speech is apparent first of all in the declamation, which but for three small passages (mm. 354, 418, 441) is entirely syllabic; not for Peri the striking melismas of Caccini's *Amarilli mia bella.* Rhythm and melody likewise imitate speech. The setting of the first line in mm. 310–311, for example, matches the accent (*Per quel va´ - go bo- schet´- to*) and approximates the durations a speaker would employ. So, too, do the unchanging B♭s, a monotone befitting the calm opening of a long and ultimately impassioned narration. Peri instead uses disruptive gestures, rests, and leaps where singers must emphasize crucial points of syntax or emotion. Thus, *la bella sposa* ("the lovely bride"), the subject that Rinuccini so achingly withholds until the end of Daphnis's first, five-line sentence, is set off in m. 320 by a rest and a leap to and from its first word. Acceleration and syncopation help heighten the delivery of agitated states, such as the moment when the snakebite is narrated in mm. 355–356, *Punsele il piè* ("bit her on the foot"): The early placement of the accented first syllable energizes the normally weak second beat. Finally, deceleration and low register can suggest despair, as in Daphnis's final phrase in mm. 405–407, *immobil gielo* ("motionless ice").

This last may also be heard as a pictorial madrigalism, its half and whole notes representing motionlessness, but it is one of very few—the others are the arrival on E♭ in mm. 329–330 during the words *o dall'acute spine* ("or from the sharp thorns," the adjective that can also mean "high") and the outline of a diminished fourth in mm. 418–419 for *di tormento* ("of torment"). Otherwise, Peri spurns every temptation of the text's imagery, jam-packed though it is with opportunities for word painting—flowing water, murmuring water, light, dark, singing, dancing, to say nothing of the serpent's bite. Not one of these images is painted in tones. There is nothing left of wit, nothing to bring a smile of recognition.

Peri's description of the bass—a basso continuo, equipped with figures and played by instruments, as in *Le nuove musiche*—further underscores the primacy of the text and the speaking-through-singing voice that delivers it. As noted, Daphnis begins her narration in a state of calm, an affect complemented by six measures (310–315) of unchanging B♭. By contrast, the resolve to save Eurydice that Orpheus displays at the end of his lament calls forth faster rhythms in mm. 451–453. As Peri also explained, bass motion in time to affect is further conditioned by the wait for an appropriate syllable with which to form a fresh consonance. More often than not this occurs on the final accent of a line, its penultimate syllable, as can be seen in the music for *Lento trascorre il fonte degl'allóri* (mm. 314–316). Deviations from this norm can highlight more important utterances or underscore stronger emotional states: The line-ending phrase *la bella sposa*, mentioned earlier, is set in further relief by the initial bass motion from C to B♭ in m. 320 and the perfect authentic cadence C–F in mm. 321–322, the latter closing off the line from what follows by resolving on the unaccented final syllable. Finally, as Peri explained, dissonances may occur as the voice part unfolds over a longer note in the bass; these occur more often and more freely than in Caccini's *Amarilli mia bella* (note the Cs against the B♭ in mm. 341–342 and the Gs against the F in mm. 345–346).

Peri did not, however, describe the text-expressive ends to which he also put harmony. Like Caccini and many madrigalists before him, he used flat-side harmonies to symbolize sweetness, as in the B♭ and E♭ triads that underpin *Dolce cantava* ("Sang sweetly") in mm. 337–338. Conversely, progressions to the sharper regions complement talk of harshness: Note the move from C to D on the word *acerba* ("bitter") in mm. 348–349, followed by the suppression of the one-flat key signature in m. 350 and the move to E in m. 351 for *Angue crudo, e spietato* ("A cruel and pitiless snake"). Nor did Peri mention his more aggressively modern harmonic practices—dissonances struck or unresolved, chromatic progressions—and the expressive ends to which he put them. For example, when Daphnis describes the cold sweat that bespattered Eurydice's face and hair, her emotion is conveyed in a shocking false relation between the B♭ in the voice and the B natural in the bass in m. 389. The moment of Eurydice's death is described with even greater, colder horror: The words *e bei sembianti* ("and her beautiful features") are set in mm. 400–402 with hideous irony, using the ugliest harmonies the composer could devise—an augmented triad followed by a blatant harmonic contradiction between voice (on B♭) and accompaniment (an E-major triad), "resolved" through a descent by a "forbidden" diminished fifth.

Orpheus's lament also features musical "modulations" to match the modulations of his mood. He goes from numb shock (*Non piango e non sospiro* / "I cry not, and I sigh not") through a sudden outpouring of grief (*O mio core, o mio speme* / "Oh my heart! Oh my hope") to firm resolve (*Tosto vedrai* / "Soon you will see"). The first section has a particularly static bass to match Orpheus's initial torpor. The second section, where lethargy gives way to active distress, is introduced by a brusque harmonic disruption: the cadential E major replaced out of nowhere in m. 437 by G minor. This most anguished section of the lament has the highest dissonance quotient. Orpheus's lines seem altogether uncoordinated with the bass harmonies. He leaves off after *Ohimè!* ("Alas!") in m. 442 with a gasp, his line dangling on an A over the bass G. The bass having changed to D as if to accommodate the A, Orpheus reenters (*Dove sei gita?* / "Where have you gone?") with a new contradiction, on E. The bass once again moves to accommodate the E, which becomes the cadence harmony. The third section begins with the same disruption as the second: a G-minor chord impinging in m. 446 on the cadential E major. This time, however, the one-flat signature is restored and the harmony moves down the circle of fifths to a cadence on F, the more gentle harmonic region complementing the optimistic resolution with which Orpheus concludes his lament.

Dafne	Daphnis
Per quel vago boschetto,	In that lovely little wood,
Ove rigando i fiori	Where, watering the flowers,
Lento trascorre il fonte degl'allori,	The laurel-strewn fount slowly flows,
Prendea dolce diletto	The lovely bride took sweet delight
Con le compagne sue la bella sposa.	With her companions.
Chi violetta, o rosa	There was she who picked violets or roses
Per far ghirland' al crine	From the field or from the sharp thorns,
Togliea dal prato, o dall'acute spine,	To make a garland for her hair,
E qual posand' il fianco	And she who, resting on her side
Sulla fiorita sponda	On the flowery bank
Dolce cantava, al mormorar dell'onda.	Sang sweetly to the murmuring of the waves.
Ma la bella Euridice	But the beautiful Eurydice
Movea danzando il piè sul verde prato	Danced on the green field
Quand' ahi, ria sorte acerba,	When ah, evil bitter fate,
Angue crudo, e spietato,	A cruel and pitiless snake,
Che celato giacea tra fiori, e l'erba	Which lay hidden amidst flowers and the grass
Punsele il piè con sì maligno dente	Bit her on the foot with so evil a tooth
Ch'impallidì repente	That she turned pale at once,
Come raggio di sol che nube adombri.	Like a ray of sun that a cloud obscures.
E dal profondo core	And from the depths of her heart
Con un sospir mortale	Cried out with a deathly sigh
Sì spaventoso, ohimè, sospinse fuore	So frightening, alas,
Che, quasi avesse l'ale,	That, as if they had wings,
Giunse ogni ninfa al doloroso suono.	Every nymph arrived to the dolorous sound,
Et ella in abbandono	And she, letting herself go,
Tutta lasciossi allor nell'altrui braccia.	Then gave herself entirely up into the arms of the others.
Spargea il bel volto, e le dorate chiome	A sweat much colder than ice.
Un sudor vie più fredd' assai che ghiaccio.	Spread over her beautiful face and golden hair
Indi s'udio 'l tuo nome	Then your name was heard
Tra le labbra sonar fredd'e tremanti.	To sound from her cold and trembling lips.
E, volti gl'occhi al cielo,	And, her eyes turned toward heaven,
Scolorito il bel volto e bei sembianti,	Her beautiful face and beautiful features
Restò tanta bellezza immobil gielo.	Remained, so much beauty, motionless ice.
Arcetro	**Arcetro**
Che narri, ohimè, che sento?	What do you narrate, alas, what do I hear?
Misera Ninfa, e più misero amante,	Miserable nymph, and more miserable lover,
Spettacol di miseria e di tormento!	Spectacle of misery and of torment!

ORFEO

Non piango e non sospiro,
O mia cara Euridice,
Che sospirar, che lacrimar non posso,
Cadavero infelice.
O mio core, o mio speme, o pace, o vita!
Ohimè, chi mi t'ha tolto,
Chi mi t'ha tolto, ohimè, dove sei gita?

Tosto vedrai ch'invano
Non chiamasti morendo il tuo consorte.
Non son, non son lontano:
Io vengo, o cara vita, o cara morte.

ORPHEUS

I cry not, and I sigh not,
Oh my dear Eurydice,
For I can not sigh, I can not cry,
Unhappy cadaver.
Oh my heart, oh my hope, oh peace, oh life!
Alas, who has taken you from me,
Who has taken you from me, alas, where
    have you gone?

Soon you will see that not in vain
Did you while dying call your consort.
I am not, I am not far:
I come, oh dear life, oh dear death.

67

Claudio Monteverdi
(1567–1643)

L'Orfeo favola in musica, Act 2 (1607)

Claudio Monteverdi's opera *Orfeo* was first performed in Mantua on 24 February 1607; it was published two years later and again in 1615. Like Peri's *Euridice*, it was a product of courtly culture. Indeed, its sponsor, Francesco Gonzaga, heir to the ducal throne of Mantua, was keenly interested in musical developments in Florence. *Orfeo*, however, was written not to celebrate a dynastic wedding but as a sort of semiprivate entertainment. It was performed before the *Accademia degli Invaghiti* ("Academy of those captivated [by the arts]"), a gathering of courtiers whose ranks included the librettist, Alessandro Striggio (ca. 1573–1630). As Rinuccini did with *Euridice*, Striggio revised the mythological subject to avoid a tragic conclusion, albeit less radically. In the myth, after losing Eurydice a second time, Orpheus turns against all women, for which reason a rioting chorus of jealous Bacchantes tears him to pieces. In the *Orfeo* libretto Orpheus's father, Apollo, the divine musician, turns Orpheus into the constellation of stars that bears his name, substituting serene apotheosis for bloody cataclysm. Act 2, given here complete, includes the same episode found in the excerpt from Peri's *Euridice*: Messenger tells Orpheus of Eurydice's death (mm. 201–228), shepherds respond (mm. 228–242), Orpheus laments (mm. 243–264).

Act 2 also shows how Monteverdi's music mirrors the implicit point of the whole *favola*, which is in essence a music-myth, a demonstration of music's power to move the affections. That power most famously manifests itself in Orpheus's singing and playing his way into the Underworld in Acts 3 and 4; in Act 2 it takes another form, a determined clash between two types of music. One is the new *stile recitativo* of Peri and his Florentine cohorts, the other an equally new genre, the *canzonetta*. The latter is a tuneful rendering of lighthearted, strophic poetry, one whose rhythms closely follow accent and verse length and whose stanzas are often framed by instrumental ritornelli.

The act begins with a celebration of the marriage of Orpheus and Eurydice. Fittingly, canzonettas abound. After an opening ritornello (mm. 1–12, here marked *Sinfonia*) Orpheus announces his return to his friends the shepherds in a single stanza (mm. 13–24). A shepherd responds with a fresh canzonetta of two stanzas (mm. 24–40, 40–53), each preceded by a ritornello, which ends with his calling on all to sing (*Ciascun sua voce snodi . . .* / "Let everyone

unleash his/her voice . . . "). A pair of shepherds answer the call in mm. 54–90; in so doing they subtly underscore the distinction between the two types of music found in virtually every opera ever written. That is, this canzonetta and the two that follow are "realistic": The characters perform the act of singing songs and are thus heard by one another—and, of course, by the audience too—to sing. By contrast, the opening canzonettas for Orpheus and the shepherd are heard as such by the audience alone. The characters hear them instead as speech, the same dichotomy that applies to recitative. Students of opera sometimes refer to the music that both the audience and the stage characters hear as such as "phenomenal" music, while that which is heard by the audience but is "inaudible" to the characters on stage they call "noumenal."

The phenomenal music, then, continues in the next canzonetta, its first stanza sung by two shepherds, its second by a chorus of same (mm. 91–112, 113–128). Though the published score—like that of *Euridice* a souvenir book of the first performance—explains that *fu sonato di dentro* ("it was played offstage"), the playing of the obbligato *flautini* (recorders), rich in pastoral associations, was likely mimed onstage. The chorus calls on Orpheus to play his lyre, and he replies in mm. 128–150 with *Vi ricorda o bosch'ombrosi*, the most elaborate canzonetta of all (four stanzas rather than two, eight-syllable lines rather than seven, the first line of each stanza repeated and recalled at stanza's end, a ritornello with four obbligato parts rather than two). In this canzonetta, moreover, Orpheus gives catchy vent to his joy by adopting the latest fashion in setting octosyllabic verse: The $\frac{6}{8}$ meter often shifts to $\frac{3}{4}$, the latter creating a hemiola for the final two syllables of each line, as in mm. 138 and 140. The ritornello, again played offstage, is now undoubtedly phenomenal: The Orphic lyre was then understood to be a bowed string instrument, and the singer who mimed its playing would create the Orphically miraculous effect of conjuring up an entire ensemble with a single instrument.

After Orpheus has finished, one of the shepherds bids him strike up another song (mm. 151–164), this time to be accompanied with a plucked instrument (*co 'l plettr' aurato* / "with your golden plectrum"); but before Orpheus can comply, the baleful "Messenger" (actually the nymph Sylvia) bursts in with the horrible news of Eurydice's death and silences the stage music for good (*Ahi caso acerbo . . .* / "Ah harsh event," mm. 164–170). But the phenomenal music is silenced only so that the noumenal music, the real music of lyric eloquence, can work its wonders on the audience. From here until Orpheus and the Messenger depart the scene (he to fetch Eurydice back, she to hide in shame at having broken such bitter news), no instrument is heard but those of the basso continuo, whose music goes symbolically "unheard" onstage. The verse, moreover, reverts to the seven- and eleven-syllable lines used for recitative.

The central business of the act is the exchange between Orpheus and the nymph Sylvia, which is clearly modeled on, but just as clearly far surpasses, the analogous scene in Peri's *Euridice*. The harmonic disparity between Orpheus's lines and Sylvia's symbolizes his resistance to the untimely news she has brought him. He breaks in on her narrative in m. 197 with G minor—*Ohimè, che odo?* ("Oh no, what am I hearing?")—as soon as she has mentioned the name of Eurydice (on an E-major harmony), as if to deflect her from the bitter message she is about to deliver, but she comes right back in m. 198 with E major and resolves the chord cadentially to A in m. 199 on the word *morta*, "dead." (For his part, Striggio introduces here a nice *coup de théâtre*: Unlike Rinuccini's Messenger, his announces Eurydice's death before narrating how it happened.) When Orpheus responds in m. 200 with another *Ohimè*, this time he takes up the same harmony where she left it and confirms it with D, the next harmony along the circle of fifths: The message has sunk in, and he must accept it.

Once again, as in *Euridice*, the same horrific events are recounted rather than portrayed (mm. 201–228), not only out of delicacy but because the aim is to portray emotions rather than events. At the same time, Striggio and Monteverdi diverge from *Euridice* by fashioning a much shorter narration, about half the length of that of Rinuccini and Peri, and their greater concision leads to another stunning moment. In mm. 228–233 a shepherd responds to the messenger by repeating, to nearly identical music, her opening couplet *Ahi caso acerbo*. . . . Such, apparently, is his shock that he can think of nothing else, but the return of previously heard material poses once more the question of noumenal and phenomenal music: By the end of the act the phrase will be heard three more times and thus will be transformed from speech-act to song-act, a vocal refrain that complements in sadness the instrumental ritornelli heard in happiness.

When Orpheus finds his voice again after temporarily becoming *un muto sasso* ("a mute stone"), as one of the shepherds puts it in m. 235, Monteverdi once more showed his reliance—but not dependence—on Peri. Thus Orpheus begins his central soliloquy (mm. 243–264) in greater agitation: He declares at once that Eurydice is dead, and his melody begins by leaping down a diminished fourth to an F♯, which clashes with the G in the basso continuo. Monteverdi heightens the tension a moment later, in m. 245, by repeating the key phrase of Striggio's text (*se' morta*/"are dead")—something Peri never did with Rinuccini's—and having it begin this time with a struck dissonance. Orpheus then resolves to rescue his bride, just as he does in *Euridice*, but his utterances are now laced with pictorial madrigalisms, a descent on *a' più profondi abissi* ("to the deepest abysses") in m. 253, an ascent on *a riveder le stelle* ("to see once more the stars," an exact quote of the last line of Dante's *Inferno*) in mm. 256–257, and another one that charts the progression *terra–cielo–sole* (earth–heaven–sun) in mm. 261–263. Once again, the music has subtly shifted from noumenal to phenomenal. Orpheus's natural mode of speech, the myth tells us, is song itself: As his courage returns, his innate musicality comes to the fore, and listeners both onstage and off hear a virtuoso madrigalist at work.

Orpheus having sung/spoken and left, the familiar *Ahi caso acerbo* returns in mm. 265–270, now intoned by a five-voice chorus. The melody that was last sung by the shepherd has moved down a fifth and become the bass, completing another noumenal-to-phenomenal transformation, as the chorus now sings a formal dirge that will return in mm. 323–328 and 353–359. The chorus then continues with a new piece in mm. 271–280 (note the change in key signature), a madrigal replete with pictorialisms on *fugge* ("flees") and *salita* ("ascent"). There follows a final outpouring of recitative from the messenger Sylvia, who reflects on the pain her tidings have caused (mm. 281–295).

The act's final section begins with a return of instrumental music, a sinfonia (mm. 296–301) that introduces a pair of shepherds. Instead of canzonettas, they sing two continuo madrigals (mm. 302–322, 328–352), a weightier genre befitting lament (whether to regard them as phenomenal or noumenal music is an open question). Each madrigal is punctuated by a choral statement of *Ahi caso acerbo*, the emotion thereby made more formalized and ritualized than the spontaneous outpourings of Silvia and Orpheus. This most affecting act of *Orfeo* closes with another masterful reminder of music's power, an instrumental ritornello (mm. 360–363) previously heard in the prologue (not included here), in which Music personified sings her own praises.

Orfeo	**Orpheus**
Ecco pur ch' a voi ritorno,	Here, then, I return to you,
Care selve e piaggie amate,	Dear forests and beloved hills,
Da quel sol fatte beate	That are made blessed by that sun
Per cui sol mie nott' han giorno.	For which alone my nights have days.
Pastore	**Shepherd**
Mira ch'a se n'alletta	Look, Orpheus, how the shade
L'ombra, Orfeo, de que' faggi,	Of those beeches entices,
Or che 'nfocati raggi	Now that Phoebus shoots
Febo da ciel saetta.	Flaming rays from heaven.
Su quell'erbosa sponda	Let us rest on that leafy bank,
Posiamci e in vari modi	And let everyone unleash his/her voice
Ciascun sua voce snodi	In various ways
Al mormorio dell'onde.	To the murmuring of the waves.
Due Pastori	**Two Shepherds**
In questo prato adorno	In this beautiful field
Ogni selvaggio Nume	Every forest god
Sovente ha per costume	Is accustomed
Di far lieto soggiorno	To take happy recreation.
Qui Pan, Dio de' Pastori,	Here Pan, god of the shepherds,
S'udì talor dolente	Was once heard mournfully
Rimembrar dolcemente	To remember, sweetly,
Suoi sventurati amori.	his misadventurous loves.
Qui le Napee vezzose,	Here the delightful nymphs,
Schiera sempre fiorita,	An always flowering group,
Con le candide dita	Were seen picking roses
Fur viste a coglier rose.	With their snow-white fingers.
Coro	**Chorus**
Dunque fa degno, Orfeo,	So, Orpheus, make worthy
Del suon della tua lira	Of the sound or your lyre
Questi campi ove spira	These fields where blows
Aura d'odor sabeo.	A breeze of Sabaean fragrance.
Orfeo	**Orpheus**
Vi ricorda, o bosch' ombrosi,	Do you remember, oh shady woods,
De miei lungh' aspri tormenti,	My long, bitter torments,
Quando i sassi ai miei lamenti	When the stones, made piteous,
Rispondean, fatti pietosi?	Responded to my lamenti?

Dite: allor non vi sembrai
Più d'ogn'altro sconsolato?
Or fortuna ha stil cangiato
Et ha volto in festa i guai.
Vissi già mesto e dolente,
Or gioisco, e quegli affanni
Che sofferti ho per tant' anni
Fan più caro il ben presente.
Sol per te, bella Euridice,
Benedico il mio tormento
Dopo 'l duol vi è più contento
Dopo 'l mal vi è più felice.

Pastore
Mira, deh mira, Orfeo, che d'ogni intorno
Ride il bosco e ride il prato,
Segui pur co 'l plettr' aurato
D'addolcir l'aria in sì beato giorno.

Messaggiera [Silvia]
Ahi caso acerbo, ahi fatt' empio e crudele,
Ahi stelle ingiuriose, ahi ciel avaro!

Pastore
Qual suon dolente il lieto dì pertuba?

Messaggiera
Lassa, dunque debb'io,
Mentre Orfeo con sue note il ciel consola,

Con le parole mie passargli il core?

Pastore
Questa è Silvia gentile,
Dolcissima compagna
Della bell' Euridice. O quanto è in vista

Dolorosa! Or che sia? Deh sommi Dei,
Non torcete da noi benigno il guardo.

Messaggiera
Pastor, lasciate il canto,
Ch'ogni nostr' allegrezza in doglia è volta.

Orfeo
D'onde vieni? Ove vai? Ninfa, che porti?

Say: did I not them seem to you
More disconsolate than any other?
Now fortune has changed style
And has turned troubles into.
I once lived sad and mournful,
Now I rejoice, and those troubles
That I suffered for many years
Make more dear the fine present.
For you alone, lovely Eurydice,
Do I bless my torment
After grief there is more contentment,
After pain there is more happiness.

Shepherd
Look, pray look, Orpheus, all around
The wood laughs and the field laughs,
Continue then with your golden plectrum
To sweeten the air on such a blessed day.

Messenger [Sylvia]
Ah harsh event, ah wicked and cruel fate,
Ah harmful stars, ah greedy heaven!

Shepherd
What sad sound disturbs the happy day?

Messenger
Alas, must I then,
While Orpheus consoles heaven with his
music
Pierce his heart with my words?

Shepherd
This is gentle Sylvia,
Most sweet companion
Of the beautiful Eurydice. Oh how her
face
Is sad! What can it be? Pray, supreme gods,
Do not turn from us your benign gaze.

Messenger
Shepherd, leave aside song,
For all our happiness is turned to sadness.

Orpheus
Whence come you? Where do you go?
Nymph, what do you bring?

Messaggiera
A te ne vengo, Orfeo,
Messaggiera infelice
Di caso più infelice e più funesto,
La tua bella Euridice . . .

Orfeo
Ohimè che odo?

Messaggiera
La tua diletta sposa è morta.

Orfeo
Ohimè.

Messaggiera
In un fiorito prato
Con l'altre sue compagne
Giva cogliendo fiori
Per farne una ghirlanda alle sue chiome,
Quand' angue insidioso
Ch'era fra l'erbe ascoso
Le punse un piè con velonoso dente:
Ed ecco immantinente
Scolorirsi il bel viso e ne suoi lumi
Sparir que' lampi, ond' ella al Sol fea scorno.

Allor noi tutte sbigottite e meste
Le fummo intorno richiamar tentando
Li spirti in lei smarriti
Con l'onda fresca e co' possenti carmi.
Ma nulla valse, ahi lassa,
Ch'ella i languidi lumi alquanto aprendo,
E te chiamando, Orfeo,
Dopo un grave sospiro
Spirò fra queste braccia, ed io rimasi
Piena il cor di pietade e di spavento.

Pastore [I]
Ahi caso acerbo, ahi fatt' empio e crudele,
Ahi stelle ingiuriose, ahi ciel avaro!

Pastore [II]
All'amara novella
Rassembra l'infelice un muto sasso
Che per troppo dolor non può dolersi.

Messenger
To you I come, Orpheus,
Unhappy messenger
Of the most unhappy and most
Your beautiful Eurydice . . .

Orpheus
Alas, what do I hear?

Messenger
Your beloved bride is dead.

Orpheus
Alas.

Messenger
In a flowery field,
With her other companions,
She went picking flowers
To make of them a garland for her hair,
When an insidious snake
Which was hidden amidst the grass
Bit her on the foot with poisonous tooth:
And here at once
Her lovely face became pale, and in her eyes
Those lights with which she outdid the
sun disappeared
Then all of us, confused and sad,
Stood around her, trying to recall
The spirits lost in her
With cool water and with powerful songs.
But nothing worked, alas,
For she, barely opening her languid eyes,
And calling you, Orpheus,
Expired in these arms,
After a heavy sigh, and I remained
My heart full of pity and terror.

Shepherd [1]
Ah harsh event, ah wicked and cruel fate,
Ah harmful stars, ah greedy heaven!

Shepherd [2]
Before the bitter news
The unhappy one seems a mute stone
Who for too much pain cannot feel pain.

Pastore [I]

Ahi, ben avrebbe un cor di tigre o d'orsa

Chi non sentissi del tuo mal pietate,
Privo d'ogni tuo ben misero amante.

Orfeo

Tu se' morta mia vita, ed io respiro?
Tu se' da me partita
Per mai più non tornare, ed io rimango?
No, che, se i versi alcuna cosa ponno
N'andrò sicuro a' più profondi abissi
E, intenerito il cor del Re dell'ombre,

Meco trarrotti a riveder le stelle.

O se ciò negherammi empio destino,
Rimarrò teco in compagnia di morte.
Addio terra, addio Cielo, e Sole, addio.

Coro

Ahi caso acerbo, ahi fatt' empio e crudele,
Ahi stelle ingiuriose, ahi ciel avaro!
Non si fidi uom mortale
Di ben caduc' e frale
Che tosto fugge, e spesso
A gran salita il precipizio è presso.

Messaggeria

Ma io ch'in questa lingua
Ho portato il coltello
C'ha svenata ad Orfeo l'anima amante,
Odiosa ai Pastori et alle Ninfe,

Odiosa a me stessa, ove m'ascondo?
Nottola infausta, il sole
Fuggirò sempre e in solitario speco
Menerò vita al mio dolor conforme.

Due Pastori

Chi ne consola, ahi lassi?
O pur chi ne concede
Negl'occhi un vivo fonte
Da poter lagrimar come conviensi
In questo mesto giorno,

Shepherd [1]

Ah, one would have the heart of a tiger or
   a bear
Not to feel pity for your pain,
Miserable lover deprived of every good.

Orpheus

You are dead, my life, and I still breathe?
You have departed from me
Never to return again, and I remain?
No, if my verses can do anything at all
I will go safe to the deepest abysses
And, having softened the heart of the
   King of shades
I will bring you with me to see once more
   the stars.
O, if cruel destiny denies me this
I will remain with you in death's company.
Farewell earth, farewell heaven, and sun,
   farewell.

Chorus

Ah harsh event, ah wicked and cruel fate,
Ah harmful stars, ah greedy heaven!
Let mortal man not trust
In goods fleeting and frail,
Which quickly flee; often
After a great ascent the precipice is near.

Messenger

But I, who with this tongue
Have brought the knife
That has killed Orpheus's loving soul,
Hateful to the shepherds and to the
   nymphs,
Hateful to myself, where shall I hide?
Like an unfortunate bat, I shall flee the sun
Forever, and in a solitary cave
Lead a life in conformity to my pain.

Two Shepherds

Who will console him, alas?
Or who will grant his eyes
A fountain of tears
To be able to cry as is necessary
In this sad day,

Quanto più lieto già tant' or più mesto?
Oggi turbo crudele
I due lumi maggiori
Di queste nostre selve,
Euridice et Orfeo,
L'una punta dall'angue,
L'altro dal duol traffitto, ahi lassi, ha spenti.

Coro

Ahi caso acerbo, ahi fatt' empio e crudele,
Ahi stelle ingiuriose, ahi ciel avaro!

Due Pastori

Ma dove, ah dove or sono
Della misera Ninfa
Le belle e fredde membra,
Dove suo degno albergo
Quella bell'alma elesse
Ch'oggi è partita in sul fiorir de' giorni.

Andiam, Pastori, andiamo
Pietosi a ritrovarle,
E di lagrime amare
Il dovuto tributo
Per noi si paghi almeno al corpo esangue.

Coro

Ahi caso acerbo, ahi fatt' empio e crudele,
Ahi stelle ingiuriose, ahi ciel avaro!

As much as it was happy now sad?
Today cruel fate disturbs
The two greatest lights
Of these forests of ours,
Eurydice and Orpheus,
The one bitten by a snake,
The other pierced by sadness, alas,

Chorus

Ah harsh event, ah wicked and cruel fate,
Ah harmful stars, ah greedy heaven!

Two Shepherds

But where, ah where are now
The beautiful and cold limbs
Of the miserable nymph,
Where is the worthy dwelling place for
That lovely elect soul
Who today has departed in the flower of
   her days.
Let us go, shepherds, let us go,
Piteously to find them,
And let us at least pay to the lifeless body
The required tribute
Of bitter tears.

Chorus

Ah harsh event, ah wicked and cruel fate,
Ah harmful stars, ah greedy heaven!

Ritornello

Questo Ritornello fu suonato di dentro da un Clavicembano, duoi Chitaroni, & duoi Violini piccioli alla Francese.

Questo ritornello fu sonato da duoi Violini ordinarii da braccio, un Basso de Viola da braccio, un Clavicembano, & duoi Chittaroni.

Ritornello

Due pastori (C4, C4)

Qui Pan Dio de' Pa - sto - ri___ S'u - di - tal - hor do - len - te___ Ri -

Qui Pan Dio de' Pa - sto - ri___ S'u - di - tal - hor do - len - te___ Ri -

-mem - brar dol - ce - men - te___ Suoi sven - tu - ra - ti a - - mo - ri.

-mem - brar dol - ce - men - te___ Suoi sven - tu - ra - ti a - - mo - ri.

Fu sonato di dentro da duoi Chitaroni un Clavicembano, & duoi Flautini.

Ritornello

Due pastori

Qui le Nap - pee vez - zo - se (Schie - ra sem - pre fio - ri - ta)

Qui le Nap - pee vez - zo - se (Schie - ra sem - pre fio - ri - ta)

Con le can - di - de di - ta___ Fur vi - ste à co - glier ro - se.

Con le can - di - de di - ta___ Fur vi - ste à co - glier ro - se.

Ritornello

122 CHORO

Dun - que fà de - gno Or - fe - o Del suon de la tua li - ra

Dun - que fà de - gno Or - fe - o Del suon de la tua li - ra

Dun - que fà de - gno Or - fe - o Del suon de la tua li - ra

Dun - que fà de - gno Or - fe - o Del suon de la tua li - ra

Dun - que fà de - gno Or - fe - o Del suon de la tua li - ra

125

Que - sti cam - pi o - ve spi - ra Au - ra d'o - dor Sa - be - o.

Que - sti cam - pi o - ve spi - ra Au - ra d'o - dor Sa - be - o.

Que - sti cam - pi o - ve spi - ra Au - ra d'o - dor Sa - be - o.

Que - sti cam - pi o - ve spi - ra Au - ra d'o - dor Sa - be - o.

Que - sti cam - pi o - ve spi - ra Au - ra d'o - dor Sa - be - o.

[V.S. Ritornello]

*Fu sonato questo Ritornello di dentro da cinque Viole da braccio,
un contrabasso, duoi Clavicembani & tre chitarroni.*

128 Ritornello

(G2)

(C1)

(C3)

(C4)

132

Orfeo (C4)

1. Vi ri - cor - da ò bo - schi om - bro - si, Vi ri - cor - da ò bo - schi om - bro - si De' miei
2. Di - te, all' hor non vi sem - bra - i, Di - te, all' hor non vi sem - bra - i Più d'o -
3. Vis - si già me - sto e do - len - te, Vi - si già mo - sto e do - len - te, Hor gio -
4. Sol per tè, bel - la Eu - ri - di - ce, Sol per tè, bel - la Eu - ri - di - ce Be - ne -

141

lun - ghi a - spri tor - men - ti Quan - do i sas - si ai miei la - men - ti Ri - spon -
-gni al - tro scon - so - la - to? Hor for - tu - na hà stil can - gia - to Et hà
-i - sco, e que - gli af - fan - ni Che sof - fer - ti hò per tan - t'an - ni Fan più
-di - co il mio tor - men - to, Do - pò'l duol viè più con - ten - to, do - pò'l

145

-dean fat - ti pie - to - si? Vi ri - cor - da ò bo - schi om - bro - si, Vi ri -
vol - to in fe - sta i guai. Di - te, all' hor non vi sem - bra - i Più d'o -
-ca ro il ben pre - sen - te. Vis - si già me - sto e do - len - te, Vi - si
mal viè più fe - li - ce. Sol per tè, bel - la Eu - ri - di - ce, Sol per

149   [1]   [4]

-cor - da o bo - schi om - bro - si.
-gni al - tro scon - so - la - to?
già me - sto e do - len - te.
tè, bel - la Eu - ri - di - ce.

68

Claudio Monteverdi
(1567–1643)

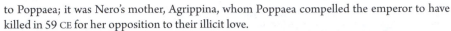

L'incoronazione di Poppea ("The Coronation
of Poppea"), Excerpts from Acts 1 and 3 (1643)

In one of the most impressive feats of self-rejuvenation in the history of music, the septuage-narian Claudio Monteverdi composed three operas for one of Venice's newly opened public theaters between 1639 and 1643. The last was *L'incoronazione di Poppea*, a historical rather than mythological fantasy, based on Tacitus and other Roman historians. The librettist was Giovanni Francesco Busenello (1598–1659), a poet active in the *Accademia degli Incogniti* (Academy of the Disguised), a society of libertines and skeptics who participated extensively in early Venetian commercial theater. Unlike those of such court operas as *Orfeo*, his libretto celebrates vice triumphant and virtue mocked. More precisely, it narrates the triumph of erotic love and the intrigue and betrayal it entails. Yet Busenello may have had a moralizing aim as well, for the *Incogniti* were patriotic Venetians, proud of their Republic and the free thought it allowed. To show Rome, Venice's rival, in the worst light, all the while enjoying the show, was to damn it with garish praise.

Busenello provided the following synopsis of the opera in his collected works published in 1656, making no secret of its deviation from historical fact:

> Nero, in love with Poppaea, who was the wife of Otho, sent him on the pretext of embassy to Portugal, in order to enjoy for himself his dear beloved one; thus Tacitus presented it. But here the facts are presented differently. Otho, desperate at seeing himself deprived of Poppaea, gives himself over to delirium and exclamations. Octavia, Nero's wife, orders Otho to kill Poppaea. Otho promises to do it, but not having sufficient courage to take the life of his adored Poppaea, disguises himself in the clothes of Drusilla, who is in love with him. Thus disguised he enters Poppaea's garden. Love [Cupid] interrupts and impedes that death. Nero repudiates Octavia, despite Seneca's advice, and takes Poppaea as his wife. Seneca dies, and Octavia is exiled from Rome.

The actual Seneca was forced to commit suicide in 65 CE for his supposed participation in a plot to overthrow Nero, not for his opposition to the emperor's marriage three years earlier to Poppaea; it was Nero's mother, Agrippina, whom Poppaea compelled the emperor to have killed in 59 CE for her opposition to their illicit love.

In setting Busenello's libretto, Monteverdi employed several flamboyant voice types foreign to court *favole*: two prima-donna roles (the virtuosic Poppea and the more poignantly monodic Octavia), two male castrato parts (the feminized emperor Nero and the stoical wronged husband Otho), and a quartet of low-born comic characters who spoof their betters (including Arnalta, Poppaea's former wet nurse, often played by a male falsettist in drag). Even the bass part for the Stoic philosopher Seneca, a nominally serious character, is laced with extravagances.

Such extravagances can be found in Act 1, Scene 6, which Busenello summarizes thus: "Seneca advises Octavia to be steadfast. Octavia's Page, for the empress's entertainment, makes fun of Seneca, to whom Octavia entrusts herself; she goes to offer prayers in the temple." Seneca's first monologue (mm. 1–87) is cast in *versi sciolti*, freely rhymed seven- and eleven-syllable lines standard for recitative throughout the period. And thus does Monteverdi begin his setting, with recitative, when Seneca first comments on Octavia's sad state (mm. 1–7) and then criticizes her for crying about it (mm. 8–19); a tonal juxtaposition, C minor to D minor (mm. 7–8), marks the shift from description to address. However, when Seneca calls on Octavia to embrace suffering as a means of building character and denounces physical beauty for its impermanence, the composer abandons recitative, unleashing, instead, devices associated with aria—triple meter (mm. 20–43, 59–74), melismas (mm. 39–41, 54–57), sequences (mm. 44–47), repeated text (passim), and madrigalisms (mm. 75–77). Only at the end (mm. 78–87), when Seneca returns to praise *la virtù costante* ("steadfast virtue"), does Monteverdi return to recitative.

Seneca's lyric outburst suggests an attempt to convince the empress to behave as a Stoic, using melodiousness as a form of intellectual seduction. The music, however, also suggests that Seneca is too much in love with his own thought, losing himself in didactic ecstasy. His biggest melisma (mm. 54–57), for example, falls not on the noun *bellezza* ("beauty") but on the essentially meaningless definite article *la* ("the") that precedes it. Octavia's reply (mm. 88–101), an austere recitative, suggests a further uncharitable reading of his character: After another harmonic shift that signals the change from description to criticism (E to D, mm. 93–94), she declares his ideas *Vanità speciose, / Studiati artifici, / Inutili rimedi a gl'infelici* ("Specious vanities, / Studied artifices, / Useless remedies to the unhappy").

The bulk of the scene belongs to Octavia's Page, who gets both the longest speech (mm. 102–203) and the last word (mm. 224–236). Typical of early Venetian opera, high tragedy and low comedy exist side by side. Here the opera's "lowest" character directly mocks Seneca, its most exalted one, in utterances marked by comic exaggeration. *Io vo' sfogar la stizza che mi move* ("I want to unleash the anger that moves me") is set repeatedly to sixteenth notes that recall the *genere concitato* (mm. 106–111); *M'accende pur a sdegno* ("[He] just ignites me to disdain") is repeated to rising sequences (mm. 116–118); Seneca's teachings are declared *canzoni* ("songs"; i.e., worth little) to the strains of the lighthearted *ciaccona* ground bass (mm. 138–149); sneezing (mm. 150–153), yawning (mm. 154–160), and laughter (mm. 169–171) are acted out; and *Sempre al contrario fa di quel ch'insegna* ("[his philosophy] always does the opposite of what it teaches") is set to contrary motion between voice and continuo (mm. 176–181). (This last rehearses a celebrated historical critique of Seneca as hypocrite.)

Elsewhere in the opera, lyric utterances and exaggerated madrigalisms represent the unabashed lust of Nero and Poppaea. Such can be seen in Act 1, Scene 10, which Busenello summarizes thus: "Poppaea and Nero speak of their past contentments, Nero remaining prey to Poppaea's beauties, promising that he wants to make her empress; Seneca being put in his bad graces by Poppaea, Nero decrees his death. Poppaea makes a vow to Love [Cupid] for the elevation of her fortunes, and all is understood and observed by Otho, who remains hidden." The scene begins with three exchanges (mm. 1–11, 12–27, 28–62), in which Poppaea questions Nero about her charms and the emperor responds ecstatically. The subject of each question, *baci* ("kisses"), *pomi* ("breasts"), and *amplessi* ("embraces," also a euphemism for intercourse) is teasingly delayed by rests (mm. 6–7, 17–20, 36–38). Monteverdi further maps the growing sexual charge by shifting to triple meter and introducing a graphic madrigalism, a quarter-note hocket between continuo and voice, to depict "the tight [*stretti*] embraces" (mm. 34–36). Nero's first two responses make use of an affective harmonic progression (mm. 8–9, 21), his C rising to C♯ as the continuo moves from F to E (i.e., an F-major triad followed by a C♯-diminished triad in first inversion). His last ends by assuming the characteristics of a small aria, with repeated affirmations (mm. 55–62) that his destiny *sta de' labbri tuoi nel bel rubino* ("resides in the beautiful ruby of your lips").

As Poppaea and Nero praise one another at greater length (mm. 63–138, 139–209), Monteverdi turns up the musical temperature still further. Poppaea's triple-meter material makes her declarations a fresh seduction. Nero's gestures include a *ciaccona* (mm. 153–175), now in its original guise as a sign of lasciviousness rather than the musical pun it was for the Page (mm. 138–149). His mention of the transcendent beauty of Poppaea's eyes brings a modulation to A minor and a six-measure ostinato in that key (mm. 179–184, 185–190). Poppaea responds at first with her own eight-measure ostinato, which she promptly abandons after two iterations (mm. 210–218, 218–226). Stark recitative (mm. 227–243), introduced by a shift to B♭, is the means by which she informs Nero that Seneca opposes their union. Nero's decision to have Seneca killed (mm. 254–272) is announced in similar recitative; only when he reassures Poppaea (mm. 273–293) of his determination to do so does the music return to triple meter.

The last three scenes of the opera feature many of the devices already discussed. The opera's most tragic moment, Octavia's farewell to Rome as she heads into exile (Act 3, Scene 6), is followed immediately by its most farcical—Arnalta's gloating at her mistress's impending elevation and her own (Act 3, Scene 7). In the tragic scene, Monteverdi once again laces his setting with exaggerated gestures, but ones that underscore austerity rather than sensuality. Octavia's stuttered first syllable of *addio* (mm. 2–3, 4–5) remains on an unchanging A, which in turn sets the tone for much of her music, often little more than a monotonal recitation (e.g., mm. 2–8, 13–14, 19–21, 49–50). The comic scene has exaggerations of a different sort. Arnalta too begins by stuttering (mm. 1–6), but in ridiculous fashion. She repeats whole words, often misaccenting them (see *di Roma*, mm. 3–4), joy leading to garrulousness. And like the Page, she sings such over-the-top madrigalisms as the rising and falling line (mm. 10–18) that traces *Ascenderò delle grandezze i gradi. / No, col volgo io non m'abbasso più* ("I shall ascend the steps of riches. No, I shall no longer lower myself with *hoi polloi*."). As soon-to-be imperial "counselor"—the post

Seneca held—she closes with a send up of Stoic thought (mm. 61–80), hoping that, if reborn, she will pass from wealth to poverty, thus to welcome death as consolation.

The aria *Pur ti miro*, which ends the opera, is both the most famous and the most disputed part of Act 3, Scene 8. Busenello does not provide text for a closing love duet for Nero and Poppaea, nor does he mention it in his summary of the scene: "Nero solemnly witnesses the CORONATION OF POPPAEA, who in the name of the Roman people and senate is crowned by consuls and tribunes; Love descends from heaven with Venus, the Graces, and Cupids, and crowns Poppaea as the goddesses of beauties on earth, and the opera finishes." Yet both of the surviving scores of the opera include the aria. Scholars have suggested that it might not be by Monteverdi but might, rather, be the work of a younger composer active in the 1640s, possibly Benedetto Ferrari or Francesco Sacrati. Whoever the composer, he had mastered the art of ground-bass composition. The outer sections of this ternary form (mm. 1–32, 96–123) employ an ostinato that descends by step from G to D. After an initial bit of antiphony from the lovers (mm. 5–9), two near-identical phrases follow (mm. 9–13, 13–17), in which the imagery of embracing and entwining is captured by the sustained A and sequential quarter notes of the two voices. The next two phrases (mm. 17–21, 21–25) are nearly identical as well; now the dissonant friction of suspensions makes the point of *Più non peno, più non moro* ("I suffer no more, I die no more"). The middle section (mm. 37–66, repeated verbatim in mm. 67–96) abandons the ground bass even as it revisits the staggered interjections of the first phrase. Only at the very end (mm. 62–66, 92–96) do the lovers sing together in parallel thirds for their final affirmation, *Sì, mio ben, sì, mio cor, mia vita sì* ("Yes, my treasure, yes, my heart, my life, yes"). The music leaves no doubt that the lovers are enacting their passion before us.

ATTO PRIMO, SCENA SESTA	ACT 1, SCENE 6
SENECA, OTTAVIA, VALLETTO	SENECA, OCTAVIA, PAGE
Seneca	**Seneca**
Ecco la sconsolata	Here is the disconsolate
Donna, assunta all'impero	Woman, brought to rule
Per patir il servaggio. O gloriosa	Only to suffer servitude. O glorious
Del mondo imperatrice,	Empress of the world,
Sovra i titoli eccelsi	Conspicuous and great over
Degl'insigni avi tuoi conspicua e grande,	The exalted titles of your illustrious ancestors,
La vanità del pianto	The vanity of tears
Degl'occhi imperiali è ufficio indegno.	Is an act unworthy of imperial eyes.
Ringrazia la Fortuna,	Thank Fortune,
Che con i colpi suoi	Which with its blows
Ti cresce gl'ornamenti.	Increases your adornments.
La cote non percossa	The unstruck flint
Non può mandar faville.	Can not send sparks.
Tu dal destin colpita	You, struck by destiny,
Produci a te medesma alti splendori	Will produce in yourself high splendors
Di vigor, di fortezza,	Of vigor, or strength,

Glorie maggiori assai che la bellezza. | Much greater glories than beauty.
La vaghezza del volto, i lineamenti | The loveliness of the face, the lines
Ch'in apparenza illustre | That shine colorful and delicate
Risplendon coloriti e delicati, | In illustrious appearance,
Da pochi ladri dì ci son rubati. | Are stolen from us by a few thieving days.
Ma la virtù costante, il fato, e 'l caso, | But steadfast virtue never sees
Giammai non vede occaso. | Fate and chance overtake it.

Ottavia

Tu mi vai promettendo | You are promising me
Balsamo dal veleno, | Balm from poison
E glorie da tormenti. | And glories from torments.
Scusami, questi son, Seneca mio, | Pardon me, these are, my Seneca,
Vanità speciose, | Specious vanities,
Studiati artifici, | Studied artifices,
Inutili rimedi a gl'infelici. | Useless remedies to the unhappy.

Valletto

Madama, con tua pace, | Madame, with your leave,
Io vo' sfogar la stizza che mi move | I want to unleash the anger that
Il filosofo astuto, il gabba Giove. | The astute philosopher, the trickster moves in me.

M'accende pur a sdegno | This painter of beautiful conceits
Questo miniator de' bei concetti. | Just ignites me to disdain.
Non posso star al segno | I can not stand around
Mentre egli incanta altrui con aurei detti. | While he bewitches others with his golden sayings.

Queste del suo cervel mere invenzioni | These are mere inventions of his brain
Le vende per misteri, e son canzoni! | That he sells as mysteries, and they are songs!

Madama, s'ei sternuta o s'ei sbadiglia | Madame, if he sneezes or if he yawns
Presume d'insegnar cose morali, | He presumes to teach morality,
E tanto l'assottiglia, | And to make it so subtle
Che moverebbe il riso a' miei stivali. | That it would move my boots to laughter.

Scaltra filosofia, dov' ella regna, | Miserable philosophy, where it rules,
Sempr' al contrario fa di quel ch'insegna. | Always does the opposite of what it teaches.
Fonda sempre il pedante | The pedant always bases
Su l'ignoranza d'altri il suo guadagno, | His earnings on the ignorance of others,
E accorto argomentante | And clever disputer
Non ha Giove per dio, ma per compagno, | He has not Jupiter for a god, but for a comrade,

E le regole sue di modo intrica, | And he twists his rules such
Ch'alfin ne anch'egli sa ciò ch'ei si dica. | That in the end not even he knows what he's saying.

Ottavia | **Octavia**

Neron tenta il ripudio | Nero is trying to repudiate
Della persona mia | My person
Per isposar Poppea. Si divertisca, | In order to marry Poppea. Let him amuse himself,

Se divertir si può sì indegno esempio. | If such an unworthy specimen can amuse himself.

Tu per me prega il popol e 'l senato, | You plead for me to the people and the senate,

Ch'io mi riduco a porger voti al tempio. | While I go to pray at the temple.

Valletto | **Page**

Se tu non dai soccorso | If you don't help
Alla nostra regina, in fede mia, | Our queen, I swear
Che vo' accenderti il foco | That I shall light a fire
E nella barba, e nella libreria. | In your beard and in your library.

Act 1, Scene 6

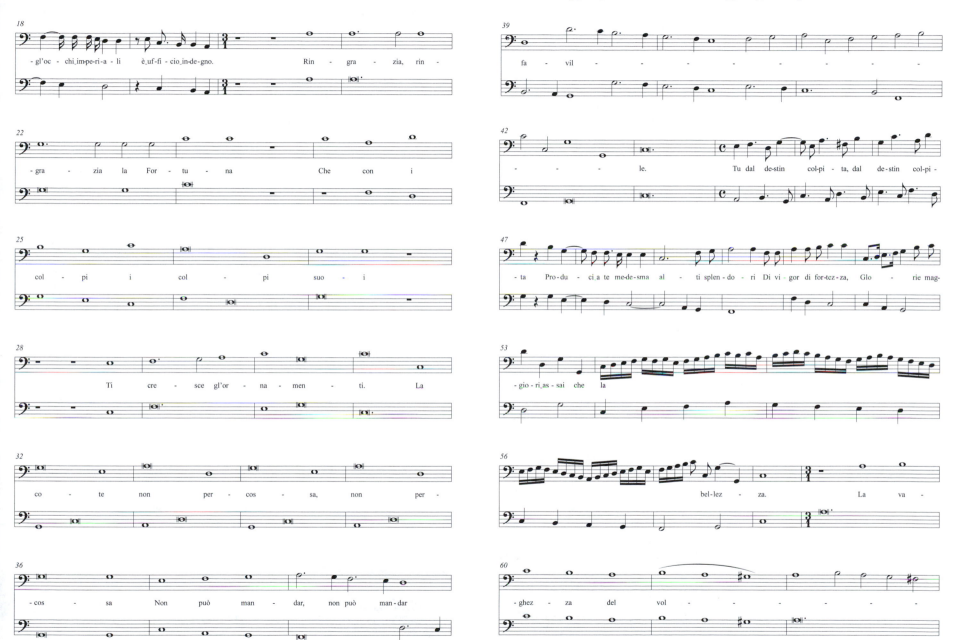

ATTO I, SCENA DECIMA

POPPEA, NERONE, OTTONE in disparte.

Poppea
Come dolci, Signor, come soavi,
Riuscirono a te la notte andata
Di questa bocca i baci?

Nerone
Più cari i più mordaci.

Poppea
Di questo seno i pomi?

Nerone
Mertan le mamme tue più dolci nomi.

Poppea
Di queste braccia gli stretti, stretti amplessi?

Nerone
Idolo mio, deh in braccio ancor t'avessi!
Poppea, respiro appena,
Miro le labbra tue,
E mirando ricupero con gl'occhi
Quello spirto infiammato,
Che nel bacciarti, o cara, in te diffusi.

Non è più in cielo il mio destino,
Ma sta dei labbri tuoi nel bel rubino.

ACT 1, SCENE 10

POPPAEA, NERO, OTHO hidden.

Poppaea
How sweet, sir, how sweet
Did the kisses from this mouth
Seem to you last night?

Nero
The most biting were the most dear.

Poppaea
The apples of this breast?

Nero
Your breasts deserve sweeter names.

Poppaea
The tight, tight embraces from these arms?

Nero
My idol, oh that I still had you in my arms!
Poppaea, I scarcely breathe,
I look at your lips,
And looking at you I recoup with my eyes
That inflamed spirit,
Which in kissing you, oh dear one, I dif-
        fused in you.
Heaven is no longer my destiny,
But resides in the beautiful ruby of your lips.

Poppea
Signor, le tue parole son sì dolci,
Ch'io nell'anima mia
Le ridico a me stessa,
E l'interno ridirle
Necessita al deliquio il cor amante.
Come parole le odo,
Come baci io le godo,
Son de' tuoi cari detti
I sensi sì soavi e sì vivaci,
Che, non contenti di blandir l'udito,

Mi passano a stampar sul cor i baci.

Nerone
Quest'eccelso diadema ond'io sovrasto
Degl'uomini e dei regni alla fortuna
Teco divider voglio,
Allor sarò felice
Quando il titolo avrai d'imperatrice.
Ma che dico, o Poppea!
Troppo picciola è Roma ai merti tuoi,
Troppo angusta è l'Italia alle tue lodi,
E al tuo bel viso è basso paragone

L'esser detta consorte di Nerone.
Ed han questo svantaggio i tuoi begl'occhi,

Che trascendendo i naturali esempi,
E per modestia non tentando i cieli,

Non ricevon tributo d'altro onore,

Che di solo silenzio e di stupore.

Poppea
A speranze sublimi il cor innalzo
Perché tu lo comandi,
E la modestia mia riceve vita.
Ma troppo s'attraversa, ed impedisce

Delle regie promesse il fin sovrano.
Seneca, il tuo maestro,
Quello stoico sagace,

Poppaea
Sir, you words are so sweet
That in my soul
I repeat them to myself
And in repeating them within
My loving heart must faint.
I hear them as words,
I enjoy them as kisses,
They are the senses so sweet and so lively
Of your dear utterances,
Which, not content with pleasing my
        hearing,
Go to imprint your kisses on my heart.

Nero
I want to share with you
This exalted crown from which I rule
The fortune of men and of kingdoms,
Then I shall be happy
When you have the title of Empress.
But what am I saying, oh Poppaea!
Roma is too small for you merits,
Italy is too narrow for you praises,
And it is a base comparison to your lovely
        face
To be called Nero's consort.
And you lovely eyes have this
        disadvantage,
That transcending natural
And for modesty not challenging the
        heavens,
They receive no other tribute of high
        honor
Than of silence alone and of stupor.

Poppaea
I raise my heart to sublime hopes
Because you command it,
And my modest state receives life.
But too much is to be crossed, and
        impedes
The sovereign end of royal promises.
Seneca, your master,
That sagacious stoic,

Quel filosofo astuto,	That astute philosopher,
Che sempre tenta persuader altrui	Who always tries to persuade others
Ch'il tuo scettro dipenda sol da lui.	That you reign depends on him alone.

Nerone / **Nero**

Che, che?	What, what?
Quel decrepito pazzo ha tanto ardire?	That decrepit madman dares that much?

Poppea / **Poppaea**

Quel, quel! ha tanto ardire.	That one, that one! he does dare that much.

Nerone / **Nero**

Olà, vada un di voi	Oh, one of you go
A Seneca volando, e imponga a lui,	Flying to Seneca, and impose on him
Ch'in questa sera ei mora.	That he die this evening.
Vuo' che da me l'arbitrio mio dipenda,	I want my will to depend on me,
Non da concetti e da sofismi altrui.	Not on others' conceits and sophistries.
Rinnegherei per poco	I would renounce in a moment
Le potenze dell'alma, s'io credessi	The powers of my soul, if I were to believe
Che servilmente indegne	That, in servile fashion unworthy,
Si movessero mai col moto d'altre.	They were ever moved by the motion of others.
Poppea, sta di buon core.	Poppaea, be of good cheer.
Oggi vedrai ciò che sa far Amore.	Today you will see that which Love can do.

Act 1, Scene 10

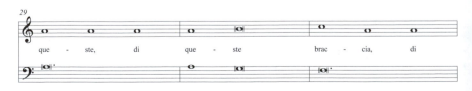

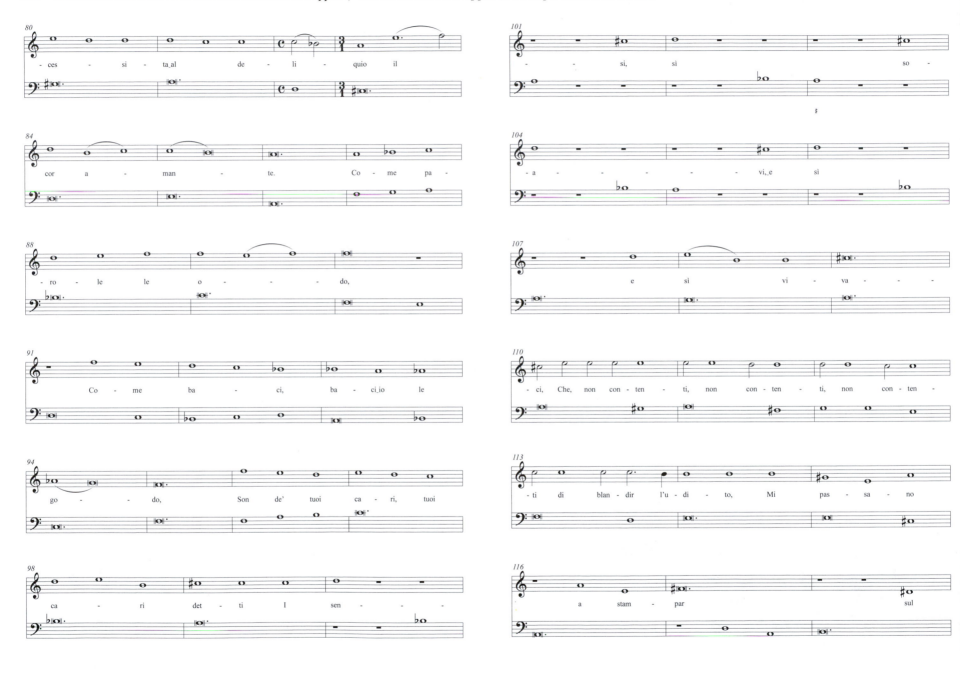

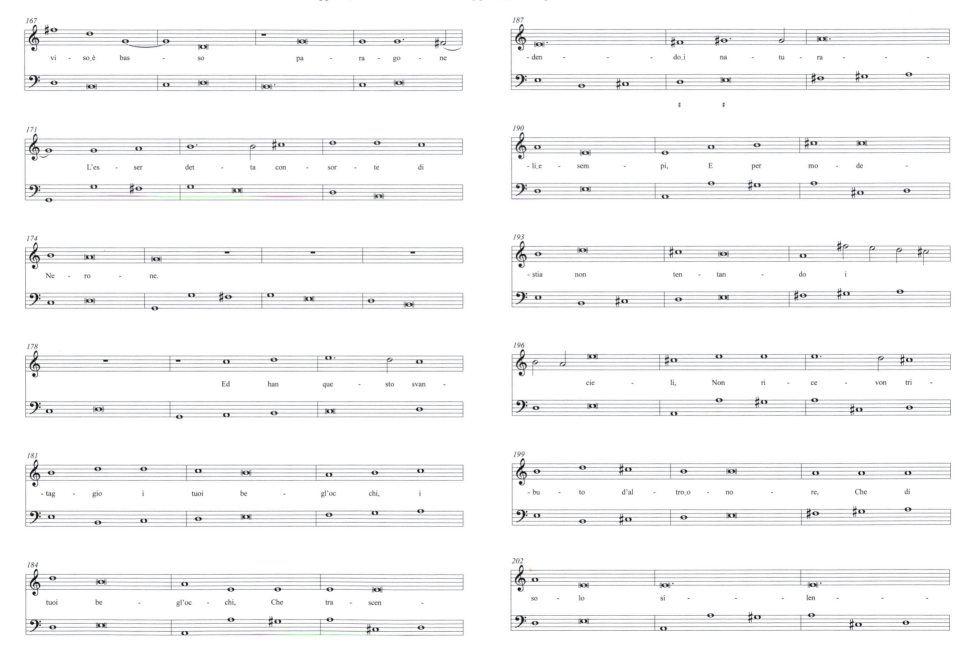

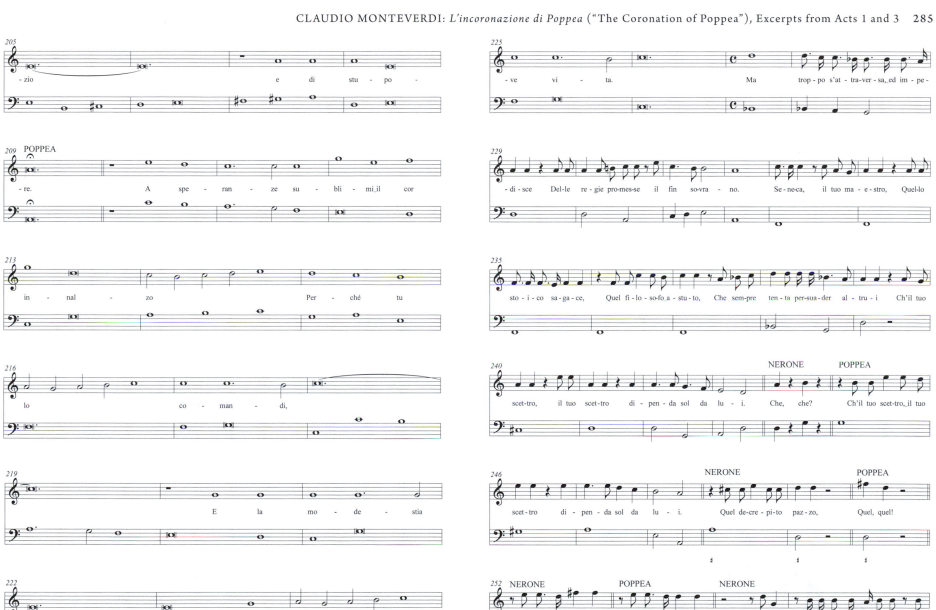

256
Se - ne - ca vo - lan - do, e im - pon - ga la lu - i Ch'in que - sto se - ra ei mo - ra. Vuo' che da me, da

260
me l'ar - bi - trio mio di - pen - da, Non da con - cet - ti e da so - fis - mi al - tru - i. Ri - ne - ghe - rei per

266
po - co Le po - ten - ze del - l'al - ma, s'io cre - des - si Che ser - vil - men - te in - de - gne Si mo - ves - se - ro

271
mai col mo - to d'al - tre.   Pop - pe - a, Pop -

275
- pe - a, sta di buon co - re, sta,

279
sta di buon co - re. O - gi,

283
og - gi ve - drai, ciò che sa

286
far A - mo - re, ve - drai, ve -

289
- drai ciò che sa far A - mo - re.

ATTO TERZO, SCENA SESTA

OTTAVIA

Ottavia

Addio Roma, addio Patria, amici, addio.

Innocente da voi partir conviene.

Vado a patir l'esilio in pianti amari,
Navigo disperata i sordi mari.
L'aria, che d'ora in ora
Riceverà i miei fiati,
Li porterà, per nome del cor mio,
A veder, a baciar le patrie mura,
Ed io starò solinga,
Alternando le mosse ai pianti, ai passi,
Insegnando pietade ai tronchi e ai sassi.

Remigate oggi mai perverse genti,
Allontanatevi omai dagli amati lidi.
Ahi, sacrilego duolo,

ACT 3, SCENE 6

OCTAVIA

Octavia

Farewell Rome, farewell homeland,
    friends, farewell.
It is time that I, innocent one, depart from
    you.
I go to suffer exile in bitter crying,
Desperate I sail the deaf seas.
The air, which again and again
Will receive my breath
Will bring, in the name of my heart,
To see, to kiss my native walls,
And I shall be alone,
Alternating between crying and wandering,
Teaching pity to the trees and to the
    stones.
Row today, twisted people,
Move away now from the beloved shores.
Ah, sacrilegious pain,

Tu m'interdici il pianto   You forbid me to cry
Quando lascio la patria,   When I leave my homeland,
Né stillar una lacrima poss'io   Nor can I shed a tear
Mentre dico ai parenti e a Roma: addio.   While I say to my kinfolk and to Rome:
    farewell.

Act 3, Scene 6

Chi lascia le grandezze	Who leaves riches
Piangendo a morte va.	Goes to death crying.
[Ma chi servendo sta,]	[But the one serving,]
Con più felice sorte	With a happier destiny
Come fin degli stenti ama la morte.	Loves death as the end of troubles.

Act 3, Scene 7

ATTO TERZO, SCENA SETTIMA	**ACT 3, SCENE 7**
ARNALTA	ARNALTA

Arnalta	**Arnalta**
Oggi sarà Poppea	Today Poppaea
Di Roma imperatrice.	Will be Empress of Rome.
Io, che son la nutrice,	I who am the nurse
Ascenderò delle grandezze i gradi.	Shall ascend the steps of riches.
No, col volgo io non m'abbasso più.	No, I shall no longer lower myself with *hoi polloi*.
Chi mi diede del tu,	Who addressed me with "thou,"
Or con nova armonia	Now with new harmony
Gorgheggierammi il "Vostra Signoria."	Will serenade me as "Your Ladyship."
Chi m'incontra per strada	Who sees me in the street
Mi dice "fresca donna e bella ancora."	Will say to me "fresh lady, and still beautiful."
Ed io, pur so che sembro	And I, even though I know I resemble
Delle Sibille il leggendario antico.	The legendary ancientness of the Sibylls.
Ma ognun così m'adula,	But everyone will adulate my thus
Credendo guadagnarmi	Believing to get me
Per interceder grazie da Poppea.	To intercede for favors from Poppaea.
Ed io, fingendo non capir le frodi,	And I, pretending not to understand the lies,
In coppa di bugie bevo le lodi.	Drink the praises in a chalice of lies.
Io nacqui serva, e morirò matrona.	I was born a servant, and shall die a lady
Mal volentier morrò.	Unwillingly I shall die.
Se rinascessi un dì,	Were I reborn one day,
Vorrei nascer matrona, e morir serva.	I would like to be born a lady, and die a servant.

ATTO TERZO, SCENA OTTAVA

Si muta la scena nella reggia di Nerone.
NERONE, POPPEA, CONSOLI,
    TRIBUNI,
AMORE, VENERE in Cielo,
e CORO D'AMORI

. . .

Poppea
Pur ti miro,

Nerone
pur ti godo,

Poppea, Nerone
Pur ti stringo, pur t'annodo,
Più non peno, più non moro,
O mia vita, o mio tesoro.

Poppea
Io son tua,

Nerone
tuo son io,

Poppea
Speme mia,

Poppea, Nerone
dillo, dì

Nerone
Tu sei pur l'idol mio

Poppea
Tu sei pur

Poppea, Nerone
Sì, mio ben, sì, mio cor, mia vita, sì.

Poppea
Pur ti miro,

Nerone
pur ti godo,

Poppea, Nerone
Pur ti stringo, pur t'annodo,
Più non peno, più non moro,
O mia vita, o mio tesoro.

ACT 3, SCENE 8

The scene changes to the Palace of Nero.
NERO, POPPAEA, CONSULS,
    TRIBUNES,
CUPID, VENUS in Heaven,
and CHORUS of CUPIDS

. . .

Poppaea
Yet I look at you,

Nero
yet I enjoy you,

Poppaea, Nero
Yet I embrace you, yet I entwine you,
I suffer no more, I die no more,
Oh my life, oh my treasure.

Poppaea
I am yours,

Nero
yours am I,

Poppaea
My hope,

Poppaea, Nero
say it, say

Nero
You are indeed my idol

Poppaea
You are indeed

Poppaea, Nero
Yes, my treasure, yes, my heart, my life, yes.

Poppaea
Yet I look at you,

Nero
yet I enjoy you,

Poppaea, Nero
Yet I embrace you, yet I entwine you,
I suffer no more, I die no more,
Oh my life, oh my treasure.

Act 3, Scene 8

69

Girolamo Frescobaldi (1583–1642)

Cento partite sopra passacagli ("A Hundred Variations on Passacagli") (1637)

Girolamo Frescobaldi, the most famous keyboardist of the early seventeenth century, held the prestigious post of organist at St. Peter's on and off for over three decades, starting in 1608. In 1637 he published *Cento partite sopra passacagli* ("A Hundred Variations on *Passacagli*")—a wonderfully misleading title, for there are not 100 variations, nor are they all on *passacaglia*—in the *Aggiunta* ("Supplement") to the fifth and final edition of his First Book of keyboard music. *Passacagli* is Italian for *passacalles,* a Spanish genre consisting of variations on cadential patterns that grew out of the habits of guitarists who accompanied courtly singers. It and other ground-bass genres became popular in Italy during the early decades of the seventeenth century—Frescobaldi himself had already published some in his Second Book of keyboard music—and the version found here was a common one, a minor-mode progression with a bass descending through scale degrees 8–7–6–5 and harmonized i–v⁶–iv⁶–V, of which the concluding dominant demands resolution, either to a fresh iteration of the ground bass or to a section-ending tonic. The triple meter—$\frac{6}{4}$ is to be understood as double measures of $\frac{3}{4}$—is configured such that second beats are frequently stressed. Frescobaldi, though, does more than simply adopt a fashionable novelty: He adds to it fresh novelties of his own, which become apparent only as the piece unfolds.

The beginning presents straightforward variations on the descending tetrachord, which remains clearly recognizable even when migrating from the bass to the middle voices (mm. 11–12) or embellished by passing tones and neighbors (mm. 13–14). The composer himself numbers the first eleven variations (mm. 1–22), and one easily follows these and the next nine (mm. 23–40). Pervasive faster rhythms in variations 16–20 (mm. 31–40), culminating in sixteenth notes, also help clarify the overall structure. Things change with variations 21–25 (mm. 41–52), where Frescobaldi inserts a *corrente*—a fast, triple-meter dance—followed by another twenty-two variations (mm. 53–131). He apparently thought of this section as a unit, giving it the additional listing *Corrente e passacagli* in the collection's Table of Contents. The generic disruption announces itself through an increase in tempo: $\frac{3}{2}$ is, if anything, a proportional sign, and the meter remains unchanged ($\frac{6}{4}$, once again understood as double measures of $\frac{3}{4}$). The

corrente's conventional two-part form, with modulation to the dominant and back, forces the variations themselves to modulate. Dance and harmonic mobility continue to make themselves felt in the *passacagli* that follow. Those marked ₵ $\frac{3}{2}$ (mm. 53–88, 103–31)—note that $\frac{3}{2}$ now indicates meter, an attribute reinforced by the mensuration sign ₵, and that the slower rhythms of these variations follow directly from the concluding measure of the *corrente*, itself configured in $\frac{3}{2}$, a cadential slowing typical of that dance. Those marked $\frac{6}{4}$ that come between, particularly the eighth-note-laden variations 38–40 (mm. 97–102) that imply $\frac{12}{8}$, suggest a gigue. Finally, variation 42 (mm. 107–110) modulates to F major, and the arrival in the new key announced by the marking *Altro tono* ("Another mode") is now maintained over the next five *passacagli* (mm. 111–131); frequent minor-mode inflections preserve the genre's tonal convention.

Frescobaldi unleashes yet another surprise at variation 48 (m. 132), where he introduces a different ground-bass pattern, the *ciaccona*. Originally a fast (and lascivious) triple-meter dance imported from the New World at the end of the sixteenth century, it became a major-mode ostinato generally built on scale degrees 1–5–6–3–4–5 harmonized I–V–vi–I⁶–IV–V. Frescobaldi's *ciaccone* contrast with his *passacagli* in other ways as well: They generally unfold in two- rather than four-measure units, and stresses remain on the downbeat, such that rhythmic patterns of 2 + 1 beats predominate, the opposite of those found in *passacagli*. Once again, the composer announces the new presence in the Table of Contents, designating a section of *Ciaccone e passacagli*, and in fact the remainder of the piece alternates three sections of the former (mm. 132–151, 174–197, 218–255) with three of the latter (mm. 152–173, 198–217, 256–326). From here on, then, the work becomes a game of contrasts, both sharp and subtle. Variation 57 (mm. 148–151), the last of the first round of *ciaccone*, modulates to C major, and the ensuing *passacagli* carry on in that key. Second-beat stresses return at once, however, announcing the shift of genre, and these are soon complemented by the minor-mode inflections that appear halfway through the initial variation 58 (m. 154) and that then become more pervasive. The next set of *ciaccone* also features a modulatory closing variation (mm. 196–197), this one leading to A minor, the generically "correct" mode for the ensuing *passacagli*. It is now the *ciaccone* that are harmonically wrong-footed: the *passacagli* remain in A minor, and the final set of *ciaccone* begins in that key, frequently adjusting scale degree 6 from F natural to F♯ in an attempt to fix the modal anomaly. Another modulating variation (mm. 236–237), confirmed by the marking *altro tono* at the beginning of the next, returns the piece to the tonic. Now, however, the *ciaccone* continue rather than yield to the *passacagli*, and the same difficulty regarding the scale degree 6—B♭ or B natural—remains (though the D-Dorian key signature, lacking flats, privileges the raised sixth degree).

The final set of *passacagli* presents new marvels (m. 256). The designation *altro tono* with which it begins (m. 256) likely refers to the new one-flat signature, since otherwise the piece remains in D minor. Frescobaldi's choice was likely symbolic, since flats could still signify languor, an affect associated with *passacagli*, and another contrast with the generally extrovert *ciaccone*. In this event, languor is clearly projected in the chromatically inflected descending tetrachord of the opening variation 102 (mm. 256–259), even as that variation retains some qualities of the *ciaccona*. Stresses on the second beat are lacking—they return in the next variation—and

B natural is still a prominent presence in the right hand. Following the example of the *ciaccone*, these final *passacagli* also change key, just as did those of the cycle that followed the *corrente*. The flat is cancelled at the beginning of the modulatory variation, 110 (m. 284), and the arrival in A minor is noted at the start of the next by the now-familiar *altro tono* (m. 286). Another modulation, up a fifth, occurs in variation 117 (mm. 306–308), with the arrival in E minor announced in its last measure. And there the piece remains, with a slowly unwinding conclusion in a foreign key.

So shocking was this closing modulatory gesture that Frescobaldi himself offered performers a way to avoid it. His final instruction to them reads, "The *Passacagli* can be played separately, in according with what pleases whom the most, by adjusting the tempo of one or another part, and so too the *ciaccone*."

70

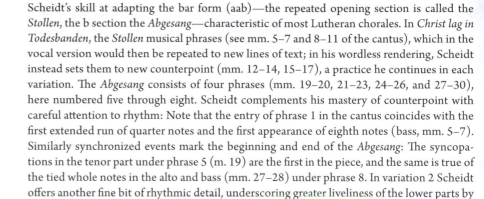

Samuel Scheidt
(1587–1654)

Christ lag in Todesbanden ("Christ lay in the bonds of death"),
SSWV 131 (1624)

The chorale partita *Christ lag in Todesbanden* ("Christ lay in the bonds of death"; see score 53 for the tune) is one of eight such pieces that Samuel Scheidt published in his *Tabulatura nova* ("New Tablature") of 1624, a monumental three-volume collection of forty-six sacred and secular organ works. The title is another manifestation of the early seventeenth century's rage for the new—think of *Le nuove musiche*—but Scheidt's title lives up to its billing more than does Caccini's. "Tablature" refers to a means of notation, and *Tabulatura nova* is the first German publication of keyboard music in open score—that is, with each "voice" (generally there are four) notated on its own five-line staff—a layout that had been used by such celebrated Italian composers as Adriano Banchieri and Girolamo Frescobaldi for their organ works. Scheidt, then, turned away from at least one aspect of both his nationality and training—he was a lifelong resident of the Saxon town of Halle and studied with the great Dutch organist Jan Pieterszoon Sweelinck (1562–1621)—and, like his conationals Heinrich Schütz and Johann Hermann Schein, looked instead to Italy as the fount of musical novelty.

Some have argued, though, that Scheidt intended *nova* to refer to the music itself rather than its notation. If this is so, *Christ lag in Todesbanden* exemplifies novelty as well as any work in the collection, for chorale partitas, variation sets on Lutheran chorales, hardly existed before Scheidt. In each variation of such pieces the traditional melody is treated strictly—that is, with little or no embellishment—as a cantus firmus in a single voice. The tune may migrate through the texture as verse succeeds verse, and the accompanying voices may vary from one to three. Sometimes the latter incorporate aspects of the chorale tune, thus integrating it into the polyphony; sometimes they contrast with it as countersubjects.

Scheidt composed five variations on this *Cantio Sacra* ("Sacred Song"), as he called it, the first two of which are closely related—both are marked *Choralis in Cantu* ("Chorale in the cantus": Scheidt conceived the work in four real voices). The first (mm. 1–30) is an integrated motet-like setting with some old-fashioned imitative foreshadowing of the cantus firmus in the accompanying voices, of a kind that Luther himself would surely have recognized. In the second (mm. 30–66), successive lines of the chorale are set in relief against a series of ever-more rhythmically active countersubjects, each treated in imitation. Both show

Scheidt's skill at adapting the bar form (aab)—the repeated opening section is called the *Stollen*, the b section the *Abgesang*—characteristic of most Lutheran chorales. In *Christ lag in Todesbanden*, the *Stollen* musical phrases (see mm. 5–7 and 8–11 of the cantus), which in the vocal version would then be repeated to new lines of text; in his wordless rendering, Scheidt instead sets them to new counterpoint (mm. 12–14, 15–17), a practice he continues in each variation. The *Abgesang* consists of four phrases (mm. 19–20, 21–23, 24–26, and 27–30), here numbered five through eight. Scheidt complements his mastery of counterpoint with careful attention to rhythm: Note that the entry of phrase 1 in the cantus coincides with the first extended run of quarter notes and the first appearance of eighth notes (bass, mm. 5–7). Similarly synchronized events mark the beginning and end of the *Abgesang*: The syncopations in the tenor part under phrase 5 (m. 19) are the first in the piece, and the same is true of the tied whole notes in the alto and bass (mm. 27–28) under phrase 8. In variation 2 Scheidt offers another fine bit of rhythmic detail, underscoring greater liveliness of the lower parts by setting the cantus firmus entirely in whole notes.

The third verse is at once the longest (mm. 67–233) and the most modestly scored, what Scheidt called a *Bicinium complexus mutui* ("Duo of mutual embrace"). Said "embrace" can be seen in the motivic fragments that precede each entry of the cantus firmus, in both their closely spaced points of imitation (mm. 71–72) and their frequent flirtations with canon (mm. 124–130). Embrace can also be seen in the treatment of the cantus firmus, each phrase of which is played first in the right hand and then an octave lower in the left. In the *Stollen*, such repetition maps onto the chorale's regular unfolding: Phrases 1 and 2 (mm. 99–103 and 104–109) return as phrases 3 and 4 (mm. 110–114 and 115–120). In the *Abgesang* Scheidt instead parts company with tradition by sounding each phrase twice (mm. 135–138 / 139–142, mm. 157–161 / 162–166, mm. 188–192 / 192–196, mm. 228–230 / 231–233). This freer treatment is signaled at the very beginning of the piece, in the changed time signature (¢ to the more up-to-date c) and the opening motive (the raised leading tone that is the second note). As the variation progresses, it also becomes a more idiomatically instrumental piece, thanks to the sixteenth notes that first appear at the end of the *Stollen* (m. 120) and pervade phrases 7 and 8 of the *Abgesang*. Finally, as if to emphasize its singularity, Scheidt ended this variation on an authentic rather than a plagal cadence.

The fourth variation (mm. 234–283) reverses some of the trends of the third, adding a voice and presenting the cantus firmus without repetitions. Nevertheless, its texture remains more modern: After a brief foreshadowing in the bass, the *Choralis in Tenore* (the "tenor" being the middle voice) is pitted against two exceptionally florid outer voices that sometimes develop countersubjects in imitation and sometimes contrast with one another as well as with the subject, creating in phrase 7 (mm. 273–277) an "obbligato" texture with a fast-flowing line above the tenor, a slower "walking bass" beneath it.

The fifth and last variation (mm. 284–371), a return to four-voice texture, offers fresh oddities. By *Choralis in Basso* Scheidt seems to have meant both tenor and bass, for whichever is the lower part at the moment quotes the cantus firmus. Thus phrases 1 and 2 are entrusted to the tenor in mm. 287–292 and 294–299; indeed, one might hear this variation as a continuation of the three-part texture of its predecessor. The entrance of the true bass in m. 300 confirms the four-part texture as it proceeds to restate the *Stollen* as phrases 3 and 4 in mm. 300–308, 309–315; its unbroken whole notes single it out even more. Rhythmic monotony, however, is offset by tonal surprise, as Scheidt transposes phrase 3 a perfect fifth below the original pitch. Phrase 4 begins with the same transposition, but from the second note to the end it continues on another, down a perfect fourth. Thus are the original closing pitches of both phrases, A and D, reversed, and Scheidt avoided strong closure on both by means of deceptive cadences. Similar transpositional games pervade the *Abgesang*: The tenor maintains the original pitches in mm. 317–320, 330–334, 343–347, and 357–359, while the bass always transposes, in mm. 322–328, 335–342, 348–356, and 360–364 (these internal repetitions recall variation 3). Scheidt moves all but one phrase down a fourth (he set phrase 6 down a fifth), such that when he ends phrase 8 with an authentic cadence, in m. 364, there is strong closure on the wrong harmony. This he remedies by repeating phrase 8 in the bass once more (mm. 365–369), now with the original pitches, a most satisfying tonal and registral close (note the unprecedented exploration of low notes).

3. Versus. Bicinium complexus mutui.

4. Versus. Choralis in Tenore.

71

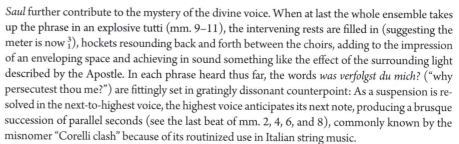

Heinrich Schütz
(1585–1672)

Symphoniae sacrae: III, Op. 12, *Saul, Saul, was verfolgst du mich*
("Saul, Saul, why do you persecute me?"), SWV 415 (1650)

Saul, Saul, was verfolgst du mich is one of the crowning masterworks of Heinrich Schütz's third and last volume of *Symphoniae sacrae*. Like the other pieces in the collection (but unlike many of those Schütz composed during the Thirty Years War), it is opulently scored, for six vocal soloists, two four-part choruses, two violins, and continuo (the last for *violone*—string bass—and organ). The text is taken from Acts of the Apostles 26, which narrates the conversion of Saul, Jewish persecutor of early Christians, to Paul, an Apostle of Christ. Paul himself recounts the journey to Damascus when it occurred:

> *13* At midday, O king, I saw in the way a light from heaven above the brightness of the sun, shining round about me, and them that were in company with me.
> *14* And when we were all fallen down on the ground, I heard a voice speaking to me in the Hebrew tongue: *"Saul, Saul, why persecutest thou me? It is hard for thee to kick against the goad."*
> *15* And I said: "Who art thou, Lord?" And the Lord answered: "I am Jesus whom thou persecutest."

Schütz sets only the italicized words in verse 14, but he does so with music designed to fill in a great deal of the surrounding narration of Paul's miraculous conversion. The words echo and reecho endlessly in the prostrate persecutor's mind, which we who hear them seem to inhabit, and the intensity of the moment is complemented by its brevity—*Saul, Saul, was verfolgst du mich* is the shortest piece in *Symphoniae sacrae* III. The echo idea is portrayed in the music not only by repetition but also by the use of explicitly indicated dynamics, something pioneered in Venice by Schütz's erstwhile teacher, Giovanni Gabrieli.

The musical phrase on which most of the concerto is built works its way quietly, indeed mysteriously, from low to high. It is first sung by a pair of basses (mm. 1–3), then by the alto and tenor (mm. 3–5), and then by the sopranos (mm. 5–7) and then is played by the pair of violins (mm. 7–9). Text accents suggest that each of these overlapping phrases be heard in measures of three breves (rather than as double measures of $\frac{3}{1}$), and the slow pacing and odd offbeat iterations of

Saul further contribute to the mystery of the divine voice. When at last the whole ensemble takes up the phrase in an explosive tutti (mm. 9–11), the intervening rests are filled in (suggesting the meter is now $\frac{3}{1}$), hockets resounding back and forth between the choirs, adding to the impression of an enveloping space and achieving in sound something like the effect of the surrounding light described by the Apostle. In each phrase heard thus far, the words *was verfolgst du mich?* ("why persecutest thou me?") are fittingly set in gratingly dissonant counterpoint: As a suspension is resolved in the next-to-highest voice, the highest voice anticipates its next note, producing a brusque succession of parallel seconds (see the last beat of mm. 2, 4, 6, and 8), commonly known by the misnomer "Corelli clash" because of its routinized use in Italian string music.

After the tutti, Schütz backs away from the climax just as suddenly. He lets *was verfolgst du mich?* echo twice (mm. 11–12) for soloists and instruments alone, marked first *mezzo piano* and then *pianissimo*. Verbal accents here transform the meter from $\frac{3}{1}$ to $\frac{3}{2}$, fleetness of delivery further complementing the rapidly fading voice. Schütz also switches from simultaneous to consecutive clashes. In mm. 10–11 he had harmonized the phrase i–V–I in G, a Picardy third raising the expected B♭ to B natural on the downbeat of m. 11. Both echoes, however, begin in G minor, forcing a chromatic slide from B natural back to B♭ (note that the sharp before the B in the tenor indicates raising the pitch a half step with respect to the previous B♭).

Having switched to duple meter in m. 12, Schütz reserves the second sentence of the text, *Es wird dir schwer werden, wider den Stachel zu löcken* ("It will be hard for thee to kick against the goads"), for the soloists, an intimate, madrigal-like treatment of Christ's statement that Saul cannot resist the call to conversion. He first sets the words to consecutive statements for tenor and alto (mm. 13–15, 15–17). Madrigalisms abound on *zu löcken* ("to kick"): an uncomfortable downward leap out of a dissonance followed by a melisma. After an abbreviated repetition of the opening (mm. 18–21), the second sentence returns with more extravagances. It now appears as a duet (mm. 22–24) in which the opening consecutive major tenths between soprano and bass create a tritone cross relation (B–F), while the succeeding melisma is longer and in imitation. Imitative duets then take over (mm. 25–28), and as the harmony of the first three measures moves inexorably down the circle of fifths to the darkness of an unusually flat region (G–C–F–B♭–E♭–A♭), Schütz makes it more dissonant as well. A surprise B natural in soprano 1 momentarily creates an augmented triad (m. 27; note another juxtaposition with B♭, in soprano 2 on the fourth beat), followed by the alto striking a G against the continuo's A♭ (m. 27, beats 5–6). The final statement of these words (mm. 28–34) brings with it the violins as well as a wonderful anticipation of the return of the first sentence (m. 33).

In the final section of the concerto, the soloists declaim the text rapidly in a manner recalling Monteverdi's *genere concitato*. Meanwhile, the tenor soloist calls repeatedly on Saul, his voice continually rising in pitch from C to D to E (mm. 36–37, 38–40, 41–43), the two choirs interpreting these pitches as dominants and reinforcing each successive elevation with a cadence, their entries marking "modulations" from F to G to A, the last preparing the final return to the initial tone center, D (m. 45). The ending, rather than the climax that might have been expected, revisits the echo effects heard earlier. Once again, it takes the form of reverberations over a fastidiously marked decrescendo to *pianissimo*, the forces scaled down from tutti to soloists plus instruments.

In a final stroke of genius, Schütz adds an extra echo for alto and tenor soloists over the continuo (mm. 48–49), followed by a final notated silence, the grand pause at the end of m. 49. The fadeout corresponds to the Apostle's "blackout," his loss of consciousness on the road to Damascus. Thus have we heard Christ's words through Saul's ears and shared his shattering religious experience.

Saul, Saul, was verfolgst du mich?　　Saul, Saul, why persecutest thou me?
Es wird dir schwer werden, wider den　　It will be hard for thee to kick against the
　　Stachel zu löcken.　　　　　　　goad.

72

Giacomo Carissimi (1605–74)

Jephte, Concluding solo and chorus (1640s)

Giacomo Carissimi, *maestro di cappella* at the Jesuit *Collegio Germanico* in Rome, composed *Jephte* no later than 1649, the date on one of its manuscript sources. Like most of his fourteen surviving Latin oratorios, it tells an Old Testament story, this one a celebrated tale of tragic expiation from the Book of Judges (chapter 11). The Israelite commander Jephthah vows that if God grants him victory over the Ammonites, he will sacrifice the first being who greets him on his return home. That turns out to be his beloved daughter, a virgin, who is duly slaughtered after spending two months in the mountains with her companions, lamenting her fate. The grim story is appropriate to the Lenten season, for which oratorios were then composed.

Carissimi ends his version with lament rather than sacrifice, setting newly written text rather than the quotations and paraphrases of Judges 11:29–38 that constitute the bulk of the work. The anonymous author of this text elaborates on the final phrase of verse 38 ("And when she was gone with her comrades and companions, she mourned her virginity in the mountains"), providing the composer with a small opera-like scene. The Daughter's lament consists of four sections, the first three of which are addressed to her natural surroundings. Each is longer than the last, and each ends with an echo of her last word, an imperative of sound, *Ululate . . . Lachrimate . . . Resonate* ("Wail . . . Weep . . . Resound"). The responses suggest that the Daughter's keening reverberates off the rocky face of the mountains and cliffs. The last section is shorter and is addressed to her companions. They, too, respond with an echo, but a much larger one that repeats nearly verbatim the Daughter's final words.

The first section (mm. 1–12) typifies Carissimi's tonal organization and the text-expressive ends to which it is used. The Daughter sings her first two verbal phrases to nearly identical music, her second utterance transposed up a fourth (mm. 1–3, 3–5); her next phrase, heard twice, is similarly repeated at the same transposition (mm. 5–8, 9–12). The first two musical phrases end on A and D, the next two on E and A, a harmonic away-and-back from tonic to subdominant to dominant to tonic. Just as important, though, is the way Carissimi connects the end of the second phrase and the beginning of the third in m. 5: The chromatic ascent D–D♯ in the basso continuo and the implied harmonic progression from a D-major triad to a B-major triad nicely underscore the words *et in afflictione cordis* ("at the affliction of my heart") as well as

the shift from the Daughter's opening imperatives to the description of her own state. The voice part also makes prominent use of the flatted second degree of each tonal level, at once invoking the mournful affect of the Phrygian mode and, in the cadences of the final two phrases, preparing the grinding cross relation between Neapolitan sixth and dominant (F to F♯ between mm. 7 and 8, B♭ to B natural between mm. 10 and 11). This progression (♭II⁶–iv⁶–i₄⁶–V–i), in turn, harmonizes the echo that follows (mm. 13–14).

Similar features are found in the second section (mm. 15–29, 30–31), which begins with a shift to G minor that sets in sharp relief the Daughter's opening reflection on her own state, *Ecce moriar virgo* ("Behold I shall die a virgin"), and that continues the tonal rivalry between A and G found throughout the work. A chromatic shift in the next phrase (mm. 17–18) sends the music back to E minor in time for a new round of imperatives, only to have the sharper key undone by a progression down the circle of fifths (mm. 20–23) to a fresh arrival on G, this by way of another Neapolitan progression (mm. 24–25). Another chromatic shift introduces a textual repetition, which ends by presenting the final musical phrase a whole step higher (mm. 26–29), reestablishing A minor.

The third section (mm. 32–53, 54–55) introduces contrast, between the Daughter's sadness and the rejoicing around her. Carissimi presents the threefold description of the latter, *In laetitia populi, in victoria Israel et gloria patris mei* ("Amidst the people's happiness, amidst Israel's victory and my father's glory"), on three successive transpositions, each a fourth higher than the last (mm. 35, 36, 37). He also fashions a madrigalism for the voice part, a trumpet-call motive that sounds out the celebration of military victory. After deploying another chromatic juxtaposition to return the Daughter to self-reflection (mm. 37–38), Carissimi introduces another first, a phrase-ending Phrygian cadences on *virgo* and *moriar*, key words heard in the previous section (mm. 39–40, 41–42); this harmonic progression will feature prominently in the remainder of the oratorio. With the return to imperatives (m. 44) the continuo line begins to restate that of the corresponding passage in the previous section, albeit to slightly different rhythms and harmonies (cf. mm. 44–52 and 19–28). Complementing the more elaborate nature of the third section, the final vocal phrase and its echo have larger melismas.

The fourth section (mm. 56–70) initially recalls the opening of the first, with which it shares the same repeated *plorate*'s. The bulk of it, though, uses material found in the previous section. The first two phrases end with Phrygian cadences, chromatically inflected (mm. 57–58, 59–60); the final word, the imperative *lamentamini* ("lament"), is set twice to the same cadence that ends the third section (mm. 64–65, 69–70), only now with its bass line moving twice as slow.

Carissimi sets the final "echo," the response of the Daughter's companions, as a six-part chorus (mm. 71–117). Its first two phrases (mm. 71–74, 74–77) recall those of the preceding solo, both ending in Phrygian cadences. Now, however, each cadence comes at the end of a descending tetrachord, the very emblem of lament, such that the chorus acts out the deploring it enjoins. Carissimi also changes the rhythms of the new material, stretching to dirge-like slowness the phrase-ending *Israel* (mm. 73–74) and *virgines* (mm. 76–77) and coordinating them with the Phrygian progressions (note, too, that all six voices are not heard until the second phrase, which contains the modified text *omnes virgines*—singers again act out meaning, as the enlarged community is called on to lament). He also begins the ground bass on E and shortens the initial descent A–G to half notes: So configured, the bass line suggests descent through scale degrees 4–3–2–1 of the Phrygian mode as much as it does an 8–7–6–5 descent in A minor (indeed, with one possible exception the chorus never comes to a V–i cadence in A minor). After a shift from E major to E minor followed by a progression up the circle of fifths from C to A (mm. 77–81) that quickly names the object of the lament—*et filiam Jephte unigenitam* ("Jephthah's only daughter")—Carissimi returns to the descending tetrachord, once more acting out the text *in carmine doloris* ("in a song of sadness," mm. 81–89). The song, however, is a small *stile antico* motet, as the descending tetrachord is now treated in six-part imitation; here the 7–6 suspensions over the initial tetrachords' penultimate Fs (mm. 73, 76) are writ large, as one is heard in nearly every measure of the passage. After the half-cadence close on E (m. 89, another suggestion of the Phrygian mode), Carissimi sets the final imperative *lamentamini* in spectacular fashion. Once again, C follows E at the beginning of a phrase (m. 90) but without the softening intervention of E minor (as in m. 77). The ensuing phrase (mm. 90–93) echoes the progression that ended the Daughter's final solo, but now in G major, the overall key of the oratorio. It is also configured such that the V$^{44}_2$ arrives with a jolt on the word's last syllable (m. 91); the 2–3 suspension resolved by the succeeding I^6 coheres beautifully with its new surroundings. A final phrase leading to the repeat sign (mm. 93–99) is more emphatic still, as the word is repeated antiphonally, with double and even triple suspensions sounded against a rising bass line. After the repetition, a final phrase begins by echoing the preceding one (cf. mm. 111–112 and 93–94) and then closes with the familiar progression (mm. 113–117), the dominant now stretched to three measures.

Filia
Plorate, colles; dolete, montes,
et in afflictione cordis mei ululate.

Daughter
Lament, hills; be sad, mountains,
and wail at the affliction of my heart.

Echo
Ululate.

Echo
Wail.

Filia
Ecce moriar virgo, et non potero morte mea

meis filiis consolari. Ingemiscite silvae,
fontes et flumina; in interitu virginis
*   lachrimate.*

Daughter
Behold I shall die a virgin, and at my
    death can not
be consoled by my children. Groan, forests,
springs, and rivers; weep for a virgin's
    destruction.

Echo
Lachrimate.

Echo
Weep.

Filia
Heu me dolentem! In laetitia populi,

in victoria Israel et gloria patris mei;

Daughter
Alas, miserable me! Amidst the people's
    happiness,
amidst Israel's victory and my father's glory;

ego sine filiis virgo, ego filia unigenita moriar,

et non vivam! Exhorrescite, rupes;
obstupescite, colles; valles et cavernae,
in sonitu horribili resonate.

I, a virgin without children, I, an only
    daughter, shall die,
and I shall not live! Shudder, rocks;
be dumbfounded, hills; valleys and caverns,
resound with horrid sound.

Echo
Resonate.

Echo
Resound.

Filia
Plorate, filii Israel, plorate virginitatem meam;

et Jephte filiam unigenitam
in carmine doloris lamentamini.

Daughter
Lament, children of Israel, lament my
    virginity;
and lament in a song of sadness
Jephthah's only daughter.

Chorus
Plorate, filii Israel, plorate omnes virgines,

et Jephte filiam unigenitam
in carmine doloris lamentamini.

Chorus
Lament, children of Israel, lament all you
    virgins,
and in a song of sadness lament
Jephthah's only daughter.

73

Barbara Strozzi
(1619–77)

Lagrime mie ("My tears") (1659)

The secular cantata *Lagrime mie* (My tears) by the Venetian singer and composer Barbara Strozzi comes from the seventh of the eight volumes of music she published between 1644 and 1664. The collection's learned and whimsical title, *Diporti di Euterpe* ("Euterpe's Recreations"), refers to the muse of lyric poetry and music, while its prosaic subtitle, *cantate & ariette a voce sola* ("Cantatas and Arias for Solo Voice"), identifies the two genres that comprise its contents.

The text is a lament by the Venetian nobleman Pietro Dolfin (1636–1709), author as well of several opera librettos. In it, a lover bemoans the loss of his beloved Lydia, locked away in her father's palace. As often happens in laments, the opening line becomes a refrain, returning to punctuate moments of high rhetorical intensity. The first return occurs after the speaker has narrated the cause of Lydia's imprisonment and the pain her pain causes him, leading him to exclaim *E voi, lumi dolenti, non piangete?* ("And you, sad eyes, do not cry?"). The second comes at the very end, after further reflections on Lydia's and his own suffering, followed by new ones on fate's desire that he cry. Most of the poem consists of *versi sciolti*, freely rhymed seven- and eleven-syllable lines that generally call for recitative. Unlike early-seventeenth-century laments, however, which consist entirely of such verse, midcentury cantata texts like this one generally deploy one or more strophic arias. Here there is one, the pair of quatrains that begins *Lidia ahimé, veggo mancarmi* ("Lydia, alas, I see is gone from me"), which Dolfin strategically places immediately following the first refrain.

Strozzi's music matches the overwrought tone of Dolfin's verse; indeed, it resembles Monteverdi's treatment of *versi sciolti* in *L'incoronazione di Poppea*. Syllabic, speech-like declamation frequently yields to melismas and outright lyrical effusions, and the setting is peppered with textual repetitions and pictorial madrigalisms of various sorts. Strozzi sets the very first word (mm. 1–3) to an extravagant example of the latter, a scalar descent representing downward-flowing tears, further enhanced by such "painful" leaps as an augmented second (D♯ to C natural) and a diminished fourth (G to D♯), this last landing dissonantly against the sustained E of the basso continuo. The bass then initiates its own decorated stepwise descent, whose arrival on B at the end of the first line (m. 8) outlines what was in this repertory an emblem of lament, the minor

descending tetrachord through scale degrees 8–7–6–5 (note that the concluding Phrygian cadence in mm. 7–8 is painfully embellished by the augmented sixth and major seventh formed against the bass by the soprano's A♯ and B). The passage features another extreme madrigalism, when in m. 6 the voice literally does what the text says, interrupting itself just before the accent-bearing penultimate syllable of the word *trattenete* ("hold back"). (Strozzi, it should be noted, suppresses this madrigalism in subsequent statements of the refrain, rewriting it to close in the tonic in mm. 63–70 and 123–130 [the latter erroneously omitted from the edition reprinted here].) Expressive dissonance continues in the second line, with the voice now sustaining an E in m. 11 on the word *dolore* ("pain") as the bass leaps from A♯ to D♯. The remainder of the setting is shot through with madrigalisms, such as the interruption on *respiro* ("breath") in mm. 12–13, 17–18 (voice acting out text), the descending scales on *rigor* ("severity") in mm. 30 and 32 (punishment hurled down from on high), and the chromatic slide on *tormenti e pene* ("torments and sufferings") in mm. 41–43.

By contrast, Strozzi deploys triple meter just twice, but in substantial passages that immediately precede the refrains, thus joining melodic and verbal intensity. The first (mm. 49–60) sets the bulk of the line *E voi, lumi dolenti, non piangete?* ("And you, sad eyes, do not cry?"), mostly to "sobbing" 7–6 suspensions over a relentless stepwise bass descent. The second (mm. 97–122) sets the reflection on fate that occupies the final three lines. Four statements of the emblematic descending tetrachord underscore a repetitive setting of the couplet *Se dunque è vero, o Dio,/Che sol del pianto mio* ("If it is true then, oh God,/That only for my crying"), the voice dissolving once more into pictorial melismas for the key word *pianto* (mm. 105, 107, 109). The music for the last line, *Il rio destino ha sete* ("Does evil destiny thirst"), reverses direction, its first phrase (mm. 112–116) bringing the voice to its highest note (*destino!*), its second repeating the passage a third lower (mm. 116–122) to close on the tonic.

The placement of these passages, which resemble small arias, is a harbinger of things to come: By the end of the century most cantatas were cast recitative–aria–recitative–aria. The actual aria in this cantata (mm. 71–87) is, paradoxically, more declamatory than lyrical, based on a rhythmic pattern used since the beginning of the seventeenth century to set octosyllabic verse. Groups of eight eighth notes, which begin on weak beats and end on strong (e.g., mm. 71–72), provide most of the material for this curiously understated section (the initial descending tetrachord is its only affective gesture); even the melismatic departures from this norm follow the verse's structure rather than its meaning: Strozzi uses them to round off each half of the quatrain, in mm. 74–75 and in mm. 78–80, the latter transposed down a fifth and repeated in mm. 82–84.

This transposition, however, reminds us that the aria was as up to date as the rest of the piece, for transposed restatements of this sort (there is another that links mm. 13–17 and mm. 17–21) were common in music of the mid-seventeenth century. Strozzi was equally up to date in her use of sequence: From the last beat of m. 75 to the downbeat of m. 77, as the melody proceeds down a third, up a step, and so on, the harmony progresses on successive quarter beats down the circle of fifths (e–A–D–G–c♯–F♯).

Lagrime mie, a che vi trattenete?	My tears, why do you hold back?
Perché non isfogate il fier dolore	Why do you not pour out the fierce pain
Che mi toglie 'l respiro e opprime il core?	That takes my breath away and oppresses my heart?
Lidia, che tant' adoro,	Because Lydia, whom I adore so much,
Perch'un guardo pietoso, ahi, mi donò,	Gave me, ah, a pitying glance,
Il paterno rigor l'imprigionò.	Paternal severity imprisoned her.
Tra due mura rinchiusa	The beautiful innocent one is
Sta la bella innocente	Enclosed between two walls
Dove giunger non può raggio di sole.	Where not a ray of sun can reach her.
E quel che più mi duole,	And that which pains me the most,
Ed accrese al mio mal tormenti e pene,	And increases the torments and sufferings of my pain
È che per mia cagione	Is that on my account
Provi male il mio bene.	My darling feels pain.
E voi, lumi dolenti, non piangete?	And you, sad eyes, do not cry?
Lagrime mie, a che vi trattenete?	My tears, why do you hold back?
Lidia, ahimé, veggo mancarmi,	Lydia, alas, I see is gone from me,
L'idol mio che tanto adoro.	My idol whom I worship so much.
Sta colei tra duri marmi	She is between hard marble walls
Per cui spiro e pur non moro.	For which I sigh and yet do not die.
Se la morte m'è gradita,	If death is welcome to me,
Or che son privo di spene,	Now that I am deprived of hope,
Deh, toglietemi la vita!	Pray, take my life!
Ve ne prego, aspre mie pene.	I beg of you, my bitter pains.
Ma ben m'accorgo che per tormentarmi	But well do I realize that to torment me
Maggiormente, la sorte	Even more, fate
Mi niega anco la morte.	Still denies me death.
Se dunque è vero, o Dio,	If it is true then, oh God,
Che sol del pianto mio	That only for my crying
Il rio destino ha sete,	Does evil destiny thirst,
Lagrime mie, a che vi trattenete?	My tears, why do you hold back?

Adagio
Aria

1. Li-dia,ahi-mè, veg-go man-car-mi, Li-dia,ahi-mè, veg-go man-car-mi. L'i-dol
2. Se la mor-te m'è gra-di-ta, se la mor-te m'è gra-di-ta, Or che

mio,che tan-to a-do - - - ro, Stà co-lei tra du-ri mar-mi per cui
son pri-va di spe - - - ne, Dhè to-glie-te-mi la vi-ta (Ve ne

spi-ro, per cui spi - ro E pur____ non mo - - ro. Stà co-lei tra du-ri
pre-go, ve ne pre - go) a - spre-mi-e pe - - ne. Dhè to-glie-te-mi la

mar-mi,per cui spi-ro, per cui spi - ro E pur____ non mo - - ro.
vi-ta,(ve ne pre-go, ve ne pre - go) a - spre-mie pe - - ne.____

-len - ti,e voi lu-mi do-len-ti, do-len - ti, non pian -

-ge - - - - - - - -te! La - - - - - - -gri-me

mi - e, à che, à che vi trat-te-ne - te?

(Repeat mm. 63-70)

74

Jean-Baptiste Lully (1632–87)

Atys, Overture and Act 3 (1676)

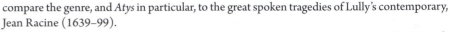

Atys is the fourth *tragédie en musique*—the genre now commonly referred to as *tragédie lyrique*—written by Jean-Baptiste Lully and his librettist, Philippe Quinault. Its story is based on an ancient Greek myth as told by the Roman poet Ovid, in a collection entitled *Fasti*. Attis, worshipped as a god of vegetation who controlled the yearly round of wintry death and vernal resurrection, was originally a beautiful youth over whom jealous goddesses fought. Cybele, the earth or mother goddess, fell in love with the unwitting and insouciant Attis and, so that none other should ever know his love, caused him to castrate himself in a sudden frenzy. In Quinault's libretto Cybele instead has a rival for the love of Attis in the person of the nymph Sangaride, to whom Attis has actually declared his affections. At the end of the opera, Cybele causes Attis to kill Sangaride in his frenzy and then to stab himself fatally. Before he can die, Cybele transforms him into a pine tree whose life is renewed yearly so that she will be able to love it forever.

As is customary, the overture—a French overture—consists of a march-like opening that is repeated (mm. 1–15; the editor of this nineteenth-century vocal score wrote out the repetition as mm. 16–30); the genre's stilted dotted rhythms became a universal code for royalty and pomp for a century and more. Equally characteristic is the fast section with imitative opening that follows (mm. 31–48; this one is gigue-like), and the return to the slow, dotted rhythms of the opening (mm. 49–55). Like most instrumental sections in *tragédies en musique*, the overture is scored for a five-part string band—violins, three types of violas, and cellos—that was performed by the celebrated *vingt-quatre violons du Roi* ("twenty-four violins of the king"), the number arrived at by assigning 6 + 4 + 4 + 4 + 6 players to a part.

The third act of *Atys,* at once the most succinct and the most varied, is a perfect model of courtly opera at the peak of its prestige. As an anonymous observer wrote of the entire opera a few months before the premier, "The whole drama unfolds thus, in half-tints: no big effects for the singers, no grand arias, but small *airs de cour* and recitatives, all with basso continuo; and it is their alternation alone that sets things in motion." Such qualities distinguish the *tragédie en musique* from contemporary Italian opera, as do its lack of castrati, comic episodes, and messy subplots. This tendency toward serenity and exalted moderation—found even in the *divertissements*, moments of spectacle for choristers and dancers—have led modern commentators to

compare the genre, and *Atys* in particular, to the great spoken tragedies of Lully's contemporary, Jean Racine (1639–99).

Scene 1 is a short soliloquy for the title character, cast as an *haute-contre*, the highest French male voice range, a soft tenor shading into falsetto. Attis laments the loss of Sangaride to her betrothed, King Celaenus of Phrygia. This little number, an *air de cour* of the type described by the anonymous observer, epitomizes Lully's deliberate avoidance of big Italianate vocal display. The text consists of a single quatrain, of which the first couplet is used as a refrain to round it off into a miniature ABA form (mm. 19–26, 26–32, 32–39). This little rounded entity is enclosed between a pair of identical *ritournelles*, themselves ABA structures (mm. 1–6, 6–14, 14–19), in which the first measure already discloses the characteristic slow triple meter with stressed second beat of the sarabande (this edition does not give the closing *ritournelle*). Thus even the vocal solos reflect the underlying basis of the French court opera in the court ballet and, beyond that, in ballroom dance itself. The setting of the text is entirely syllabic and is responsive to the contours, stresses, and lengths of the spoken language, reflecting the other underlying basis of the court opera, namely, high-style theatrical declamation.

In Scene 2 the nymph Doris and her brother Idas enter to urge Attis to act on his passion and spurn his official duty as Celaenus's protégé and chief sacrificer to Cybele, thus crystallizing the moral dilemma on which the drama turns. Like most scenes of dialogue, it is carried by a recitative that employs both four-beat and three-beat measures. But when the two confidants come to their principal argument, *Dans l'empire amoureux,/Le devoir n'a point de puissance* ("In the empire of love/Duty has no power"), they come together in another short *air* in minuet tempo (mm. 32–63), into and out of which they slip almost imperceptibly—thus the deft "alternation . . . that sets things in motion" to which the anonymous writer referred. And when they win Attis over, he joins them in a tiny trio (mm. 68–90) in the style of an allemande, with dotted rhythms recalling the imperious strains of the overture.

Attis is left alone in Scene 3 to reflect on his amorous prospects. After another sarabande-like *ritournelle* (mm. 1–10), he launches what promises to be an extended *air* based on the same dance (mm. 10–17); two statements of a descending major tetrachord, often a symbol of amorous desire (as in the final duet of Monteverdi's *L'incoronazione di Poppea*), suggest the start of ground-bass aria. But Attis is quickly distracted by the counterclaim of duty and lapses into a recitative, from which he finally lapses into sleep.

Scene 4 is an enchanted slumber that Cybele has engineered in order to apprise Attis of her love without having to degrade herself by confessing it. The scene, which requires a set change to Sleep's enchanted cave, is the most famous in the opera, a "sleep scene" so widely copied by later composers and librettists that it became a standard feature of the *tragédie en musique*. It begins with a Prelude (mm. 1–57) in which soft, sweet-toned *flûtes* (i.e., recorders) are spotlighted in a somewhat concerto-like dialogue with the string band. The rocking rhythms, slurred in groups of two (the markings were changed by the editor of the vocal score) and surely performed with the characteristic French lilt (the so-called *notes inégales*), as well as the long pedal tones that support oscillating tonic–dominant harmonies (mm. 23–25, 35–39) cradle the entranced title character and serve as the prologue to a charmed vision of Sleep himself. The latter, another haute-contre, sings a hypnotic refrain, the first statement of which (mm. 58–70) is followed by replies from two of his three sons, the haute-contre Morpheus (mm. 71–102) and the bass Phobetor (mm. 105–133). Adding to the dreamlike nature of these unusual events is one other: The *flûtes* play while Phobetor sings. Sleep then repeats his refrain (mm. 134–146), which is followed by an expanded restatement from all three sons (mm. 146–180), who now include the tenor Phantasmus ("Dream").

After the opening sinfonia is repeated (not given in this edition), Pleasant Dreams enter, and Morpheus has a short recitative (mm. 181–195) in which he informs Attis that he has the honor of being loved by the exalted Cybele. The three sons of Sleep then sing a quatrain (mm. 196–205) that reminds Attis that Cybele's love exacts duty and constancy in return. Phantasmus follows with a minuet-like *air* (mm. 206–221) in praise of Love's charms, and his melody becomes the basis of a ballet of Pleasant Dreams (mm. 222–261). The whole sequence is then repeated, with new recitative for Phobetor (mm. 262–276), the same quatrain for the three sons (mm. 277–286), a second stanza of Phantasmus's *air* (mm. 297–312), and a repetition of the ballet (mm. 303–332).

Baleful Dreams enter during this last; and when the ballet ends, one of their number suddenly warns against offending a divine love (mm. 333–347). They then dance to the strains of an allemande in pompous overture style (mm. 348–378), its regal rhythms reflecting the high station of the goddess at whose behest the nightmares have appeared. The chorus that follows (mm. 379–406) issues a further warning, driven home by the rapid-fire patter of its delivery. The Baleful Dreams then launch into a lusty *courante* (mm. 407–452), full not only of the usual hemiolas but of rattling military tattoos as well.

The nightmare is dispelled when Attis awakes with a start. The palace setting returns, Cybele herself arrives, and Scene 5 begins. She comforts him, distressed though she is to learn, through an exchange of minuscule airs (mm. 12–37, 44–63), that Attis properly reveres her but does not return her passion. Sangaride enters for Scene 6, a nearly unbroken stretch of recitative that encloses the drama's turning point, when Cybele (alas, only temporarily) promises to aid her rival out of unselfish love for Attis. Her crucial decision is rendered as a maxim: *Les Dieux sont les protecteurs / De la liberté des coeurs* ("The gods are the protectors / Of freedom of the heart"), set as a tiny march, or allemande, for the goddess, immediately repeated by the mortal pair (mm. 16–21, 21–26). Sangaride and Attis exit to seek the aid of Sangaride's father, the river Sangarus.

Cybele's confidant, the priestess Melissa, enters in Scene 7 to console the unhappy goddess, whose complaint that *L'ingrat Atys ne m'aime pas* ("the ungrateful Attis does not love me") is set against the all-but-inevitable chromatically descending tetrachord in the continuo (mm. 4–7). She sings in recitative style throughout, while Melissa's attempts to console her take the form of two *airs* (mm. 21–34, 50–69); the first, with its two-quarter upbeat in "cut time," is readily identifiable as a gavotte. In the concluding Scene 8, Melissa leaves Cybele alone on stage and the goddess delivers herself of an impassioned yet dignified lament, the most extended solo turn in the opera. Introduced and concluded by a *ritournelle* in an elegiac sarabande style (mm. 1–11; the concluding statement is not given here), Cybele's lament is a recitative built around a threefold textual and musical refrain (mm. 11–14, 24–27, 37–40): *Espoir si cher et si doux, / Ah! pourquoi me trompez-vous?* ("Hope so dear and so sweet, / Ah! why do you deceive me?") Each

time, Lully places a quarter rest after the exclamation "Ah!" and repeats the word before completing the line to which it belongs. The rare fragmentary repetition heightens the poignancy of Cybele's desperation.

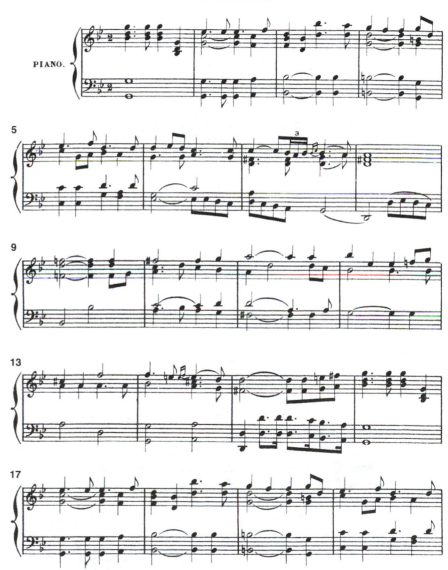

OUVERTURE.

en $\frac{6}{4}$ dans la Partition.

Lentement.

ACTE III
Le Palais du Grand Sacrificateur de Cybèle.

SCÈNE PREMIERE
ATYS seul.

Atys
Que servent les faveurs que nous fait la Fortune,
Quand l'Amour nous rend malheureux?
Je pers l'unique bien qui peut combler mes
*   voeux,*
Et tout autre bien m'importune.
Que servent les faveurs que nous fait la
*   Fortune,*
Quand l'Amour nous rend malheureux?

SCÈNE SECONDE
IDAS, DORIS, ATYS.

Idas
Peut-on ici parler sans feindre?

Atys
Je commande en ces lieux, vous n'y devez
*   rien craindre.*

Doris
Mon frere est votre ami.

Idas
Fiez-vous a ma soeur.

Atys
Vous devez avec moi partager mon bonheur.

Idas et Doris
Nous venons partager vos mortelles allarmes;
Sangaride, les yeux en larmes,
Nous vient d'ouvrir son coeur.

Atys
L'heure aproche où l'Hymen voudra qu'elle
*   se livre,*
Au pouvoir d'un heureux Epoux.

Idas et Doris
Elle ne peut vivre
Pour un autre que pour vous.

ACT 3
The Palace of the Great Sacrificer of Cybele.

SCENE 1
ATTIS alone.

Attis
What good are the favors Fortune grants us,
When love makes us unhappy?
I lost the only treasure that can satisfy my
    wishes,
And every other treasure just vexes me.
What good are the favors Fortune grants
    us,
When love makes us unhappy?

SCENE 2
IDAS, DORIS, ATTIS.

Idas
Can one speak here without fear?

Attis
I command in this place; you need not
    fear.

Doris
My brother is your friend.

Idas
Believe my sister.

Attis
You must share my good fortune with me.

Idas and Doris
We come to share your mortal distress;
Sangaride, tears in her eyes,
Came to open her heart to us.

Attis
The hour approaches where Hymen wants
    her delivered
To the power of a happy husband.

Idas and Doris
She can not live
For anyone other than for you.

Atys
Qui peut la dégager du devoir qui la presse?

Idas et Doris
Elle veut elle-même, aux pieds de la Déesse,
Declarer hautement vos secretes amours.

Atys
Cybèle pour moi s'interresse,
J'ose tout esperer de son divin secours.
Mais, quoi, trahir le Roi? tromper son
*   esperance!*
De tant de biens reçûs, est-ce la recompense?

Idas et Doris
Dans l'empire amoureux,
Le devoir n'a point de puissance;
L'amour dispense,
Les rivaux d'estre genereux;
Il faut souvent, pour de venir heureux,
Qu'il en coûte un peu d'innocence.

Atys
Je souhaite, je crains, je veux, je me repens.

Idas et Doris
Verrez-vous un Rival heureux à vos depens?

Atys
Je ne puis me resoudre à cette violence.

Atys, Idas et Doris
En vain, un coeur, incertain de son choix,
Met en balance mille fois,
L'Amour et le reconnaissance,
L'Amour toujours emporte la balance.

Atys
Le plus juste parti céde enfin au plus fort.

Allez, prenez soin de mon sort,
Que Sangaride ici se rende en diligence.

Attis
Who can release her from the duty that
    oppresses her?

Idas and Doris
She herself wants, at the feet of the goddess,
To declare aloud your secret loves.

Attis
Cybele looks out for me,
I dare hope everything from her divine help.
But, what, betray the king? deceive his
    hope!
Is this the repayment for so many goods
    received?

Idas and Doris
In the empire of love
Duty has no power;
Love exempts
Rivals from being generous;
It is custom, for happiness to come,
That a bit of innocence be put aside.

Attis
I hope, I fear, I want, I repent.

Idas and Doris
Would you like a rival happy at your
    expense?

Attis
I can not resort to this violence.

Attis, Idas, and Doris
In vain, a heart, uncertain of its choice,
Puts in the balance a thousand times
Love and gratitude.
Love always tips the balance.

Attis
The more just party always cedes to the
    stronger.
Go, take care of my fate.
Let Sangaride come here quickly.

SCÈNE TROISIÈME
ATYS seul.

Atys
Nous pouvons nous flater de l'espoir le plus
*   doux,*
Cybèle et l'Amour sont pour nous;
Mais du Devoir trahi j'entens la voix pressante,

Qui m'accuse et qui m'épouvante.
Laisse mon coeur en paix, impuissante Vertu,
N'ai-je point assez combattu?
Quand l'Amour, malgré toi, me contraint à
*   me rendre,*
Que me demandes-tu?
Puisque tu ne peux me deffendre,
Que me sert-il d'entendre
Les vains reproches que tu fais?
Impuissante Vertu, laisse mon coeur en paix.
Mais le sommeil vient me surprendre,
Je combats vainement sa charmante douceur.
Il faut laisser suspendre,
Les troubles de mon coeur.
*   (ATYS s'endort)*

SCÈNE QUARTRIÈME
(Le Théâtre change, et represente un Antre
*   ensouré de Pavots et de Ruisseaux, où le*
*   Dieu du Sommeil se vient rendre,*
*   accompagné des Songes agréable, et funestes.*

ATYS dormant, LE SOMMEIL, MORPHÉE,
PHOBÉTOR, PHANTASE, LES
SONGES AGRÉABLES, LES SONGES
FUNESTSES.

Le Sommeil
Dormons, dormons tous;
Ah que le repos est doux!

Morphée
Regnez, divin Sommeil, regnez sur tout
*   le monde,*
Répandez vos pavots les plus assoupissants,
Calmez les soins, charmez les sens,

SCENE 3
ATTIS alone.

Attis
I can flatter myself with the sweetest
        hope:
Cybele and Love are on my side.
But I hear the pressing voice of Duty
        betrayed,
Which accuses me and which frightens me.
Leave my heart in peace, impotent Virtue,
Have I not struggled enough?
When Love, despite you, forces me to
        yield,
What would you ask of me?
Since you can not defend me,
What does it help me listening
To the vain reproaches that you make?
Impotent Virtue, leave my heart in peace.
But sleep comes to overtake me,
Vainly I fight its charming sweetness.
My heart's troubles
Must be suspended.
        (ATTIS falls asleep)

SCENE 4
The scene changes, and represents a cave
        surrounded by poppies and brooks,
        where the God of Sleep comes, accom-
        panied by Pleasant and Baleful Dreams.)

ATTIS sleeping, SLEEP, MORPHEUS,
PHOBETOR, PHANTASMUS,
PLEASANT DREAMS, BALEFUL
DREAMS.

Sleep
Let us sleep, let us all sleep;
Ah, but rest is sweet!

Morpheus
Rule, divine Sleep, rule over all the world,

your most soporific poppies,
Calm cares, charm the senses,

Retenez tous les coeurs dans une paix profonde.

Phobétor
Ne vous faites point violence,
Coûlez, murmurez, clairs ruisseaux,
Il n'est permis qu'au bruit des eaux
De troubler la doucer d'un si charmant silence.

Le Sommeil
Dormons, dormons tous;
Ah que le repos est doux!

Morphée, Phobétor
*   et Phantase*
Dormons, dormons tous;
Ah que le repos est doux!

(Les Songes agréables aprochent d'Atys, et
*   par leurs danses, lui font connaître l'amour*
*   de Cybèle, et le bonheur qu'il en doit*
*   esperer.)*

Morphée
Écoute, écoute Atys, la gloire qui t'appelle,
Sois sensible à l'honneur d'être aimé de
*   Cybèle,*
Jouis, heureux Atys, de ta felicité.

Morphée, Phobétor,
*   et Phantase*
Maissouviens-toique la beauté,
Quand elle est immortelle,
Demande la fidelité
D'une amour eternelle.

Phantase
Que l'Amour a d'attraits
Lorsqu'il commence,
A faire sentir sa puissance!
Que l'Amour a d'attraits
Lorsqu'il commence,
Pour ne finir jamais!

Phobétor
Goûte en paix chaque jour une douceur
*   nouvelle,*

Hold all hearts in profound peace.

Phobetor
Do not make a disturbance.
Flow, murmur, clear brooks.
It is not permitted that the waters' sound
Trouble the sweetness of such charming
        silence.

Sleep
Let us sleep, let us all sleep;
Ah, but rest is sweet!

Morpheus, Phobetor, and
    Phantasmus
Let us sleep, let us all sleep;
Ah, but rest is sweet!

(Pleasant Dreams approach Attis, and with
        their dances let him know of Cybele's
        love, and the happiness which he
        may hope from it.)

Morpheus
Hear, hear, Attis, the glory that calls you,
Be sensible to the honor of being loved by
        Cybele,
Rejoice, fortunate Attis, in your happiness.

Morpheus, Phobetor, and
    Phantasmus
But remember that beauty,
When it is immortal,
Demands the faithfulness
Of an eternal love.

Phantasmus
What attractions has Love
As soon as he begins
To make his power felt!
What attractions has Love
As soon as he begins,
Never to finish!

Phobetor
Savor in peace a new sweetness every day,

Partage l'heureux sort d'une Divinité,
Ne vante plus la liberté,
Il n'en est point du prix d'une chaîne si belle.

Morphée, Phobétor,
  et Phantase
Maissouviens-toique la beauté,
Quand elle est immortelle,
Demande la fidelité,
D'une amour eternelle.

Phantase
Trop heureux un Amant
Qu'Amour exempte
Des peines d'une longue attente!
Trop heureux un Amant
Qu'Amour exempte
De crainte et de tourment!

(*Les Songes funestes approchent d'Atys, et*
  le menaçent de la vangeance de Cybèle,
  s'il méprise son amour, et s'il ne l'aime pas
  avec fidelité.)

Un Songe Funeste
Garde-toi d'offenser un amour glorieux,
C'est pour toi que Cybèle abandonne
  les cieux,
Ne trahi point son esperance.
Il n'est point pour les Dieux de mépris
  innocent,
Ils sont jaloux des coeurs, ils aiment la
  vangeance,
Il est dangereux qu'on offence
Un amour tout puissant.

Choeur Des Songes Funestes
L'amour qu'on outrage,
Se transforme en rage,
Et ne pardonne pas
Aux plus charmants appas.
Si tu n'aime point Cybèle,
D'une amour fidèle,
Malheureux que tu souffriras!

Partake of the happy fate of a Divinity,
Vaunt no more your liberty,
There is no prize equal to so beautiful a
  chain.

Morpheus, Phobetor, and
  Phantasmus
But remember that beauty,
When it is immortal,
Demands the faithfulness
Of an eternal love.

Phantasmus
Too happy is a lover
Whom Love exempts
From the pains of a long wait!
Too happy is a lover
Whom Love exempts
From fear and torment!

(Baleful Dreams approach Attis, and
  threaten him with Cybele's vengeance
  if he disdains her love, and if he does
  not love her faithfully.)

A Baleful Dream
Beware of offending a glorious love,
It is for you that Cybele abandoned
  heaven,
Do not betray her hope.
For the Gods there is not innocent
  contempt.
They are jealous hearts, they love
  vengeance,
It is dangerous when one offends
An all-powerful love.

Chorus of Baleful Dreams
The love that one outrages
Is transformed into rage,
And does not forgive
The most beguiling charms.
If you do not love Cybele
With a faithful love,
Unhappy one, you will suffer,

Tu periras:
Crain une vangeance crudelle,
Tremble, crain un affreux trépas.

(*Atys épouvanté par les Songes funestes,*
  saréveille en sursaut, le Sommeil et les
  Songes disparoissent avec l'Antre où ils
  étointe, et Atys se retrouve dans le même
  Palais où il s'étoit endormi.)

SCÈNE CINQUIÈME
ATYS, CYBÈLE.

Atys
Venez à mon secours, o Dieux! o justes Dieux!

Cybèle
Atys ne craignez rien, Cybèle est en ces lieux.

Atys
Pardonnez au desordre où mon coeur
  s'abandonne;
C'est un songe . . .

Cybèle
Parlez, quel songe vous étonne?
Expliquez-moi votre embaras.

Atys
Les songes sont trompeurs, et je ne les
  croy pas.
Les plaisirs et les peines,
Dont en dormant on est seduit,
Sont des chimeres vaines,
Que le réveil détruit.

Cybèle
Ne méprisez pas tant les songes,
L'Amour peut emprunter leur voix;
S'ils font souvent des mensonges,
Ils disent vrai quelque fois.
Ils parloient par mon ordre, et vous le devez
  croire.

Atys
O Ciel!

You will die:
Fear a cruel vengeance,
Tremble, fear an awful death.

(Attis, frightened by the Baleful Dreams,
  awakes startled, Sleep and the Dreams
  with the cave disappear along with the
  cave where they were, and Attis finds
  himself once more in the same Palace
  where he fell asleep.)

SCENE 5
ATTIS, CYBELE.

Attis
Come to my aid, oh Gods, oh just Gods!

Cybele
Attis, do not fear, Cybele is here.

Attis
Forgive the disorder to which my heart
  abandoned itself.
It was a dream . . .

Cybele
Speak, what dream astonished you?
Explain your distress to me.

Attis
Dreams are deceivers, and I do not
  believe them.
The pleasures and the pains
By which one when sleeping is seduced
Are vain chimeras
That awakening destroys.

Cybele
Do not scorn dreams so much,
Love can borrow their voice;
If they usually lie,
Sometimes they speak the truth.
They spoke on my order, and you must
  believe them.

Attis
O heaven!

Cybèle
N'endoutez point connaissez votre gloire,
Répondez avec liberté,
Je vous demandé un coeur qui depend de
lui-même.

Atys
Une grande Divinité
Doit assurer toujours de mon respect extreme.

Cybèle
Les Dieux dans leur grandeur supreme,
Receiving tant l'honneur quails en sont
rebates.
Ils se lassen souvent, d'être trop respected,

Ils sont plus contents qu'on les aimé.

Atys
Je say trop ce que je vous dois
Pour manquer de reconnaissance.

SCÈNE SIXIÈME
SANGARIDE, CYBÈLE, ATYS.

Sangaride
J'ai recours à votre puissance,
Reine des Dieux protegez-moi.
L'interest d'Atys vous en presse. . . .

Atys (interrompant Sangaride.)
Je parlerai pour vous: que votre crainte cesse.

Sangaride
Tous deux unis des pluys beaux noeuds. . . .

Atys (interrompant Sangaride.)
Le sang et l'amitié nous unissent tous deux.
Que vôtre secours la delivre,
Des loix d'un hymen rigoureux,
Ce sont les plus doux de ses voeux
De pouvoir à jamais vous servir, et vous suivre.

Cybèle
Les Dieux sont les protecteurs

Cybele
Do not doubt knowing your glory,
Answer freely,
I ask of you a heart that is independent.

Attis
A great divinity
Must always be assured of my highest
respect.

Cybele
The gods in their supreme grandeur
Receive so many honors that then are
repelled by them.
They are usually bored by being respected
so much,
They are more content when they are loved.

Attis
I know too well that which I owe you
To lack gratitude.

SCENE 6
SANGARIDE, CYBELE, ATTIS.

Sangaride
I call upon your power,
Queen of the Gods protect me.
Attis's interest demands it of you . . .

Attis (interrupting Sangaride.)
I shall speak for you: let your fear cease.

Sangaride
Both united by the most beautiful knots . . .

Attis (interrupting Sangaride.)
Blood and friendship unite us both.
May your help deliver her
From the laws of a strict marriage.
These are the sweetest of her wishes:
To be able always to serve you and to
follow you.

Cybele
The gods are the protectors

De la liberté des coeurs.
Allez ne craignez point le Roi, ni sa colere.

J'aurai soin d'appaiser
Le Fleuve Sangar vôtre Pere;
Atys veut vous favoriser,
Cybèle, en sa faveur, ne peut rien refuser.

Atys
Ah! c'en est trop . . .

Cybèle
Non, non, il n'est pas necessaire
Que vous cachiez vôtre bonheur,
Je ne prétens point faire,
Un vain mystere
D'un amour qui vous fait honneur:
Ce n'est point à Cybèle à craindre d'en
trop dire.
Il est vrai, j'aime Atys, pour lui j'ai tout quitté
Sans lui je ne veux point de grandeur ni
d'Empire
Pour ma felicité
Son coeur seul peut suffire.
Allez, Atys lui-même ira vous garantir
De la fatale violence
Où vous ne pouvez consentir.
Laissez nous.

(Sangaride se retire.)

Cybèle (à Atys)
Attendez mes ordres pour partir,
Je prétens vous armer de ma toute puissance.

SCÈNE SEPTIÈME
CYBÈLE, MÉLISSE

Cybèle
Qu'Atys dans ses respects mêle d'indifference!

L'ingrat Atys ne m'aime pas;
L'amour veut de l'amour, tout autre prix
l'offence;
Et souvent le respect et la reconnaissance
Sont l'excuse des coeurs ingrats.

Of freedom of the heart.
Go and do not fear the King, nor his
wrath.

I will take care to appease
The River Sangarius your father
Attis wants to favor you,
Cybele, in his favor, can not refuse.

Attis
Ah! that is too much . . .

Cybele
No, no, it is not necessary
That you should hide your happiness,
I do not want to make
A vain mystery
Of a love that does you honor:
It is not for Cybele to fear saying too
much.
It is true, I love Attis,
Without him I need neither grandeur nor
empire.
For my happiness
His heart alone can suffice.
Go, Attis himself will go to protect you
From the fatal violence
To which can not consent.
Leave us.

(Sangaride exits.)

Cybele (to Attis)
Await my orders to depart,
I presume to arm you with all my power.

SCENE 7
CYBELE, MELISSA

Cybele
How Attis mixes his respect with
indifference!
The ungrateful Attis does not love me;
Love wants love, anything else offends it;

And often respect and gratitude
Are the excuse of ungrateful hearts.

Mélisse

Ce n'est pas un si grand crime
De ne s'exprimer pas bien:
Un coeur qui n'aima jamais rien
Sçait peu comment l'amour s'exprime.

Cybèle

Sangaride est aimable, Atys peut tout
* charmer,*
Ils témoignent trop s'estimer,

Et de simples parents ont moins d'intelligence:
Ils se sont aimez dés l'enfance,

Ils pourroient enfin trop s'aimer.

Je crains un amitié, que tant d'ardeur anime.

Rien n'est si trompeur que l'estime:
C'est un nom supposé
Qu'on donne quelque fois à l'amour déguisé.
Je prétens m'éclaircir, leur feinte sera vaine.

Mélisse

Quels secrets par le Dieux ne sont point
* penetrez?*
Deux coeurs à feindre preparez
Ont beau cacher leur chaîne;
On abuse avec peine
Les Dieux par l'Amour éclairez.

Cybèle

Va, Mélisse, donne ordre à l'aimable Zephire
D'accomplir promtement tout ce qu'Atys desire.

SCÈNE HUITIÈME
CYBÈLE seule.

Cybèle

Espoir si cher et si doux,
Ah! pourquoi me trompez-vous?
Des suprêmes grandeurs vous m'avez fait
* descendre,*

Melissa

It is not so great a crime
Not to express oneself well:
A heart that has never loved
Knows little about how love is expressed.

Cybele

Sangaride is adorable, Attis can charm
  everyone,
They show too much regard for one
  another,
And mere relatives have less understanding:
They have loved one another since
  childhood,
They could in the end love one another
  too much.
I fear a friendship that is animated by so
  much ardor.
Nothing is so deceiving as esteem:
It is an assumed name
That is sometimes given to disguised love.
I intend to clarify for myself; their feint
  will be vain.

Melissa

What secrets are not penetrated by the
  gods?
Two hearts prepare to feign
Hide well their chain.
One with difficulty deceives
The Gods are clear about Love.

Cybele

Go, Melissa, order gentle Zephyr
To do promptly all that Attis desires.

SCENE 8
CYBELE alone.

Cybele

Hope so dear and so sweet,
Ah! why do you deceive me?
You made me descend from supreme
  heights,

Mille coeurs m'adoroient, je les neglige tous,

Je n'en demande qu'un, il a peine à se rendre;

Je ne sens que chagrin et que soupçons jaloux;

Est-ce le sort charmant que je devois attendre?

Espoir si cher et si doux,
Ah! pourquoi me trompez-vous?
Helas! par tant d'attraits falloit-il me
* surprendre?*
Heureuse si toûjours j'avois pû me deffendre!
L'amour, qui me fattoit, me cachoit son
* courroux:*
C'est donc pour me frapper des plus funestes
* coups,*
Que le cruel Amour m'a fait un coeur si
* tendre!*
Espoir si cher et si doux,
Ah! pourquoi me trompez-vous?

A thousand hearts worship me, I neglect
  them all.
I ask for but one, it barely surrenders
  itself;
I feel nothing but vexation and jealous
  suspicions.
Is this the charming fate that I had to
  await?
Hope so dear and so sweet,
Ah! why do you deceive me?
Alas! must I be surprised by so much
  beguilement?
Happy was I when I could protect myself!
Love, which beguiled me, hid from me his
  torments:
Thus it was to strike me the most baleful
  blows,
Since cruel love gave me so tender a
  heart!
Hope so dear and so sweet,
Ah! why do you deceive me?

ACTE III

Le théâtre représente le Palais du grand Sacrificateur de Cybèle.

SCÈNE I.

ATYS Seul.

SCÈNE II.

DORIS, ATYS, IDAS.

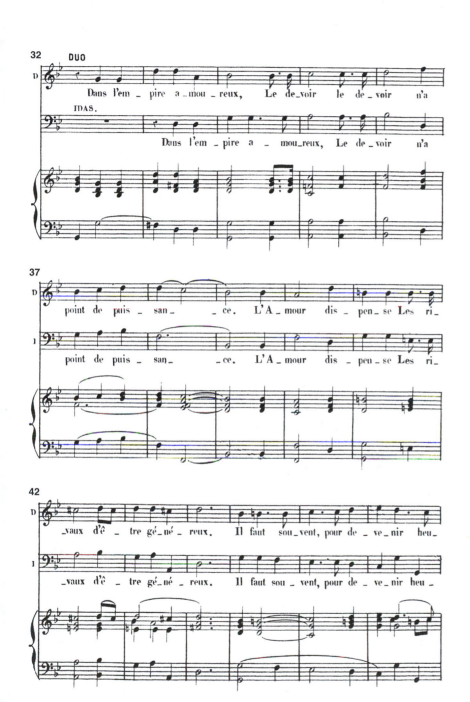

86

_mour   l'A_mour toujours em _ por _ te   la ba_ lan _ ce

_mour   l'A_mour toujours em _ por_te   la ba _ lan _ ce

_lan _ ce   L'A_mour toujours em _ por_te   la ba _ lan _ ce

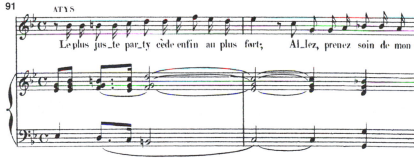

91   ATYS

Le plus jus_te par_ty cède enfin au plus fort;   Al_lez, prenez soin de mon

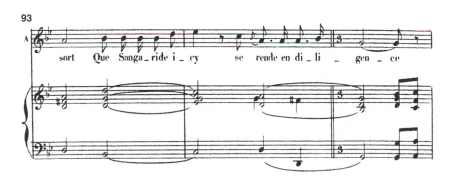

93

sort   Que Sanga_ride i _ cy   se rende en di _ li _ gen _ ce

SCÈNE III

ATYS seul.

RITOURNELLE.

PIANO.

5

10   ATYS

Nous pou_vons nous flat_ter   de l'es_poir le plus doux; Cy _ bèle et l'A_

16

_mour sont pour   nous Mais du devoir tra _ hy j'entends la voix pres_

SCÈNE IV

Le théâtre change et représente un autre entouré de Pavots et de ruisseaux où le Dieu du Sommeil se vient rendre accompagné des Songes agréables et funestes.

ATYS *dormant*, LE SOMMEIL, MORPHÉE PHOBÉTOR, PHANTASE.
LES SONGES AGRÉABLES, LES SONGES FUNESTES.

PIANO.

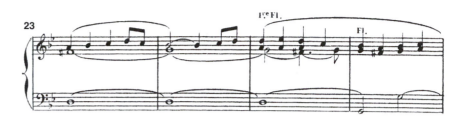

ENTRÉE DES SONGES AGRÉABLES

PHOB.

Goûte en paix cha_que jour u_ne dou_ceur nou_vel _ le, Par_

_ta _ ge l'heu_reux sort d'u_ne Divi_ni _ té.   Ne van_te

en ³⁄₂ dans la partition

plus la li_ber _ té, Il n'en est point du prix d'u_ne chai _ ne si

en ³⁄₂

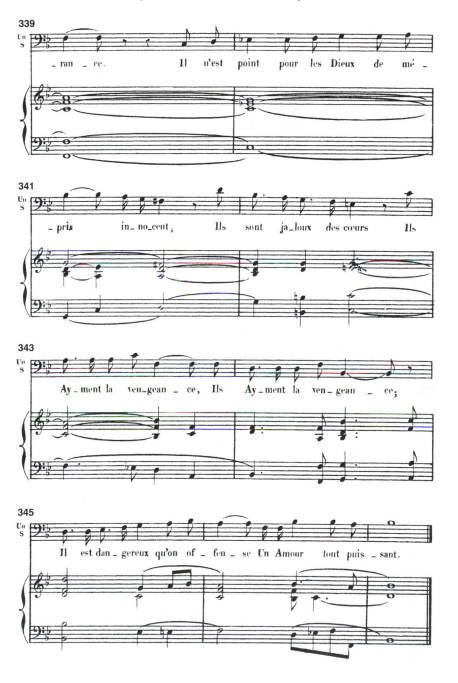

UN SONGE FUNESTE

Gar _ de-toi d'of_fen _ ser un A_mour glo_ri _ eux. C'est pour toy que Cy_

_bèle a_ban_don _ ne les Cieux. Ne tra_his pas son es_pé _

_ran _ ce. Il n'est point pour les Dieux de mé _

_pris in _ no_cent; Ils sont ja_loux des cœurs Ils

Ay _ ment la ven_gean _ ce, Ils Ay _ ment la ven_gean _ ce;

Il est dan _ gereux qu'on of _ fen _ se Un Amour tout puis _ sant.

ENTRÉE DES SONGES FUNESTES

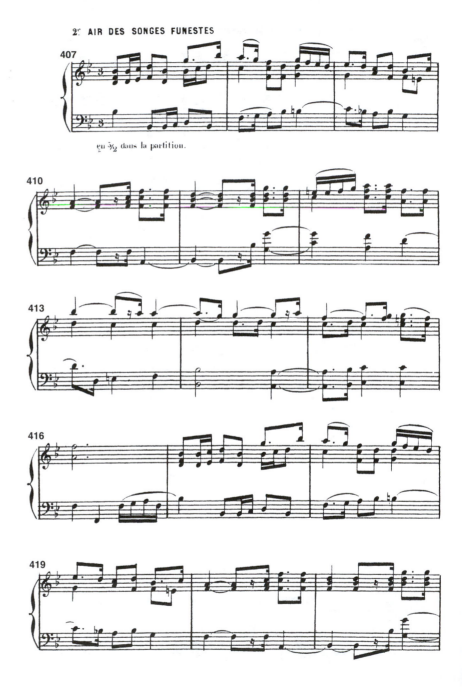

Atys, epouvanté par les Songes funestes, se réveille en sursaut; le Sommeil et les Songes disparaissent avec l'Antre ou ils estaient et Atys se retrouve dans le mesme Palais où il s'estait endormy.

SCÈNE V

CYBÈLE. ATYS.

SCÈNE VII

CYBÈLE, MÉLISSE.

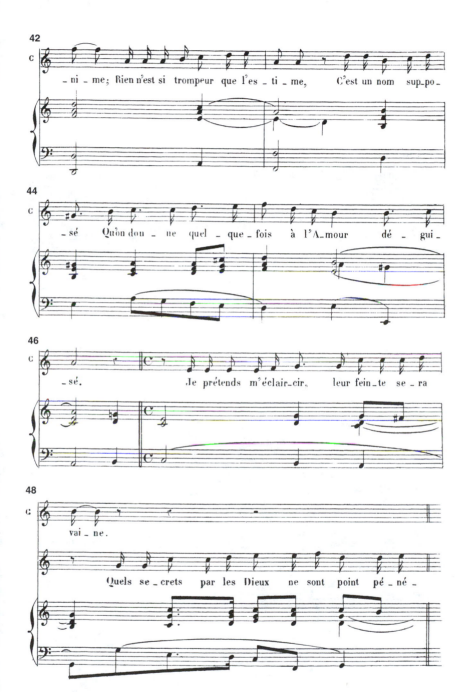

SCÈNE VIII.

75

Jean-Philippe Rameau
(1683–1764)

Castor et Pollux, Act 5, Scene 7, *ariette* (1737)

In the 1730s, when Jean-Philippe Rameau began to compose *tragédies en musique*, those of Jean-Baptiste Lully still held the stage. Their unprecedented longevity was born of an arch-conservative taste that measured new works against old, such as *Atys*. Thus the stylistic changes that less hidebound repertories had undergone during the previous half century and that Rameau introduced into his operas—among them more complex harmonies, more demanding vocal parts, more varied instrumentation—were at once condemned and applauded. *Hippolyte et Aricie* (1733), his first *tragédie en musique*, is apparently the first musical work to which the adjective "baroque" (in its original, pejorative sense) was attached. Rameau's prodigality of invention and complexity of style were taken by some as offensive to the memory of the great founder, Lully, whose works were in effect the first true "classics" in the history of music, sacramentally perpetuated in repertory. Others found his novelties refreshing; in good Gallic fashion, a fierce polemic ensued.

Castor et Pollux, Rameau's second opera, came on the heels of the disputes between *Lullistes* and *Ramistes*. Like *Atys*, its plot is drawn from myth. The title characters are twin brothers, born of the same mother impregnated by two fathers: Pollux is immortal by virtue of having been sired by Jupiter; Castor is not. In various tellings of the myth, Castor is slain and Pollux journeys to the Underworld to plead for Castor's return to the living, offering in exchange to take his place among the dead. Their heroism is rewarded by transformation into stars, part of the constellation Gemini. As in *Atys*, the libretto by Pierre-Joseph-Justin Bernard adds amorous complications (Pollux loves Telaira, who loves Castor, etc.); tragedy is averted (as it was in most of Lully's operas, *Atys* being an exception) by the arrival of a *deus ex machina*, when Jupiter himself descends on an eagle and effects the cosmic metamorphosis.

The *ariette* given here is found midway through the final scene, an immense *fête de l'univers* of some 500 measures that contains many of the same elements as the sleep scene in *Atys*. Instrumental music, dance, and choral song all play large roles and feature the stylistic innovations just described. In the *ariette*, the contrast with Lully is heard at once. The opening ritornello (mm. 1–14) is longer and more demanding than those of the *airs* in *Atys*, and it bears little if any resemblance to dance. If anything, it recalls the slashing virtuosity of contemporary Italian

string music (another feature sure to have annoyed Francophile *Lullistes*); equally Italianate are the cascading sequences that run from the arrival in the relative major A (m. 6) until the beginning of the cadential formula in the tonic F♯ minor (m. 10). In the latter, Rameau the master harmonist is also on display, setting the same melody to changing accompaniments (mm. 10–12, 12–14).

Even by Rameau's standards, though, the vocal part is extremely elaborate, embodying a virtuosity otherwise uncalled for in the opera. Here, too, Italy supplied the model for what is literally an otherworldly moment, a singing planet greeting a new constellation. Not surprisingly, Rameau deploys his virtuoso demands with considerable subtlety. The first difficult turn occurs on the phrase *régnez sur l'onde!* ("rule over the waves!"; mm. 18–19); though confined to the first word, it is clearly a madrigalism (this, coming just after the ornamented syncopated quarter notes of the violins are revealed as pictorialisms of the stars the singer commands to shine, is another bit of Italophilia). The rapid shift to the relative major in the orchestra (mm. 20–21) and the restatement of the text that follows suggest a second ritornello and solo—in short, the unfolding of another Italian import, the da capo aria. This time, however, *régnez sur l'onde* is shorn of its long melisma (mm. 25–26), and its apparent conclusion of the second solo with a perfect authentic cadence on A on the first syllable of the last word is immediately undercut by the harmonization of the second syllable with an F♯-minor triad in first inversion. New text, *Guidez les mortels sur les flots!* ("Guide mortals at sea!"), heard this one time and set to a Phrygian cadence on the dominant C♯ (mm. 26–28), confirms that the second solo has not ended, and its continuation offers two increasingly extravagant statement of *régnez sur l'onde* (mm. 30–33, 35–39), the latter adding a melisma to *l'onde*. The B section (mm. 46–56) is less idiosyncratic, its single traversal of its text culminating in another virtuoso turn on *La gloire d'être utile au monde!* ("The glory of being useful to the world!"), the melodic descent a madrigalism for starlight's earthward direction.

Despite (or maybe because of) its novelties, *Castor et Pollux* was a triumph, perhaps Rameau's greatest. In the end, his style was seen not to challenge Lully's but to intensify it. Proof of that sentiment is found in one of music history's great ironic reversals. When a revised version was mounted in 1754, it was held up as a model of French music, a rallying point for conservative taste against the encroachments of a still newer Italian style, that of the comic intermezzo.

ACTE CINQUIÈME	**ACT 5**
Une vue agréable aux environs de Sparte.	A pleasant view of Sparta's surroundings.
. . .	. . .
SCÈNE SEPTIÈME	**SCENE 7**
(Les cieux s'ouvrent, et laissent voir le Zodiaque; le Soleil sur son char commence à le parcourir; dans les nuages du fond on découvre le palais de l'Olympe, où les Dieux sont assemblés.)	(The heavens open, and allow the Zodiac to be seen; the Sun in its chariot begins to traverse it; in the clouds in background is revealed the palace of Olympus, where the Gods are assembled.)

JUPITER, CASTOR, TÉLAÏRE, POLLUX,
LES ASTRES, LES PLANÊTES,
LES SATELLITES, LES DIEUX

. . .

Une Planète

Brillez, brillez, astres nouveaux!
Parez les cieux, régnez sur l'onde!
Guidez les mortels sur les flots!
Triomphez de la nuit,
Suivez l'astre du jour
Et disputez-vous tour à tour
La gloire d'être utile au monde!

JUPITER, CASTOR, TELAIRA,
POLLUX, STARS, PLANETS,
SATELLITES, GODS

. . .

A Planet

Shine, shine, new stars!
Adorn the heavens, rule over the waves!
Guide mortals at sea!
Triumph over the night,
Follow the day star
And contend with each other
The glory of being useful to the world!

76

François Couperin
(1668–1733)

Le Rossignol en amour (The Nightingale in Love) and *Rossignol double* (1722)

Between 1713 and 1730 François Couperin published four books of harpsichord pieces. Together they comprise twenty-seven *ordres*, suite-like gatherings of movements joined by a common key. Some *ordres* follow the customary sequence of dances, like that found in J. S. Bach's French Suite No. 5; still more, however, depart from this model, united (if at all) by the programmatic titles that Couperin supplied for nearly all the approximately 220 pieces found across the collections. *Le Rossignol en amour* ("The Nightingale in Love") and its embellished repeat, *Rossignol double*, open the fourteenth *ordre*, and are followed by several other representations of birds, *La linotte éffarouchée* ("The Startled Finch"), *Les fauvettes plaintives* ("Plaintive Warblers"), and *Le Rossignol vainqueur* ("The Victorious Nightingale").

Given their rocking $\frac{6}{8}$ meter, binary form, and imitative opening, *Le Rossignol en amour* and its *double* seem at first glance to be gigues. But since the conventional quick tempo of a gigue contradicts tenderness or languor, Couperin had to countermand it with a very detailed verbal indication, directing the performer to play *Lentement, et très tendrement, quoi que mesuré* ("Slowly, and very tenderly, although basically in time"). Thus they are not really dances at all but "character pieces," or (to use Couperin's own word) "portraits" in tones, cast in a conventional form inherited from dance music. The subject portrayed is ostensibly a bird, and the decorative surface of the music teems with embellishments that seem delightfully to imitate the bird's singing. But since the bird in question is incongruously experiencing a human emotion, the musical imitation is simultaneously to be "read" as a metaphor—a portrait not just of the bird but of the emotion, too, in all its tenderness, its languorousness, its "sweet sorrow."

At the stipulated tempo there is room for a great wealth of *agréments* (embellishments), all indicated with little shorthand signs. The first sign in order of appearance, which Couperin called the *pincée* (a "pinched note," or mordent), is a rapid alternation of the written note with its lower neighbor on the scale. The second, which Couperin called *tremblement* ("trembling," or short trill or shake), is a rapid and repeated alternation of the written note with its upper neighbor, starting on the upper neighbor. Though such ornaments were learned "orally" (by listening to one's teacher and imitating) and deployed improvisationally, Couperin—like Caccini

a century earlier—fought against both tendencies. He published tables of ornaments in his First Book of harpsichord pieces and his didactic treatise *L'art de toucher le clavecin* ("The Art of Playing the Harpsichord") of 1716, which indicate precisely how to execute these and other *agréments*. More notably, he railed against those who ornamented freely: In the Preface to the Third Book itself he described himself as "surprised" by those who disregarded his ornamentation in favor in their own: "It is unpardonable negligence, all the more so as the placement of such *agréments* is not arbitrary. I declare then that my pieces must be played as I have marked them, and that they will never make a real impression on people of true taste unless one observes exactly what I have marked, without adding or subtracting."

Beneath the highly ornamented surface, often compared to the contemporaneous *rococo* style in the visual arts, lies the simplest of shapes. The opening section falls neatly into two four-measure phrases, the first of which is built from the same commonplaces of the nascent galant style found in the Allemande of Bach's French Suite No. 5. That is, the opening melodic ascent A–D–E–F♯ outlines in its core tones the same ascent from scale degree 1 to scale degree 3 in D major. Likewise, the remainder of the phrase descends (mm. 2–4) from scale degree 6 to scale degree 3 in the right hand (B–A–G–F♯) over a parallel descent from 4 to 1 (G–F♯–E–D) in the left. Though the second phrase begins like the first, it quickly introduces E major (m. 5), the dominant of the dominant; the harmony momentarily touches A minor (m. 7) on its way to a conventional section-ending close in A major. A shift in mode shortly before a cadence is not unusual—Bach's Allemande again provides an example—but here it nicely complements the portrayal of a lovesick nightingale. Indeed, after the first section is repeated, minor mode comes to the fore in the second section, further expressing the *très tendrement* affect Couperin calls for. The second section opens quite unusually in E minor; a shift from G natural to G♯ (m. 9) restores A as the momentary tonic, and another G natural (m. 10) seems to lead things back to D major, as suggested by the half cadence on A that concludes the phrase (m. 12). Couperin, however, proposes E minor once more (mm. 12–13), and, after what seems to be another approach to D major (m. 14 restates m. 10), he presents new amorous languors. For the first and only time in the piece he abandons four-measure phrasing, introducing a somewhat bizarre digression: The bass line moves from G natural back up to A while the right hand repeats the motive A–E (mm. 14–15), a realistic imitation of the bird's *accents plaintifs* breaking through the heretofore-affective representation. Couperin then begins the wayward passage again (m. 16 restates m. 14), now continuing it with a normative cadence in the tonic (mm. 17–18). After the second section is repeated, a second ending leads to a repetition of the final four measures (mm. 19–23). Here Couperin resorts to specifically composed embellishments, a means of presenting an especially spontaneous—or especially ornithological—burst of feeling. In place of the "plaintive accents" heard earlier, he composes a written-out trill, the speed of whose notes he directs to be *augmentés, par gradations imperceptibles* ("increased by imperceptible degrees").

In the *double* that follows, the surface becomes a real welter of notes. *Agréments* are still used plentifully, but they are supplemented with turns and runs that have no conventional shorthand notation, and it becomes the supreme mark of skillful performance to keep the contours of the original melody in the foreground. Perhaps that is why Couperin remarks in a footnote that the piece could also be played as a flute solo, for the flutist can use flexible dynamic shading and a true legato, while a harpsichordist must "fake" both. Whatever the case, the footnote also makes clear that however strict Couperin was about playing ornaments as written, he was not so about tempo, at least here: "One must not be too precisely attached to the beat in the *Double*. . . . Everything must be sacrificed to taste," presumably the same good taste that would lead one to follow his ornaments.

77

Henry Purcell
(1659–95)

Dido and Aeneas, Act 3, Conclusion (1689)

Henry Purcell's *Dido and Aeneas* is often described, incorrectly, as the first English opera (that distinction probably belongs to *Venus and Adonis* [1683] by John Blow, one of Purcell's teachers). There can be no doubt, however, that it is the first masterpiece of the genre. Its one documented performance during the composer's lifetime took place in 1689 at a London girls' school ("Mr. Josias Priest's Boarding-School at Chelsey," as the libretto's title page says). Its rapid succession of song, dance, and chorus and its overall brevity recall that typically English courtly entertainment, the masque. The surviving libretto contains an allegorical prologue (for which no music survives) that celebrates the ascension to the throne, after James's overthrow in the Glorious Revolution, of William and Mary.

Whether the opera itself is an allegory on contemporary politics is a vexed historical question. However it was intended, the plot was adapted by the poet Nahum Tate from the fourth book of the *Aeneid*, the Roman poet Virgil's epic poem that tells of the hero Aeneas's return from the Trojan War. On the way he stops at Carthage, in North Africa, where the Queen, Dido, having given him hospitality, conceives a passionate love for him. But the gods send Mercury to bid the hero continue on his journey (in Virgil, that is; in the libretto it is a false Mercury sent by scheming witches) and Aeneas departs, leaving Dido bereft. She dies (that is, kills herself) out of grief and shame.

The conclusion of Act 3, given here, is the opera's dénouement. It opens with a dramatic recitative (No. 40 in this edition), in which Aeneas takes leave of the forlorn and lovesick Queen and which displays Purcell's mastery of English declamation. The language's unusual accentuation patterns, in which stressed syllables and long syllables do not necessarily coincide the way they do in Italian, pose a special challenge. Purcell meets it by using short-long rhythms ("Lombards," or "Scotch snaps") on accented beats, as, for example, in the last two lines of Dido's first speech ("To fate I sue, of *other* means bereft, / The only *refuge* for the wretched left"), where the words in italics are so set (mm. 11, 13). Elsewhere, he makes use of madrigalisms (downward leap of a diminished fourth on "Weeps," m. 25) and affective harmonies (juxtaposed B♭-major and D-major triads on "By all that's *good, no* more!" m. 30—Dido's effectively mocking Aeneas's attempted reconciliation), still the *lingua franca* of European vocal music.

Purcell employs another familiar device in the sadly sympathetic comment from the chorus that follows (No. 41). To map the first line's move from positive ("Great minds") to negative ("against themselves conspire"), he moves in the first seven measures from B♭ major to D, the dominant of G minor. To do so he composes out the opening of a *Romanesca* progression, the B♭–F bass/D–C melody of m. 1 completed by the G–D bass/B♭–A melody of mm. 6–7 (*Romanesca*, like *ciaccona* and *passacaglia*, was one of the common ground-bass patterns). An equally subtle bit of text expression opens the next line. Two measures of oscillating dominant–tonic harmonies over a pedal D (mm. 7–8), with an imitative duet for soprano and tenor, lead at last to a cadential formula, literally "shunning the cure," putting off the end of the phrase ("desire") until m. 9, on which fresh imitation between bass and alto further defers the close. Repeated fragments of text heighten the sense of delay.

Dido's final recitative (No. 42) continues the embrace of death that ended her previous utterance. Here Purcell employs some conventional symbolism, starting in C minor and setting "darkness shades me" to the flattest harmony heard thus far (mm. 2–3); only with the concluding Phrygian cadence on D does he reestablish G minor. The ground-bass aria that follows (No. 43) is built on a chromatic version of the descending minor tetrachord that Monteverdi and his Venetian successors of the 1630s and 1640s had pioneered as an "emblem of lament." Purcell, however, modifies this conventional device in striking fashion. The descent itself, which begins with a pickup half-note G and ends with a whole-note D, is three rather than four measures long; a cadential formula lasting two more measures then follows, B♭–C–D–G. Instead of a four-measure module that ends on the dominant, then, a five-measure module that ends on the tonic results.

Above this asymmetrical yet strongly closed ostinato Purcell fashions a vocal line of haunting irregularity. For example, the voice enters at the conclusion of the first statement, the downbeat of m. 6 rather than the upbeat to m. 7. This "early" entry leads Dido to sing "am laid" twice. Purcell could just as easily have set "When I" to a half-note pickup and whole-note downbeat in mm. 6–7 and then continued with the music as is, but his version brilliantly diminishes Dido's importance, "I" relegated to a weak second beat, and the burial that awaits her emphasized instead through repetition. He sets the remainder of the first two lines more conventionally. The madrigalism "laid in earth" ends in sync with the Phrygian cadence that concludes the ostinato's descent (mm. 8–9), as does the remainder of the line ("may my wrongs create") with the perfect cadence that concludes the module (m. 11). The next line ("No trouble in thy breast") is still more tightly coordinated with the first three measures of the ostinato, beginning with the pickup and ending with the Phrygian cadence (mm. 11–14). After the cadential formula and a repetition of mm. 6–15 in mm. 16–25, the despondent refrain ("Remember me, but ah forget my fate") is set with more striking irregularity. Its opening phrase is again placed at the conclusion of a module (mm. 25–26) and then echoed two measures later. The Ds are now dissonant against the E natural/E♭ of the ostinato (m. 28), and only with the exclamation "ah!" is D finally resolved to C (m. 30). The melisma that follows pushes the conclusion of the line ("forget my fate") beyond that of this ostinato and into the first full measure of the next (m. 32). "Remember me" returns again over the E-natural/E♭ (m. 33), but it is now on a consonant high G and immediately proceeds to finish the line, thus getting the resolution "right" on the downbeat of m. 34. Thus Dido has had to try twice to make her plea musically coherent. Finally, mm. 36–46 are a near-identical restatement of mm. 26–36, but because of the coordinated end of the previous vocal phrase and ostinato, Purcell moves the first two "Remember me's" one measure "to the right" (mm. 36–37 instead of 35–36, mm. 38–39 instead of 37–38). As a result, the second one is now consonant with the bass's D–B♭ (m. 39), and the continuation ("but ah! . . .") occurs immediately, without pause. The final ritornello (m. 46—No. 44, m. 1) continues the distinctively dissonant, suspension-saturated harmony of the aria, further enhancing it with additional chromatic descents.

A final chorus of lamentation (No. 44) and a dance for Cupids (for which there is no music) end the opera (Dido's suicide will take place after the curtain falls). The long diatonic stepwise descents with which the chorus opens complement the chromatic descents of the previous arias and provide "With drooping wings" a touching madrigalism. Eighth notes on "To scatter roses" (mm. 10–13) and quarter-note sighing motives on "Soft" (mm. 14–20) continue the word painting, while the sterner final command to the Cupids ("Keep here your watch and never part") is set in a chordal declamatory fashion (mm. 22–30).

(*Enter Dido, Belinda, and train.*)

Dido
Your counsel all is urg'd in vain,
To earth and heav'n I will complain.
To earth and heav'n why do I call?
Earth and heav'n conspire my fall.
To fate I sue, of other means bereft,
The only refuge for the wretched left.

Belinda
See, madam, where the Prince appears,
Such sorrow in his looks he bears,
(*Aeneas enters.*)
As would convince you still he's true.

Aeneas
What shall lost Aeneas do?
How, royal fair, shall I impart
The gods' decree and tell you we must part?

Dido
Thus on the fatal banks of Nile,
Weeps the deceitful crocodile.
Thus hypocrites that murder act,
Make heav'n and gods the authors of the fact!

Aeneas
By all that's good,

Dido
By all that's good, no more,
All that's good you have forswore.
To your promised empire fly,
And let forsaken Dido die.

Aeneas
In spite of Jove's command I'll stay,
Offend the gods, and Love obey.

Dido
No, faithless man, thy course pursue,
I'm now resolv'd as well as you.
No repentance shall reclaim
The injured Dido's slighted flame.
For 'tis enough whate'er you now decree,
That you had once a thought of leaving me.

Aeneas
Let Jove say what he will, I'll stay.

Dido
Away!
(*Exit Aeneas.*)
To death I'll fly, if longer you delay.
But death, alas, I cannot shun,
Death must come when he is gone.

Chorus
Great minds against themselves conspire,
And shun the cure they most desire.

Dido
Thy hand, Belinda, darkness shades me,
On thy bosom let me rest.
(*Cupids appear in the clouds o'er her tomb.*)
More I would but death invades me.
Death is now a welcome guest.
When I am laid in earth, may my wrongs create

No trouble in thy breast,

Remember me, but ah! forget my fate.

Chorus

With drooping wings you Cupids come

To scatter roses on her tomb.

Soft and gentle as her heart,

Keep here your watch and never part.

(Cupids dance.)

40. Enter Dido, Belinda, and Train/ *Dido, Belinda und Gefolge.*

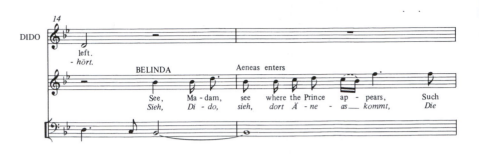

Cupids appear in the Clouds o'er her Tomb/ *Amoretten erscheinen in den Wolken über ihrem Grab*

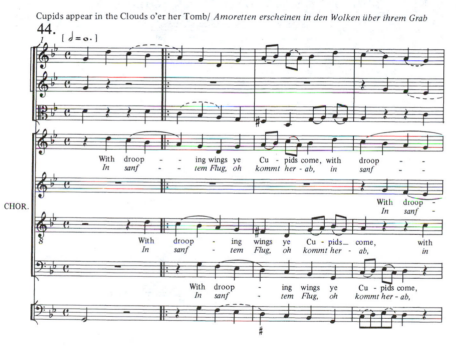

78

Alessandro Scarlatti
(1660–1725)

Andate, o miei sospiri ("Go, oh my sighs") (1712)

The cantata *Andate, o miei sospiri, al cor d'Irene* (Go, oh my sighs, to Irene's heart) is among the more idiosyncratic of the approximately 800 that Alessandro Scarlatti composed. He wrote it in 1712, in friendly competition with his younger contemporary Francesco Gasparini: Each had to compose two settings of the same text, as different from one another as possible. The one given here is Scarlatti's second, composed, as he put it on the title page, "with inhuman idea, but in a regulated chromatic style; it is not for every practitioner." The extravagances to which he refers are found in the first and third movements, the recitatives, and consist of chromatic motion in the basso continuo, dissonant harmonizations, striking harmonic progressions, and odd intervals in the voice. These elements, nicely suited to portraying the poetic speaker's amorous desperation, are not new; some can be found in Barbara Strozzi's cantata *Lagrime mie, a che vi trattenete*, as well as in the more outlandish madrigals from the turn of the seventeenth century. It is, rather, the density of such events—at least one in virtually every measure—that astonishes.

Such can be seen at the very opening (mm. 1–2), which requires the voice to sing two successive tritones on the repeated word *Andate* ("Go") while the continuo descends from F♯ to E♯. The harmony is equally strange: The initial F♯-minor harmony is followed in the second half of m. 1 by an implied V♯$^4_2$ of C♯. While the progression is not unheard of (it featured prominently in the final chorus of Carissimi's *Jephte*), it is an unusual opening, implying modulation in a piece that has just begun. Arrival on C♯, moreover, is immediately undercut by the next harmony, a diminished-seventh chord over the E♯ (note that the leading tone B♯ of the previous harmony has moved down to B natural) followed by a C♯-diminished triad in first inversion over the succeeding E natural. Only in the next two measures (3–4) do things become more familiar, as F♯ is reestablished and confirmed by an authentic cadence (note that the voice arrives on the tonic, while the continuo, still on dominant, resolves a beat later, a common mannerism in Scarlatti's recitatives). Here, too, things turn immediately strange, as the continuo now moves up a half step, creating a E♭-major triad in first inversion, which becomes the dominant of the extremely remote A♭ minor; the latter, coinciding with the word *pene* ("pains"), is confirmed in m. 5 by another half-step ascent to A♭ in the continuo, followed by an authentic cadence.

Bizarre as it is, though, the movement suggests that Scarlatti meant what he said about regulated chromaticism. The bass never moves more than two consecutive half steps in the same direction, and the first two times it does so, F♯–E♯–E natural (mm. 1–2) and F♯–G–A♭ (mm. 4–5), the pitches are the highest of a group bounded by a perfect fourth and ending with an authentic cadence (F♯ to C♯ in mm. 1–5, A♭ to E♭ in mm. 5–6; the second A♭ in m. 6 may be thought of as having been transposed an octave down—note that the next phrase begins in the lower register with A–G♯ before returning to the higher register with F♯ and E in mm. 8–10). In addition to adapting that durable emblem of lament, the descending tetrachord, Scarlatti may have been gently pulling Gasparini's leg with a sly allusion to the chromatic tetrachord—semitone–semitone–minor third—of ancient and Renaissance music theory (*idea inumana* also implies a send up of Medieval theory's *musica humana*). Four years earlier his rival had become known as a theorist by publishing the important basso continuo treatise *L'armonico pratico al cimbalo* ("The Practical Harmonist at the Harpsichord").

Similar subtleties, in the form of musical puns, are found in the second recitative. Its still more overwrought opening—the first triad in second inversion, a unique descent of three half steps—again comes to momentary rest after the bass has descended a perfect fourth, G♯ (=A♭) to E♭ (mm. 1–3). And it is this, the enharmonic respelling of the same note, that runs through the rest of the movement. At first, such respelling is done with an eye toward convention, a flatted note indicating descent, a sharped one ascent (cf. A–A♭–G [mm. 3–5] and G–G♯–A [m. 6]). However, when the singer declaims *Ma fingerà, qual fin ad ora ha finto* ("But she will feign, as she has feigned till now") and the continuo moves down a half step from B natural and back again (mm. 7–8), Scarlatti spells the lower note B♭, "feigning" a descent that does not come (note the A♯ that takes its place when the same bass motion is repeated in mm. 8–10).

This cantata is otherwise highly conventional, both in its overall structure—four movements that alternate recitative–aria–recitative–aria—and in the da capo form of its arias. Hints of the four-movement structure are found in earlier cantatas, such as Strozzi's, but it was not until Scarlatti's time that it became the norm. The da capo form of the arias, which Italian composers developed in the final decades of the seventeenth century, likely out of earlier ternary structures, would remain the principal aria form for the bulk of eighteenth century.

The first aria exemplifies da capo form at its most conventional, in which three instrumental ritornelli alternate with two vocal solos in the A section of the larger ABA form. The continuo plays the first ritornello (mm. 1–7; when they are used, obbligato instruments play here as well). It is followed by the first solo (mm. 7–32), in which the voice sings the first syntactic unit (here it consists of four lines) and ends after a modulation to the dominant (some minor-mode pieces move to the relative major; this one does not). Somewhat exceptionally, neither this solo nor the next uses material from the ritornello. Madrigalisms are not unheard of: *Pien del solito rigore* ("Full of its accustomed strictness") is largely set to 2–3 suspensions (mm. 13–16, 17–20), an element of the strict style of composition (and presumably another allusion to Gasparini's theoretical acumen). The second ritornello (mm. 32–34) is much shorter and begins in the new key of F♯ minor; by the time the second solo (mm. 34–61) begins, it has already returned to B minor. All these are conventional gestures, though the return to the tonic is often delayed until solo 2, which in any case repeats the text heard in solo 1: Scarlatti, probably working in even greater haste than usual, likely found it easier to launch it in the home key. Indeed, the first nine and a half measures of solo 2 restate those of solo 1 exactly (cf. mm. 34–43 and 7–16), and its next eleven and a half measures follow a later passage, but now in the tonic (cf. mm. 44–55 and mm. 21–32); an additional six and a half measures (mm. 55–61) confirm the customary return. The third and final ritornello (mm. 61–67) remains in the tonic, though after the initial B, Scarlatti moves briefly toward the subdominant (mm. 61–63). The middle section (the B section of the ABA form; mm. 68–101) follows custom as well. It is shorter, begins and ends off-tonic, and delivers the remainder of the text. The words *da capo* ("from the top"), written at its conclusion direct the performers to repeat the first section either in its entirety or to the word *fine* ("end"); the unwritten repeat offered opportunities for, or rather demanded, spontaneous embellishment.

The second aria belongs to a type that was particularly characteristic of Scarlatti and of Neapolitan music in general. Identifiable by compound meter ($\frac{6}{8}$ or, more commonly, $\frac{12}{8}$), leisurely or languid tempo, lilting rhythms (with much use of the figure ♪♩♪) and (usually) by an eighth-note pickup, such an aria was called a *siciliana* and is often assumed, although without any real evidence, to stem from a jig-like Sicilian folk or popular dance. Very often, too, *siciliana* arias exhibit at their cadences the "Neapolitan sixth" harmony that emerges when the flatted second degree in the tune coincides with the fourth degree in the bass. This distinctive harmonic mannerism reinforces the impression that the *siciliana* may have originated in some local musical dialect (to be sure, it is also found in such earlier and different music as Carissimi's *Jephte*); as it happens, this aria has just one, in the penultimate measure of the middle section. The first section has a few idiosyncrasies of its own: Solo 1 (mm. 5–9) ends in E rather than A major or C# minor, solo 2 (mm. 10–22) is more than twice its length, and there is no third ritornello.

Andate, o miei sospiri, al cor d'Irene,	Go, oh my sighs, to Irene's heart,
Esso del mio le pene	Let it know the pains of mine
Sappia da voi. Ben le saprà se dite	From you. It will know them well if you say
Che, per aver ristoro al suo dolore,	That, to have relief from its pain,
Tutto con voi sen viene, anche il mio core.	All of it goes with you, even my heart.
Andate e a quel bel seno,	Go, and to that lovely breast,
Tanto ch'un sol almeno	Such that she receive
Essa n'accolga pien del mio foco,	At least one, full of my fire,
Ognun di voi s'aggiri.	Let every one of you get going.
Andate al cor d'Irene, o miei sospiri!	Go to Irene's heart, oh my sighs!
Se vedrete il cor di lei	If you should see her heart
Pien del solito rigore,	Full of its accustomed strictness,
Sfortunati non lo dite	Unlucky ones, do not say
Che partite dal mio cor.	That you come from my heart.
Ma se poi dimostra a voi	But if she then shows you
Di gradire il vostro ardor,	That she appreciates your ardor,
Dite allor che siete miei	Then say that you are mine,

E che a lei vi manda Amor.	And that Love sends you to her.
Ma di che mi lusingo, oh Dio, che penso?	But with what do I flatter myself, oh God, what am I thinking?
V'udirà la crudele,	The cruel one will hear you,
Vedrà le vostre fiamme,	Will see your flames,
E saprà che l'accese il suo bel ciglio,	And will know that her lovely eyes ignited it,
Ma fingerà, qual fin ad ora ha finto,	But she will feign, as she has feigned till now,
Ch'ella non vi conosce o non v'intende.	That she does not know you or does not understand you.
E pur sa, quell'ingrata,	And yet she knows, that ungrateful one,
Lo sa con suo piacer, che miei voi siete	She knows to her contentment that you are mine,
E intende, ma s'infinge	And understands, but that barbarous heart of hers
Quel suo barbaro cor ciò che chiedete.	Feigns to do that which you ask.
Se non v'accoglie in seno,	If she does not receive you in her breast,
Restar potrete almeno	You can at least remain
Della mia bella al piè.	At my lovely's feet.
Infin ch'un dì rimiri	Let her see at last one day
In voi qualsia mia fè,	In you what is my faith,
E un sol de' suoi sospiri	And let her release just one
Sparga colei per me.	Of her sighs for me.

79

Arcangelo Corelli
(1653–1713)

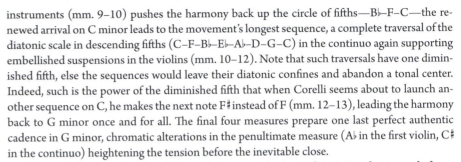

Trio Sonata in G Minor, Op. 3, No. 11 (1689)

The twelve trio sonatas of Arcangelo Corelli's Opus 3, like those of his Opus 1, are commonly referred to as *Sonate da chiesa* ("Church Sonatas"), although the composer titled them *Sonate a tre* ("Sonatas for Three"). And though such works were used in secular settings, they differ from those of Opp. 2 and 4, which he called *Sonate da camera* ("Chamber Sonatas"). The latter consist largely of binary-form dance movements, while in Opp. 1 and 3 none are so labeled. Instead, all feature at least one imitative movement, which suggests an ecclesiastical style. In the seventeenth and eighteenth centuries, moreover, instrumental music was often played during Mass to accompany liturgical actions: typical placements were between the scripture readings (in place of the Gradual), at the collection (in place of the Offertory), or at Communion. At Vespers they could be played before Psalms in place of antiphons. As for the term *Sonate a tre*, Corelli and his contemporaries meant a work for three instrumental parts plus basso continuo; hence the subtitle calling for four instruments: "two violins and violone [a cello or cello-like instrument] or archlute [a larger version of the lute], with basso [continuo] for the organ." In Corelli's sonatas, though, the continuo doubles the lowest instrument almost without exception.

As with most of the sonatas in Opp. 1 and 3, the work given here consists of four movements in alternating tempi, slow–fast–slow–fast. The first movement features several typically Corellian elements, chief among them a strong tonal focus—indeed, common-practice tonality is often said to begin with Corelli's music. An early move from G minor toward C minor (mm. 2–3) is at once turned back to the tonic by a prominent Phrygian cadence on its dominant, D (mm. 3–4); G minor is further confirmed on the first beat of m. 5, with all parts then pausing for an eighth rest. Another common Corellian gesture follows: sequential motion down the circle of fifths. At first the composer moves just one notch, again to C minor (mm. 5–6), before returning once more to G minor (mm. 6–7). This time the arrival on the tonic is prepared by another, more rapid circle-of-fifths progression, the bass instruments moving in quarter notes, A–D–G, while the violins proceed in imitation, a short series of decorated suspensions that are also a common bit of Corelliana. G having been securely established on the third beat of m. 7, the music at last moves toward a new tonal region, a perfect authentic cadence locking on to the relative major, B♭ (m. 9, beat 3). After some rare imitation between first violin and bass

instruments (mm. 9–10) pushes the harmony back up the circle of fifths—B♭–F–C—the renewed arrival on C minor leads to the movement's longest sequence, a complete traversal of the diatonic scale in descending fifths (C–F–B♭–E♭–A♭–D–G–C) in the continuo again supporting embellished suspensions in the violins (mm. 10–12). Note that such traversals have one diminished fifth, else the sequences would leave their diatonic confines and abandon a tonal center. Indeed, such is the power of the diminished fifth that when Corelli seems about to launch another sequence on C, he makes the next note F♯ instead of F (mm. 12–13), leading the harmony back to G minor once and for all. The final four measures prepare one last perfect authentic cadence in G minor, chromatic alterations in the penultimate measure (A♭ in the first violin, C♯ in the continuo) heightening the tension before the inevitable close.

Typical of a *sonate da chiesa*, the second movement begins with imitation, but instead of constructing a three-part fugue on a subject at least two measures long, as he usually does, Corelli deploys a short point of imitation (three quarter notes and a quarter rest) for the violins alone, while the bass instruments proceed in eighth notes. He also marks the movement *Presto*, an equally rare tempo indication, which together with the duple meter and opening leap upward of a fourth gives the movement a more-than-passing resemblance to some of the gavottes in the *sonate da camera*, a reminder not to assume too neat a distinction between church and chamber sonatas. Despite its idiosyncrasies, however, the movement displays virtually the full range of Corelli's style. The opening exchange between the violins (mm. 1–2) again offers strong tonal focus, this time by alternating tonic, dominant, and tonic. A sequence down the circle of fifths, G–C–F–B♭, follows immediately (mm. 2–3), and Corelli then introduces 2–3 suspensions in the violins at precisely the moment he breaks the sequence (m. 4). After some hocket-like imitation between the violins and a rising sequence (mm. 7–10) followed by a Phrygian cadence on D (mm. 10–11), Corelli again launches a series of sequences down the circle of fifths (mm. 11–17), arriving at last at a perfect authentic cadence on B♭ in m. 17. Having securely established the relative major, Corelli at once wrenches his music back to G (mm. 17–18) and then to D minor (mm. 20–21). The opening material is then restated in the new key (cf. mm. 21–23 and 1–3), but with subtle adjustments that allow a return to G minor, with the opening material now repeated at pitch (cf. mm. 24–26 and mm. 4–6) instead of in transposition. Having regained the tonic with such remarkable subtlety, Corelli then breaks off all pretense at imitation: a Phrygian cadence on D is followed by silence in the bass instruments and triplet parallel thirds in the violins; a single D in the bass then launches their repetition (mm. 26–27, 27–28). After this respite from the movement's otherwise-frenetic motion, the texture is reconstituted: The bass instruments reenter (m. 28), briefly restating the same figure they had sounded just before the Phrygian cadence (cf. mm. 29 and 26), heightening the sense that the triplets were an interruption. The new continuation (mm. 28–30) features another common Corellian routine, a bass line rising by step—the unembellished version would be half notes D–E♭–F–G–A—and harmonized as an alternating series of $\frac{5}{3}$ and $\frac{6}{3}$ sonorities. After another, identical approach to B♭ major (cf. mm. 31–32 and 16–17), Corelli initiates another rising sequence (mm. 32–34) that leads to yet another descending circle-of-fifths progression (mm. 34–37) that is finally broken off for the cadential formula in the last three measures that once and for all reestablishes G as the tonic.

Much of what has been observed thus far can be applied to the last two movements as well. In addition, the conventionally languorous third movement has two common features, slow tempo and triple meter. By contrast, its off-tonic, E♭ major beginning is unusual, as is the apparent move to C minor, at once declined, that follows. Equally strange for this repertory are the various resemblances it bears to the first movement: the Phrygian cadence on D followed by the bass line D–E natural, F–G, G–A–B natural–C (mm. 6–7, 7–9, 9–11), events occurring in the same order as they had in the opening.

Corelli mixes familiar and unfamiliar in the last movement as well. It, too, is imitative, more conventionally so for the participation of the bass instruments in the texture. Yet once again there is a surprise: The binary form with repeats again suggests a dance piece, in this case the gigue. Indeed, the motive's inverted contour at the beginning of the second part also recalls a common strategy of imitative gigues, and of course the gigue was often the closing movement in *sonate da camera*. But it is another feature that deserves the last word, for it was one of the great wellsprings of form in the century that followed. In the second part, immediately after the perfect cadence in the relative major (mm. 26–27), the opening motive is heard once more: Indeed, mm. 27–45 essentially restate mm. 1–12, altered so as to end in the tonic instead of the dominant. Rounded binary form, of which this is so fine an example, offered composers of the eighteenth century one of the principal strategies out of which they devised what a later age called sonata form.

80

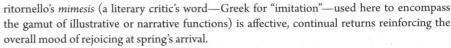

Antonio Vivaldi
(1678–1741)

La primavera ("Spring") (1725)

In 1725 the Venetian violinist, composer, and priest Antonio Vivaldi published a book of twelve concerti that he rather fancifully titled *Il cimento dell'armonia e dell'inventione* (something like "The challenge of technique and of inspiration"), Op. 8. Thanks in large part to the first four items, arranged in a set called *Le quattro stagioni* (The Four Seasons), it made a sensation. Each of the four, accompanied by a *sonetto dimostrativo*, or "explanatory sonnet," that spells out its imagery, is an inventively detailed evocation or "imitation" of nature as manifested in spring, summer, autumn, and winter.

La primavera quickly became the most popular one of the lot; since the rediscovery of Vivaldi's music in the 1930s, it has regained that distinction. Its first movement in particular shows that the late Baroque concerto form (three movements, fast–slow–fast), with its constant and fluid components, proved easy to adapt to illustrative or narrative purposes. As Vivaldi himself declared to the volume's dedicatee, *The Four Seasons* had been around "for quite some time" but that he had now added the sonnets as "a most clear declaration of all the things that are narrated in them." The letters running down the left margin are original, and mark the exact spots in the score to which the words refer—or conversely, the exact spots where the music is designed to mime the words in question. Though the imitations are obvious and hardly need pointing out, it is worthwhile to consider the precise relationship at various points between the musical and verbal imagery.

The first and second quatrains describe the first movement, which, as expected of a first movement, is in ritornello form. Letter A corresponds to the rather unusual ritornello (mm. 1–13; note that Vivaldi printed each letter with its accompanying sonnet text in the score as well). Whereas most ritornelli consisted of a theme that was spun out elaborately to a cadence, this one is a simple bouncy tune in binary form—an imitation folk song, as it were, whose implied words, as if sung by some implied peasants who will actually appear and dance in the last movement, are suggested by the sonnet's first line. Its periodic returns (mm. 27–31, 40–44, 55–59, 76–82) also suggest song: Except for transpositions to the dominant and the relative minor, they always provide unaltered statements of the second phrase. At the same time, the ritornello's *mimesis* (a literary critic's word—Greek for "imitation"—used here to encompass the gamut of illustrative or narrative functions) is affective, continual returns reinforcing the overall mood of rejoicing at spring's arrival.

The remaining images, **B** through **E**, correspond exactly to the four episodes that come between the ritornelli. Letter **B**, the singing of the birds (mm. 13–27), is rendered in the most straightforward way that music, the art of combining sounds, has at its disposal: *onomatopoeia*, direct "sound-alike" imitation. Note that in addition to the letter **B**, Vivaldi added the explanatory phrase *Il canto degl' uccelli* ("The song of the birds") to m. 13. Letter **C**, the episode of the brook and breezes (mm. 31–40; note the added phrase *Scorrono i fonti*—"the streams flow"), takes us back almost a century and a half, to the heyday of the madrigal, when the same textual images found the same mimetic response. The rendering of water by the use of wavelike motion was a stock device, the kind of thing we now call "madrigalism." And madrigalism would not be a bad term to characterize Vivaldi's mimetic devices as well, despite the transfer to the instrumental medium. Using it would signal the easily overlooked, somewhat paradoxical fact that to embrace the new practice of incorporating mimesis into an instrumental concerto was actually to fall back on an old practice.

Letter **D**, the sudden storm (mm. 44–55), juxtaposes low *tremolandi* for the ripieni (the full orchestra), mimicking thunder (note the added word *Tuoni*), with high arpeggios that depict lightning. Thunder, like birdsong, is onomatopoeia—sound imitating sound. But how can music imitate lightning, which is a visual, not an aural phenomenon? The answer is that the adjectives one might use to describe the violin arpeggios—bright, quick, even "flashy"—apply to lightning as well; the shared attributes are what link music and image (in an example of what is called *metonymy*, the representation of an object through one of its attributes). Following the storm, the ritornello takes on its minor-mode coloration, as if an affective reflection on the spoiling of the day.

Letter **E**, the birds' return (59–76), is the masterstroke: The way the solo violins steal in diffidently on chromatic-scale fragments, as if checking the weather before resuming their song, adds a "psychological" dimension to the onomatopoetical. The work of an expert musical dramatist, it gives the lie to those who later dismissed such effects as cheap. Vivaldi was a prolific composer of opera, and what obviously lies behind Vivaldi's mimetic practices is the opera house, where winds and storms, birds, rustic song, and all the rest were regularly evoked and compared—in the ritornelli of "simile arias"—with dramatic situations and the emotions to which they gave rise.

The second and third movements feature less narrative detail. Each corresponds to one of the sonnet's tercets, whose identifying letter (**F**, **G**) Vivaldi simply placed over the first measure. Nevertheless, the sharply contrasting middle movement—minor mode, lower strings and continuo silent, ritornelli abandoned in favor of unbroken solo melody—is a mimetic tour de force, in which the techniques just surveyed appear simultaneously rather than consecutively. The languorous melody of the solo violin, given the additional marking *Il capraro che dorme* ("the sleeping goatherd"), is an affective representation of sleep. Against it Vivaldi sets the metonymy of the ripieno violins, an undulating depiction of the *Mormorio di frondi e pianti* ("murmur of fronds and plants"), and the onomatopoeia of the viola, *Il cane che grida* ("the barking dog"), the last achieved by playing *sempre molto forte, e strappato* (literally, a kind of "torn" bowing).

In the third movement, built on the familiar alternation of ritornello (mm. 1–12, 22–34, 58–71, 79–89) and solo (mm. 12–22, 34–58, 71–78), music itself is the subject of imitation. The tempo, meter, and rhythm of the *Danza pastorale* make it a gigue, while the sustained notes in the lower strings and continuo represent the droning bagpipe. The latter is heard as well in the double stops of the second solo. Alongside such hyperrealism, though, is affective mimesis of the most touching sort: In the midst of joy is a hint of melancholy (a common theme in pastoral art and literature) in the switch to minor mode early in the third ritornello (m. 61), especially the chromatically embellished descending tetrachord in the lower strings and continuo (mm. 68–71). The violin sustains the mood throughout its final solo, joy restored at last by the succeeding ritornello.

A *Giunt'è la primavera, e festosetti*	Spring has arrived and festively
B *La salutan gli augei con lieto canto,*	The birds greet it with happy song,
C *E i fonti allo spirar de' zeffiretti*	And meanwhile at the blowing of the little zephyrs
Con dolce mormorio scorrono intanto.	The streams flow with sweet murmuring.
D *Vengon coprendo l'aer di nero amanto*	Lightning and thunder, chosen to announce it,
E lampi, e tuoni ad annuntiarla eletti.	Cover the air in a black cloak.
E *Indi, tacendo questi, gli augelletti*	Then, these quieting, the little birds
Tornan di nuovo al lor canoro incanto.	Return again to their songful enchanting.
F *E quindi sul fiorito ameno prato*	And so, on the flowering, pleasant field,
Al caro mormorio di fronde e piante	At the dear murmuring of branches and plants,
Dorme 'l caprar col fido can' a lato.	Sleeps the goatherd with faithful dog at his side.
G *Di pastoral zampogna al suon festante*	At the festive sound of pastoral bagpipe
Danzan ninfe e pastor nel tetto amato	Nymphs and shepherds dance under the beloved sky
Di primavera all'apparir brillante.	At the brilliant appearance of spring.

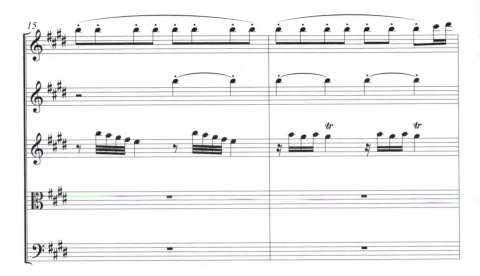

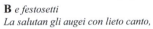

B *e festosetti*
La salutan gli augei con lieto canto,

Il canto degl' uccelli

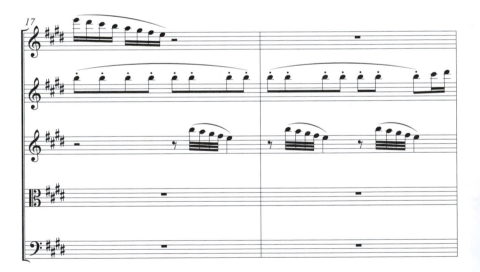

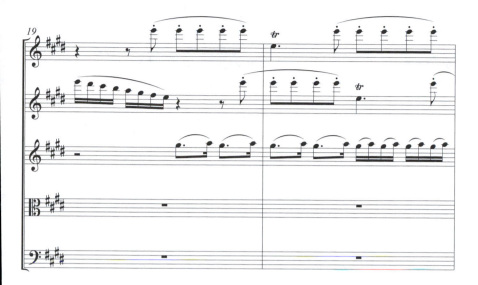

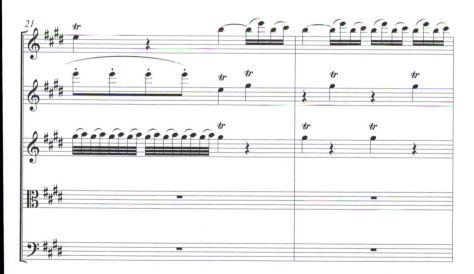

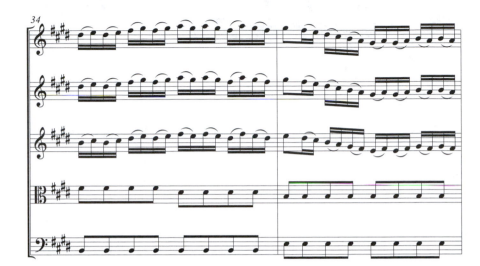

C *E i fonti allo spirar de' zeffiretti*
Con dolce mormorio scorrono intanto.

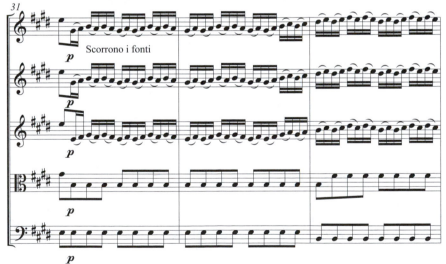

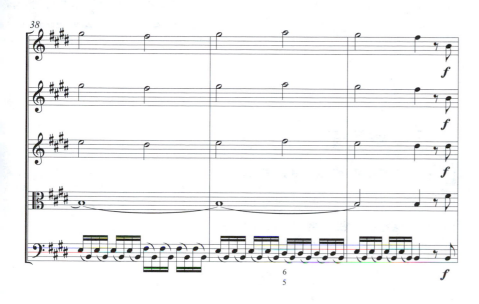

D *Vengon coprendo l'aer di nero amanto*
E lampi, e tuoni ad annuntiarla eletti.

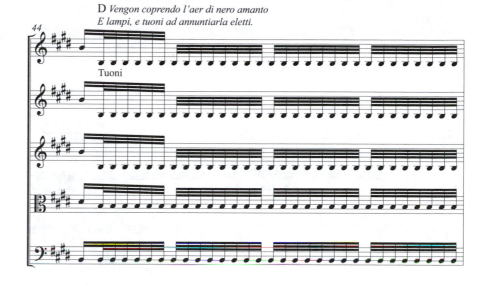

Tuoni

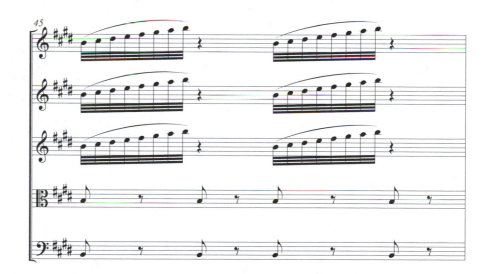

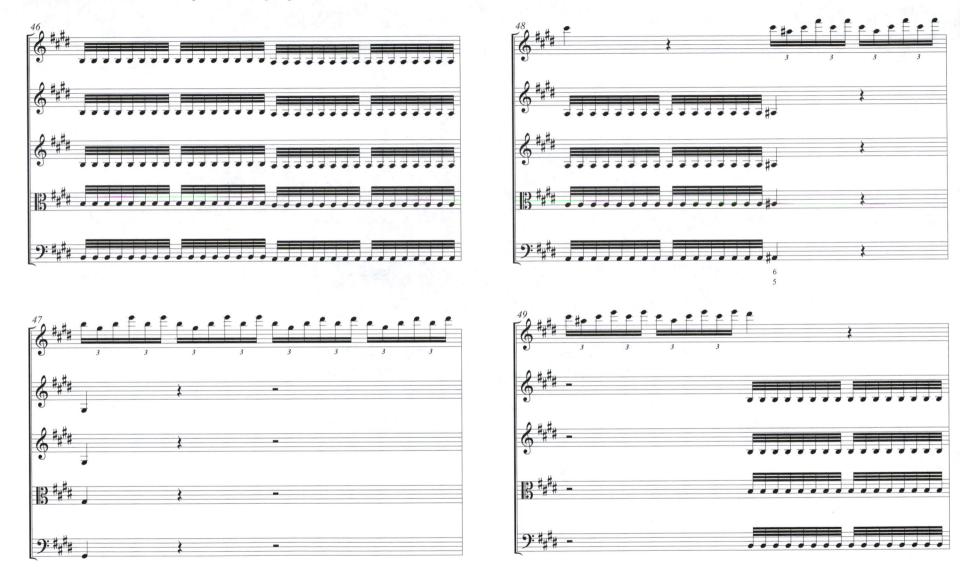

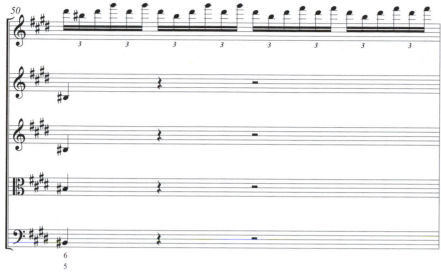

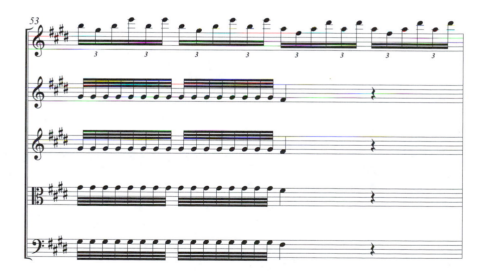

E *Indi, tacendo questi, gli augelletti*
Tornan di nuovo al lor canoro incanto.

Canto degl' uccelli

Tasto solo

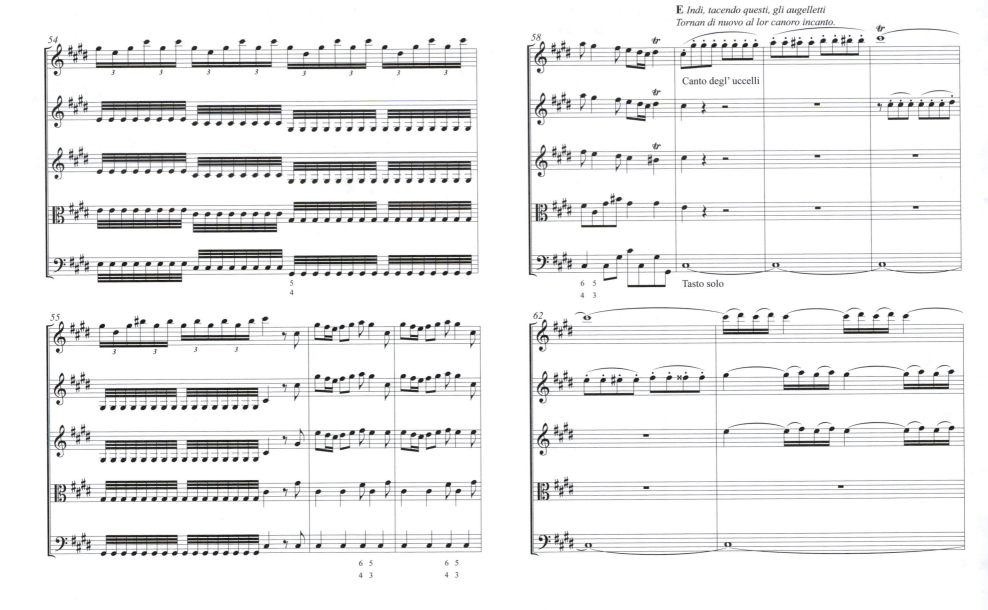

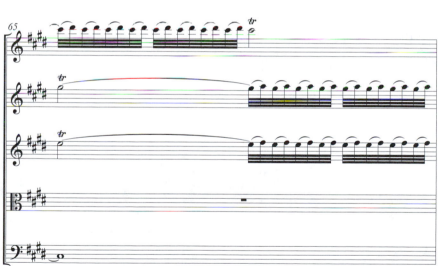

2. Largo

F *E quindi sul fiorito ameno prato*
Al caro mormorio di fronde e piante
Dorme 'l caprar col fido can' a lato.

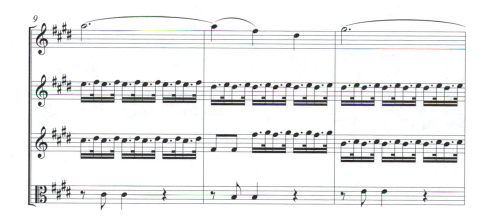

G *Di pastoral zampogna al suon festante*
Danzan ninfe e pastor nel tetto amato
Di primavera all'apparir brillante.

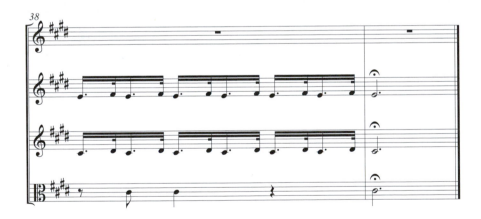

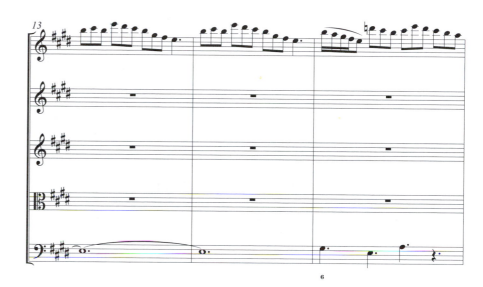

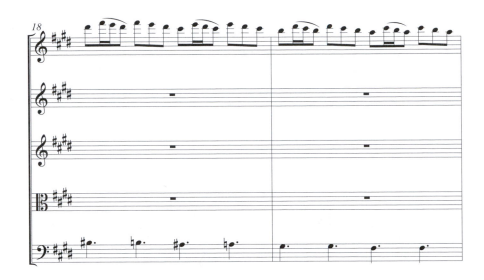

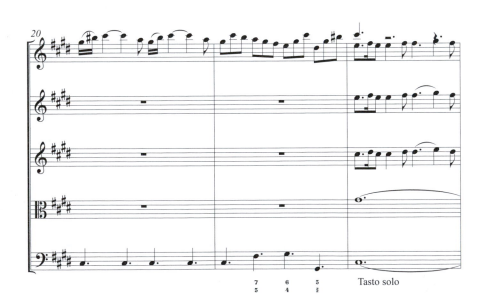

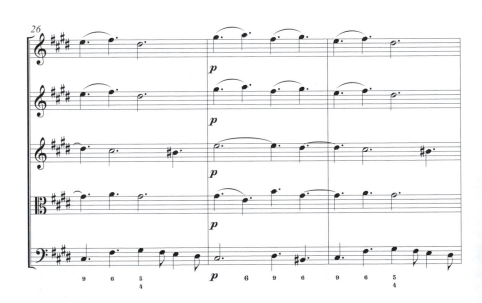

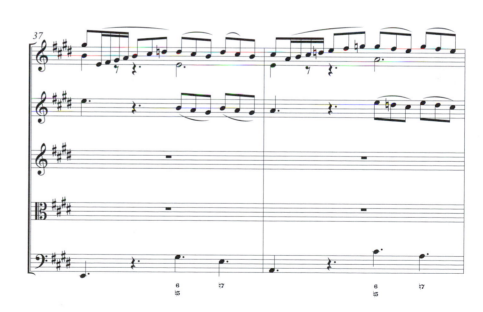

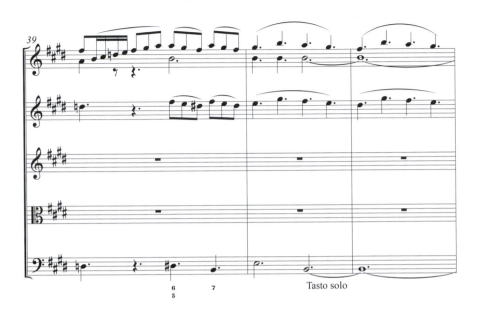

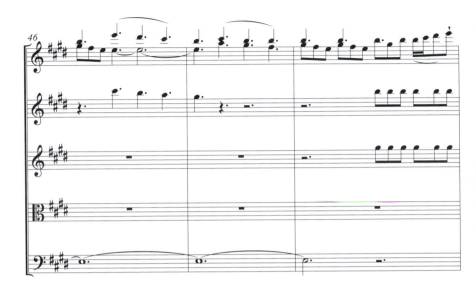

Tasto solo

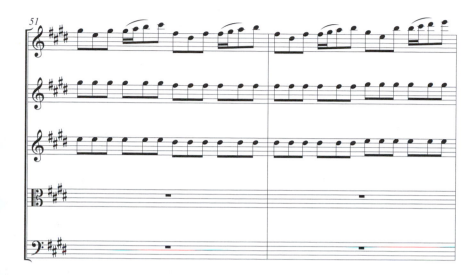

Tasto solo

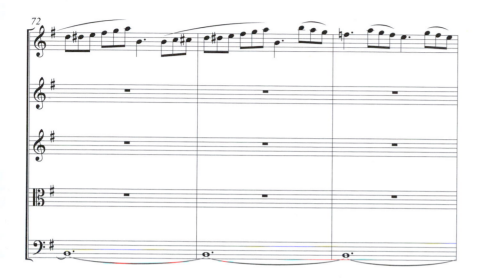

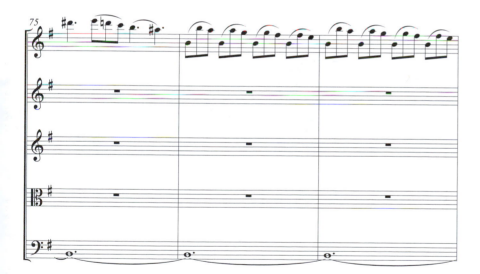

81

Two Chorale Preludes on *Durch Adams Fall ist ganz verderbt* ("Through Adam's Fall We Are Condemned")

The *Choralvorspiel,* or "chorale prelude," is one of several genres of Lutheran organ music that were popular in the seventeenth and eighteenth centuries. Its distinguishing feature, in addition to the modest length of its single-verse setting, is that the chorale melody appears complete in only one voice. It may be treated strictly as a cantus firmus, or else melodically embellished, or else played off against a ritornello or a ground bass, or else elaborated "motet-style" into points of fugal imitation based on its constituent phrases. Among its uses were as a cue for the congregation to sing and as an accompaniment to silent meditation.

Dietrich Buxtehude (1637–1707) and Johann Sebastian Bach (1685–1750), leading Lutheran organists a generation apart, each composed a chorale prelude on *Durch Adams Fall ist ganz verderbt* ("Through Adam's fall [human nature and essence] is completely defiled"), whose text is among the grimmest in the repertory. The first line refers to what for Christians was the greatest catastrophe in human history—Adam and Eve's eating of the forbidden fruit from the tree of knowledge and the fallen state of mankind that resulted. And though the real subject of the chorale's text is God's mercy by which man may be redeemed from Adam's original sin through faith in Jesus Christ, it is the first line that sets the tone for the setting, since the first verse is the one directly introduced by the prelude.

Both settings are tinged with grief, thanks to the affective counterpoints that surround the chorale melody. An example in Buxtehude's piece is the chromatic descent in the pedal in mm. 14–15, anticipated by the "tenor" a beat earlier and imitated by the "alto" in mm. 16–17; another is the complementary chromatic ascent in mm. 20–22. The descents also symbolize the fall itself: Note the three falling fifths that accompany the first phrase of the chorale in the bass in mm. 2 and 4–5 (that the chromatic descent accompanies the third phrase, a restatement of the first, is hardly coincidental). Other affective touches include the frequent ornamentation of the chorale melody in the "soprano," especially in the last three phrases (mm. 31–35, 37–41, and 43–49) of the *Abgesang* (the b section of the chorale's bar form), which suggests impassioned solo singing rather than choral performance.

Bach's setting is found in his *Orgelbüchlein* ("Little organ book"), which dates from the end of his Weimar period (though some scholars have argued that *Durch Adams Fall* may have been composed as early as 1708–12). Ever the encyclopedist and the synthesizer, the composer set about collecting his chorale preludes into a liturgical cycle that would cover the whole year's services. He had inscribed only 46 items out of a projected 164 in this manuscript when he was called away to Cöthen. But in their variety, the ones entered fully justify Bach's claim on the manuscript's title page, that in his little book "a beginner at the organ is given instruction in developing a chorale in many diverse ways." Bach also claimed here that the player will "acquire facility in the study of the pedal, since in the chorales contained herein, the pedal is treated as wholly *obbligato,*" that is, as an independent voice.

Bach's setting fulfills both goals, fairly easy for the manuals, more difficult for the pedal. The upper parts, in fact, are in some ways more modest than Buxtehude's: The melody is unadorned and confined to the soprano part, the two phrases of the *Stollen* (the a section of the bar form) are repeated unchanged, and phrase 6—identical to phrase 1—receives the same accompaniment in mm. 6–8. Yet the pedal part is a powerful surprise and is further evidence of Bach's unique imaginative boldness. It consists almost entirely of dissonant drops of a seventh—Adam's fall made audible! And not just the fall but also the attendant pain and suffering are depicted (and, in a way, evoked), since so many of those sevenths are diminished. A rank madrigalism, the fall is given emotional force through sheer harmonic audacity and is then made the primary unifying motive of the composition. Again the union of illustration and construction, symbolic image and feeling, "form" and "content" is complete. Even Bach's didacticism complements his imagery: All but the last two pedal phrases feature identical rhythms, helping students to attend more to the tricky leaps while setting off the climax in mm. 11–12, a delayed entry and an eighth-note stretto of three uninterrupted descents. And if, as seems likely, Bach knew Buxtehude's particular work, we have another case of his propensity to emulate—to adopt a model and then to surpass it to an outlandish degree, amounting to a virtual difference in kind.

Bach's extravagance extends to the inner parts as well. The alto part begins with a stepwise descent that anticipates that of the chorale tune, while the florid tenor part, largely a series of descending sixteenth notes, creates a second madrigalistic representation of the fall. A last bit of symbolic-contrapuntal ingenuity should be noted at the beginning of the *Abgesang,* in the last beat and a half of m. 4b. The tenor C–D–E♭–F–E natural inverts the opening alto line A–G–F♯–E–F natural: The momentarily ascending line no doubt acknowledges the momentary shift in the text, that all would be lost *Ohn Gottes Trost der uns erlöst* ("without God's solace that redeems us").

a. Dietrich Buxtehude, BuxWV 183

b. Johann Sebastian Bach, BWV 637, from *Orgel-Büchlein*
(ca. 1715)

82

Johann Sebastian Bach
(1685–1750)

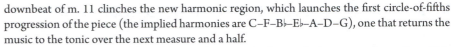

Fugue in G Minor, BWV 578 (before 1707?)

This work for organ is one of Bach's earliest; scholars believe the composer wrote it while still employed at his first full-time post, which he held in Arnstadt from 1703 to 1707. The loss of the autograph makes precise dating of the piece difficult, but Bach's elder brother, Johann Christoph, had a copy of it made between about 1710 and 1715. As might be expected, BWV 578 lacks the complexities of Johann Sebastian's later fugues, but for this reason it offers an excellent introduction to the genre. What it lacks in intricacy, moreover, it more than makes up for in attractiveness.

A fugue may be usefully thought of as an elaboration of a single point of imitation, called the *subject*. As often happens in such works, the subject of the Fugue in G Minor first enters in the "soprano" (mm. 1–5)—for the sake of convenience, each of the work's four parts shall be referred to as if they were voices—and is followed by successively lower entries, in the alto (mm. 6–10), the tenor (mm. 12–17), and the bass (mm. 17–22, this last played by the pedal). Whatever the disposition of voices, though, each entrance must follow a prescribed set of trans-positions. That is, the second entry plays the subject "at the fifth" (meaning up a fifth or, as here, down a fourth); when thus transposed, it is called the *answer*. The subject then returns in its original form, here down an octave, followed by another answer a fourth lower.

Fugal writing also requires another element in the opening presentation of subjects and answers. As the answer enters in m. 6, the soprano continues in counterpoint with new mate-rial, called the *countersubject*. This material, suitably modified, appears against each subsequent subject or answer, and its use reveals the young Bach's extraordinary strengths (and occasional weaknesses). For example, the end of the subject (m. 5, notes 1–9), duly transposed, becomes the opening of the countersubject (m. 6, notes 1–9). The sixteenth notes that fill out the re-mainder of m. 5, a codetta that prepares the D-minor answer by means of a raised E natural, also anticipate the countersubject's rising eighth-note figure at the end of m. 6. When in turn answer and countersubject conclude on the third beat of m. 10, an extended codetta returns the music to the tonic, such that the subject can enter where it must in m. 12. Bach crafted the passage with customary ingenuity: The raised B natural in the alto at the end of m. 10 becomes the leading tone of C minor rather than the second scale degree of A minor. The soprano's surprise E♭ on the

downbeat of m. 11 clinches the new harmonic region, which launches the first circle-of-fifths progression of the piece (the implied harmonies are C–F–B♭–E♭–A–D–G), one that returns the music to the tonic over the next measure and a half.

With the entrance of the subject in the tenor, Bach reveals the one weakness for which this piece has been criticized: a less than fully developed contrapuntal texture. That is, despite the entrance of a third voice in m. 12, a two-voice texture prevails. The countersubject, now in the alto, does not enter until m. 13; when it does, the soprano goes silent. The countersubject is then passed to the soprano on the third beat of m. 14, the alto reduced to sounding a series of filler eighth notes, while from the third beat of m. 15 the countersubject is simply split between soprano and alto. Similarly, the entrance of the fourth voice in m. 17, the bass's answer, creates a three-voice texture, the alto having gone silent. Two voices often prevail here as well, though, for a good portion of the soprano consists of nothing more than a sustained A (mm. 19–21).

Yet however meager his invention is here, relative to the masterpieces of his riper years, Bach ingeniously reworks this three-voice complex of subject–countersubject–sustained note over the course of the piece. Such can be seen first in the way he brings the answer to its conclusion on the downbeat of m. 22. Here ends the fugal exposition, the section in which the subject is introduced in every voice, and Bach strengthens its sense of closure by modifying the last four beats of answer and countersubject so that they form an authentic cadence; The eighth and quarter notes that replace the sixteenths in the answer also make the part more playable on the pedal.

As the rhythms of the lower parts slow, the soprano instead accelerates, abandoning its sustained A in the second half of m. 21 for a sixteenth-note motive first heard in the countersub-ject (cf. mm. 7, 14, and 19). The livelier rhythm helps launch a new section (mm. 22–25), called an *episode*, in which the subject is withheld; as in any fugue, the remainder of BWV 578 will alternate episodes with returns of the subject. This first episode consists of another three-voice complex, in which the lowest part takes up the sixteenth-note motive just heard in the soprano and treats it sequentially, initiating a long circle-of-fifths progression (D–G–C–F–B♭–E♭–A–D–G) that concludes with the return of the subject in the tonic in m. 25. Said progression now makes explicit the one implied by the codetta of mm. 10–12, and Bach further intensifies the return of G minor by doubling the harmonic rhythm—one change per quarter note in place of one change per half note—in the episode's final measure (m. 24). Finally, the episode clarifies another tendency implicit from the start of the piece. The rapid lower part and the more stately imitative upper ones create rhythms and textures reminiscent of the Italian trio sonata, thereby complementing the oft-remarked-on violinistic nature of the subject.

The subject and countersubject return in m. 25 in the tenor and soprano, respectively, but in the second half of the measure the countersubject continues in sixteenth rather than eighth notes, and the same rhythms then infect the subject in the first half of m. 26. By the second half of the measure the voices have exchanged material, such that for the first time in the piece the subject appears in a higher voice than does the countersubject. By holding back this first bit of what is called *invertible counterpoint* until the third beat of the subject, Bach cleverly avoids the lone transgression of dissonance treatment that would otherwise have occurred. That is, had he stated the inverted subject–countersubject complex complete, a quarter-note D on beat 2 of the soprano would have been struck over an A in the tenor, creating the dissonant interval (in two-part counterpoint) of a perfect fourth. The appearance of a third voice in the bass at the end of m. 26 introduces another bit of contrapuntal cleverness. When the part becomes a sustained low D (mm. 27–30), it sounds what had been the soprano part of the material first heard at the end of the exposition (mm. 19–21). Bach thus expands the purview of his invertible counterpoint to three voices; in each subsequent return of the subject he restates this texture, rearranging it such that each voice appears at least once as the highest, the lowest, and the middle part. This technique also makes BWV 578 an example of what is called a *permutation fugue.*

The remainder of the piece can be described more concisely. The brief second episode (mm. 30–32) modulates to the relative major, whereupon the subject returns first in the alto (mm. 33–34) before shifting to the tenor on the last beat of m. 34. There follows another appearance of the three-voice complex in mm. 34–37, with the sustained note now taking the middle part and the countersubject the highest.

The third episode (mm. 37–40) elaborates on material first heard in the codetta of mm. 11–12. After a momentary feint towards E♭ major (note the A♭ in m. 39 of the soprano), the subject returns once more in the relative major. As it had at the end of the fugal exposition, it appears in the bass (mm. 41–45), and Bach once again modifies the final notes to create an authentic cadence and to avoid unnecessary difficulties for the pedal (cf. mm. 21–22 and 44–45). The countersubject instead begins in the soprano, only to shift down an octave and continue in m. 43 in the alto. This shift, cleverly masked by the extensive parallel sixths in mm. 42–43, allows the soprano to sound the sustained F during the return of the three-voice complex.

The fourth episode (mm. 45–50), which uses the same material as the first, again employs permutation, switching the soprano and tenor parts. The episode is also the first passage in which all four voices are heard together, and Bach takes advantage of the full texture to introduce a harmonic sleight of hand. The pedal's initial B♭ is followed on the downbeat of m. 46 by C rather than the expected E♭, and the tenor is likewise modified here to accommodate the new harmony. These changes create a circle-of-fifths progression whose origin and goal is C minor (mm. 46–49), whereupon the subject is heard in this key (mm. 50–55). For a second time the subject appears above the countersubject (soprano and alto, respectively), and this time Bach solves the problem of the struck perfect fourth by holding a low G in the pedal, such that an acceptable $\frac{8}{5}$ sonority is created over the bass. The countersubject then migrates to the bass for the first and only time (mm. 51–55), and this most difficult moment for the pedal coincides with a maximally permuted three-voice complex: Each part appears in a different register with respect to its first appearance in mm. 19–21.

The fifth and final episode (mm. 55–63), the longest and most difficult, continues this extravagance. After an initial circle-of-fifths progression from C to G (mm. 55–57), a sixteenth-note embellishment of the subject's opening quarter notes appears in the tenor (m. 58), the alto (m. 58), and the soprano (m. 59). Such overlapping is a rudimentary form of a foreshortening device called the *stretto* (Italian for "straitened"—tightened or made stricter), which is usually found near the end of a fugue. The remainder of the episode provides an effective climax to the piece as a whole: The rising sequence in the soprano and alto (mm. 59–61) is underpinned in the tenor by the piece's lone chromatic ascent and is followed by the piece's highest, longest-sustained note, the B♭ in the soprano (mm. 61–62). The final return of the subject in the pedal (mm. 63–68) contributes to this sense of valediction, at last allowing all four parts to sound at once.

83

Johann Sebastian Bach (1685–1750)

Das Wohltemperierte Klavier ("The Well-Tempered Clavier"), Book 1 (1722)

Bach completed the first volume of *Das Wohltemperierte Klavier* ("The Well-Tempered Clavier," hereafter WTC) in 1722; he assembled a second volume between 1738 and 1742. Its subtitle reads "Praeludia und Fugen durch alle Tone und Semitonia," or "Preludes and Fugues through all the Tones and Semitones." This means that each of the books making up Bach's famous "Forty-Eight" consists of a prelude-and-fugue pair in all the keys of the newly elaborated complete tonal system, alternating major and minor and ascending by semitones from C major to B minor (thus: C, c, C♯, c♯, D, d, and so on). Only a keyboard tuned in a "well temperament" can play passably throughout such a complete traversal of keys. (Bach's own preferred tuning remains a subject of debate.) A likely model for the WTC is a work that the south German organist Johann Caspar Ferdinand Fischer published in 1702: *Ariadne musica*, a collection of twenty prelude-and-fugue pairs cast in nineteen keys plus one in E Phrygian; those missing are the "remote" C♯, d♯, F♯, g♯, and a♯. Bach paid him tribute of quoting the subject of his E major fugue in WTC II.

Something of the range of technique and intensity of style of the WTC may be gleaned by juxtaposing the very beginning and the very end of the first book: the C-major prelude and the B-minor fugue. These are both famous pieces, albeit for very different reasons.

a. Prelude No. 1 in C, BWV 846

The C-major prelude is a piece that every pianist encounters as a child. It is in a classic "preludizing" style that goes back to the lutenists of the sixteenth century. That style had been kept alive through the seventeenth century by the French court harpsichordists (or *clavecinistes*), who took over from their lutenist colleagues like the great Parisian virtuoso Denis Gaultier (1603–72) both the practice of composing suites of dances for their instrument and also many "lutenistic" mannerisms, such as the strumming or arpeggiated style Bach's prelude continues to exemplify. The French called it the *style brisé*, or "broken [chord] style"; early written examples, like those of the *claveciniste* Louis Couperin (ca. 1626–61), preserve many aspects of

what was originally an impromptu performance practice akin to the old lute ricercar, in which the player prefaced the main piece with a bit of preparatory strumming to capture the listeners' attention and to establish the key.

Thus, descending from a literally improvisatory practice, the C-major prelude is cast in a purely harmonic, "tuneless" idiom. (It was so tuneless as to strike later musicians as beautiful but incomplete. The French opera composer Charles Gounod [1818–93] actually wrote a melody, to the words of the prayer *Ave Maria*, to accompany—or, rather, to be accompanied by—Bach's prelude.) Even without a tune, though, Bach's prelude has a very clearly articulated form—as well it might, since it is harmony that chiefly articulates the form of "tonal" music even when melody is present. The first four measures establish the key by preparing and resolving a cadence on the tonic. Measures 5–11 prepare and resolve a cadence on the dominant. And note that even though all the chords are "broken," the implied contrapuntal "voice leading" is very scrupulously respected. Dissonances, chiefly passing tones and suspensions, are always resolved in the same "voice." Thus the suspended bass note C in m. 6 resolves to B in the next measure; the suspended B in m. 8 resolves to A in m. 9; the suspended G in the middle of the texture in m. 9 (its "voice" identifiable as the one represented by the fourth note in the arpeggio—let's call it the alto) resolves to F♯ in m. 10; while the suspended C in the soprano in that same measure resolves to B in m. 11.

Measures 12–19 lead the harmony back to the tonic, characteristically employing a few chromaticized harmonies as a feint, to boost the harmonic tension prior to its final resolution. That resolution turns out not to be final, however: The tonic chord sprouts a dissonant seventh, turning it into a dominant of the subdominant; and the subdominant F in the bass, having passed (mm. 21–24) through a fairly wrenching chromatic double neighbor (F♯/A♭—note that the latter [m. 23] is especially dissonant by virtue of its C, the only repeated passing tone in the piece), settles on G, which is held as a dominant pedal for a remarkable eight measures before making its resolution—a resolution accompanied by more harmonic feinting so that full repose is achieved only after four more measures. This apparently simple and old-fashioned composition conceals a wealth of craftsmanship, and, in particular, it displays great virtuosity in the new art of manipulating tonal harmony.

b. Fugue No. 24 in B Minor, BWV 869

The B-minor fugue is instead famous for its chromatic saturation and its attendant sense of pathos—a pathos achieved by harmony alone, without any use of words (unless one counts the marking "Largo," which more likely meant "broadly" rather than "very slow" and which makes this the only fugue in WTC I to bear an expressive indication). The three-measure subject is celebrated in its own right for containing within its short span every degree of the chromatic or semitonal scale, which at the same time symbolically consummates the progress of the whole cycle "through all the tones and semitones." What gives the subject, and the whole fugue, its remarkably poignant affect is not just the high level of chromaticism but also the way in which that chromaticism is coordinated with what, even on their first "unharmonized" appearance, are obviously dissonant leaps—known technically as *appoggiaturas* ("leaning notes"). The two leaps of a diminished seventh in the second measure are the most obviously dissonant. The jarring interval is clearly meant to be heard as an embellishment "leaning on" the minor sixth that is achieved when the first note in the slurred pair resolves by half step: C natural to B, D to C♯. But, in fact, as the ensuing counterpoint reveals, *every* first note of a slurred pair is (or can be treated as) a dissonant appoggiatura.

Measures 9–15, encompassing the entries of the third voice (bass) and the fourth voice (soprano), feature an astonishing level of dissonance on the strong beats, where the appoggiaturas fall. The bass G in m. 9 is harmonized with a tritone; the B on the next beat clashes with the C♯ above; the E on the downbeat of m. 10 makes the same clash against the F♯ above; the C that follows is harmonized with a tritone; the F♯ that comes next, with a fourth and a second; and the D on the fourth beat creates a seventh against the suspended C♯. Most of these dissonances are created not by suspensions but by direct leaps—the strongest kind of dissonance one can have in tonal music. Turning now to the soprano entrance in m. 13, we find a tritone and a diminished seventh against the D on the third beat; a leapt-to seventh on the fourth; a simultaneous clash of tritone, seventh, and fourth on the ensuing downbeat of m. 14; a tritone against the sustained B on the second beat; another leapt-to seventh on the third beat, and so it goes.

These slurred descending pairs with dissonant beginnings were known as *Seufzer*—"sighs" or "groans"—and had originated as a kind of madrigalism. The transfer of vivid illustrative effects into "abstract" musical forms shows that those forms, at least as handled by Bach, were not abstract at all but fraught with a maximum of emotional baggage. What is most remarkable is the way Bach consistently contrives to let the illustrative idea that bears the "affective" significance serve simultaneously as the motive from which the musical stuff is spun out. Indeed, he heightens the pathos of this material by fashioning episodes—passages in which the subject is absent—that contrast with it in the strongest way possible. Thus the first episode, which runs from the second half of m. 17 until the downbeat of m. 21, features the sunniest of harmonic progressions, two sequences down the circle of fifths, and the most conventional of dissonance treatments, suspensions; the same material, transposed to the subdominant, recurs as the second episode in mm. 26–30.

Bach does not, however, do without the contrapuntal sleights of hand for which he was legendary. Note, for example, the treatment of the countersubject, which first appears against the answer in mm. 4–7. When it returns, set against the subject in mm. 9–12, it is split between two voices, beginning—in inversion!—in the highest part (the first three beats of m. 9) and then continuing with its original contour in the middle part (the descending quarter notes). This two-voice configuration becomes the norm, as can be seen in mm. 53–56, where it is set against an F♯-minor statement of the subject. This lone statement of the subject in the dominant in turn calls attention to Bach's profound attention to overall structure—much of the piece has a strong subdominant pull, starting with the answer in mm. 4–7. Note that though the subject begins here as a typically tonal answer (B–A–F♯), the "proper" response to a subject that begins on the fifth scale degree (F♯–D–B), it quickly veers off to E minor (note the continuation D–B–E–D♯ instead of D–C♯–F♯–E♯ in the remainder of m. 4). This "downward" pull—which complements the subject's internal movement upward, toward the dominant—is writ large in the transposition of the sequential episode, noted earlier, as well as in the final complete statement of the subject in mm. 70–72, again in E minor.

84

Johann Sebastian Bach
(1685–1750)

French Suite No. 5 in G, BWV 816 (1722–23, rev. 1725)

Bach composed his six French Suites for keyboard in the 1720s. The title originated after his death and tells us nothing about their style, as they are no more or less "French" than his other works in the keyboard-suite genre (these include six English Suites—another misleading posthumous title—and six Partitas). They were probably composed for the private enjoyment of his family and the instruction of his children. French Suites 1–5 are found in the *Clavier-Büchlein vor Anna Magdalena Bach*, one of the music books of the composer's second wife. The manuscript itself may well have been a wedding present: The couple was married late in 1721, and the *Clavier-Büchlein* is dated 1722. Despite the date, however, Bach finished writing out the fifth suite in 1723, after moving to Leipzig, and he revised the work around 1725.

As with all of Bach's keyboard suites, the core consists of an allemande, a courante, a sarabande, and a gigue, augmented by a trio of slighter dances (a gavotte, a bourrée, and a loure) interpolated before the gigue. Bach himself used the term *Galanterien* (from the French *galanteries*) to classify the interpolated dances in a suite and to distinguish them from the core. Even though the word *galanterie* can be translated as "a trifle," it denotes a very important aesthetic category. It is derived from what the French called the *style galant*, which stemmed in turn from the old French verb *galer*, which meant "to amuse" in a tasteful, courtly sort of way, with refined wit, elegant manners, and easy grace. It was a quality of art—and life—far removed from the stern world of the traditional Lutheran Church, and Bach's mastery of both idioms is yet another testament to his genius.

The allemande bears witness to the sheer persistence of the old *style brisé*, in which the harpsichord apes the elegant strumming of a lute. Derived from French keyboard practice, it informs much of the piece, and it can be seen at its most essential in the left-hand figuration in mm. 3–4. Like all the movements of French Suite No. 5, though, the allemande is shot through with up-to-date features: One might say that it is as *galant* as the *galanteries*. Bach places the opening motive over a variant of a common galant exordium: in the customary configuration the bass's stepwise ascent G–A–B occurs in the melody, the middle part's embellished G–F♯–G in the bass. The material after the pickup to m. 2 is a still more common reply, which Bach now presents in an entirely straightforward manner. Innumerable galant pieces deploy as their

second gesture a stepwise descent from scale degree 4 to 1 in the bass (here, C–B–A–G) supporting a parallel descent from scale degree 6 to 3 in the melody (E–D– C–B, here ornamented with sixteenth notes); the leap from C up to A and back in the right hand is, moreover, a virtual cliché of galant cadences.

The overall form follows a plan that became ever more popular in the course of the eighteenth century. The familiar binary structure, in which the harmony modulates from tonic to dominant in the first section (mm. 1–12) and back again in the second (mm. 13–24), is articulated in several important ways. The opening motive returns at the beginning of the second section, in the newly established dominant. This section then follows an independent course, coming to a cadence on the submediant E on the third beat of m. 18 before beginning the journey back to the tonic with renewed force. The submediant (vi) is the most common destination for this harmonic "far out point"—henceforth FOP—a phenomenon in the second sections of binary and related forms that we shall encounter in instrumental music throughout the century. Another contemporary touch occurs at the close, where the last three measures of the first section—striking in their chromaticism—are restated in the tonic (compare mm. 10–12 and 22–24).

The other movements in the French Suite all confirm this basic pattern of harmonic motion, in which the simple "binary" there-and-back is amplified and extended by means of an initial closure on the tonic to emphasize departure toward the dominant, and an excursion to a FOP on the way back from the dominant to the tonic, thus: Here-there-FOP-back. In the courante, the cadential points are distributed with perfect regularity, as follows: m. 8 (I), m. 16 (V), m. 24 (vi), m. 32 (I). By comparison with the stately old-style French courante, this one is an Italianate type, a corrente. By virtue of its rhythmic evenness, its regular cadences, and its uncomplicated, predominantly two-voiced texture, it is practically a *galanterie*. This being Bach, however, the learned and the fashionable are made to lie down together. Note the imitation between right hand and left hand in mm. 1–2 and 2–3, which puts one in mind of a two-part invention, or the return of the opening motive in inversion in mm. 23–26.

In the sarabande, the cadence points again evenly divide the first half. In contrast, the second half is elaborately subdivided into sections cadencing on ii in m. 20 and vi in m. 24 (the FOP); the trip back to the tonic is subarticulated with stops on the subdominant (m. 28) and the dominant (m. 36) before finally touching down at the end (m. 40). The result is a colorfully lengthened, but also strengthened, harmonic structure.

While of course slighter, the *galanteries* observe similar tonal proportions. The *gavotte*, a buoyant dance with beats on the half note and a characteristic two-quarter pickup, has cadences on mm. 4 (I), 8 (V), 16 (vi), and 24 (I). Notice that the tendency to expand the second half, already apparent in the sarabande, is maintained here as well by doubling the phrase lengths, though without the addition of any supplementary cadence points. The *bourrée*, a rambunctious stylized peasant dance in two quick beats per bar, has its cadences more irregularly placed: mm. 4 (I), 10 (V), 18 (vi), 30 (I). That irregularity is part of its *galant*, or witty charm: Each phrase is longer than the last, and the listener is kept guessing how much longer.

The *loure*, one of the rarer dances, might be described as a heavy (*lourd*) or rustic gigue in doubled note values. (In the sixteenth century the word *loure* was used for a certain kind of bagpipe, but whether that is the source of the dance's name is unclear.) Its meter and note values resemble those of the "true" French courante, but its rhythms—particularly the pattern ♩♪♩—are gigue-like. Altogether unlike those of the courante just discussed, the cadences of Bach's loure are distributed with perfect regularity (mm. 4, 8, 12, 16). The supertonic (ii), somewhat unusually, is used in place of the submediant (vi) as FOP.

Finally comes the gigue. With its 56-measure length (distributed 24 + 32) and its fugal expositions in three real parts, it is the most elaborate dance of all. Tracking cadences here is complicated by the behavior of the fugal writing, which has its own pendular rhythm. The first fugal exposition makes its final tonic cadence on the third beat of m. 9, and the dominant is reached by the third beat of m. 14, when the bass enters with the subject. Final confirmation of arrival on V comes, after a lengthy episode, in m. 24. The second half begins, as Bach's gigues often do, with an inversion. As befits a dance (if not a fugue), this inverted exposition ends, somewhat indefinitely, on either vi in m. 37 or ii in m. 38. The bass then enters with the subject on the dominant of vi, the FOP on vi arrives on the downbeat of m. 44 to start steering the course toward home.

85

Johann Sebastian Bach (1685–1750)

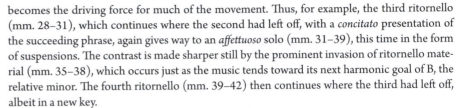

Brandenburg Concerto No. 5 in D, BWV 1050 (1721)

This concerto calls for three soloists: transverse flute (the wooden ancestor of the modern metal flute), violin, and harpsichord. It is apparently the earliest of all concerti to treat this last as more than simply a continuo instrument. The harpsichord in fact plays two roles throughout: In the ritornelli, where it is marked *accompagnement* and the left hand alone is notated and provided with figures, it is a traditional continuo instrument; in the solos, where both hands are notated and figures are lacking, it becomes a soloist.

The harpsichord's new role, however, is not immediately apparent. One who watches as well as listens to a performance for the first time might mistake the work for a solo flute concerto. It alone is missing from the fiery opening ritornello (mm. 1–9), and it initiates the imitative dialogue with the violin that launches the first solo episode (mm. 9–19). And just as it quickly becomes clear that the flute and violin are soloists of equal import, the harpsichord has not yet gained that status: Continuo players often improvised elaborate right-hand parts in chamber music, and Bach himself was especially adept at doing so. Only the triplets in the right hand (m. 10) suggest that the harpsichord is to be no mere accompanist. These create an embellished, inverted version of the imitative motive just heard in the flute and violin, which soon take up the new motive in imitation (mm. 13–16).

With the arrival on the dominant and the return of the tutti (mm. 19–20) Bach displays the remarkable integration of ritornelli and solo episodes that characterizes so much of his work in this genre. Already in the first episode he sets fragments of the ritornello against the solo instruments (see the ripieno violins in mm. 10–11 and 13, which correspond to mm. 1 and 2). Now, after the second ritornello has stated its lone phrase, the flute continues (mm. 20–21), with the same pitches that would have followed in the ripieno violins had the ritornello continued, B–C♯–B–D–C♯–F♯. Bach changes these, though, from repeated sixteenth notes to single eighth notes slurred in pairs, thereby giving the flute its own idiomatic version of the ritornello (repeated sixteenth notes would be virtually unplayable on the flute) and creating a stunning transformation in affect. The agitated ritornello recalls the dramatic *concitato* style that goes all the way back to Monteverdi, while the "sighing" eighth notes that pervade the whole of the second solo episode (mm. 20–28) conjure up a tender, *affettuoso* style. Contrast of characters

becomes the driving force for much of the movement. Thus, for example, the third ritornello (mm. 28–31), which continues where the second had left off, with a *concitato* presentation of the succeeding phrase, again gives way to an *affettuoso* solo (mm. 31–39), this time in the form of suspensions. The contrast is made sharper still by the prominent invasion of ritornello material (mm. 35–38), which occurs just as the music tends toward its next harmonic goal of B, the relative minor. The fourth ritornello (mm. 39–42) then continues where the third had left off, albeit in a new key.

This contrast, between rival versions of the same material, is never resolved. For its part, the harpsichord now becomes a disruptive element, further impeding reconciliation as it becomes ever more prominent. In the fourth solo (mm. 42–58) the instrument makes it clear that it will not be content with its usual service role; indeed, it is determined to dominate the show. In m. 47 the harpsichord actually abandons the bass line (leaving it to the viola and ripieno violin) and launches into a toccata-like riff in thirty-second notes that lasts for only three measures but that ultimately succeeds in knocking things for a loop. At first, things seem "normal": The sighing eighth notes return to fill out the remainder of the solo, and the fifth ritornello (mm. 58–61) appears in the tonic, a note-for-note restatement of mm. 2–5. Even the deceptive cadence (to I♭7 in first inversion instead of I) that launches the fifth solo in m. 61 revisits the same progression that featured prominently in the opening ritornello, on the third beat of m. 7.

But it is this solo that becomes exceedingly strange. After ten measures of familiar material there follows a long dreamlike section (mm. 71–101) that marks the movement's harmonic "far out point" (FOP; see Vol 1-84) in the very unusual mediant key of F♯ minor. A new theme, related neither to the ritornello nor to the original soloist's material, is traded off between the flute and violin soloists while the harpsichord keeps up a relentless tramp of sixteenth notes. Eventually the other soloists' stamina gives out and the music becomes entirely harmonic, a slow march around the circle of fifths in which nothing sounds but arpeggios at various levels of speed. At m. 95 the motion is further arrested, with the long-held dissonances in the flute and violin, trilled *pianissimo*, seeming to go out of time as if everyone were falling asleep—everyone, that is, except the harpsichord and its continuo cohort, the cello.

At m. 101 all snap out of their trance with a ritornello (the sixth) on the dominant that seems to be pointing the way toward home. In the sixth solo the flute and violin conspire to direct the harmony tonicward with a sequential episode (mm. 102–110; note that here the harpsichord again officially maintains its continuo role within a solo section) and succeed in bringing about a return to the tonic that the harpsichord seems to abet with an entrance that apes its very first solo. The flute and violin join in with reminiscences of *their* first solos (mm. 110–121), and when the ripieno chimes in to cap things off with a full repetition of the opening ritornello (mm. 121–125)—the normal ending for a movement like this—the piece seems about to end on the expected note of fully achieved concord.

But it has all been a diabolical ruse, and the movement, which has already reached more or less average Vivaldian length, turns out to be only half over. On the third beat of m. 125 the end so agreeably promised is aborted by a deceptive cadence, the same one heard in mm. 5 and 61, but with the I♭7 chord now in third inversion: The bass assaults the tonic D with a fiercely

426

dissonant and chromatic C natural that drives the music out of its tonal bed, so to speak, and forces it to keep going at least long enough to repair the abruption (mm. 125–136). A new purchase on the same ritornello (mm. 136–139) is thwarted again, now by the tamer, first-inversion form of the deceptive cadence.

There will be no more attempts at closure for a long time, because the harpsichord, as if seizing its moment, launches once again into the toccata riff it had initiated some ninety or so measures earlier, and this time it proves to be truly irrepressible. The thirty-second notes keep up for fifteen measures (mm. 139–153), changing in figuration from scales to decorated slow arpeggios to very wide and rapid arpeggios. With every new phase in the harpsichord's antics comes a corresponding loss of energy in the other instruments (now clearly their former accompanist's accompanists), until they simply drop out, leaving their obstreperous companion alone in play.

What follows is something no eighteenth-century listener could ever have anticipated. It had no precedents of any kind in ensemble music, and it would have no successors, either. The unimaginably lengthy passage for the *cembalo solo senza stromenti* ("harpsichord alone without [the other] instruments"; mm. 154–219), is a unique event in this repertory. It is often called a *cadenza*, on a vague analogy to the kind of pyrotechnics that opera singers indulged in before the final ritornello in an opera seria aria. But the actual style of the solo is more in keeping with what Bach's contemporaries would have called a *capriccio*—a willfully bizarre instrumental composition that makes a show of departing from the usual norms of style. Bach's capriccio begins by joining the motive of the flute and violin to that of the harpsichord itself (compare mm. 154–155 to mm. 9–10) and then greatly expanding it (to mm. 184). There follows a return to the relentless tread of sixteenth notes that had accompanied the F♯-minor episode described earlier (mm. 184–195, anticipated in mm. 163–165). Finally, there is a mind-boggling explosion of toccata fireworks that lasts nearly twenty measures (mm. 195–214) before resuming the earlier thematic elaboration and bringing it at last to cadence (mm. 214–219). By the time it has run its course and allowed the tutti finally to repeat its opening ritornello one last time (mm. 219–227) and bring the movement to a belated close, the harpsichord's cadenza/capriccio/toccata has lasted sixty-five measures, close to one-third the length of the entire movement, and completely distorted its shape.

The remaining movements have nothing to compare with this disruption; the harpsichord, having made its point, calmly alternates its roles of accompanist and soloist. The middle movement, explicitly marked *affettuoso*, is at once chamber music (it is scored for the soloists alone) and a concerto. When the harpsichord acts as the continuo (mm. 1–5, 10–14, 20–23, 30–34, 45–49), the ensemble becomes a ritornello, a recurring trio sonata in different tonal areas. When instead the figured bass disappears and notated music for the right hand appears, new melodic material emerges, in the manner of a solo: thus the slurred, "sighing" sixteenth notes in mm. 6–9 of the right hand. In passages such as these, the writing for the flute and violin often becomes sparser, such as the antiphony into silence of mm. 7–9 or 24–27. Only rarely is a full quartet texture joined, as in the opening of the first "solo" (mm. 5–6) and the close of the third (mm. 28–29) and fourth (mm. 43–44).

The final movement is an excellent example of "fused" genres. It seems to have a hard time deciding whether it is a fugue, a gigue, or a concerto. But of course it is all of those things at once.

We have already seen how often the two sections of a gigue begin with little fugal expositions. In the Fifth Brandenburg Concerto, the exposition is extended into quite an elaborate affair—in four parts, two of them assigned to the harpsichord—that lasts twenty-eight measures before the ripieno joins in to second it with another extended exposition of fifty measures' length, the whole seventy-eight-measure complex in effect making up one huge ritornello. After a long central section in B minor (mm. 79–232), the opening material returns (mm. 233–310) to close out the piece; yet another genre, the da capo aria, is thereby referenced.

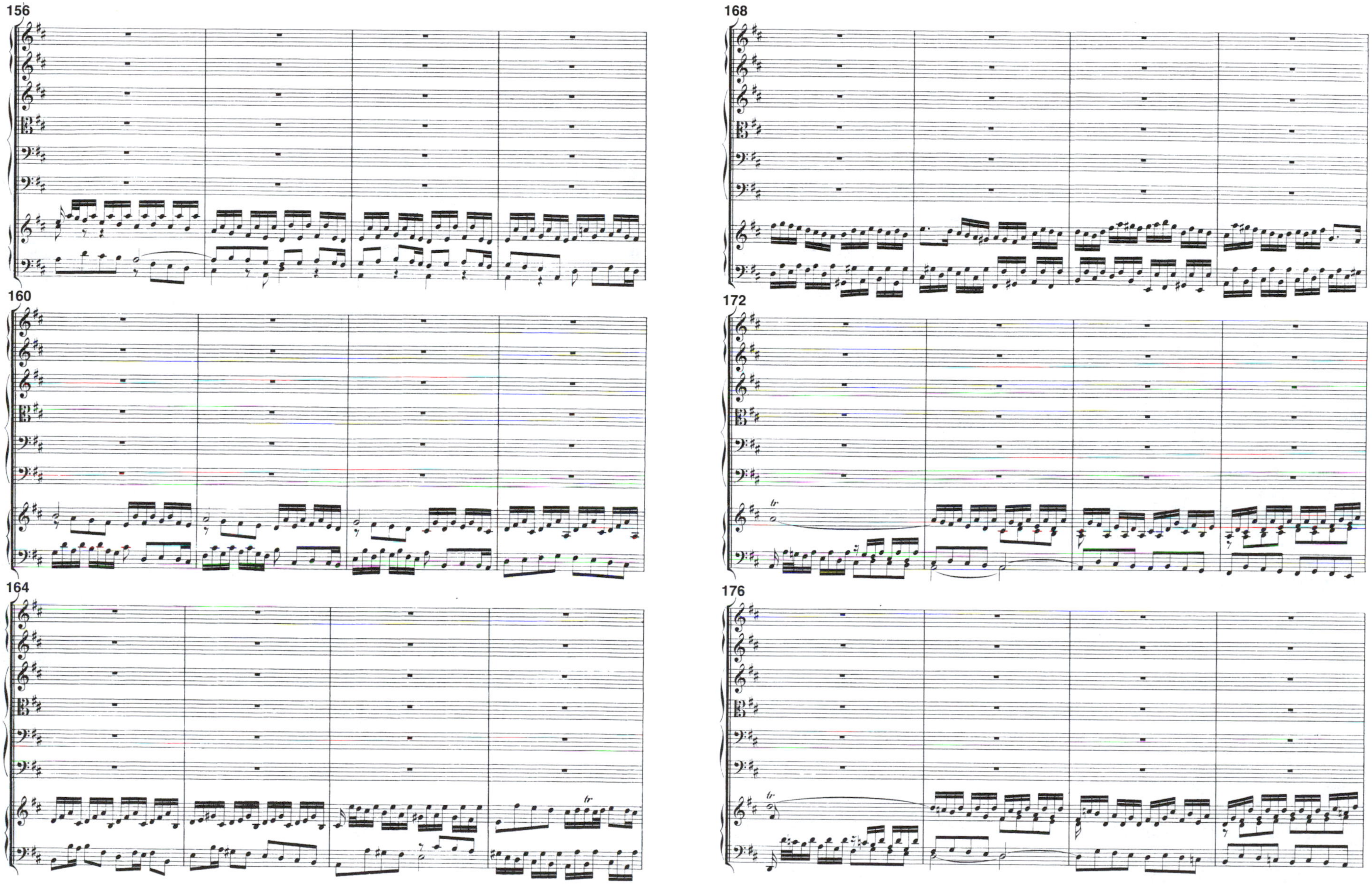
156
160
164
168
172
176
tr

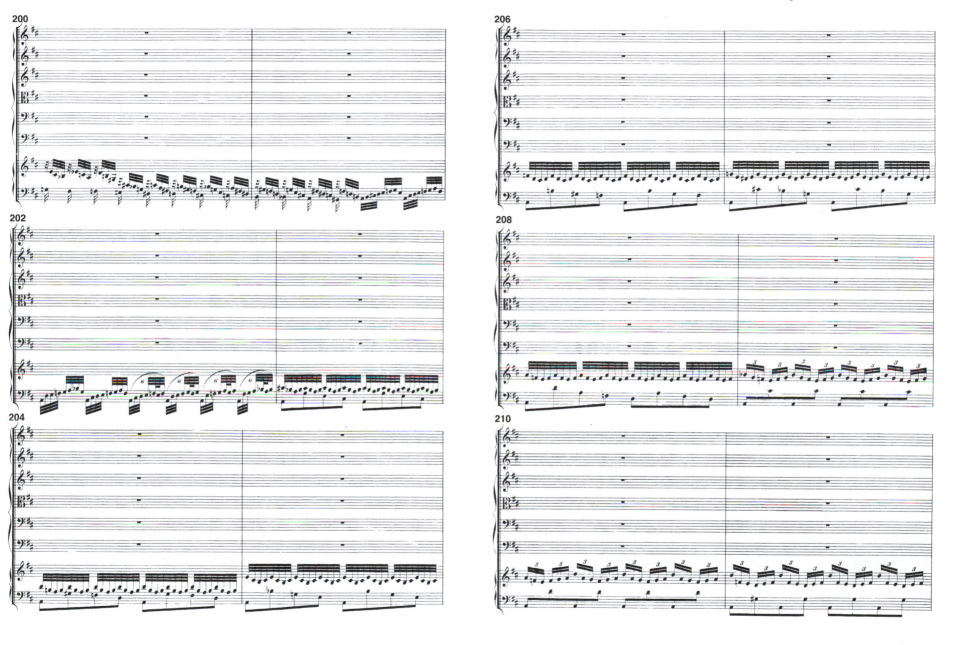

Flauto traverso.

Violino principale.

Violino
di ripieno.

Viola
di ripieno.

Violoncello.

Violone.

Cembalo concertato.

76
(cantabile)
piano
(piano)
85
piano
(cantabile)
forte
Solo
pianissimo
(piano)
93
forte
Solo
piano
pianissimo
(pianissimo)
(pianissimo)
(cantabile)
101
forte
forte
forte
(forte)
(forte)
110
tr
119
tr

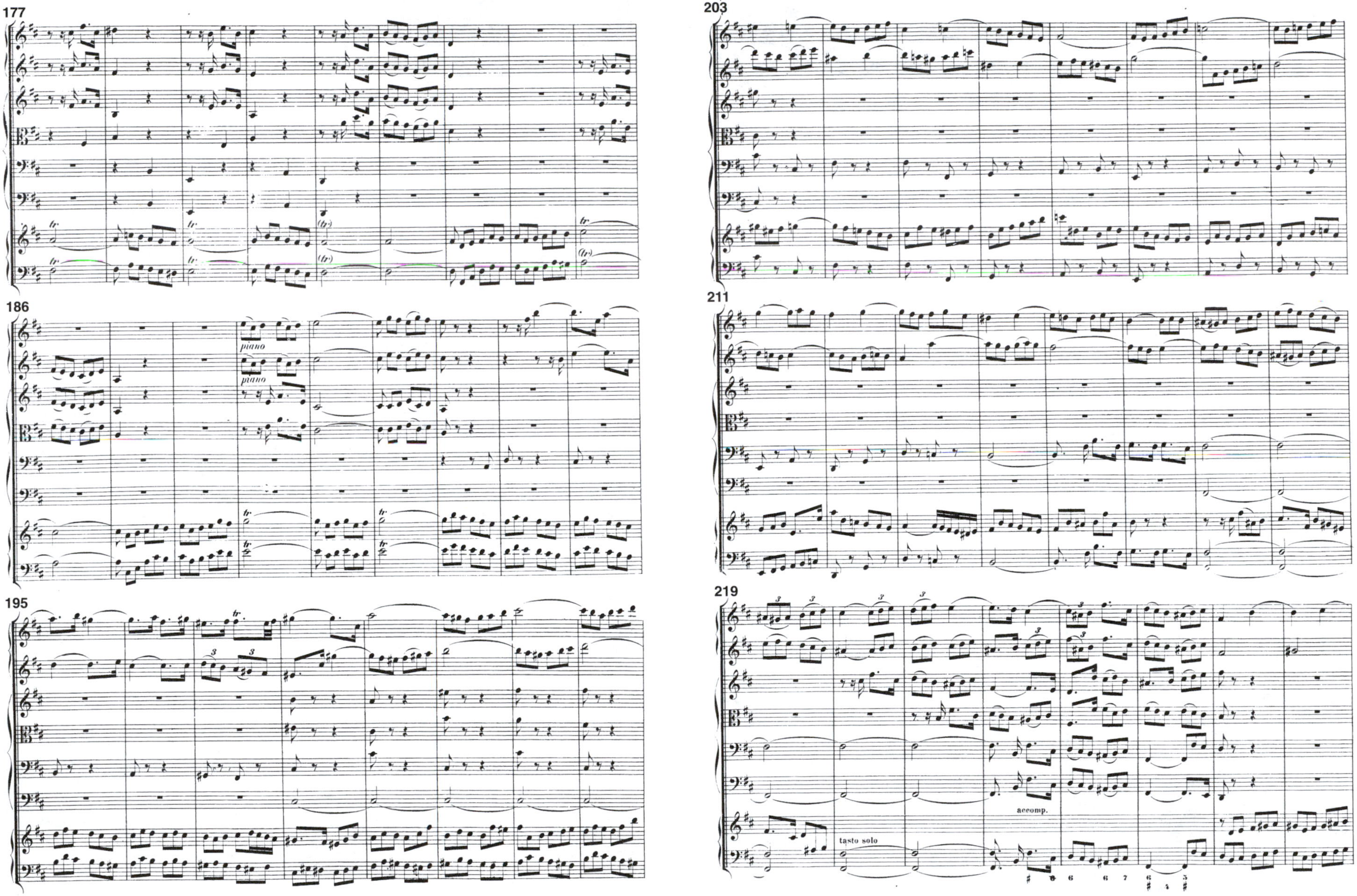
177
186
piano
piano
195
203
211
219
accomp.
tasto solo

86

Johann Sebastian Bach
(1685–1750)

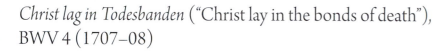

Christ lag in Todesbanden ("Christ lay in the bonds of death"),
BWV 4 (1707–08)

This chorale cantata is one of Bach's earliest. It may have had its first performance in Mühlhausen on Easter Sunday (24 April) 1707, as part of his application for the organist's post there. Bach also reused it during his Leipzig years, performing it on the same feast day in 1724 and 1725. It consists of a set of variations on Luther's venerable chorale *Christ lag in Todesbanden* ("Christ Lay in the Bonds of Death"; see Vol 1–53 for the tune). Its text is exactly that of the chorale, its seven vocal movements corresponding to the seven verses of the hymn, the whole preceded by a diminutive *sinfonia*. As such, it resembles the chorale-based compositions of such seventeenth-century masters as Dietrich Buxtehude more than it does the ones that Bach composed after the genre was reformed in the 1710s (these abound with recitatives, da capo arias, extensive instrumental ritornelli, and freshly authored poetry not found here). And as with so much Lutheran music of the period, it proclaims its allegiance to tradition while incorporating the styles of the day.

The *sinfonia*, which serves a kind of "preluding" function, is cleverly constructed out of materials from the chorale melody. The first line of the tune is quoted by the first violin in mm. 5–7; the second line, minus its cadential notes, is played by the second violin in mm. 8–10; the expected cadence is finally made by the first violins at the end. The first four measures are built on a neighbor-note motif derived from the melody's incipit (first in the continuo, then in the first violins). The obsessive repetitions, a seeming stutter before the first line of the tune is allowed to progress, effectively suggest constraint—"death's bondage."

The elaborate first chorus is a cantus firmus composition in "motet style," in which the successive lines of the unadorned chorale tune in the soprano are pitted against faster-moving, imitative lower voices. (Some of these are "*Vorimitationen*," pre-echoes of the next line, such as those found in the marvelously recomposed repeat of the *Stollen*, where lines 3 and 4 feature elaborate lead-ins [mm. 13–19, 23–30] not found in lines 1 and 2.) The procedure dates back to Lutheran music of the sixteenth century, although Bach clothes it in a contemporary harmonic idiom and adds an intensely motivic instrumental figuration (often drawn from the neighbor-note incipit). For the final *Hallelujah!* (mm. 68–94), he livens things up by doubling the tempo and shifting over to an integrated motet style in which all parts now move at the same healthy speed.

The music for verse 2 is unabashedly up to date. A lightly ornamented version of the chorale melody in the soprano is shadowed by a somewhat freer alto counterpart, and both are set over a walking bass that largely moves stepwise in broken octaves. The movement, like most of those that follow it, also features a rather striking madrigalism. The melody for line 7, which proclaims that death *Hielt uns in seinem Reich gefangen* ("Held us captive in its kingdom"), ends on a low E (mm. 41–43); here Bach places the alto above the tune-bearing soprano part, the higher part "captured" (*gefangen*) beneath the lower.

The style of verse 3, with its neatly layered counterpoint, is like that of an organ chorale prelude: The tenor sings the cantus firmus in the "left hand," while the massed violins play something like a ritornello in the "right hand," and the frequently cadencing continuo supplies the "pedal." Once again, talk of death triggers a madrigalism: Following line 5, which proclaims that Christ has taken away *All sein Recht und sein Gewalt* ("All its rights and its force") the violins dig in with forceful multiple stops and the continuo breaks out into no less forceful sixteenth notes (mm. 24–26).

Verse 4 is the most austere. It is another cantus firmus setting (tune in the alto, in B minor rather than E minor) against motet-like imitations, with a very lengthy *Vorimitation* at the beginning that takes in two lines of the chorale (mm. 1–5, repetition for lines 3 and 4 in mm. 12–16). The continuo is of the *basso seguente* variety, following (in somewhat simplified form) the lowest sung voice whichever it may be, very rarely asserting an independent melodic function of its own. When it does so, it is as part of another death-inspired madrigalism: *Wie ein Tod den andern fraß* ("How one death devoured the other"—i.e., Christ's death on the cross led to salvation) is set to a canon for soprano, tenor, bass, and basso continuo (mm. 29–31). The closely knit imitation (at the quarter note) and the repeated motive suggest one part consumed by another. Later, hocket-like figuration (mm. 35–37) mimics the taunting described by the first two words of line 7, *Ein Spott aus dem Tod ist worden* ("A mockery is made of death").

Verse 4 is also the middle stanza, and Luther made it the turning point of his text: After narrating original sin and the coming of Christ in stanzas 1–3 he describes the commemoration of Easter in stanzas 5–7. For his part, Bach creates several musical symmetries. Having isolated verse 4 by means of unique scoring and tonality, he revisits (in reverse order) the instrumentation of verses 1–3: Verse 5 is for solo voice and strings, verse 6 is for two voices and continuo, and verse 7 was originally (so scholars believe) a repeat of the opening chorus.

Unlike verse 3, however, verse 5 recasts the chorale as an operatic lament. The opening chromatically embellished descending tetrachord in the continuo sets the tone, while the triple meter recalls the more lyrical utterances of opera and cantata. Once again, Bach sets the really morbid textual imagery to madrigalisms: Here he seems literally to have tortured the vocal part, forcing it unexpectedly to leap downward a twelfth, to a grotesquely sustained low E♯ on *Tode* ("death") in mm. 64–67, and to leap up almost two octaves to an equally unexpected, even lengthier high D on *Würger* ("murderer") while the violins suddenly break into a rash of unprecedented sixteenth notes in mm. 70–73.

In verse 6, Bach incorporates the characteristic regal rhythms of the French overture as a way of reflecting the meaning of *So feiern wir das hohe Fest* ("Thus we celebrate the high feast"), which connotes an air of great solemnity and ceremony. Now it is the more joyous imagery that triggers word painting, such as the triplet melismas on *Wonne* ("delight"), *Sonne* ("sun"), *Gnaden* ("grace"), and *Herzen* ("hearts") in mm. 6–8, 13–15, 19–20, and 22–24. Bach also fashions a more subtle pictorialism between the first and second statement of the *Stollen*: He entrusts the melody of lines 1 and 2 to the soprano and tenor, respectively (mm. 1–3, 5–8), but reverses the roles for lines 3 and 4 (tenor in mm. 8–10, soprano in mm. 12–15). Thus the *uns* ("us"—here below) on whom the *Sonne* ("sun") shines is set to music an octave lower than that heard the first time (cf. tenor, m. 9 and soprano, m. 2), while the sun is pitched an octave higher (cf. soprano, m. 14 and tenor, m. 7).

The final verse, which was likely recomposed for the Leipzig performance, is set as a *Cantionalsatz*, or "hymnbook setting," the kind of simple "Bach chorale" harmonization one finds in books meant for congregational singing. Bach ended many cantatas with such settings, and it is possible that the congregation was invited to join in. We do not know this for a fact, but it does make sense in terms of Leipzig practice as Bach once described it, where "alternate preluding and singing of chorales" by the congregation customarily followed the performance of the "composition."

Christ lag in Todesbanden	Christ lay in the bonds of death
Für unsre Sünd gegeben,	Sacrificed for our sins,
Er ist wieder erstanden	He rose again
Und hat uns bracht das Leben;	And brought us life;
Des wir sollen fröhlich sein,	For this we should be happy,
Gott loben und ihm dankbar sein	Praise God and be thankful to him
Und singen halleluja.	And sing Hallelujah.
Halleluja!	Hallelujah!
Den Tod niemand zwingen kunnt	Nobody could overcome death
Bei allen Menschenkindern,	Among all mankind,
Das macht' alles unsre Sünd,	Our sin caused all this
Kein Unschuld war zu finden.	No innocence was to be found.
Davon kam der Tod so bald	For this death came so soon
Und nahm über uns Gewalt,	And took power over us,
Hielt uns in seinem Reich gefangen.	Held us captive in its kingdom.
Halleluja!	Hallelujah!
Jesus Christus, Gottes Sohn,	Jesus Christ, God's son,
An unser Statt ist kommen	Came in our stead
Und hat die Sünden weggetan,	And cast aside sin
Damit dem Tod genommen	Thereby taking from death
All sein Recht und sein Gewalt,	All its rights and its force,
Da bleibet nichts denn Tods Gestalt,	Nothing remains except death's form,

Den Stach'l hat er verloren.	It has lost its sting.
Halleluja!	Hallelujah!
Es war ein wunderlicher Krieg,	There was a marvelous war
Da Tod und Leben rungen	Fought by death and life
Das Leben behielt den Sieg,	Life grasped the victory
Es hat den Tod verschlungen.	It vanquished death.
Die Schrift hat verkündigt das,	Scripture announced it,
Wie ein Tod den andern fraß,	How one death devoured the other,
Ein Spott aus dem Tod ist worden.	A mockery is made of death.
Halleluja!	Hallelujah!
Hier ist da rechte Osterlamm,	Here is the true Passover lamb,
Davon Gott hat geboten,	That God has commanded
Das ist hoch an des Kreuzes Stamm	High on the cross's shaft
In heißer Lieb gebraten,	Roasted in ardent love,
Das Blut zeichnet unsre Tür,	The blood marks our doors,
Das hält der Glaub dem Tode für,	Faith holds it before death,
Der Würger kann uns nicht mehr schaden.	The murderer can no longer harm us.
Halleluja!	Hallelujah!
So feiern wir das hohe Fest	Thus we celebrate the high feast
Mit Herzensfreud und Wonne,	With heart's joy and delight,
Das uns der Herre scheinen läßt,	That the Lord lets shine upon us,
Er ist selber die Sonne,	He himself is the son
Der durch seiner Gnade Glanz	Who through the brilliance of his grace
Erleuchtet unsre Herzen ganz,	Illuminates our hearts completely,
Der Sünden Nacht ist verschwunden.	The night of sin has disappeared.
Halleluja!	Hallelujah!
Wir essen und leben wohl	We eat and live well
In rechten Osterfladen,	With the true unleavened Passover bread,
Der alte Sauerteig nicht soll	The old leaven shall not
Sein bei dem Wort der Gnaden,	Be with the word of grace,
Christus will die Koste sein	Christ will be the meal
Und speisen die Seel allein,	And would alone feed the soul,
Der Glaub will keins andern leben.	Faith wants no other life.
Halleluja!	Hallelujah!

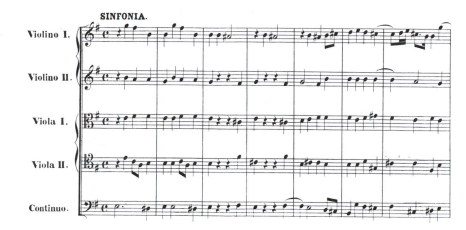

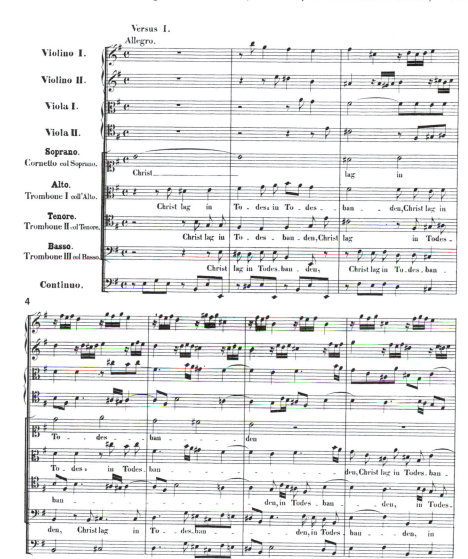

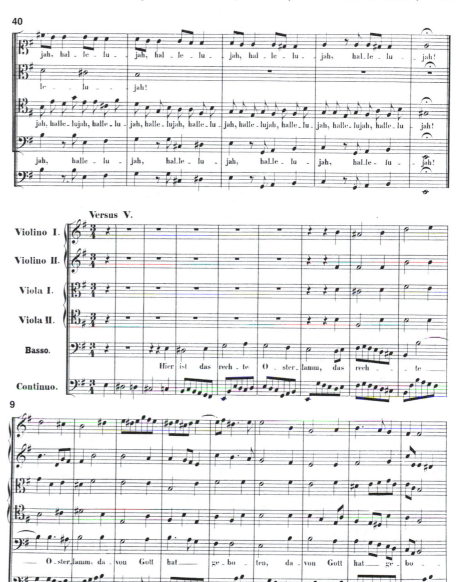

87

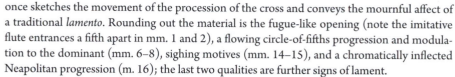

Johann Sebastian Bach
(1685–1750)

St. Matthew Passion, BWV 244, Opening
Chorus (1727, rev. 1736)

Bach's Passion oratorios were written for church use on the afternoon of Good Friday, the most solemn day in the Christian year. The St. Matthew Passion was composed in 1727, heard again in 1729 (the performance long thought to have been the first), and revised in 1736. Bach preserved this latter version in a lavish calligraphic score, replete with inks of different colors, a gesture that bespeaks the high regard in which he held the work.

The first movement makes it easy to see why. The text is by the Leipzig lawyer and playwright Christian Friedrich Henrici (1700–64), a friend of Bach's who wrote under the name Picander and who also provided the texts for many of his cantatas. Here he ingeniously joined two of the three textual types found in passion libretti, chorale and aria (direct biblical quotation is the third). *O Lamm Gottes, unschuldig*, a celebrated sixteenth-century German paraphrase of the *Agnus Dei* by Nikolaus Decius, represents the former, and it is printed here in bold type. Picander's own *Kommt, ihr Töchter, helft mir klagen*, whose verse he wove between those of the chorale—it is probably no accident that both poems consist of seven lines—is at once a da capo aria (his term—the return of lines 1–3 is printed in our edition) and a dialogue for "The Daughter Zion and the Faithful" (his title). The former—an allegory either of Jerusalem, its inhabitants, or the early followers of Jesus—calls on the latter to help her mourn and, by answering their questions, explains the tragic scene at Golgotha. Moreover, Picander's poem comments on both the story about to unfold and the chorale text: Note that the *Stollen* inspired shared words, *Lamm* in Picander's line 3 and Decius's line 1 and *Geduld / geduldig* ("forbearance" / "forbearing") in Picander's line 4 and Decius's line 3; the *Abgesänge* elicited shared concepts, *Schuld / Sünde* ("guilt" / "sins") in Picander's line 5 and Decius's line 5 (for once attributes of the believers rather than of Jesus), while Jesus's *Lieb und Huld* ("love and grace") in Picander's line 6 underscore the chorale's final call that he *Erbarm dich unser* ("Have mercy upon us").

Bach responded with a setting that masterfully combines the formal characteristics of da capo aria and chorale fantasy; he supplied each interlocutor with its own forces, a four-part chorus and orchestra each for Zion and the Believers, soprano and organ for the chorale. Common to both forms is an opening ritornello (mm. 1–17); this one features a broad $^{12}_{8}$ meter and a frequently static bass (cf. mm. 1–5, 9–13) with a high degree of resultant dissonance that at

once sketches the movement of the procession of the cross and conveys the mournful affect of a traditional *lamento*. Rounding out the material is the fugue-like opening (note the imitative flute entrances a fifth apart in mm. 1 and 2), a flowing circle-of-fifths progression and modulation to the dominant (mm. 6–8), sighing motives (mm. 14–15), and a chromatically inflected Neapolitan progression (m. 16); the last two qualities are further signs of lament.

The entrance of the "Zion" chorus in turn strongly recalls the first solo section of a da capo aria. Its first nine measures (mm. 17–25) elaborate on the first eight of the ritornello, a common generic trait. The frequent long melismas on the word *klagen* ("lament") similarly recall the aria, forming stunning madrigalisms of crying. Generic purity is pierced, however, when Bach sets the dialogue in Picander's lines 2 and 3 (mm. 26–29). New material appears, with the punctuating questions assigned to the second chorus. The circle-of-fifths progression and sequential descent also give rise to the bass line E–D–C–B in the bass of the Believers' chorus, a descending tetrachord that was the archetypical emblem of lament.

After the cadence on E on the word *Lamm* in m. 30, the music for the *Stollen* unfolds (mm. 30–32, 34–37); here and throughout, the chorale tune is treated as a cantus firmus, just as it would have been in the first movement of a chorale cantata. Thus the music heard up to this point lends itself to reinterpretation, recalling the opening instrumental and vocal utterances of a chorale fantasy. As if to make manifest the double significance mm. 1–30 have now achieved, Bach further integrates da capo aria and chorale fantasy in ingenious ways. That is, during the *Stollen* the Zion and Believers' choruses restate a foreshortened setting of Picander's lines 1–3, modulating from E minor to G major in the process. This move to the relative major fulfills a generic obligation of the first solo in a minor-mode da capo aria, while at the same time the G-major chorale tune arrives at its "correct" harmonization over the course of mm. 30–37. This harmonic reconciliation is of a piece with Bach's near-miraculous ability to have made his own music for Picander's text work in counterpoint against the preexisting chorale melody.

Similar generic interplay characterizes the repetition of the *Stollen* (mm. 44–46, 48–51). This is preceded not by the wholesale repetition of mm. 1–30, the generic norm in a chorale fantasy, but by a considerably foreshortened ritornello in the relative major (mm. 38–41, drawing on mm. 6–8); the gesture is of a piece with the second ritornello of da capo aria. Yet the chorale, too, has its generic say, as the return of the two choruses in m. 42 sets new material, line 4 of Picander's text, *Sehet*, (G.) *Was?* (Z.) *seht die Geduld* ("See [F.] What? [Z.] see his forbearance"), instead of restating the opening lines in the manner of a well-formed second solo. The line is an outlier—it does not return in the modified da capo with which the movement closes—serving to create the *Geduld / geduldig* pairing noted earlier.

The *Stollen* concluded, elements of chorale fantasy and da capo aria continue to comingle. The succeeding orchestral ritornello (mm. 52–56) recalls the former, continuing in G major and avoiding there turn to E minor that would have occurred after the second solo in a da capo aria. Nevertheless, as the choruses resume their dialogue for Picander's line 5 (mm. 57–70), Bach introduces new material, whose contrast recalls that of a da capo aria's middle section. Staccato rather than legato eighth notes dominate the orchestral parts, three-note units alternating in equal-voiced antiphony (mm. 57–63, 67–68). Similarly, the Believers' chorus becomes more active, repeating its single question *Who in?* ("Where?") and foreshadowing the greater role it will presently assume. Tonal instability, another marker of da capo B sections, distinguishes the music for the first two lines of the *Abgesang*: That for the first (mm. 61–64) begins in E minor and ends in B minor, while that for the second (mm. 67–69) begins in B minor and ends in the midst of a progression that later concludes in A minor (m. 72).

And it is here that Bach unleashes a stunning *coup de théâtre*, a grand synthesis of the elements heard thus far. First, he entrusts Picander's last two lines (mm. 72–82) to both choruses. The poet had assigned them to the Daughter Zion alone; in Bach's setting she and the Believers abandon their dialogue and together describe Jesus, this while the final line of the chorale (mm. 76–79) begs his mercy. Bach further intensifies this outward turn—to us, the listeners—by anticipating Picander's da capo, setting this final couplet to the music of the opening. Yet as this last utterance is united to the musical call to mourning, the da capo is at first imperfect, in the subdominant A minor rather than the tonic. Only when the chorale has finished does Bach return the music to its original transposition: mm. 80–82, which round off the melisma on the concluding word, *tragen*, track precisely with mm. 7–9 of the opening ritornello. The remainder of the movement finishes the ritornello (cf. mm. 82–90 and 9–17), while both choruses continue to sing as one for Picander's first line and in dialogue for his lines 2–3.

Die Tochter Zion und die Gläubigen	*The Daughter Zion and the Faithful*
(Z.) Kommt, ihr Töchter, helft mir klagen,	(Z.) Come, you daughters, help me lament,
Sehet (G.) Wen? (Z.) den Bräutigam,	See (F.) Whom? (Z.) the bridegroom,
Seht ihn (G.) Wie? (Z.) als wie ein Lamm.	See him (F.) How? (Z.) like a lamb.
O Lamm Gottes, unschuldig	**Oh lamb of God, innocent**
Am Stamm des Kreuzes geschlachtet,	**Slaughtered on the trunk of the cross,**
(Z.) Sehet, (G.) Was? (Z.) seht die Geduld,	(Z.) See (F.) What? (Z.) see his forbearance,
Allzeit erfunden geduldig,	**Forever seen as forbearing,**
Wiewohl du warest verachtet.	**How much were you despised.**
(Z.) Seht (G.) Wohin? (Z.) auf unsre	(Z.) See (F.) Where? (Z.) upon our guilt
Schuld,	
All Sünd hast du getragen,	**You have borne away all sins,**
Sonst müßten wir verzagen.	**Else must we have despaired.**
(Z.) Sehet ihn aus Lieb und Huld	(Z.) See him out of love and grace
Holz zum Kreuze selber tragen!	bear the wood of the cross himself!
Erbarm dich unser, o Jesu!	**Have mercy upon us, oh Jesus!**
(Z.) Kommt, ihr Töchter, helft mir klagen,	(Z.) Come, you daughters, help me lament,
Sehet (G.) Wen? (Z.) den Bräutigam,	See (F.) Whom? (Z.) the bridegroom,
Seh tihn (G.) Wie?(Z.) als wie ein Lamm.	See him (F.) How? (Z.) like a lamb.

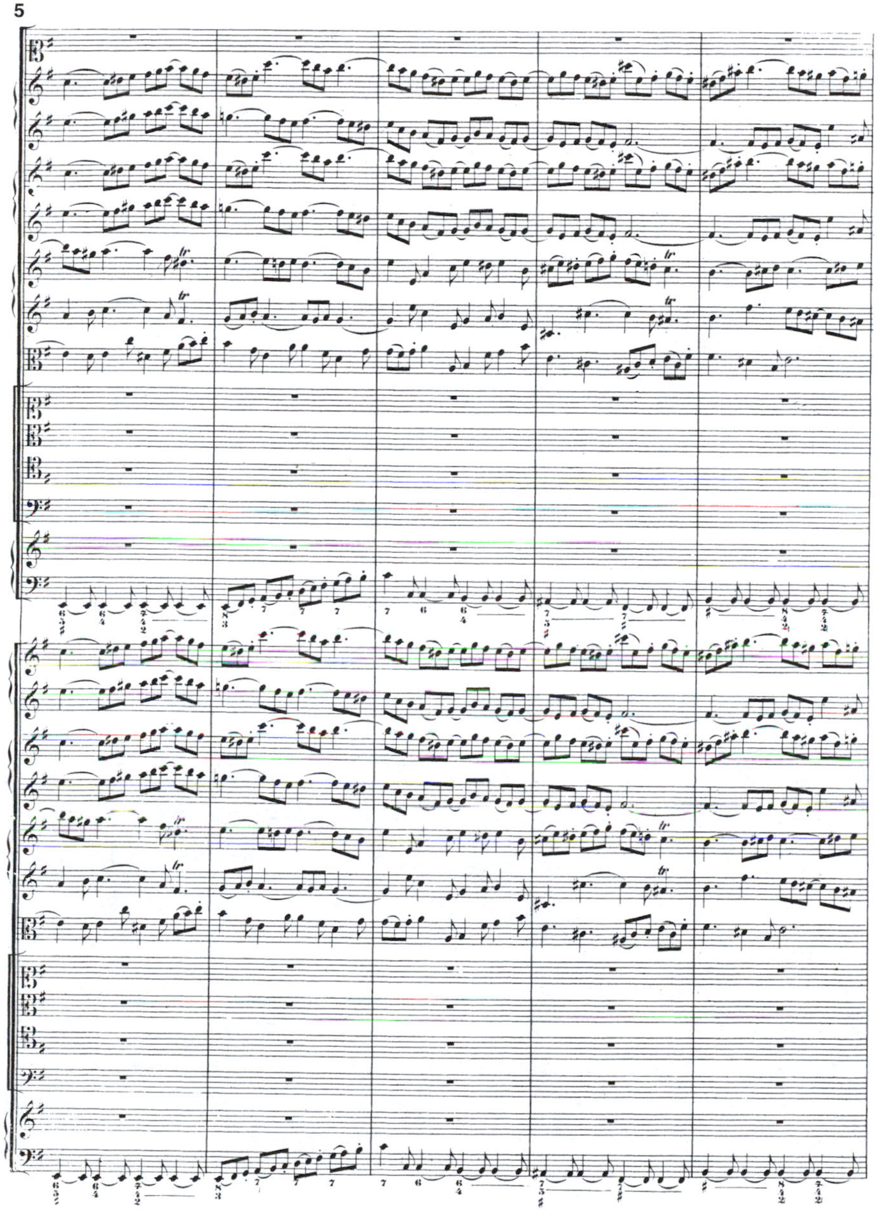
5

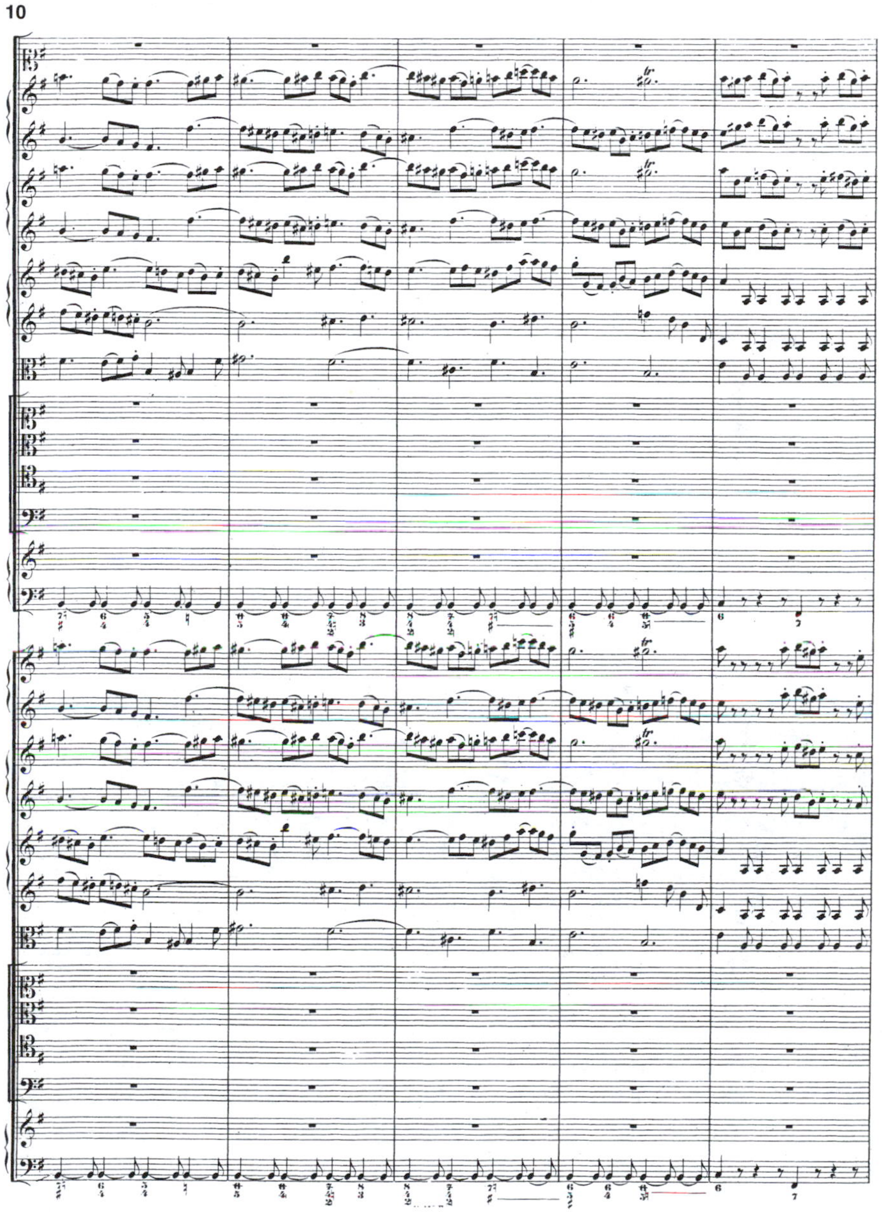
10

15
m.f.
tr
Kommt, ihr Töch - ter, helft mir kla - gen
Kommt, kommt, kommt,
Kommt, kommt, kommt, ihr
Kommt, ihr Töch - ter, helft mir kla - gen, kommt, ihr
19
helft mir kla - gen, kommt, ihr Töch - ter, helft mir kla
ihr Töch - ter, helft mir kla
Töch - ter, helft mir kla - gen, helft mir kla - gen, kommt, ihr Töch - ter, helft mir kla
Töch - ter, helft mir kla - gen, kommt, ihr Töch - ter, helft mir kla - gen, kommt, ihr Töchter, helft mir

23

gen, helft mir kla - gen, se - het den Bräu - ti -
gen, se - het den Bräu - ti -
gen, helft mir kla - gen, se - het den Bräu - ti -
kla - gen, kommt, ihr Töch - ter, helft mir kla - gen, helft mir kla - gen, se - het den Bräu - ti -
Wen?

27

O Lamm Got
gam, seht ihn als wie ein Lamm, se - het den Bräuti - gam, seht ihn als wie ein Lamm, kommt, ihr Töchter, helft mir
Wie?
Wen?

31
tes un - schul - dig, am Stamm des
kla - gen, se - het den Bräu - ti -
kla - gen, helft mir kla - gen, helft mir kla - gen, se - het den Bräu - ti -
kla - gen, helft mir kla - gen, kommt, ihr Töch - ter, helft mir kla - gen, se - het den Bräu - ti -
kla - gen, helft mir kla - gen, se - het den Bräu - ti -
Wen?
Wen?
Wen?
Wen?

35
Kreu - zes geschlach - tet,
gam, seht ihn als wie ein Lamm, se - het den Bräu - ti - gam, seht ihn als wie ein Lamm.
gam, seht ihn als wie ein Lamm, se - het den Bräu - ti - gam, seht ihn als wie ein Lamm.
gam, seht ihn als wie ein Lamm, se - het den Bräu - ti - gam, seht ihn als wie ein Lamm.
gam, seht ihn als wie ein Lamm, se - het den Bräu - ti - gam, seht ihn als wie ein Lamm.
Wie? Wen? Wie?
Wie? Wen? Wie?
Wie? Wen? Wie?
Wie? Wen? Wie?

39
43
all zeit er fundn ge dul dig
Se het, seht die Ge
duld, se het, seht die Ge duld, se het die Ge duld, se
Was?

47

wie - wohl du wa - rest ver - ach - - - tet.
- het die Ge - duld, se - het; seht die Ge - duld, se - het, seht die Ge - duld, se - het, seht die Ge-
— die Ge - duld, se - - het die Ge - duld, — se - het, seht die Ge - duld, se - het, seht die Ge - duld, se - het, seht die Geduld, se - - het die Ge - duld, se - het, seht die Ge - duld, se - het, seht die Ge - duld, se - het, seht die Ge-
se - het, se - het die Ge - duld, se - het, seht die Ge - duld, se - het, seht die Ge - duld, se - het, seht die Ge-
Was? Was? Was?
Was? Was? Was?
Was? Was? Was?
Was? Was? Was?

51

duld, se - het, seht die Ge - duld,
duld, se - het, seht die Ge - duld,
duld, se - het, seht die Ge - duld,
duld, se - het, seht die Ge - duld,
Was?
Was?
Was?
Was?

56

seht
auf un-sre Schuld,
Wohin? Wo-hin?

61

All' Sünd' hast du ge-tra-gen,
auf un-sre Schuld,
seht
hin?
Wohin? Wohin? Wo-hin?

66
sonst müss - ten wir ver - za - - gen;
seht, seht auf un - sre Schuld, auf un - sre
Wo-hin? Wo-hin? Wo-hin? Wo-hin?
70
Schuld.
Se - het ihn
Se - het ihn aus Lieb und Huld Holz zum Kreu - ze sel - ber
Se - het ihn aus Lieb und Huld Holz zum Kreu - ze
Se - het,

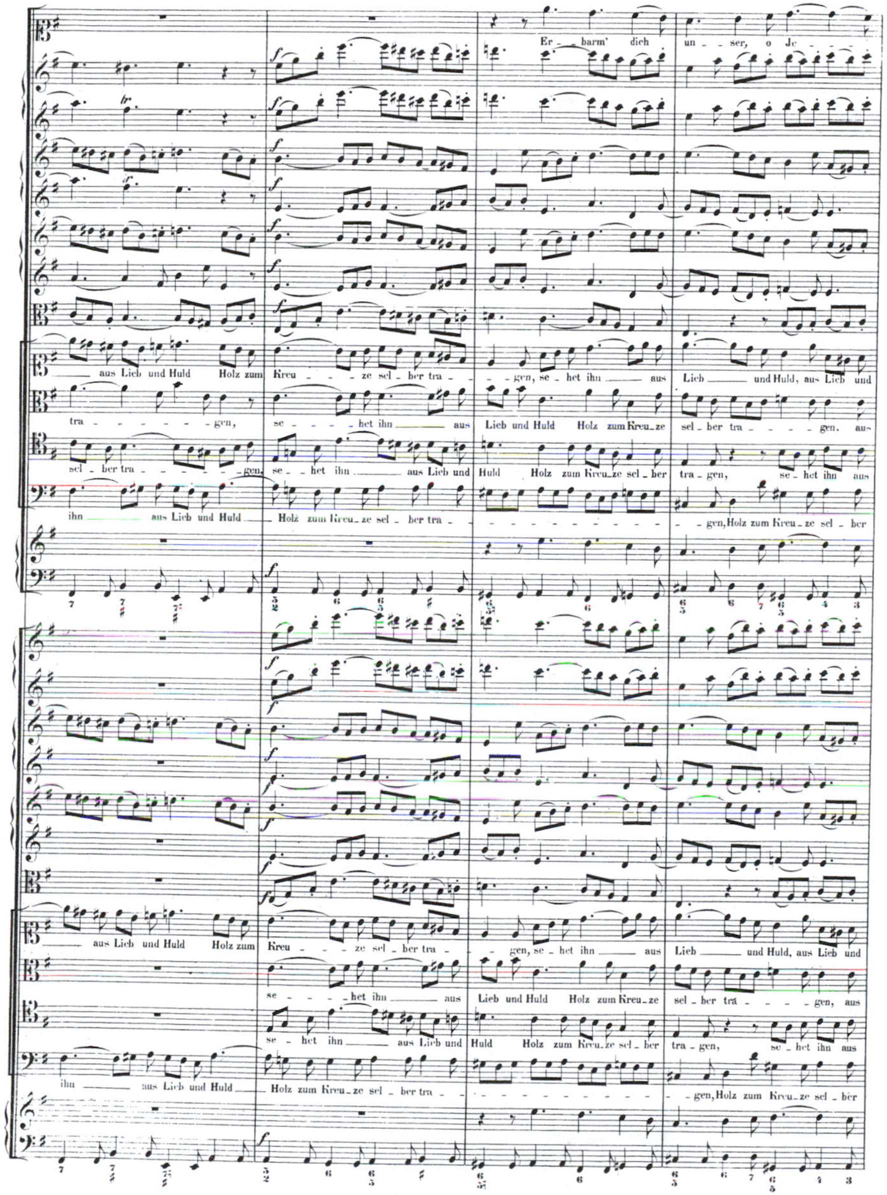

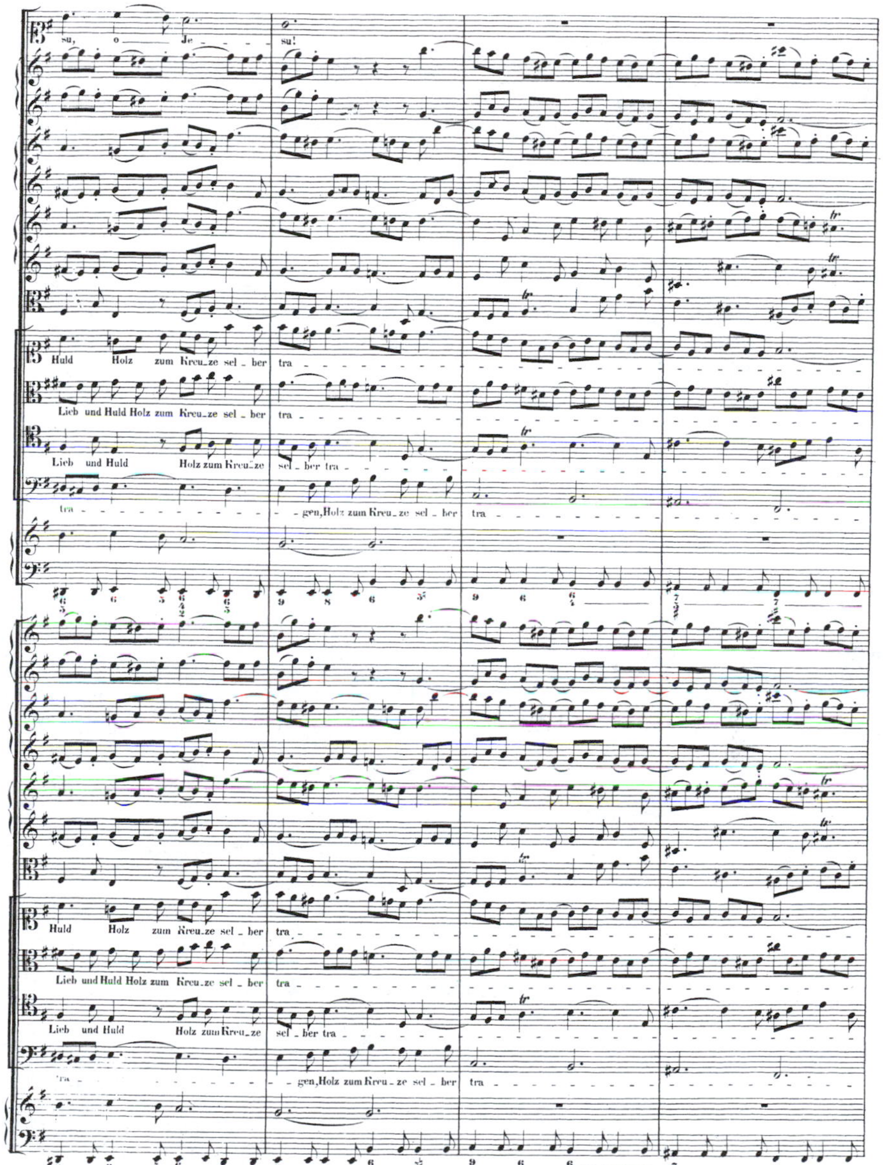

82
gen. Kommt, ihr Töch - ter, helft mir kla - - gen, kommt, ihr Töch-ter, helft mir kla
gen. Kommt, ihr Töch - ter, helft mir kla - - gen, kommt, ihr Töch - ter, helft mir kla
gen. Kommt, ihr Töch - ter, helft mir kla
gen. Kommt, ihr
gen. Kommt, ihr Töch - ter, helft mir kla - - gen, kommt, ihr Töch-ter, helft mir kla
gen. Kommt, ihr Töch - ter, helft mir kla - - gen, kommt, ihr Töch - ter, helft mir kla
gen. Kommt, ihr Töch - ter, helft mir kla
gen. Kommt, ihr

86
gen, se - het den Bräu - ti - gam, seht ihn als wie ein Lamm, als wie ein Lamm.
gen, se - het den Bräu - ti - gam, seht ihn als wie ein Lamm, als wie ein Lamm.
gen, helft mir kla - gen, se - het den Bräu - ti - gam, seht ihn als wie ein Lamm, als wie ein Lamm, wie ein Lamm.
Töch - ter, helft mir kla - gen, helft mir kla - gen, se - het den Bräu - ti - gam, seht ihn als wie ein Lamm, als wie ein Lamm.
gen. Wen? Wie? als wie ein Lamm.
gen. Wen? Wie? als wie ein Lamm.
gen, helft mir kla - gen. Wen? Wie? als wie ein Lamm.
Töch - ter, helft mir kla - gen, helft mir kla - gen. Wen? Wie? als wie ein Lamm.

88

George Frideric Handel (1685–1759)

Giulio Cesare in Egitto, HWV 17, Act 1, Scene 3, "Empio, dirò, tu sei" ("Evil you are, I say") (1724)

An opera-seria role consists of attitudes struck in reaction to the complicated but conventionalized unfolding of a moralizing plot. The great opera-seria composer was the one who could give the cut-and-dried, obligatory attitudes a freshly vivid embodiment and who could convey them essentially without words. Nothing illustrates such greatness better than this da capo aria from *Giulio Cesare in Egitto*, one of Handel's most successful operas, first performed in London at the King's Theatre on 20 February 1724, right in the brilliant middle of his operatic career, and revived several times thereafter. The libretto was an adaptation—by one of Handel's chief literary collaborators, Nicola Francesco Haym, an expatriate Italian Jew who also acted as theater manager, stage director, and continuo cellist—of an earlier opera libretto, produced in Venice in the 1670s, that was based on ancient accounts of the life of Julius Caesar.

The aria comes from the first scene. Caesar, having vanquished his enemy Pompey, has entered Egypt in triumph. The Egyptian king, Ptolemy, thinking to curry favor with the victor, has had Pompey decapitated; his general Achillas has just presented Caesar with the severed head. Caesar, magnanimous opera-seria ruler that he was, had planned to forgive Pompey, but he now flies into a rage, denouncing Ptolemy before setting off to confront him. As was customary in such arias, Handel uses the first ritornello (mm. 1–9) to represent the aria's affect—in this case stormy indignation and thundering wrath—and does so in a variety of ways: minor mode, rapid tempo, and, in the violins, downward-rushing scales (m. 1, made more brutal by their restatement in parallel octaves with the continuo) followed by a near-continuous stream of sixteenth notes, frequently repeated and often requiring frenzied string crossings (mm. 3–7; note that mm. 3–5 of the continuo part also require string crossings for the cello), and in both parts a jagged leap to B natural followed by a grand pause (m. 8) before the closing cadential formula. Not surprisingly, this material resembles the onomatopoetical writing found in the storm episode in the first movement of Vivaldi's "Spring" concerto.

The most spectacular representation of rage, however, is reserved for the singer. The first solo (mm. 10–17) begins as convention dictates, the voice taking the ritornello's descending scale, of which it then offers two varied restatements in mm. 11–12. And it is here that Handel introduces the first of several formal peculiarities, which suggest the derangement that comes with extreme anger. In just these three measures the singer delivers all three lines of text assigned to the A section, and the music modulates to E♭, the relative major. Both events, conventional goals of the first solo, have come "too quickly": Brusqueness, though, is an attribute of fury. To maintain the intensity, Handel reintroduces the violins' repeated-note, string-crossing motive in mm. 12–14, against which the voice now repeats its last line. Having finished it a second time, the voice launches its own frenzy of sixteenth notes, a long melisma on the last syllable of *crudeltà* ("cruelty"; mm. 13–16). The fierce and florid coloratura in the A section coincides on every occurrence with that word, the "cruelty" that Caesar denounces. Each time, the outburst silences the violins' sixteenth notes—or, better, it continues them in a way that is idiomatic to the voice. A final declamatory statement of *Sei tutto crudeltà* ("You are nothing but cruelty") in mm. 16–17 leads to another cadence on E♭, now concluding a "properly" proportioned first solo and leading to the second ritornello.

As often happens, this ritornello (mm. 17–19) is considerably shorter than the first; the real surprise, however, is the omission of the descending-scale head motive. By beginning directly with the sixteenth-note material, Handel again suggests disorder. At this point, listeners may wonder whether the second ritornello has in fact begun or (since it resembles the earlier arrival on E♭) whether it had begun back at m. 12. However confusing his musical surroundings, though, the singer asserts the start of the second solo in m. 20 by launching a fresh statement of line 1. Fresh surprises follow as well. As the violins continue their sixteenth notes, the voice repeats the first line in declamatory fashion, beginning a modulatory sequence that leads not to the expected tonic, C minor, but to the dominant, G minor, which is confirmed after a still more intense melisma on *crudeltà* (the violins do not rest this time but continue with their own string-crossing eighth notes in mm. 24–25) by the cadence in m. 27. Handel again represents disorder in stunning fashion: The appearance of the missing descending-scale motive can suggest a much-delayed second ritornello (not so, as it is in the wrong key) or even the start of a third one. The latter possibility immediately collapses, though, as the raised notes A natural and B natural wrench the scale to C minor, G now the dominant to the aria's tonic key; we have been in the second solo all along. The tonic is confirmed when the voice returns to sing lines 1 and 2 in mm. 29–30, only to see itself undercut a final time. As if not satisfied with this proper destination, the voice restates the first line in m. 31, but with the harmony now veering toward F minor. Only with its final melisma (mm. 33–35) does the voice confirm the tonic for good, the last four measures of the solo (mm. 35–38) actually tracking with those of the first ritornello (mm. 6–9). The third and final ritornello (mm. 39–42), though truncated, rounds off the A section in conventional manner.

By custom, the B section (mm. 43–58), which sets the remaining text, is considerably shorter than the A section; and so it is here. B sections, though, also tend to present contrasting affects; not so here. So all-encompassing is Caesar's rage that it carries with it the material heard in the A section: The show-stopping melismas (mm. 48–49, 53–56) now fall on *pietà*, the "pity" that Ptolemy lacks. The return of the A section offers one final thrill, and that is the surprise at just how the singer would ornament his already-difficult part. Handel wrote this one for the celebrated alto castrato Francesco Bernardi, better known by his nickname, Senesino, and audiences in eighteenth-century London were sure to have been treated to astonishments.

The aria, in short, is a triumph of dramatically structured music—or of musically structured drama. The "purely musical" or structural aspects of the piece and the representational or expressive ones are utterly enmeshed. There is no way of describing the one without invoking the other. An intricately worked-out and monumentally unified, thus potentially self-sufficient, musical structure serves to enhance and elevate the playing out of a climactic dramatic scene. And the structure, in its lapidary wholeness, enables the singer-actor to reach a pitch that is both literally and figuratively beyond the range of spoken delivery.

Cesare	Caesar
Empio, dirò, tu sei,	Evil you are, I say:
Togliti dagli occhi miei	Get out of my sight,
Sei tutto crudeltà.	You are nothing but cruelty.
Non è dal Re quel cor	The heart that is given to harshness,
Che donasi al rigor	That has not mercy in its breast
Che in sen non ha pietà.	Is not that of a king.
(parte)	(exits)

89

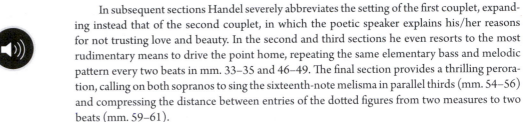

George Frideric Handel
(1685–1759)

An Example of Self-Borrowing

Nothing better illustrates the secular, Italianate idiom that informed so much of Handel's sacred music than a comparison between a little-known cantata (*No, di voi non vo' fidarmi*) and the immensely famous oratorio chorus based on it ("For unto us a Child is born"). In July 1741 Handel composed the former, a duet for two sopranos and continuo. In its text, the poetic speaker reproaches Eros (Cupid) himself, the fickle god of amorous desire. Equally typical is the treatment of the two voices, whose frequent imitative overlappings suggest a metaphor for amorous embrace.

The movement traverses the poem's first stanza four times, in mm. 1–24, 24–36, 36–51, and 51–65. A close look at the first section shows how Handel made the most out of a handful of musical ideas. He fashions the opening soprano solo out of two formulas common to eighteenth-century music. The first (mm. 1–2) sets line 1 to a melodic descent that outlines scale degrees 5–4–3 (D–C–B) in two-beat units over the harmonic progression I–ii–V–I. The second (mm. 2–6) sets line 2 twice to an ascending melodic sequence—down a third, up a fourth—that outlines scale degrees 1–6–2–7–3–1–4–2 (G–E–A–F♯–B–G–C–A), again in two-beat units, over the progression I–IV–ii–V–iii–vi–IV; the complementary harmonic sequence—root motion up a fourth, down a third—is broken with the arrival on V on the downbeat of m. 6. Handel bases every subsequent statement of the opening couplet on this material, enriching it with imitation and virtuosic embellishment. Thus, when the second soprano repeats the same pair of formulas in mm. 6–12, the first soprano replies imitatively in m. 7 (note that in mm. 7–8 the second soprano rests for four beats instead of two to allow the new entry) and then launches a sixteenth-note melisma over the rising sequence. The voices then exchange parts and repeat this material in D in mm. 12–18 (note the delightful hocket caused by the extra "no" in the first soprano, which launches the new phrase on a note of greater urgency). When the sequence concludes, this time on A, Handel repeats the bass line of mm. 16–17, embellished and reharmonized, to underpin new interjections of *Cieco Amor, crudel Beltà* in mm. 18–19. Finally, a new rising melodic sequence, this time in dotted rhythms, reverses the frenzy of the previous melismas as it sets the closing couplet in mm. 20–24.

In subsequent sections Handel severely abbreviates the setting of the first couplet, expanding instead that of the second couplet, in which the poetic speaker explains his/her reasons for not trusting love and beauty. In the second and third sections he even resorts to the most rudimentary means to drive the point home, repeating the same elementary bass and melodic pattern every two beats in mm. 33–35 and 46–49. The final section provides a thrilling peroration, calling on both sopranos to sing the sixteenth-note melisma in parallel thirds (mm. 54–56) and compressing the distance between entries of the dotted figures from two measures to two beats (mm. 59–61).

Two months later Handel, hard at work on *Messiah*, drew on this duet to compose the chorus "For unto us a Child is born," a setting of Isaiah 9:6 (he also turned to its last movement to fashion another chorus, "All we, like sheep, have gone astray"). Aside from basing a brief instrumental introduction and conclusion on material from the duet's fourth section (mm. 51–54), Handel follows his model closely: Like the duet, the chorus consists of four sections (mm. 7–37, 37–53, 53–72, and 72–91), the bulk of each based on the corresponding section of *No, di voi non vo' fidarmi*. Once again, a close look at the first section sheds light on the composer's working method. In the main, Handel tosses the duet material as a unit between the high male/female pair and the low one. Thus the solo statement in mm. 1–6 of the duet goes to the choral sopranos (mm. 7–12), the two-voice continuation in mm. 6–12 to sopranos and tenors (mm. 12–18), the expanded restatement in the dominant in mm. 12–20 to altos and basses (mm. 18–26), and the dotted rhythms in mm. 20–23 back to sopranos and tenors (mm. 26–29). Handel then introduces new material to accommodate his biblical text. Before examining it, a word about his text setting is in order.

The opening word is notoriously misaccented, falling on a downbeat when natural speech demands that "For unto us a child is born" begin with an unaccented syllable. Yet Handel was not as inept as is sometimes alleged. Note that both *No, di voi non vo' fidarmi* and "For unto us a Child is born" consist of eight syllables, with the difference that the Italian verse is trochaic (accented syllable–unaccented syllable, etc.), whereas the biblical verse is the opposite, iambic. Stuck with the opening clash of musical downbeat and unaccented syllable, Handel nonetheless skillfully adjusts the remainder of his setting by replacing the eighth-note rest found in the duet with an eighth note, thereby moving syllables 2–8 to their correct accentuation one eighth note "to the left" (compare mm. 1–2 of the duet and mm. 7–8 of the chorus: The final word, "born," is correctly accented but sung to two eighth notes). Thereafter things remain unproblematic, as the accentuation of "unto us" and "a child is given" matches that of *cieco Amor* and *crudel Beltà*. Finally, "and the government shall be upon his shoulder" matches *Troppo siete menzognere / Lusinghiere* stress for stress, but the biblical text gives rise to a fortuitous madrigalism that may explain why Handel chose this duet in the first place: Dotted rhythms, the most prominent feature of the French overture, were often used to set texts that speak of kingship, and thus mm. 20–23 of the duet take on new meaning when transferred to mm. 26–29 of the chorus. Indeed, it is here that Handel parts company with his model, setting "and the government shall be upon his shoulder" once more in mm. 30–31, expanding the texture to three voices and then to four for completely new music for the words "and his name shall be called Wonderful, Counsellor

The mighty God, The everlasting Father, The Prince of Peace" (mm. 31–37). Dotted rhythms appropriately launch the section, and the violins add to the sense of majesty by taking up their own sixteenth-note figuration.

Handel follows the same strategy in the three remaining sections, moving in each from a closely modeled opening to a newly composed conclusion (note the slight modifications in the third section, where mm. 36–45 of the duet are expanded to mm. 53–65 of the chorus by means of an additional entrance [mm. 55–56] and two extra beats [mm. 60–61]; and in the fourth section, where mm. 51–61 of the duet are compressed to mm. 72–81 through the suppression of a measure [mm. 78–79 of the chorus skip from m. 57 to 59 of the duet]). Thus does the chorus retain its secular origin—which has given rise to discomfort on the part of commentators who ignore the fact that Handel's oratorios were born as theatrical entertainments—while closing with a grandiosity that came to dominate subsequent reception of the work.

a. *No, di voi non vo' fidarmi*, HWV 189, Movement 1

No, di voi non vo' fidarmi,
Cieco Amor, crudel Beltà!
Troppo siete menzognere,
Lusinghiere Deità.

No, I do not want to trust you
Blind Love, cruel Beauty!
Too much are you lying
Flattering Goddesses.

b. *Messiah*, HWV 56, Part 1, "For unto us a Child is born" (1742)

For unto us a child is born, unto us a son is given: and the government shall be upon his shoulder: and his name shall be called Wonderful, Counsellor, The mighty God, The everlasting Father, The Prince of Peace.

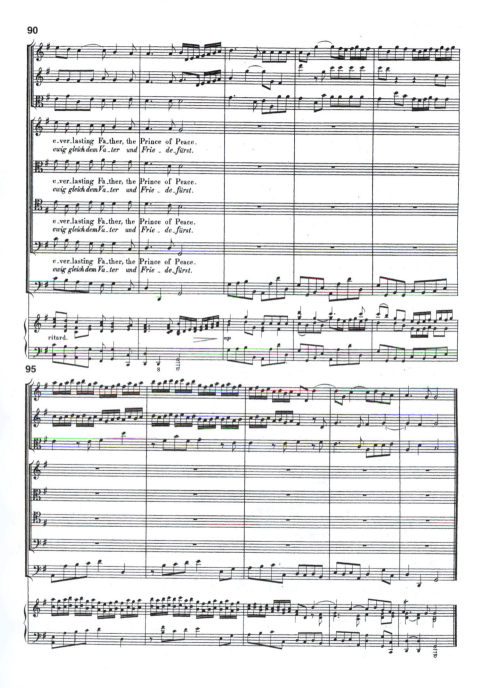

Source Notes

1. Reproduced from Apollo's Lyre: Greek Music and Music Theory in Antiquity and the Middle Ages by Thomas J. Mathiesen by permission of the University of Nebraska Press. Copyright © 1999 by the University of Nebraska Press.
2. a. Public domain.
2. b. Reproduced by permission of St. Bonabenture Publications.
2. c. Public domain.
2. d. Public domain.
3. a. Public domain.
3. b. Public domain.
4. a. Reproduced by permission of St. Bonabenture Publications.
4. b. Reproduced by permission of St. Bonabenture Publications.
4. c. Reproduced by permission of St. Bonabenture Publications.
4. d. Reproduced by permission of St. Bonabenture Publications.
4. e. Reproduced by permission of St. Bonabenture Publications.
4. f. Reproduced by permission of St. Bonabenture Publications.
5. a. Public domain.
5. b. Public domain.
6. Reprinted from Abbess Hildegard of Bingen: Sequences and Hymns, edited by Christopher Page (Antico Edition, 1983).
7. a. Public domain.
7. b. Public domain.
7. c. Public domain.
8. a. Public domain.
8. b. Public domain.
9. a. Public domain.
9. b. Public domain.
10. Reproduced by permission of David J. Rothenberg.
11. Hendrik Van der Werf, The Extant Troubadour Melodies: Transcriptions and Essays for Performers and Scholars. Rochester, NY: Published by the author, 1984. p. 226
12. Public domain.
13. Public domain.
14. Public domain.
15. Public domain.
16. Public domain.
17. Reproduced with permission from The University of Melbourne.
18. Reproduced with permission from The University of Melbourne.
19. Public domain.
20. Public domain.
21. Public domain.
22. Public domain.
23. Reproduced with permission from The University of Melbourne.
24. Reproduced with permission from The University of Melbourne.
25. a. Public domain.
25. b. Public domain.
25. c. Public domain.
26. Reproduced with permission from The University of Melbourne.
27. Reproduced with permission from The University of Melbourne.
28. Reproduced with permission from The University of Melbourne.
29. Public domain.
30. a. Reproduced with permission from The University of Melbourne.
30. b. Reproduced with permission from The University of Melbourne.
31. Public domain.
32. Reproduced with permission from The University of Melbourne
33. Reproduced by permission of the American Institute of Musicology, Inc., Middleton, Wisc.
34. Reproduced with permission from The University of Melbourne.
35. Reproduced with permission from The University of Melbourne.
36. ed. Manfred Bukofzer, rev. Margaret Bent, Ian Bent, and Brian Trowell. Copyright © 1970, American Musicological Society. Used by permission. All rights reserved.
37. Public domain.
38. Public domain.
39. Reproduced by permission of the American Institute of Musicology, Inc., Middleton, Wisc.
40. Reproduced by kind permission of the KVNM.
41. a. © 1990 by The Broude Trust; reproduced by arrangement with the Trust.
41. b. © 1990 by The Broude Trust; reproduced by arrangement with the Trust.
42. The Motet Books of Andrea Antico, edited with an Introduction by Martin Picker. Monuments of Renaissance Music VIII. Chicago & London: The University of Chicago Press, 1987. © 1987 by The University of Chicago.
43. Reproduced by permission of the American Institute of Musicology, Inc., Middleton, Wisc.
44. Public domain.
45. Reproduced by permission of the American Institute of Musicology, Inc., Middleton, Wisc.
46. Copyright by Alejandro Enrique Planchart.
47. Public domain.
48. Institute of Mediaeval Music.
49. Reproduced by permission of the American Institute of Musicology, Inc., Middleton, Wisc.
50. Istituto Italiano per la Storia della Musica.
51. Istituto Italiano per la Storia della Musica.
52. a. Agnus Dei (Mass for Four Voices), William Bryd, ed. Philip Brett, © 1981 Stainer & Bell Ltd, London, England, www.stainer.co.uk, from "Masses", Bryd Edition Volume 4, (London, 1981).
52. b. Agnus Dei (Mass for Four Voices), William Bryd, ed. Philip Brett, © 1981 Stainer & Bell Ltd, London, England, www.stainer.co.uk, from "Masses", Bryd Edition Volume 4, (London, 1981).
53. Johann Walter, Sämtliche Werke, Vol. 3, edited by Otto Schröder. Kassel: Bärenreiter-Verlag, 1955, pp. 6–7.

54. Reproduced by permission of the American Institute of Musicology, Inc., Middleton, Wisc.
55. Public domain.
56. Reproduced by permission of the American Institute of Musicology, Inc., Middleton, Wisc.
57. a. From Jane A. Bernstein, The Sixteenth-Century Chanson, Vol. 12, Orlando de Lassus (New York: Garland, 1987), 77–78.
57. b. London Pro Musica Edition, England. Order Number EML 212.
57. c. London Pro Musica Edition, England. Order Number LPM TM36.
57. d. London Pro Musica Edition, England.
58. Reproduced by permission of the American Institute of Musicology, Inc., Middleton, Wisc.
59. Reproduced by permission of the American Institute of Musicology, Inc., Middleton, Wisc.
60. © 1996 by Gaudia Music and Arts.
61. © Copyright 2003 Ut Orpheus Edizioni S.r.l.—Bologna (Italy).
62. Deutscher Verlag für Musik, Leipzig.
63. Public domain.
64. As Vesta was from Latmos Hill descending. Thomas Weelkes, ed. E.H. Fellowes, rev. Thurston Dart © 1916, 1965 Stainer & Bell Ltd, London, England, www.stainer.co.uk, from English Madrigalists Volume 13, (London, 1965).
65. Giulio Caccini: Le nuove musiche, 2nd ed., edited by H. Wiley Hitchcock, Recent Researches in the Music of the Baroque Era, vol. 9. Middleton, Wisc.: A-R Editions, Inc., 2009.
66. Jacopo Peri: Euridice, An Opera in One Act, Five Scenes, edited by Howard Mayer Brown, Recent Researches in the Music of the Baroque Era, vols. 36-37. Madison, WI: A-R Editions, Inc., 1981.
67. Early Music Company Ltd.
68. Public domain.
69. Frescobaldi, CENTO PARTITE SOPRA PASSACAGLIA, Orgel- und Klavierwerke, Bd. III: Das erste Buch der Toccaten, Partiten, Editor Pierre Pidoux, © Copyright 1961 by Bärenreiter, Kassel.
70. Public domain.
71. Public domain.
72. Public domain.
73. Public domain.
74. "Cantata: Lagrime Mie" by Barbara Strozzi, from THE SOLO SONG: 1580–1730, edited by Carol MacClintock. Copyright © 1973 by W. W. Norton & Company, Inc.
75. Public domain.
76. Public domain.
77. Copyright © 1987 Oxford University Press.
78. Public domain.
79. Public domain.
80. Public domain.
81. a. Public domain.
81. b. Public domain.
82. Public domain.
83. Public domain.
84. Public domain.
85. Public domain.
86. Public domain.
87. Public domain.
88. Public domain.
89. a. Public domain.
89. b. Public domain.
90. Public domain.
91. Public domain.

Index of Names

Page numbers in **bold** indicate detailed discussions of compositions.

Index of Terms